MINING FOR THE NATION

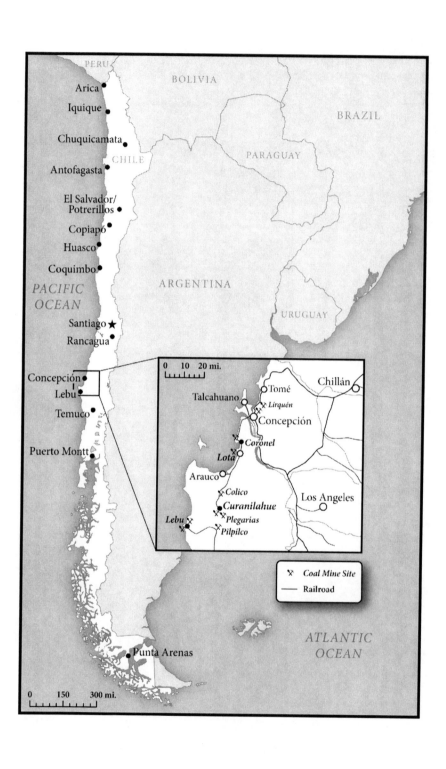

PERU

BOLIVIA

BRAZIL

CHILE

PARAGUAY

Arica

Iquique

Chuquicamata

Antofagasta

El Salvador/
Potrerillos

Copiapó

Huasco

Coquimbo

ARGENTINA

URUGUAY

PACIFIC
OCEAN

Santiago

Rancagua

0   10   20 mi.

Concepción

Chillán

Lebu

Talcahuano

Tomé

Temuco

Lirquén

Concepción

Puerto Montt

Coronel

Lota

Arauco

Colico

Curanilahue

Los Angeles

Lebu

Plegarias

Pilpilco

✗ Coal Mine Site

— Railroad

ATLANTIC
OCEAN

Punta Arenas

0   150   300 mi.

MINING FOR THE NATION

THE POLITICS OF CHILE'S COAL COMMUNITIES FROM THE POPULAR FRONT TO THE COLD WAR

JODY PAVILACK

The Pennsylvania State University Press
University Park, Pennsylvania

Several excerpts have been reproduced from Pablo Neruda,
Canto General, trans. Jack Schmitt, © 1991 by the Fundación
Pablo Neruda and the Regents of the University of California,
published by the University of California Press. Fragmentos de
"Canto General" © Fundación Pablo Neruda, 2009.

Library of Congress Cataloging-in-Publication Data

Pavilack, Jody.
Mining for the nation : the politics of Chile's coal communities from the popular front to
the Cold War / Jody Pavilack.
    p. cm.
Includes bibliographical references and index.
Summary: "Examines the politics of coal miners in Chile during the 1930s and '40s, when
they supported the Communist Party in a project of cross-class alliances aimed at defeating
fascism, promoting national development, and deepening Chilean democracy"—Provided
by publisher.
ISBN 978-0-271-03769-1 (cloth : alk. paper)
ISBN 978-0-271-03770-7 (pbk : alk. paper)
1. Coal miners—Political activity—Chile—
History—20th century.
2. Communists—Chile—History—20th century.
I. Title.
HD8039.M62C56   2011
322'.2—dc22
2010041774

Copyright © 2011 The Pennsylvania State University
All rights reserved
Printed in the United States of America
Published by The Pennsylvania State University Press,
University Park, PA 16802-1003

The Pennsylvania State University Press is a member of the
Association of American University Presses.

It is the policy of The Pennsylvania State University Press to
use acid-free paper. Publications on uncoated stock satisfy
the minimum requirements of American National Standard
for Information Sciences—Permanence of Paper for Printed
Library Material, ANSI Z39.48-1992.

Frontispiece: Location of coal-mining region in Chile. Map by Erin Greb.

TO *John D. French*

CONTENTS

PREFACE: BEGINNING AT THE END

Mining for the Nation tells the history of a group of people who continue to inspire with their resilience and, at times, resistance. These are the coal miners of southern Chile, descendants of Mapuche and mestizo campesinos who migrated to emergent mining settlements in the latter half of the nineteenth century. They were legendary within Chile for their political role as a Communist base of support—indeed, their region became known as a "Red zone." They were also renowned among Latin American workers for their social solidarity and combative grassroots actions. With their proximity to Concepción, the birthplace of the Revolutionary Left Movement (Movimiento de Izquierda Revolucionaria; MIR), it is not surprising that the people of the coal communities actively mobilized during the radical years of the 1960s and 1970s.

In 1970–73, the coal mining zone emerged as a stronghold of support for President Salvador Allende and his leftist Popular Unity coalition, which tried to implement Socialist reforms within the bounds of constitutional democracy. As part of this project, in December 1970, the Chilean national development agency CORFO (Corporación de Fomento de la Producción de Chile) became the majority shareholder of the country's largest coal mining company, Carbonífera Lota-Schwager, thus moving the coal industry into the public sector. This period of dramatic experimentation with new social, political, and economic arrangements ended abruptly with a military coup on September 11, 1973, led by Augusto Pinochet. During the sixteen-year dictatorship that followed, the coal mining communities experienced brutal repression, with thousands of people arrested and tortured and hundreds executed.

On my first trip to Chile, in July 1996, less than a decade after the country began its long road back to democracy, coal miners and their families flooded the streets of Santiago on strike against the National Coal Mining Company (Empresa Nacional del Carbón; ENACAR), created under Allende, which was now insolvent and on the verge of shutting down at any moment. Given the centrality of miners in Chile, both as an economic force and as a symbol in the national imagination, an entire era of Chilean history appeared to be coming to an end. The coal miners' strike became the focus of popular and intellectual debate throughout the country, as reflected in a Sunday feature entitled "Coal Conflict: The End of Working-Class Culture?" in Chile's leading newspaper, *El Mercurio*.[1] Here sociologist Elena Irrázabal presented the coal miners as the last vestige of a tradition of radical working-class politics forged in Chile in the twentieth century.

Powerful public images of coal mining derive in part from vivid portrayals—most notably in Baldomero Lillo's classic 1904 novel *Subterra*—of the arduous work conditions in mines extending deep beneath the Pacific Ocean. Equally important is the region's historical assertion of a distinct and strong cultural and political identity through which "the Lota coal miners" have appeared as a singular cultural and political force within the nation, particularly at critical junctures. As its historically dominant town, Lota has stood for a diverse region structured around the extraction and transportation of coal.

By mid-1997, all of the large coal mines in the country had shut down, and the region struggled to find viable projects of economic development. Newly created industrial parks tried to attract business, while workers sought retraining to cope with the new economic realities. The famous Lota slope mine known as the "Devil's Tunnel" (el Chiflón del Diablo) became a tourist site where former miners led underground walking tours. A nearby mansion built for company administrators was converted into a museum, staffed by working-class women dressed up as matrons of the late nineteenth-century local elite. State agencies and nonprofit organizations promoted such projects as a way to "preserve" the region's unique history and create jobs at the same time.[2]

Despite these efforts, the coal mining region quickly fell to the bottom nationwide in all indicators of social and economic well-being. Elderly coal miners now sat in the central plaza reminiscing about the region's past, as they watched their grandchildren head north to Santiago or the copper mines in search of work. In the coal mining town of Curanilahue,

1. Elena Irarrázabal, "Conflicto del carbón: ¿El fin de la cultura obrera?" *El Mercurio* (Santiago), July 21, 1996. Throughout the volume, translations from Spanish-language sources are mine unless otherwise noted.

2. For an overview of Lota's historical preservation program (Programa de Rescate Patrimonial), see the Web site http://www.lotasorprendente.cl/index.html/ (accessed July 2010), which includes historical and contemporary photographs of many of the places described in *Mining for the Nation*.

a new, fully equipped industrial park stood empty, and people soon began to notice a form of reverse migration. Those whose ancestors had migrated from the countryside to the burgeoning coal mines in the late nineteenth and early twentieth century were now heading back to family plots or agricultural estates to eke out a living. With a powerful historical identity and highly charged memories, the coal mining region presented a tragic tale of the social and cultural destruction wrought by adherence to a neoliberal socioeconomic model.

In July 1996, winter in the Southern Hemisphere, I sat in Lota's huge, dilapidated union hall (fig. 1) talking to desperate coal miners and their leaders as they fought what looked to be their last fight, negotiating for the best possible terms as the industry shut down. It was clear to me that the historical significance of these changes would emerge only through a deep understanding of the politics of industrial relations and class struggle during the region's twentieth-century heyday. Over the next several years, I studied the coal miners' role in Chile's national development model, which began in the 1920s and came to an end with Pinochet's structural readjustment policies in 1975. *Mining for the Nation* focuses particularly on the coal miners' heightened participation in local, national, and international politics during the turbulent 1930s and 1940s. It seeks

Fig. 1 Coal Miners' Union Hall (Sindicato 7), Lota Bajo, 1996. Photo by Jody Pavilack.

to show how their collective agency contributed to a deepening of the participatory and socioeconomic dimensions of Chilean democracy.

Several recent events highlight the significance of Chile's first major period of Center-Left governing coalitions. On June 12, 2009, former first lady Rosa Markmann, wife of Gabriel González Videla, died at age 101, and the Chilean press and public debated the legacy of this presidential couple with an interest not seen for decades. In 1947, President González Videla had sent Army troops into the coal mines to repress worker activism and had then outlawed the Communist Party, which remained illegal for the next ten years.

Also in June 2009, Chilean political scientist Carlos Huneeus published the first major study of the late 1940s, *La guerra fría chilena: Gabriel González Videla y la ley maldita* (The Chilean Cold War: Gabriel González Videla and the "Damned Law"). The book caused a great stir both in Chilean academic and political circles and in broader Internet forums, partly due to its timing: it coincided not only with the death of Rosa Markmann but also with the signing of a historic pact between the Chilean Communist Party (Partido Comunista de Chile; PCCh) and the centrist governing coalition, the Concertación. Known as the "Agreement Against Exclusion," the pact was designed to circumvent prejudicial aspects of Chile's electoral system, which particularly hinders smaller parties such as today's PCCh. Its signing prompted renewed public reflection about Chile's prior experiences with coalition politics aimed at making society more democratic, less exclusionary, and more equitable. The story of the coal mining communities in the 1930s and 1940s brings to life one of Chilean history's least-studied democratic experiments.

ACKNOWLEDGMENTS

Mining for the Nation is dedicated to John D. French, who has inspired, challenged, and guided all of my intellectual endeavors of the past decades. John's commitment to knowledge, critical thinking, and a politics of justice is extraordinary. So, too, is his generosity and enthusiasm for collaboration. From my master's thesis to this manuscript, he has read countless iterations of everything I have written; his sage comments and tireless discussions have powerfully shaped my work, and his friendship enhances my life. John's wife, anthropologist Jan French, has also been a wonderful friend and supportive colleague.

My second mentor, Danny James, has contributed greatly to my understanding and love of Latin American history; he is an innovative thinker, a beautiful writer, and a dedicated teacher. I am especially grateful to Danny for introducing me to the complexities of oral history and memory studies. At each stage of my education, I have benefited from the guidance of many other professors, especially Jorge Domínguez, Damián Fernández, Leon Fink, Greg Grandin, Malachi Hacohen, Michael Hardt, Alberto Moreiras, Jocelyn Olcott, Gunther Peck, Brian Peterson, and John Womack. During my doctoral studies, the University of North Carolina–Duke Consortium in Latin American and Caribbean Studies, run by Natalie Hartman, provided a second home.

Another person without whom this book would not have been possible is historian Mario Garcés Durán, author of several major works and director of the nonprofit agency Educación y Comunicaciones (ECO). During the years I lived in Chile (1996–2001), Mario introduced me to people, places, and critical themes; he provided professional opportunities and practical assistance; and he was a brilliant intellectual and cultural interlocutor. The staff of ECO, as well as Mario's colleagues, friends, and family, have shown me great kindness and support. Mario's daughters taught me about Chile, transcribed interviews, and contributed to my work in myriad ways. I especially thank human rights lawyer Magdalena Garcés

Fuentes and her daughter, Javiera, who invited me to live with them in 2005.

I am also grateful to Bianca Premo—a preeminent historian of colonial Latin America and an exceptional person. Little of anything I have accomplished over the past decade would have been possible without her. Her husband, Barry, and daughter, Anna Clair, have supported our friendship in the most generous ways. I first met Bianca in North Carolina's Research Triangle, where she became one of a strong cohort of helpful scholars and friends that included Antonio Arce, Jon Beasley-Murray, Adriana Brodsky, Vince Brown, Anne Curtis, Jan French, Mark Healey, Tom Rogers, David Sartorius, Alejandro Velasco, and Ivonne Wallace-Fuentes. In wider circles, I also thank Dirk Burgdorf, Leslie DeWall, Jon Hiskey, Nancy Reynolds, and the women of Kingsley.

When I first began to study Chilean history, I was privileged to find myself walking in the footsteps of a prolific generation of U.S. scholars who have reinvigorated research in Chile in the wake of the Pinochet dictatorship. Patrick Barr-Melej, Janet Finn, Lessie Jo Frazier, Elizabeth Hutchison, Tom Klubock, Corinne A. Pernet, Margaret Powers, Karin Rosemblatt, J. Pablo Silva, Joel Stillerman, and Heidi Tinsman, among others, have provided a dynamic milieu for my intellectual development. These scholars have also been generous with their support and friendship. When I was in Santiago frantically trying to prepare my first class, Liz lent me her lecture notes; Lessie Jo invited me to her home for weekend writing retreats; and Patrick rescued me on the Paseo Peatonal Ahumada. I am also thankful for the collaborative spirit of "younger" Chileanists Tracy Jaffe and Angela Vergara.

I and all of the more recent U.S. scholars of Chile are indebted to a rich body of work by our senior colleagues. In my case, Andrew Barnard, Paul Drake, Brian Loveman, Florencia Mallon, Steve Stern, and Peter Winn have especially inspired my thinking about Chilean history. Professors Stern and Mallon provided encouragement at several points in my career, and Professor Winn has consistently offered his knowledge and support; most recently, he read this manuscript in its entirety and provided very wise suggestions.

Brian Loveman's probing studies of Chilean, Latin American, and U.S. political history inspire my truest admiration, especially his profound understanding of the deeply conflictive history of Chilean democracy, as reflected in works written with his frequent co-author Elizabeth Lira. Professor Loveman has been exceedingly generous with his time, knowledge, and support over many years. Most recently, he, too, read this manuscript and offered extensive and wise comments. I also thank all the conference commentators and audiences who have contributed to my work, and especially the anonymous readers, who, along with Professors Winn and Loveman, provided meticulous and judicious suggestions, which I have tried, however imperfectly, to address in this book. Finally, I thank editor Sandy Thatcher, editorial assistant Kathryn B. Yahner, managing editor Laura Reed-Morrisson, and all the staff at Penn State University Press for their efficiency, kindness, and enthusiasm. Jeffrey Lockridge provided exceptionally dedicated and astute copyediting, which improved the book immensely.

During my years of research in Chile, I received assistance from many institutions and people. Beginning with my first visit in 1996, the Facultad Latinoamericana de Ciencias Sociales (FLACSO) offered affiliation, office space, and collegiality; I especially thank Carlos Martín Faus, who welcomed me into his home. Over the years, a number of Chile's leading scholars warmly shared their knowledge of Chilean history and their advice with me. I especially thank Enrique Fernández, Alicia Frohmann, Sergio Grez, María Angélica Illanes, Elizabeth Lira, Pedro Milos, Tomás Moulian, Luis Ortega Martínez, Oscar Ortiz V., Samuel Palma, Julio Pinto, Alfredo Riquelme, and Jorge Rojas Flores, all of whom took time out of their busy lives to contribute to my work in different ways. Several Chilean graduate students also assisted me, especially Consuelo Figueroa, Juan Rodrigo Ortiz, and Michael Reynolds.

Everyone I encountered in Santiago's archives and libraries was professional, kind, and helpful, in particular, Ana María Pino at the Biblioteca del Congreso Nacional; Marcela Cavada at the Archivo Siglo XX (now Archivo Nacional de la Administración Central del Estado); and the staff of the Salón de Investigadores at the Biblioteca Nacional. Other gracious assistance was provided by Florrie Snow, of the Centro de Documentación de la Iglesia Metodista Episcopal; Teresa Galleguillos, of the Servicio Electoral; and Juan de Dios Beltrán and Soledad Moreira, in the Labor Relations Department of the Dirección General del Trabajo.

When I began my research in Chile, the country's major coal mines had recently shut down, and the fate of company records and other local materials was in doubt. It was not clear what sources even existed in the coal mining towns, let alone where they were located or who had proprietary rights over them. Many different actors were on the ground in the coal mining zone—the national coal company, ENACAR (Empresa Nacional del Carbón), the national development agency, CORFO (Corporación de Fomento de la Producción de Chile), nonprofit groups, and private parties. At the time, however, they had more pressing concerns than what to do with basements full of soot-covered tomes. Preservation of coal mining zone history as part of the national patrimony was on everyone's mind, but what would be thrown out, what would be saved, and how it would be made accessible were far from clear in 1997.

In this context, a number of people provided me access to documents, arranged for my trips into the mines, put me in contact with interviewees, and generally facilitated my research. My first significant contact in the region was Gregorio Corvalán, a Coronel native who worked in the Intendancy of Concepción and had long studied the region's history and folklore. Gregorio opened his collection of materials to me and spent many afternoons discussing events and issues. Also very helpful were the mayor of Lota, Jorge Venegas Troncoso, and other municipal employees— Pablo Gaete Villegas, Tito Gutierrez, María Díaz, and Grecia Quiero. The Coronel labor inspector, Víctor Muñoz Eyppert, gave me access to documents and shared his knowledge of the region's history. Also in Coronel, Marta Cuevas and Alejandro Lagos allowed me to spend weeks in their office reading through municipal acts.

José Naín Zambrano, an engineer for ENACAR, taught me much about mining as we toured the interior of Trongol Norte. Bernardo Alarcón Rojas, then personnel director of ENACAR–Lota, gave me permission to consult the company personnel files; his assistant, Juan Venegas, was kind enough to meet me each morning at the entrance to the dynamite bunker where stacks of unsorted folders lined the walls. José Luis Díaz and José Ruminot of the ENACAR Employees' Union arranged one of my trips into the Lota mines and gave me a wealth of information. Enso LaMura and Marcos Rissetti, who were working in 1997–98 to develop a museum in Lota, allowed me to review boxes of company documents. Juan O'Brien, a historian also working on a patrimonial preservation project, arranged for another of my visits into the Lota mines. Stephen Bosworth, then a doctoral student at the University of Texas, was a wonderful in-field colleague.

None of my work in the coal towns would have been possible without the many people who shared their stories, memories, and knowledge with me in formal and informal conversations. The people I interviewed who wished to be named are included in the bibliography; I am grateful to each of them. Several people in the coal mining zone also offered hospitality and friendship: Berta Quiero in Concepción and the family of Juana Riquelme and Víctor Iturra in Lota opened their homes to me—then a total stranger—on my first visit south. Over the next years, I was warmly welcomed into the homes of Adela Serra and Bernardo Reyes in Concepción; of Dr. Hugo Monsalvez and Johanna Urea in Coronel; and of the Pagueguy family in Curanilahue, all of whom helped me in numerous ways. In her capacity as a social worker, Adela Serra introduced me to people and places in Lota and beyond, greatly enriching the ethnographic and testimonial dimensions of my study.

My various research trips and extended residence in Chile were supported by the following grants and fellowships: Ford Foundation, FLACSO–Chile, Duke–University of North Carolina Program in Latin American Studies (DUNCPLAS) Pre-Dissertation Research Fellowship (1996); Mellon Foundation Sawyer Seminar Pre-Doctoral Fellowship (1996–97); Fulbright-Hays Doctoral Dissertation Research Fellowship (1997–98); Aleanne-Webb Dissertation Improvement Award (1999); Duke University Graduate School Dissertation Write-up Fellowship (2000); Ford Foundation, FLACSO–Chile, DUNCPLAS Dissertation Fellowship (2000–2001).

Since 2004, the University of Montana has provided a supportive environment for my teaching, research, and writing, including a grant that enabled me to return to Chile for two months in 2005. I am especially thankful to my colleagues in the History Department and our wonderful office administrator, Diane Rapp. Several exceptional undergraduate and graduate students have offered significant intellectual dialogue and friendship, especially Happy Avery, David Brooks, Greg Gordon, and Max Granger. A gifted editor, Happy read the manuscript in its entirety and improved the writing greatly. My work over the past few years has also been supported by wonderful friends and neighbors: Susan Soltau, the Klein-Podoll family, the Depuy family, the Wiltse family, the Open Way sangha, and fellow historians Pamela Voekel and Bethany Moreton, "our favorite Missoulians."

A special note of thanks to Esther Pérez and the Centro Memorial Martin Luther King Jr. in Havana, Cuba, and to Valeria Rezende, of the Escola de Formação Quilombo dos Palmares (EQUIP) in Recife, Brazil. I also want to convey my deepest appreciation to my father, Larry Pavilack, to his wife, Donna Robertson, to my brother, Brooks Pavilack, and his family—Sherri, Derek, and Trevor—to my stepfather, Jim Getty, and to my in-laws Terry Cohea and Phil Cohea. My mother, Carol Ann McGrew Pavilack Getty, is the most extraordinary woman I have known; I am so fortunate to be her daughter. Finally, to the Parkside gang—Clyde, Zumbí, and above all, my husband, Cy, and my son, Sam—all my love and gratitude.

ABBREVIATIONS

ANCh	Archivo Nacional de Chile; Chilean National Archive
ARNAD	Archivo Nacional de la Administración Central del Estado; National Archive of the Central State Administration (formerly Archivo Siglo XX; Twentieth-Century Archive)
BCNCh	Biblioteca del Congreso Nacional de Chile; Chilean National Library of Congress
BML	Biblioteca Municipal de Lota; Lota Municipal Library
BNCh	Biblioteca Nacional de Chile; National Library of Chile
CCIL	Compañía Carbonífera e Industrial de Lota; Coal Mining and Industrial Company of Lota
CDIME	Centro de Documentación de la Iglesia Metodista Episcopal; Documentation Center of the Methodist Episcopal Church
CEN	Comité Ejecutivo Nacional; National Executive Commitee (Radical Party)
CESOC	Centro de Estudios Sociales; Center for Social Studies
CORFO	Corporación de Fomento de la Producción de Chile; Chilean Economic Development Agency
CTAL	Confederación de Trabajadores de América Latina; Confederation of Latin American Workers
CTCh	Confederación de Trabajadores de Chile; Confederation of Chilean Workers
DGT	Director General del Trabajo; director general of labor; also Dirección del Trabajo; General Directorate of Labor
DIBAM	Dirección de Bibliotecas, Archivos y Museos; Office of Libraries, Archives, and Museums (Ministry of Education)
ECO	Educación y Comunicaciones; Education and Communications
ENACAR	Empresa Nacional del Carbón; National Coal Mining Company
FDGT	Fondo de Dirección General del Trabajo; General Directorate of Labor Records

FGGV	Fondo de Gabriel González Videla; Gabriel González Videla Collection
FIC	Fondo de Intendencia de Concepción; Intendancy of Concepción Records
FLACSO	Facultad Latinoamericana de Ciencias Sociales; Latin American Faculty of Social Sciences
FMI	Fondo de Ministerio del Interior; Interior Ministry Records
FNM	Federación Nacional Minera; National Miners' Federation
FOCh	Federación de Obreros de Chile; Federation of Chilean Workers
FPAC	Fondo de Pedro Aguirre Cerda; Pedro Aguirre Cerda Collection
ICAL	Instituto de Ciencias Alejandro Lipschutz; Alejandro Lipschutz Institute of Sciences
ICT	Inspector Comunal del Trabajo; communal labor inspector
IDT	Inspector Departmental del Trabajo; departmental labor inspector
INSORA	Instituto de Organización y Administración; Institute of Organization and Administration
IPT	Inspector Provincial del Trabajo; provincial labor inspector
LDPD	Ley de Defensa Permanente de la Democracia; Law for the Permanent Defense of Democracy
MEMCh	Movimiento Pro-Emancipación de la Mujer Chilena; Movement for the Emancipation of the Chilean Woman
MNS	Movimiento Nacional Socialista; National Socialist Party
PCCh	Partido Comunista de Chile; Chilean Communist Party
PD	Partido Demócrata; Democrat Party
PD-co	Partido Democratico; Democratic Party
PDU	Partido Democrático Unificado; Unified Democratic Party
POS	Partido Obrero Socialista; Socialist Workers' Party
PR	Partido Radical; Radical Party
PS	Partido Socialista; Socialist Party
PSA	Partido Socialista Auténtico; Authentic Socialist Party
PST	Partido Socialista de los Trabajadores; Workers' Socialist Party
RJAIC	Robert J. Alexander Papers: Interview Collection
Schwager	Compañía Carbonífera y de Fundición Schwager; Schwager Coal Mining and Foundry Company
SERCh	Servicio Electoral República de Chile; Chilean Electoral Service
USNA, RG 59	United States National Archives, Record Group 59

INTRODUCTION:

COMMUNISTS, COAL MINERS, AND CHILEAN DEMOCRACY

On October 4, 1947, when nearly eighteen thousand workers in Chile's coal industry began a legally authorized strike, they met with the most thorough and severe repression ever experienced in the coal mining region. Army, Navy, and Air Force personnel took total control of the mines, towns, and surrounding countryside. Over the next days, weeks, and months, they sent hundreds of people to military prison camps and banished thousands more from the region.[1]

Many previous strikes in Chile had been broken by force, but on few other occasions had the head of state ordered a full military assault on an entire region of the nation. This was a key moment in twentieth-century Chilean history, when the Cold War exploded on the domestic scene with the violent quelling of a powerful regional workers' movement that had pushed for more inclusive democracy and greater socioeconomic justice. What made this experience even more shocking for the working-class men and women of the coal mines and around the country was that the man responsible for these acts, Gabriel González Videla, was not a despotic enemy of democracy or an oppressor of the common people, but rather the very man who had solicited their votes "with tears in his eyes," promising "that under his government there would no longer be so much suffering."[2] Indeed, this was the man for whom Communist Senator Pablo Neruda had crisscrossed the country declaring in speeches and a poem, "The people call you Gabriel" ("El pueblo lo llama Gabriel").[3]

1. For a full discussion of the miners' strike of October 1947 and its aftermath, see chapter 9.

2. Interview with Pastor Manuel Cifuentes.

3. "El pueblo lo llama Gabriel" is the title of a poem Neruda wrote for a campaign rally in Santiago in mid-1946 but refused to publish after González Videla turned against the Communists (see chapter 8, note 2). Neruda had begun publishing volumes of poetry in 1923, at age nineteen. He received the National Prize in Literature in 1945, the same year he was elected to the Senate. By the time of González Videla's 1946 presidential campaign, Neruda was quite a prestigious literary figure.

Now, just over a year later, González Videla accused Pablo Neruda of treasonous defamation and had him stripped of his congressional immunity. After fleeing across the Andes to escape arrest, Neruda lambasted his former ally in every possible forum. In articles and pamphlets, and even in his poetic masterwork *Canto general*, Neruda reviled González Videla as a traitor, Judas, clown, a "miserable mixture of monkey and rat, whose tail is combed with a gold pomade on Wall Street."[4]

Shortly after the assault on the coal mining region, President González Videla secured passage of one of the most draconian internal state security laws in the Americas at the time. Formally directed against the Communist Party, the highly controversial 1948 "Law for the Permanent Defense of Democracy" disenfranchised nearly forty thousand voters nationwide. Largely from the working class, these men and women were not only removed from electoral registers but also barred from belonging to unions, going on strike, and enjoying other hard-won rights as workers and as citizens. Dubbing it "the Damned Law," people across the political spectrum denounced this legislation as threatening the very foundations of Chilean democracy. In the words of Socialist Senator and future President Salvador Allende Gossens, this "initiative of the Executive" was "an atomic bomb dropped in the midst of our republican principles, habits, and customs."[5] Roughly 15 percent of the persecuted and excluded citizens hailed from the coal mining zone in southern Chile, where González Videla's policy aimed not only to repress Communists and labor leaders, but to unravel the entire social, political, and cultural fabric of the region, which had come to symbolize a threat to existing hierarchies of power and distribution of resources.

González Videla's presidency (1946–52) marked the transition from an era of radical democratic promise to the exclusionary politics of the Cold War.[6] His was the third in a series of Center-Left governments in Chile that gained power beginning in the mid-1930s, amid global depression,

---

4. Neruda, *Canto general*, 201. In total, nearly a quarter of the passages in *Canto general* refer to the coal miners, González Videla's betrayal, or both; see, for example, pp. 145, 168, 129–70, 196–201, 207, 232, 239, 245, 250, 260, 276–79, 321–27, 332–35.

5. Salvador Allende Gossens, Senate Session, June 18, 1948, 722–23, BCNCh.

6. González Videla has received surprisingly little scholarly attention. I know of no English-language works dedicated to his biography or his presidency and very few in Spanish, most notably *Gabriel González Videla*, a short hagiography published by Guzmán Hernández in 1946. Only in the 1990s did Chilean scholars begin to address the president's 1947–48 about-face; see, for example, Sala de Tourón, "La guerra fría"; Etchepare Jensen, "El advenimiento"; and Valdés Urrutia, "Chile, ruido de sables." Not until 2009 did Carlos Huneeus publish the first monograph focused on the González Videla administration, *La guerra fría chilena*.

rising Fascism, and a looming world war. In this context, Communists across Latin America responded to the call of the Moscow-led International to form alliances with presumably progressive bourgeois parties, a strategy known as the "Popular Front." This move away from strident class warfare was tied both to international anti-Fascism and to nationalist plans for industrial growth developed in the midst of the Great Depression.

The strategy of Center-Left alliances achieved notable results in various countries, but only in Chile did a Popular Front along European lines succeed in winning the presidency.[7] In 1938, an electoral coalition of Socialists, Communists, the centrist Radical Party, and other smaller groups successfully rallied behind the moderate Radical candidate Pedro Aguirre Cerda. Its victory marked the beginning of three coalition governments, which generated new possibilities—politically, institutionally, and discursively—for Chilean popular sectors to forge collective identities and assert their interests. Democracy and capitalism took on new social reform dimensions, as Marxist parties and their working-class followers increased their power by acting within rather than against existing systems. The election of three consecutive Radicals was no minor feat in Chile, where the executive had been controlled almost continuously by right-wing Liberals and Conservatives since Chile's consolidation as a sovereign nation-state after 1830.

The Chilean Popular Front in its original and strictest form began with political discussions in 1935–36 and endured through the end of 1940, when the Socialists withdrew from the coalition. Marxist parties, however, continued to support centrist politicians throughout World War II in ever-shifting and often quite volatile alliances. *Mining for the Nation*

---

7. The Communist promotion of Popular Front–type alliances in other Latin American countries in the 1930s and 1940s had varying degrees of success. On Cuba, see, for example, Ameringer, *Cuban Democratic Experience* (2000); Thomas, book VII, "The Age of Democracy, 1934–52," in *Cuba* (1998), 689–786; and Whitney, *State and Revolution* (2001). On Mexico, see Carr, *Marxism* (1993); Knight, "Mexico, 1930–1946" (1990) and "Cardenismo" (1994); Niblo, *Mexico in the 1940s* (1999); and Olcott, *Revolutionary Women* (2005). On Costa Rica, see Miller, "Labour" (1990); Cerdas Cruz, *La otra cara* (1998); and Molina Jiménez, *Anticomunismo reformista* (2007). On Venezuela, see Steve Ellner, "Venezuelan Left" (1979) and *Los partidos políticos* (1980). On Brazil, see works by John D. French, esp. "Workers and the Rise" (1988) and *Brazilian Workers' ABC* (1992). Several monographs and edited collections provide comparative perspective on the 1930s and 1940s. See Humphreys, *Latin America* (1981); Bethell and Roxborough, *Latin America* (1992); Rock, *Latin America* (1994); and Leonard and Bratzel, *Latin America* (2007). For a broad and ambitious comparative analysis of Latin American labor politics across the twentieth century, see Collier and Collier, *Shaping the Political Arena* (2002). The only case beyond Chile addressed in *Mining for the Nation* is Argentina, and even that is with great brevity.

covers the "Popular Front era" in the broader sense, referring to the series of coalition governments that achieved power in the mid-twentieth century and the social bases that underlay them. Framed in its international context, the era began around the time of Hitler's rise to power in the years leading up to the Seventh Congress of the Comintern (1935), when the formation of Popular Fronts was officially promoted as Communist strategy. It came to an end in the wake of World War II, when new lines of global division and alliance began to take shape around an increasingly intractable U.S.–Soviet conflict. In terms of Chilean administrations, the broadly conceived Popular Front era included (1) President Aguirre Cerda's original Popular Front (1938–40) and the remainder of his presidency until his death in late 1941; (2) the Democratic Alliance of Juan Antonio Ríos Morales (1942–46), in which Communists, Socialists, Radicals, and even Liberals offered and withheld their support at various points; and (3) the first year of Gabriel González Videla's presidency (1946–47), when he governed with a highly unusual and unstable "National Unity" cabinet that included Radicals, Liberals, and—for the first time in the Americas—Communists.[8]

The story then continues through the late 1940s, when González Videla moved violently against Communists, coal miners, and other popular sectors, putting an end to what had promised to be one of the most progressive episodes of governance in the Americas. The chapters that follow recount the dramatic history of this period of democratic coalitions and tragic betrayal from the perspective of the men and women who produced Chile's domestic coal, a fuel so vital for midcentury industrialization that it was frequently referred to as "black gold." A distinct region—la zona carbonífera—rose up in the late nineteenth and early twentieth centuries, comprising towns, ports, and railroads born of the coal mines, together with the surrounding fields and forests that fed the workers and timbered the tunnels. This region came to be marked not only by interwoven sites of production but also by a strong collective identity that historically influenced both the development of industrial relations and the direction of national politics and culture. As the coal miners organized and mobilized in conjunction with the Communist Party, the land of the "black gold" came to be seen in the national imagination as Chile's foremost "Red zone" or "Little Moscow."

8. In Cuba in 1944, at the height of the Anglo-American-Soviet alliance, Fulgencio Batista named two Communists to his wartime cabinet in what has also been described as a "Popular Front government"; these ministers, however, were "without portfolio." See chapter 8, note 21. In Chile, by contrast, Communists headed the powerful Ministries of Public Works, Agriculture, and Lands and Colonization.

Beginning about 30 kilometers (some 20 miles) south of Concepción, Chile's second largest city, the historical coal mining region stretches down the Gulf of Arauco from the Bío-Bío River to the coastal town of Lebu, as shown in the frontispiece map. In 1940, over 135,000 residents lived in and around more than a dozen urban, urbanizing, and rural communities, each linked to coal in various ways. The region's demographic and economic core was the adjacent towns of Lota and Coronel. Nearly sixteen thousand people, or 11 percent of the regional population, worked directly for one of several private coal mining companies, which, unlike Chile's copper mines, were exclusively owned by domestic capital.[9] Yet, even as regional identity centered around the extraction of black gold, a more complex weave of productive, social, and cultural dynamics shaped its contours. In addition to its mines, the region's ports, railroads, factories, markets, farms, vineyards, forests, and fishing villages were all distinct productive sites where people forged occupational, community, and political affiliations.

When the Great Depression shattered Chile's export-based economy, and the nation embarked on a path of industrialization, domestic coal became such a vital commodity that its scarcity would severely affect the entire country. Public concern with coal production intensified further during World War II, when Great Britain and the United States, Chile's principal sources of imported coal, had no surplus to sell. Chileans of all walks of life began to ardently discuss not only issues of productivity and work processes in the mines, but also the balance of political forces in the coal region and conditions of daily life there, including housing, sanitation, alcoholism, and violence.

The battle for greater inclusion and social justice waged in the coal mining zone during the Popular Front period was only the latest episode in a much longer process. Following closely on the heels of northern nitrate and port workers, the coal miners and their neighbors developed strong traditions of labor organization and political mobilization beginning in the closing decades of the nineteenth century. As sketched in chapter 1, workers of the coal mining region provided significant support to the Democrat Party (Partido Demócrata; PD), founded in 1887, and shortly afterward to a leftist breakaway called the Socialist Workers' Party (Partido Obrero Socialista; POS). When the POS voted to become the Chilean Communist Party (Partido Comunista de Chile; PCCh) in 1922, coal miners enthusiastically endorsed the move into the international Marxist

9. Dirección General de Estadísticas, Censo de 1940, BNCh.

camp. By the mid-1940s, the miners' ability to act as the vanguard of a broadly inclusive "coal mining zone" thus rested on the vital importance of domestic coal to the national economy, on their high degree of organization, and on their strong political affiliation.

The coal miners also made optimal use of the legal rights and political avenues accorded to them in Chile's modern industrial relations system, embodied in the 1931 Labor Code, which most of the workers' movement had warily accepted a decade before. The series of 1920s laws and decrees that were consolidated in the Labor Code laid the foundation for a tripartite system in which labor, capitalists, and state actors would each play theoretically equal roles in affairs such as contract negotiations and conflict resolutions. State institutions and actors were called on to justly regulate society as was required by organized capitalism.

In the mid-1930s, when leftist parties and labor organizations mobilized their supporters to participate in electoral politics, they quickly began to win public offices of all types, at the local, regional, and national levels. And, as leftist parties joined with the governing coalitions, they also gained an unprecedented number of appointed positions. With such increased representation, the Chilean coal miners, and millions of other workers across the county believed they finally had access to significant policy-making arenas. They pushed to make representational politics effectively serve the interests of the popular sectors, not just those of the oligarchic and bourgeois elites or foreign investors. There was a sense of democracy in the air at the larger rallies of the Popular Front years—as when U.S. Vice President Henry Wallace visited the coal mines in 1943 or when González Videla made his campaign stop in Lota in 1946.

The coal miners felt that they now had powerful advocates and greater opportunities to pursue their interests, to direct their own lives, and perhaps even to influence the country and the world. Local notions of democratization were integrally tied to a growing sense of empowerment, or awareness of one's historical agency, that swept through the coal towns in the Popular Front era—even as residents continued to struggle with poor living and working conditions and myriad capitalist abuses. Committed to the defeat of Fascism during the war, the coal miners also fought for their own rights and well-being and insisted on their full participation in the shaping of postwar democracy. They were not easily dissuaded from pursuing state-led reform toward greater inclusiveness and social justice, even as they repeatedly came up against continued forms of class antagonism and the capitalists' powerful influence over (and symbiosis with) government leaders.

Personal narratives of the 1930s and 1940s highlight the emotional dimension, the "structures of feeling," the sense of hope, purpose, and excitement generated in the hearts and minds of millions of Chileans when President Pedro Aguirre Cerda shouted his slogans "Bread, Roof, Overcoat!" and "To Govern Is to Educate!" The memories of leftist artists and intellectuals about the Popular Front era also emphasize a change in "the spirit of the times," with an upsurge in café debates and populist cultural productions. The writers and dramatists of the "Generation of '38," poet Gonzalo Rojas recalled, saw themselves as part of, or at least representing, the euphoric rise of the Chilean masses.[10]

The sense of democratic possibilities, of new opportunities for Chilean workers, engendered by the Popular Front was not simply a matter of populist rhetoric or political enthusiasm. Throughout the country, but particularly in the coal mining region, Communists and Socialists—most often from the working class themselves—were elected and appointed to key positions in government and civil society. As mayors and governors, national deputies and senators, labor department officials and school-teachers, as leaders of labor unions, athletic clubs, and even religious groups, these new actors changed the tone and content of politics in the coal communities, where open town councils, for example, were regularly held as a way to democratize municipal decisions. They also transformed the government's mediation of industrial conflicts, interpreting the rules in new ways and strengthening workers' confidence in the legal unions and the official labor relations system developed in the 1920s. In the words of Chilean sociologist Jorge Marambio, "The interval between the triumph of the Popular Front and the strike of 1947 presented a situation where, for the first time, particularly in the government of Pedro Aguirre Cerda, the coal mining world fully place[d] its hopes in the State, as an agent for mediating, and ultimately resolving, disputes."[11]

The Popular Front project of national development was to be achieved through an alliance of the proletariat and the progressive bourgeoisie, with the impartial mediation of an interventionist state. What Marambio points out here is that this model was not simply imposed on the Chilean people. For labor leaders, politicians, and activists of the coal mining zone, this venture in no way implied an immediate end to class conflict or suppression of workers' class-based interests. Quite to the contrary,

10. Gonzalo Rojas, television interview, "Off the Record," Channel 5 (Universidad Católica de Valparaíso), January 14, 2001.
11. Marambio, *Identidad cultural*, 78.

workers would now have access to the political and governmental actors and institutions with the power and, they believed, the will, to resolve conflicts in their favor.

In the 1940s, Communist-led coal miners emerged at the fore of a broad movement to deepen democracy and to use their newfound power in the public sphere to increase the pace and scope of social reform. This movement enjoyed the support of many community residents who did not work in the coal mines, including fishermen, bakers, shopkeepers, schoolteachers, and civil employees. The miners' consciousness and actions also developed in connection with workers of the region's forests, lumberyards, railroads, docks, breweries, and the nation's first hydroelectric plant, Chivilingo. Beyond the coal region itself, miners certainly paid close attention to the affairs of workers at the Chiguayante textile mills, the ceramics factory in Penco, and further afield, the northern ports, nitrate and copper mines, as well as burgeoning industries around Santiago.

The Chilean Communist Party (PCCh) served as a unifying umbrella for large segments of workers in all these different occupations and places. The party also provided leadership and backing for groups organized on generational, gender, and community lines, such as the Communist Youth of Chile (Juventudes Comunistas de Chile; JJCC), the Movement for the Emancipation of the Chilean Woman (Movimiento Pro-Emancipación de la Mujer Chilena; MEMCh), and neighborhood associations (*juntas de vecinos*). Through their local offices, these groups—together with Communist-sponsored athletic and social clubs—were key forums through which the PCCh influenced the culture of the coal towns and recruited and socialized the next generation of regional workers. Many people I interviewed highlighted the significance of such organizations in their early political and social formation.

Perhaps above all, the coal miners—and all Chilean workers in industrial sectors—had a strong interest in the outcome of what Brian Loveman describes as Chile's "struggle in the countryside."[12] Tenant farmers and wage laborers on agricultural estates had long fought for the right to organize, but Chile's entrenched landed interests had repeatedly, and often brutally, stymied their efforts. The Chilean Communist Party was one of several groups trying for decades to get a foothold among rural

---

12. *Struggle in the Countryside* is Loveman's now-classic 1976 study of rural politics and social relations in Chile from 1919 to 1973. See also the Loveman companion volume *Documentary Supplement*.

sectors. As the Communists gained power and momentum in the Popular Front era, it was their attempts to organize rural labor, even more than their activities in the coal mines or other industrial areas, that most alarmed the political Right. After all, the Liberal and Conservative Parties did not expect to gain a majority of votes in the coal towns, but loss of votes in rural provinces, where they dominated, would decrease their numbers in Congress—their only hope to prevent more rapid reforms after 1938.

The gains and possibilities opened for the coal miners in the Popular Front era were predicated in large part both on tacit agreements and on formal decrees that prevented advances for rural workers and tenant farmers. Throughout the 1932–64 period, Loveman explains, estate owners (*hacendados*) were able to preserve the rural status quo by making "concessions to urban interests in matters involving industrialization and economic policy in exchange for nonintervention of the state in the countryside—except to aid the hacendados and, particularly, to assist them in the repression of rural labor."[13] In other words, the coal miners, though significant players in the struggle for greater inclusion and social justice in mid-twentieth-century Chile, were not the most critical threat to the political equilibrium of Chile's formal democracy.

Yet, even though urban workers won concessions when their leaders and political representatives ceded ground on "the rural question," they themselves participated actively in efforts to organize tenant farmers and estate workers. Such organizing efforts were especially strong in 1938 and early 1939, at the beginning of Aguirre Cerda's presidency (1938–41), and again in 1946–47, when President González Videla created a temporary opening for renewed mobilization. With their high degree of party loyalty and combativeness, the workers of the coal mining zone provided an important base of support for a more radical agenda in the countryside, where most miners still had strong family ties. And, at times, as in the story of the Colicheu estate recounted below, miners even mobilized directly as the Communist Party's shock troops in agrarian conflicts.

Mining the Fields

In early 1942, a group of coal miners traveled to Cabrero, a small town 80 kilometers (about 50 miles) inland from Lota, to converse with tenant

13. Loveman, *Struggle*, xxviii.

farmers (*inquilinos*) who had been evicted from the nearby Colicheu estate. The owner of this property was a former presidential candidate, Liberal politician Enrique Zañartu Prieto, who was so outraged that he wrote to the precinct police chief:

> I must warn you: they tell me that when the Communists said goodbye to the tenant farmers at Cabrero yesterday, they told them they would return with more people from Lota, to leave them installed at the Estate. I bring this to your attention because, if I find any one of them [from Lota], even in town, I'll shoot him with all the weapons I have, which, though not a lot, will be enough to leave some of them on the ground. Since it is better to prevent than to cure, I thought it appropriate to inform you of the situation.[14]

This was certainly not the first time coal miners had participated in rural organizing and resistance efforts. In Zañartu Prieto's denunciation, "comrades from Concepción and Lota" had long been pushing his tenants "to follow the Communist line [*consigna*]." Under such instigation, he reported, some of his tenants had attacked, robbed, and sabotaged those who "refused to be deceived by the seditious elements [*revoltosos*]"; they had even set fire to a briar patch near his son's wheat fields. Family members of the evicted tenants were mounting a campaign of "permanent agitation," Zañartu Prieto claimed, and he requested that police forces be sent to round them up. Landowners' resort to violence, even inflicted by their own hands, was also not a new phenomenon in Chile. Yet the particular way Zañartu Prieto worded his threat in 1942 points toward an interesting configuration in the Popular Front period. Although clearly enraged at the tenant farmers on his estate, he saved his most bitter denunciations for Communist coal miners and urban workers as external agitators. Without their involvement, Zañartu Prieto knew he would have a much easier time maintaining a compliant, atomized workforce—as his ancestors had done for more than a century.

In the context of the national development model of the 1930s and 1940s, access to (or influence over) state actors became one of the major points of contention between workers and their employers, both urban and rural. Thus, at the same time that he wrote to the police lieutenant

---

14. Letter from Zañartu Prieto to Cabrero Police Lieutenant, February 4, 1942; see also a report, dated February 1942 [no day given], from ICT (Inspector Comunal del Trabajo; Communal Labor Inspector) to IPT (Inspector Provincial del Trabajo; Provincial Labor Inspector), both in FIC, vol. 2255, ANCh.

calling for state force to protect his private property, Zañartu Prieto also wrote to his "esteemed old friend" Desiderio González, intendant of the province of Concepción, a public official appointed by the president. Zañartu Prieto first thanked González "for the kindness you have shown us with regard to the workers' conflict that is becoming endemic in Colicheu and threatens to spread to the entire zone."[15] He then condemned the subdelegate of Cabrero, Francisco Viveros—another executive appointee—for "head[ing] the Communist agitation, disturbing the work of the farmers, and issuing slanderous documents that he makes the workers sign."[16] In both this letter and the one he sent to the police chief, Zañartu Prieto claimed that Viveros's drugstore (*botica*) was the central meeting place for the Communists who arrived from Concepción and Lota, and that his house was always filled with "a seditious crowd [*un choclón sedicioso*]."

The poor lieutenant who ran police operations for the rural district around Cabrero must have felt a bit overwhelmed when he received this letter. After all, it did not come from just any irate hacendado, but from Enrique Zañartu Prieto—a powerful Liberal Party leader. Zañartu Prieto had served as finance minister in Carlos Dávila's short-lived government in 1932, when he had also run for president "as a more reformist candidate of the elites."[17] Though relatively progressive, Zañartu Prieto represented the landed aristocracy, precisely the sector with which President Aguirre Cerda and the Popular Front parties made a tacit pact to suspend rural unionization in March 1939. In the early months of the Popular Front government, as Loveman explains, "a massive wave of labor conflict and unionization" swept the countryside, instigated largely by Communist, Trotskyist, and Socialist activists. This raised serious alarm among "the Conservative-Liberal opposition" and even among "members of the President's own party."[18] Aguirre Cerda responded by issuing Ministerial Order no. 34, in March 1939, which instructed labor department officials to "suspend all activity [*tramitación*] related to the constitution of agricultural unions." This order effectively blocked the creation of rural unions and

15. Letter from Zañartu Prieto to Cabrero Police Lieutenant, February 4, 1942, FIC, vol. 2255, ANCh.

16. Technically, subdelegates were named by departmental governors, who were themselves "named by the president of the Republic on the recommendation of the intendente of the province." Loveman, *Struggle*, xix.

17. Drake, *Socialism and Populism*, 91. See also Millas, *En tiempos*, 215. After winning only 12.4 percent of the national vote in the 1932 presidential elections, Zañartu Prieto was reelected senator for Concepción.

18. Loveman, *Chile*, 212.

the presentation of collective demands; it would remain in effect until November 1946.[19]

The Communist and Socialist Parties, as well as the Confederation of Chilean Workers (Confederación de Trabajadores de Chile; CTCh), initially accepted the president's March 1939 decree, even though it violated the 1931 Labor Code.[20] In return, the National Agricultural Society (Sociedad Nacional de Agricultura; SNA), representing the landowners, "agreed to try to prevent its members from dismissing workers and throwing them off the land, as they had been doing in retaliation for unionization and the presentation of labor petitions."[21] In the case of Zañartu Prieto in 1942, the SNA clearly failed to prevent such reprisals. The only group to protest from the beginning against "the government's acquiescence to landowner demands" was a Trotskyist breakaway from the Chilean Communist Party, led by deputy Emilio Zapata Díaz, who formed Chile's first national peasant league. By 1940, the Trotskyists were joined by a group of deputies from the Socialist Party (later dubbed the "Nonconformists"), who also opposed the ban on rural unionization.

In the midst of mounting tension, in mid-1940, President Aguirre Cerda reiterated his insistence that agrarian conflicts would not be tolerated, and, through a circular order issued by the interior minister, he "instructed the *carabineros* [national police] to repress the activity of 'professional agitators who provoke problems in the countryside and industrial centers.'"[22] This greatly angered workers throughout the country, as well as most Socialists and Communists, who dominated the Confederation of Chilean Workers, which had formed in 1936.

In the coal mining town of Curanilahue, for example, Communists held a rally in October 1940 to hear from their delegate, José Cruz Delgado, who had just returned from the national PCCh convention in Santiago. When Cruz finished his report, the Curanilahue Communists unanimously adopted a series of resolutions, the first of which insisted both that the government rescind the interior minister's circular ordering the national police to suppress unionization in the countryside (and elsewhere) and that it facilitate the formation of rural unions; their fifth and

---

19. Loveman, *Struggle*, 119. A copy of Ministerial Order no. 34 is in Loveman, *Documentary Supplement*, 102–3. A significant precedent for this 1939 de facto executive ban on rural unions was a telegram-circular issued by the administration of Arturo Alessandri Palma in 1933, which ordered labor officials "to refrain from assisting in the constitution of organizations of this type." As Loveman notes in *Struggle*, 115, "No new rural unions gained legal recognition until 1937."

20. Loveman, *Chile*, 212–13, and *Struggle*, 118–19.

21. Loveman, *Struggle*, 118.

22. Loveman, *Chile*, 214.

final resolution supported all measures taken by the CTCh to promote rural unionization. The Communists also voted to reinvigorate the work of local brigades who traveled to the countryside to help organize their compatriots ("Brigadas de Obreros Organizados a Constituir Sindicatos Agrícolas").[23]

Just a few months later, in early 1941, Schwager miners gathered to hear a report from their delegates to the provincial CTCh meeting in Concepción. One of the proposals they were asked to vote on was whether to contribute 10 centavos (0.10 peso) per member toward a fund that would enable the confederation to hire a paid consultant to coordinate the rural organizing campaign. The Schwager miners overwhelmingly agreed, as did the majority of CTCh member unions throughout the province.[24] Despite such efforts to oppose and circumvent it, the ban on rural organizing would be maintained and enforced by Aguirre Cerda's successor, Juan Antonio Ríos Morales (1942–46), an even more conservative Radical closely tied to landed interests, especially in his home province of Arauco, where the Curanilahue and Lebu coal mines were located.

This was the context in which the conflict in Colicheu had erupted in 1942. According to Max Jiménez, the provincial labor inspector (Inspector Provincial del Trabajo; IPT) for Concepción, over one hundred workers, out of a total of four hundred and eighty on the estate, had submitted a contract petition. Since this was less than the required two-thirds, the petition was ruled illegal, and the owner quickly "took the initiative of firing more or less eighty-four workers," whom he deemed to be rabble-rousers.[25] The workers denounced Zañartu Prieto not only for these reprisals but also for violating other labor laws. According to Inspector Jiménez, the main problem was that Zañartu Prieto owed his workers thirteen months of back pay, totaling 145,443.45 pesos. At the inspector's insistence, Zañartu Prieto finally did pay these wages, but then—in "a clear violation of the Law"—he demanded that the eighty-four laid-off workers leave the estate within twenty-four hours. Jiménez eventually brokered an agreement that gave the workers two months to vacate the property. Meanwhile, the questions of the legitimacy of the contract petitions and of the estate owner's right to dismiss tenant workers in retaliation were

---

23. *Frente Popular* (Concepción), October 19, 1940, 8.

24. Report on Schwager Union Assembly of January 26, 1941, prepared by Chief of Community Security Juan Mococaín H., Schwager Welfare Department, January 27, 1941, FIC, vol. 2228, ANCh.

25. Report from ICT to IPT, February 1942; Telegram no. 612, from Interior Minister, February 13, 1942, both in FIC, vol. 2255, ANCh.

turned over to the Permanent Conciliation Board of the department of Yumbel.

In some ways, time stood still in the Chilean countryside during the Popular Front years, as a series of agreements and decrees at the presidential level effectively blocked rural union organizing. Yet, beneath the illusory stillness, seething conflicts were taken up by a generation of civil servants with new political alignments and policy views. The IPT for Concepción, Max Jiménez, for example, represented the now decades-old, yet still growing cadre of professional (some leftist and Left-leaning) labor bureaucrats, who sought to uphold Chile's progressive social legislation—the "constitutionalists" of the Ministry of Labor.[26] Though officials such as Jiménez (whether of Communist, Socialist, Democratic, Radical, or other political persuasion) were still beleaguered in many places, it was due in no small part to their efforts that hacendados such as Zañartu Prieto had lost absolute control over the people and occurrences on their rural property. This was a key factor behind Zañartu Prieto's threats of violence. As Loveman explains,

> For these landowners, private property meant that governmental regulation did not extend into the territory of their proprietary domain. The use of force by landowners also indicated, however, that in some cases, despite all efforts to evade or subvert application of labor law, labor inspectors insisted on compliance. Physical force, the least subtle and, over the long run, the least effective manner of resistance to labor legislation in the Chilean context, represented an anachronistic response by landowners unable to otherwise impede the increasing restriction of proprietary authority contained in labor law.[27]

As discussed throughout this book, especially in chapter 5, coal mine owners also reacted in often rash and defensive ways when dealing with what they perceived as undue state encroachments on their relations with

---

26. Another quite progressive member of the growing corps of professional labor officials was Héctor Escríbar Mandiola, the head of the Ministry of Labor's legal section in 1939, who "persistently rejected . . . the legal validity" of the executive ban on rural unions. Loveman, *Struggle*, 119. In 1946, when President González Videla finally repealed the ban, he chose Escríbar to head the Ministry of Labor, as director general of labor (Director General del Trabajo; DGT). For a glimpse of a slightly less progressive paragon of the labor bureaucracy, see the discussion of Mariano Bustos Lagos in chapter 4.

27. Loveman, *Struggle*, 105.

their workers and control of "their towns," or fiefdoms, as the Communists alleged. In addition to similarities (and differences) between how landed elites and mining capitalists experienced the expanded state role in social relations, the story of the Chilean countryside provides a significant backdrop to the coal miners' story for a number of reasons. First, almost all miners and other urban residents had relatives, often immediate family members, who worked in near or distant fields and forests. Many miners had themselves migrated from the countryside, or at least their parents had, and, throughout the 1940s, coal companies and provincial government officials continued to complain about the high numbers of urban workers who just abandoned their jobs at harvesttime.[28]

Second, the coal companies themselves were the largest landowners in the vicinity, with huge tracts of forest, crops, and grazing land. The Coal Mining and Industrial Company of Lota (Compáñia Carbonifera e Industrial de Lota; CCIL) alone owned over 60,000 hectares (about 150,000 acres) in the province of Concepción and had a vast workforce of tenant farmers and rural wage laborers.[29] The company's tree plantations, begun in the 1880s, had grown by the mid-1940s to more than 30,000 hectares (about 75,000 acres) of eucalyptus for timbering the mines and several varieties of pine for manufacturing boards and shipping crates. The spread of these artificial forests pushed small farmers off their land, contributing to the pool of people who, over decades, came to depend on the coal mining companies for their livelihood.

Juan Sánchez Guerrero's 1963 novel *Hijo de las piedras* tells the story of one rural family forced into the mining life when the CCIL expanded its forest holdings. "We lived happily working well our own land," the mother tells her son. "We had everything in our home. We were free. . . . One bad day, covered in clouds of dust, your father pulling the yoke and me, with you in my arms, up in the cart, we entered the precincts of the mine company . . . and committed ourselves to a life sentence, just as our land was conquered by pine trees."[30] Urban and rural workers were indeed

28. In 1942, for example, a labor official estimated that coal production was down by 40,000 to 50,000 tons due to the flight of workers to the countryside. It was especially important to avoid "a repetition of these occurrences," the official noted, "since it is vital that national coal replace a portion of the combustible petroleum that we cannot import." Oficio no. 2666, November 28, 1942, FDGT, 1943 Oficios, vol. 3, ARNAD (my knowledge of this document comes from Brian Loveman). The hundreds of CCIL personnel files I read also showed significant instances of temporary migration of coal company employees back and forth from the countryside.

29. For a summary breakdown of the CCIL's landholdings, see Astorquiza, *Lota* (1929), 156–57; *Lota* (1942), 164–65; Astorquiza and Galleguillos V., *Cien años*, 260.

30. Sánchez Guerrero, *Hijo*, 30–31, 36.

not entirely separate groups of people. As with these evicted tenant farmers, many families moved from countryside to town, as did quite a few young boys who began planting tree seedlings or clearing forests and worked their way up to jobs in the mines—with higher pay and greater risks.[31] In the other direction, coal miners were often transferred, voluntarily or punitively, to the company's forests, fields, lumberyards, and road and canal construction sites.

In addition to the forests, the coal companies' agricultural holdings also grew rapidly. By the mid-1940s, CCIL-owned estates, such as Los Rios, Maquehua, and Quilachanquín (roughly 4,000 hectares, or about 10,000 acres, each, in the province of Arauco), provided pasture for thousands of cows, sheep, and horses; other smaller properties grew vegetables and grains. On the company's Hacienda Escuadrón, just north of Coronel, 7,000 hectares (17,000 acres) were dedicated to dairy cows, with a mechanized milking and processing plant since 1932. According to CCIL Welfare Chief Octavio Astorquiza, this property produced roughly 700,000 liters (185,000 gallons) of milk annually in the mid-1940s, most of which was distributed to company employees in the coal towns and throughout the region at below-market prices.[32]

Workers on the company's rural properties—as well as farmers who had been pushed off of them—were people with whom the miners had strong connections, including both their food supply and a shared employer, not to mention bloodlines. They were thus usually the first workers that "brigades" of Communists from Concepción, Lota, or Curanilahue sought to organize. On the CCIL's 20,000-hectare (50,000-acre) Fundo Colcura, Schwager's Fundo Calabozo, the Lebu coal company's Fundo Trongol, among many others, efforts to form unions and to present collective demands provoked continual conflict in the 1930s and 1940s. Organizing momentum, often led by Communist militants from mining towns, was particularly intense at the beginning of both the Aguirre Cerda and González Videla presidencies.

In 1946–47, all of the CCIL's agricultural and forestry operations were transferred to a new company, the Sociedad Agrícola y Forestal Colcura (SAFC; Colcura Agricultural and Forestry Society). Workers of the SAFC

---

31. Of the 320 CCIL personnel files I reviewed, 233 specified the workers' means of livelihood before their employment at the CCIL. Of these 233 workers, 92, or 39 percent, had been working in some capacity in agriculture and forestry. The real proportion of workers coming from rural areas was likely much higher and included many whose previous occupation was not specified, especially the children who had not worked before and seemed to come from campesino families.

32. Astorquiza, Lota (1942), 165; Astorquiza and Galleguillos V., Cien años, 260.

quickly formed two new industrial unions, one based in Lota and one in Curanilahue.[33] The first president of the Curanilahue union was Victoriano Pérez Torres, a former leader of the Schwager miners' union, who had worked his way up in the local and provincial Confederation of Chilean Workers, eventually serving on its Agrarian Commission. Though he seems to have had roots in Curanilahue, Pérez Torres's decision to apply for a job in the SAFC certainly related to his intent to organize, again indicating the significance of coal miners in spearheading the regional movement.[34]

Despite the efforts of miners and other workers around the country to organize their rural counterparts and to pressure the government to break its compromising ties with agrarian elites, the executive ban on rural unions would remain in effect until November 1946. Then, to the great satisfaction of his Communist allies, President González Videla finally rescinded the 1939 policy, giving rise to new hopes and a flurry of mobilization. As one of the first signs of his imminent betrayal, however, González Videla quickly renewed repressive restrictions on rural labor, first with Law no. 8811 of mid-1947, followed by the Law for the Permanent Defense of Democracy (Ley de Defensa Permanente de la Democracia; LDPD) in mid-1948, both of which again halted leftist momentum in the countryside. On the Lota SAFC union, two out of five leaders would be banished from the coal region during the October 1947 strike, and four of them would be charged as Communists and placed on the LDPD blacklists. Though Chile's twentieth-century rural politics and social relations are not the focus of this book, this far-from-idyllic pastoral history was a significant counterpart to the coal miners' story.

Based on extensive archival research and oral histories, *Mining for the Nation* challenges portrayals of the Popular Front as a passive experience for workers, revealing instead a decade of complex, Communist-led organization and mobilization around a project of participatory democracy and

33. The executives and board of directors for the Colcura Agricultural and Forestry Society (SAFC) were almost identical to those of the CCIL. The structure of SAFC unions also paralleled that of the CCIL miners, who had separate unions in Lota and Curanilahue. On the constitution of the SAFC Lota union, see Oficio no. 2474, July 31, 1947, and on the Curanilahue union, "Acta de Constitución," July 20, 1947, both in FDGT, 1947 Providencias, vol. 29, ARNAD. See also Astorquiza and Galleguillos V., *Cien años*, 143, 255.

34. On Victoriano Pérez Torres, see Report on Schwager Union Assembly of January 26, 1941, prepared by Chief of Community Security Juan Mococaín H., Schwager Welfare Department, January 27, 1941, FIC, vol. 2228, ANCh. Victoriano's roots were likely in Curanilahue since his brother, Juan de Dios, was a Communist councilman there in the 1940s, who was elected president of the Curanilahue Industrial Union of CCIL Workers in June 1947.

social justice. When Chile's centrist actors moved away from the Communist Party and the working class and back into open coordination with right-wing forces, they were responding primarily not to international pressure, but rather to assertions of popular protagonism developed over the preceding decade. The working class had begun to escape the Radicals' control in ways that alarmed even progressive elements of the party. The Center-Right perception of an empowered movement from below— one that threatened the status quo in the countryside—explains the fury of domestic repression at the beginning of the Cold War and provides depth for understanding the radicalization of the popular sectors from the 1950s through the Popular Unity government of the 1970s.

Many scholars have recognized the significance of domestic social conflict, especially of strong movements from below, to explain cycles of reaction and reconciliation in Chilean history. Few studies, however, have delved deeply into the dynamics of the 1930s and 1940s, and almost none of these has addressed national politics and culture in these decades from a regional and local perspective. Thomas Klubock's *Contested Communities*, which relates the lived experiences of copper miners, is a notable exception. The most detailed account of the early years is still John Reese Stevenson's 1942 *The Chilean Popular Front*, which highlights national political wrangling, as do works by Paul Drake on the Socialists, Andrew Barnard on the Communists, and several Chilean analyses of the Radicals.[35] Other scholarship from the 1950s–1990s has been excessively shaped by intra-Left or Left-Right debates, often explaining domestic events in terms of an international chess game.[36] In more recent years, Klubock and other historians of mid-twentieth-century Chile have moved beyond Cold War accounts by turning their attention to new terrain, such as the cultural politics of middle-class reformers, the gendered politics of rural social relations, memory and state formation, and the environment.[37]

35. See Drake, *Socialism and Populism* (1978) and "Chile, 1930–1958" (1993); Barnard, "Chilean Communist Party" (1977), "Chilean Communists" (1981), and "Chile" (1992). On the Radical Party, see Durán Bernales, *El Partido Radical* (1958); Palma Zúniga, *Historia del Partido* (1967); Zemelman Merino, "El movimiento" (1977); Urzúa Valenzuela, *La democracia* (1987); Reyes Alvarez, "El presidente" (1989); Couyoumdjian, "'La Hora'" (1998).

36. Among the largely anti-Communist accounts published in the United States, see Blasier "Chile" (1950); Abbott, "Contemporary Political Parties" (1951); Alba, *Historia del Frente Popular* (1959); Halperin *Nationalism* (1967); and Alexander Communism (1957) and *Labor Relations* (1962).

37. See, for example, Antezana-Pernet, "Peace in the World" (1994), "El MEMCh en provincia" (1995) and "Mobilizing Women" (1996); Barr-Melej, *Reforming Chile* (2001) and "Sowing 'Seeds'" (2003); Frazier, *Salt in the Sand* (2007); Hutchison, *Labors Appropriate* (2001); Klubock, *Contested Communities* (1998) and "Politics of Forests" (2006); Rosemblatt, *Gendered*

In 2009, Chilean political scientist Carlos Huneeus published the first full-length monograph about the 1947–52 period: *La guerra fría chilena: Gabriel González Videla y la ley maldita*. Providing great detail and sharp analysis, this work focuses largely on internecine national politics, downplaying the significance of both international connections and local class struggles. Brian Loveman's decades of prolific writing, including his recent works co-authored with Elizabeth Lira, contribute greatly to our understanding of the country's deeper patterns of conflict and compromise. This is also true of the analyses offered by eminent sociologist Tomás Moulian and many other Chilean scholars. The politics of the 1930s and 1940s, however, is not the central focus of these works, and although most observers recognize the significance of the October 1947 coal miners' strike, no one writing in English or Spanish has fully studied developments in the region before, during, and after this cataclysmic event.

Chilean historiography still lacks detailed studies of the 1930s and 1940s in the vein advanced by Klubock in *Contested Communities* on gendered class formation at the El Teniente copper mines and by Peter Winn for the later Popular Unity period in his study of Yarur textile workers, *Weavers of Revolution*. In addition, although abundant work has been done on Chilean copper and nitrate sectors, surprisingly few book-length studies have been written about the political history of Chile's coal mining zone.[38] Local and regional experiences of the Popular Front era help us understand the historical meanings of Chile's first experiment with Center-Left alliances and the tragedy of González Videla's swing to the Right.

Although the global context played a significant role, what occurred in Chile in the 1930s and 1940s was in large part a struggle over definitions of democracy and citizenship, the outcome of which would dramatically affect social relations and hierarchies of power. As Greg Grandin observed, the significance of the Cold War in Latin America involved a move away from the participatory promise of the Popular Front era, when many people considered at least some degree of social justice to be an integral

---

Compromises (2000) and "Charity, Rights, and Entitlement" (2001); and Tinsman, *Partners in Conflict* (2002).

38. Over the years, a number of Chilean theses and dissertations have focused on different aspects of the history of the coal mining zone. Among the more interesting, see Molina Urra, *Condición económico-social* (1948), Silva Torres, "Impacto de la actividad carbonífera" (1986), Fernández Darraz, "Carbón y sociedad" (1991), Figueroa Garavagno, *Revelación del subsole* (1999/2009), and Reynolds Neira, "Movimiento mancomunal" (2006). The only published history dedicated entirely to the coal mining zone is *Carbón: Cien años de historia (1848-1960)*, written by two Chilean journalists, Enrique Figueroa and Carlos Sandoval, in 1987. Based on local and national newspapers, it offers an interesting, but cursory (and at times inaccurate) overview of the industry, the region, and the workers.

element of democracy. What the United States achieved in the aftermath of World War II was the hegemonic ascent in its sphere of influence of a restricted notion of democracy "in the astringent terms of personal freedom rather than social security."[39]

Mining for the Nation builds on Grandin's call for critical study of the potential convergence of democratic and Socialist projects in the 1930s and 1940s, to illuminate what was at stake in the political realignments of the early Cold War years. "To the degree that Latin America today may be considered democratic," Grandin writes, "it was the left, including the Marxist left, that made it so." In mid-twentieth-century Chile, a contest over democracy was waged from below, and almost won, before powerful centrist forces turned away from progressive possibilities to a reactionary agenda aimed at demobilizing and disempowering Communist-led popular sectors. When the Chilean Radicals moved into alignment with right-wing forces in both Chile and the United States, they betrayed a project of deep and expansive democratization, for which hundreds of thousands of working-class Chileans had mobilized.

Many scholars and political observers have described the Popular Front as an example of failed reformism, which became mired in political wrangling and abandoned the interests and protagonism of Chile's working-class sectors. Tomás Moulian, for example, argues that though a "road was opened for important changes," these were to be "carried out from above, by the State, with scant participation of the masses." Looking from the vantage of national politics, Moulian and others find that the "passive character" of the Popular Front project meant that it "did not transform into social movements," but rather was marked by "interparty, and not infrequently, intraparty conflicts that were resolved in [Congress] or were diluted in public debate."[40]

It is certainly true that internecine battles racked Chilean politics in these years, but this fact does not adequately capture changes taking place at the local level—in working-class homes, streets, and job sites—where the struggles for more progressive democracy were waged daily. After alleging mass passivity during the Popular Front era, Moulian runs into apparent contradiction when he tries to explain González Videla's abrupt 1947 shift. Without discounting global influences, Moulian emphasizes "the fear of the mobilizations fostered by the Communists,"

39. Grandin, *Last Colonial Massacre*, xii–xv.
40. Moulian, "Líneas estratégicas," 8–9. See also Moulian's *Fracturas* (2006), a synthesis of his decades of extensive analysis of Chilean history, where he describes the 1938–47 period as one in which Chile's dominant sectors engaged in a "strategy of defensive containment" of popular participation in the nation's economic and political life.

which "put in danger the passive nature of the process," or, in other words, "the 'popular front' line came into crisis because the center became fearful of the plebeian irruption."[41] Yet, if the Center-Left coalitions of the era had truly failed to generate any kind of social movement, from where did the seemingly imminent plebeian irruption arise? In the view of Moulian and many others, mass mobilization appeared suddenly at the end of the World War II, when international Communism moved away from coalition politics toward a new strategy of working-class offensive.[42] By focusing on one of Chile's most strategic and politicized working-class regions, this book shows rather that the palpable sense of a threat from below derived from a decade of complex grassroots organizing and political activism.

} argument

Mining for the Nation draws on an array of primary documents, both governmental and nongovernmental, including company books and personnel files; church and municipal records; and transcripts of congressional debates. Finding scant political party and union records (most of which have been lost or destroyed), I delved into the holdings of the General Labor Office, the Ministry of the Interior, and the Arauco and Concepción Intendancies. Local, regional, national, and international media coverage complemented detailed reports from U.S. State Department officials. I learned a great deal from a series of interviews conducted by Robert J. Alexander in the 1940s and 1950s and from a variety of published testimonies. Most useful were the thirty-eight formal interviews I conducted, together with many informal encounters. Works by local artists and authors also contributed to my understanding of the coal region's history, folklore, and culture.

   Mining for the Nation is divided into three parts, each portraying a different phase in the dramatic events of the 1930s and 1940s. Part I—"Hopes and Promises"—opens with an introduction to the Chilean coal mining zone, an area south of Concepción, where dozens of different towns and rural properties provided livelihood for nearly a hundred and fifty thousand residents in the 1930s and 1940s.[43] Chapter 1 describes how industrial coal mining was first established by Chilean capitalists in the 1850s and how a strong working-class movement developed in the region by the turn of the century. Together with their counterparts in the northern nitrate region, the coal miners were crucial actors in the creation of Marxist

41. Moulian, "Líneas estratégicas," 11.
42. Moulian, "Evolución histórica," 12–13, and *Fracturas,* 144.
43. Dirección General de Estadísticas, Censo de 1940, BNCh.

political parties and radical labor organizations. The period of class struggle, when coal miners mobilized as "soldiers of revolution," peaked in a series of major strikes in the early 1920s. Thereafter, coal miners and other workers around the country came to accept social legislation, legal unions, and electoral participation, insisting on their full rights as citizen workers.

Chapters 2 and 3 recount and analyze the difficult creation of Popular Front alliances in the coal region and at the national level in the mid-1930s, highlighting the sense of promise and opportunity generated as leftist labor and political leaders swept into key positions in the government (from labor inspectors to national senators) and in civil society (from heads of labor unions to leaders of diverse cultural organizations). People such as Lota's Mayor Santos Medel and Deputy Damián Uribe Cárdenas—both former coal miners and loyal Communists—changed the tone and content of politics in the coal communities, challenging the exclusion of popular sectors and promoting the Popular Front as a radical democratic project. Leftists in key government posts also influenced the outcome of industrial conflicts, at times advancing the workers' interests in ways that strengthened their faith in the official labor relations system.

The Popular Front project that swept onto the national scene with the hard-won election of Pedro Aguirre Cerda in 1938 promoted an ideal of industrial development in which the proletariat and the domestic bourgeoisie would work together with the mediation of an interventionist state. This model did not readily placate the coal miners, who neither renounced class conflict nor saw their capitalist bosses as allies. Rather, with organization, leadership, and ever greater electoral weight, the coal miners became increasingly empowered to take advantage of political openings and to influence government policies.

As they set out to assert their rights and to advance their interests in this era of Center-Left governments, however, workers of the coal region repeatedly came up against the limits of the ideal. Part II of *Mining for the Nation*—"Collaboration and Conflict"—delves into the challenges, tensions, contradictions, and open clashes that occurred among labor, capital, and the state during the ostensibly harmonious years of the 1940s. Throughout the war, Chilean coal miners expressed patriotic commitment to national production and the defeat of Fascism, while simultaneously fighting for their own rights and insisting on their full participation in both wartime and postwar democracy. This historical period was marked by a powerful convergence of Communist internationalism with its putative opposite, patriotic nationalism. Indeed, as described in chapter 6, when U.S. Vice President Henry Wallace, chief torchbearer of the New Deal, visited Chile in March 1943, he hailed the Communist-led coal miners as "soldiers of democracy."

By the early 1940s, representatives of the Popular Front parties, especially the Communists, had won significant leadership positions throughout the coal region; indeed, they held majorities on every major labor union and municipal council. Former coal miners even reached the halls of the national Congress and occupied various posts in the executive branch. Empowered by this political representation, and backed by their strong organization and importance to the economy, workers of the coal region not only pressed the state to intervene on their behalf in industrial disputes, but also spoke out about community problems, such as alcoholism, sanitation, and housing, as well as national and international affairs.

The coalition governments of the 1940s, however, were operating in a twofold fashion: while they employed populist language and championed inclusion, conciliation, and social reform, they also used state resources to carry on long-standing practices of limiting and controlling working-class participation in economic and political life. Chapters 4–7 illuminate these two faces of the Popular Front as they played out in several government interventions in the coal region in the early 1940s—from the mixed results of agreements reached among unions, companies, and the state in 1941 to the equally contradictory recommendations of the 1941 Berguño Report, an investigation of the coal mining zone, commissioned by the president. At the end of 1942, as recounted in chapter 5, national police troops gunned down unarmed men and women at a union rally in Lota, giving rise to another complex government investigation, this one conducted by Raúl Rettig and Osvaldo Pazols.

These episodes show how the government's response to "the coal problem" in the war years consisted of intertwined strands: traditional modes of repression together with new promises that the state would address at least some of the workers' grievances. The workers and their leaders construed these promises as affirming the rightness of their positions; their small victories encouraged them to further appeal to state actors and institutions. Thus, even though powerful sectors of society, including forces within the Center-Left coalition, worked against substantial reforms, organized popular sectors still found ample opportunity to press their demands and pursue their aspirations.

Part III—"Rupture and Betrayal"—addresses the breakdown of this hopeful era for Chilean democracy in the wake of World War II, when

workers and their families expressed growing frustration over the unfulfilled promises of the previous decade. At the same time, centrist politicians who had accepted the Communists' professed commitment to
democracy during the war now began to distrust the motives of their
erstwhile allies. President González Videla and many of his fellow Radicals
came to see Communist-led popular sectors as a threat to the status quo.
As he shifted his political allegiance to right-wing forces in Chile and the
United States, the president moved violently to disband the most organized and militant workers in the country, beginning with the coal
miners.

The significance of González Videla's turn to the Right in the late 1940s
was not that the Chilean government acquiesced to U.S. pressure, though
it certainly did so. Rather, it was that the most radical democratic Chilean
government until then moved to check, or even reverse, the growing
gains of the popular sectors in Chilean political culture, social relations,
and state institutions. This conjuncture reentrenched a limited liberal
notion of democracy that would provoke increasingly aggressive challenges over the next decades, culminating in the Popular Unity government of 1970–73. Chapter 9 offers the first full account of the Chilean coal
miners' dramatic strike of October 1947, while chapter 10 gives a sense of
the human dimensions of the repression that followed. Taken as a whole,
chapters 8–10 tell the story of World War II and the early Cold War as
lived in Chile from the ground up, and even from beneath the ground,
where Chilean coal was mined.

Mining for the Nation shows how and why the Communists gained such
a loyal following in the coal region, and how the workers advanced their
interests in the often subtle politics of the war years, during which self-
proclaimed progressive administrations moved, at best, at cross-purposes
and, at worst, in reactionary directions. It explains why the most Left-
leaning of the Radical presidents, Gabriel González Videla, who had given
three cabinet posts to Communists for the first time in the Americas,
turned against both the Communists and the mobilized working-class
sectors with such fury.

Stepping away from their origins as anticapitalist revolutionaries,
Chile's strong Marxist parties not only participated actively in electoral
politics and the state industrial relations system in the 1930s and 1940s,
but did so in alliance with centrist-bourgeois parties. By working in coalitions, they sought to advance a program of modernization to include
both industrial development and a transformation of Chilean democracy—deepening its socioeconomic dimensions and expanding its inclusion of previously marginal working-class sectors. In doing so, leftist

politicians hoped to ensure their continued influence over, if not eventual control of, state policy making. By definition, this project required popular participation, and, with their high degree of organization and loyalty to the Communist Party, the coal miners emerged as crucial actors.

This period of intense and rapid expansion then contraction of democracy—with rising hopes and active participation followed by severe repression—profoundly affected the subsequent course of Chilean history. Almost all key actors in the drama of the 1960s–1990s emerged from the political fire of the Popular Front's rise and collapse, including Pablo Neruda, Eduardo Frei Montalva, Salvador Allende, Augusto Pinochet, and Raúl Rettig, chairman of Chile's 1991 Truth and Reconciliation Commission, who had been appointed by President Ríos Morales to investigate the killing of coal miners by police at a public rally in 1942. *Mining for the Nation* provides a deeper understanding of those remembered as the important political actors in twentieth-century Chile by telling the story of the coal mining region, with its miners and foremen, fishermen and bakers, homemakers and children, whose individual stories may never be known, but only glimpsed and surmised. Interweaving local, national, and international politics as lived in the coal mining region, it highlights both the democratic potential and the deep contradictions and challenges faced by Chilean workers in their mid-twentieth-century experiences with Center-Left coalitions.

PART I

HOPES AND PROMISES

FROM SOLDIERS OF REVOLUTION TO CITIZEN WORKERS

In a plaza between the mines and the administration buildings of the Coal Mining Company of Lota, the illustrious founder, Matías Cousiño, towers in bronze, "serenely observing the productive work of the mines." The statue was erected after Cousiño's death in 1863 as an expression of "the admiration and gratitude of his fellow citizens."[1] Beneath Cousiño's feet, a miner descends a ladder; with the bottom half of his legs hidden from view, he appears to be kneeling (fig. 2).

An observer in the early 1940s gave a different reading of the statue: "Capital and labor, forged together in bronze, perpetuate the glory of an exemplary citizen and his faithful, intelligent, and selfless collaborator."[2] Even in this rhetoric of patriotic alliance, the terms of hierarchy are clear: whereas the capitalist is a citizen, the miner, his "collaborator," kneels beneath him. Battles over citizenship—who was included and what privileges and responsibilities it bestowed—were central to the democratic strivings of the Chilean working class in the 1930s and 1940s, as was also true in the United States from the New Deal to the end of the World War II. How would long-entrenched inequalities and injustices in social relations respond to the new calls for progress, justice, and democracy that were spreading across Chile and the globe? This question was particularly pressing for the men, women, and children of the coal mines, who passed beneath the gaze of the bronze Cousiño in the course of their

1. *El Sur* (Concepción), September 12, 1942, 2.
2. Ibid.

Fig. 2 Statue of Matías Cousiño and a coal miner, Lota Alto, 1996. Photo (altered to remove graffiti) by Jody Pavilack.

daily commutes, perhaps pausing to rest their exhausted backs and limbs against the rungs of the miner's ladder.

At the heart of Chile's tumultuous social relations of the 1930s and 1940s were deep divisions over the definition and practical content of democracy. When it came to socioeconomic, political, and cultural equality, how much priority should be given to individual rights—including the right to private property and its profitable development—and how much to collective, or class-based, rights? Shared histories of subjugation led to popular notions of democracy as an inclusive, empowering process, which would enable the residents of the coal mining towns to become vital actors in the polity, not merely as workers, but as citizen workers. As they embraced the language and practices of democratic politics, however, workers of the coal mining zone came into often incendiary conflict with the rigid social hierarchy embodied in the Cousiño statue.

Adjacent to this symbol of inequality was the most opulent park in the nation, extending across a 14-hectare (35-acre) peninsula overlooking the mines to the north and the beaches and docks of Lota Bajo to the south. The park was developed between 1862 and 1873 by the company founder's son, Luis Cousiño, and his wife, Isidora Goyenechea Gallo. It was supplied with native and imported trees and plants (as well as birds), which lined its walkways and grew lushly around its fountains, gazebos, and marble statues of Greek and Roman gods, reflecting the Europhile tastes of the Chilean elite. Renowned throughout the country, the Lota Alto Park boasted a lighthouse, a weather station, and a conservatory for tropical plants. With its bucolic paths, the park resembled an English country garden, except for the greater lushness and diversity of its vegetation. Out for an evening stroll, the Cousiños' visiting relatives, friends, and company shareholders likely marveled at the more exotic plant species and certainly must have paused to admire the coal mine's steel hoisting frames rising hundreds of feet above the Pacific coastline, just to the north of the park (fig. 3).

The European pretensions of the national coal mining capitalists were evident not only in the architectural and operational models they adopted, but also in their frequent employment of Europeans and direct European descendants as administrators, engineers, and other white-collar employees. Thus the Cousiño park in Lota Alto was designed and maintained largely by Irish botanists and English landscapers. In a 1929 discussion of the park's origins, Octavio Astorquiza, head of the company's Welfare Department, gestured to the nationalist sentiment of the

Fig. 3   View of coal mine hoisting frames from the Lota Alto Park, 1996. Photo by Jody Pavilack.

day, claiming that the park's foreign designers had combined the best of imported and indigenous elements "to form a harmonic whole."[3]

By far the most impressive construction in Lota, comparable to any feat of wealth in the nation, was a palace built in the 1870s for Luis Cousiño and Isidora Goyenechea at the entrance to their private park (fig. 4). Modeled loosely after an English castle, this extravagant two-story palace combined an array of styles, using materials, furnishings, and pieces of art imported from around the world. Different hardwoods, for example, were selected from Latin America, Asia, and Africa and sent to France to be handcrafted into parquet tiles, which were then shipped to Chile to grace the palace's twelve main-level rooms, ranging from the Golden Ballroom to the Weapons Salon. Also imported were the palace's crystal chandeliers, marble staircases, and fireplace mantels, Italian hand-painted tiles, and French brocade and silk furnishings. Referring to the Mapuche origins of the name Lota—*louta*, meaning "little village"—one author reflected that the opulence of the Cousiño's park and palace "left far behind the 'louta' that the Mapuches of this continent had developed on that stretch of coast."[4]

3. Astorquiza, *Lota* (1929), 196.
4. *Arquitecturas del Sur* (Universidad del Bío-Bío, Concepción), no. 1 (1983): 6–7. The Cousiño palace in Lota was severely damaged in a major earthquake in 1939 and entirely

Fig. 4 Cousiño palace in Lota Alto. Photo reproduced from Octavio Astorquiza and Oscar Galleguillos V., *Cien años del carbón de Lota, 1852–1952*, Compañía Carbonífera e Industrial de Lota, 1952.

In 1897, as finishing touches were being put on the as yet unoccupied palace, the long-widowed Isidora Goyenechea de Cousiño died in Paris, and her remains were sent back to Chile for burial. The stately residence in Lota sat empty for the next two decades, until 1921, when a restructuring of the company moved the park and palace out of the private Cousiño estate.[5] After the palace's lavish rooms were turned into administrative

---

demolished after another quake in 1960. See http://www.lotasorpredente.cl/Palacio Cousino.html/ (accessed June 2010). A replica of the Lota palace, built in Santiago in the 1870s, is today a museum, which can be seen at http://www.palaciocousino.co.cl/ (accessed June 2010).

5. In 1921, the Lota company became the Compañía Minera e Industrial de Chile (CMIC; Mining and Industrial Company of Chile), under the presidency of the founder's grandson, Carlos Cousiño. See note 38 on the company's name changes.

offices for the new, publicly owned company, its costly art objects and furnishings gradually fell victim to neglect or pilfering. A point of local pride for some, the affluence of the park and palace also stood as clear refutation of the company's perennial response to workers' petitions— that its profits were insufficient to grant wage raises, to increase benefits, or to improve working and living conditions.

As coal miners and their families walked past them every day, these sites of wealth became critical features of the landscape in which cultural and political perspectives were generated. The statue, park, and palace—as well as the swimming pool, social clubs, and houses for white-collar employees—were visible reminders of the ideological and material contours of the company's paternalism, beginning in the late nineteenth century, and of the limits to its progressivism in the mid-twentieth century. In the 1930s and 1940s, the country's move toward industrial development and anti-Fascist alliances opened up possibilities for a new kind of national politics. Yet, in Lota, the Popular Front, or any such cross-class project, came up against the reality and symbolic violence of the Cousiño palace, towering over the workers whose labor produced the nation's wealth.

In the coal mining region, any group seeking to mobilize masses of people or to represent the local working class would have to challenge the company's domination of the mining towns and the lives within them. Generations of miners and their leaders rose from their knees to do just that, from the first coal miners' strike in the 1850s through the Communist heyday of the mid-1940s. This chapter provides background on the development of the coal industry and its workforce in the late nineteenth and early twentieth centuries. Over these decades, large segments of the national labor movement, including the coal miners, followed a political trajectory that eventually led them to close affiliation with the Chilean Communist Party (PCCh), though Democrats, anarchists, and, later, Trotskyists and Socialists would continue to play significant roles.

From the turn of the century through the early 1920s, the major labor and political organizations representing the coal miners and other workers around the country promoted strategies of class warfare. This climaxed in a massive wave of strikes in 1920–22 that were violently repressed. As recounted below, the Great Strike of 1920 in the coal mining zone prompted the companies to create modern welfare departments to help socialize and control workers (and their families). Likewise, at the national level, many elite political and military leaders became convinced of the desirability of modern labor legislation and government institutions to channel, if not resolve, class conflict. With the passage of Chile's first "social laws" in 1924 (later consolidated in the 1931 Labor Code), division on the Left continued. Within the Chilean Communist Party (by then the dominant force in the coal mining zone), the position that won out was "qualified acceptance" of the system of legal unions regulated by the 1931 code and monitored by Ministry of Labor officials. Though many groups on the Left continued to dissent, the system of social welfare and industrial relations forged in the 1920s became the principal arena in which working-class politics played out in the Popular Front decade, when, as recounted in later chapters, coal miners persistently tried to use the new system to their advantage.

The Development of Industrial Coal Mining and a Mobilized Workforce

Chilean coal had long been mined for fuel by pre-Columbian indigenous peoples. Surface and rudimentary tunnel extraction continued throughout the country's colonial era and well after independence at sites south of the Bío-Bío River, territory that remained under the control of Chile's seemingly unconquerable native groups, predominantly the Mapuche. After adopting the "authoritarian" Constitution of 1833, Chile came to be seen as a "model of political stability and economic growth in the nineteenth century," which "set it apart from its sister republics."[6] Chilean and foreign entrepreneurs increased their import of machinery and technology to process copper ore, build railroads, expand shipping and port operations, and install public gas lighting. This progress raised the demand for fuel and sparked commercial interest in Chile's domestic coal reserves to diminish the country's dependence on imported British coal.[7] By the 1840s, the Chilean state began to expand its territorial control southward. Chilean and European entrepreneurs were able to acquire land

6. Loveman, *Chile*, 109–10. Loveman's numerous works, including more recent books co-authored and co-edited with Elizabeth Lira, and works by several other Chileanists have persuasively challenged the long-standing myth of Chilean exceptionalism—the misconception that the country experienced nearly two centuries of stable and peaceful democracy before the military coup of 1973. *Mining for the Nation* adds to this conversation by showing the high degree of tumult that racked Chile during the supposedly harmonious 1930s and 1940s. Still, even Loveman notes in *Chile*, 111, that, at least in the nineteenth century, "Chile would largely avoid the chaos and instability of the rest of Latin America . . . by imposing a modified version of 'benevolent' despotism."

7. Lobos Araya, "La legislación carbonífera," 50.

in the frontier region of the Gulf of Arauco, often purchasing it from local caciques in order to extract coal in greater and more reliable amounts (map 1).[8] They did so despite the assessment of Charles Darwin, who, having surveyed various mine sites from 1832 to 1836, found Chilean coal unfit for industrial use.[9]

After British steamship operator William Wheelwright successfully used coal from Penco in the early 1840s, "the main breakthrough in coal mining," as described by historian Maurice Zeitlin, "came with the colossal investments of Matías Cousiño, perhaps the embodiment par excellence of the development of Chilean capitalism at mid-century."[10] After reaping substantial profits from copper and silver mines to the north, Cousiño turned his attention to capitalizing coal extraction from the suboceanic deposits at Lota, "utilizing English steam-driven machinery, Scottish technicians, and Chilean labor." To give further impetus to his rising business, "Cousiño built a copper smelter at Lota that had the highest capacity in South America and consumed, on the average, a third of Lota's entire coal output."

By the end of the 1850s, "coal production [at Lota] and in the neighboring mines at Coronel was competing effectively against British coal. . . . Lota now had a population of 5,000, and visitors from England or Wales could easily believe they had been transported back to a corner of their own blackened countryside."[11] For the next several decades, Chile's infant coal companies struggled to forge stable, skilled, and malleable workforces out of peripatetic migrants from the southern countryside and northern mines. As one of the early entrepreneurs of the industry, Juan MacKay, wrote,

> Miners were improvised from the workers who flowed in from the fields, attracted by better wages, though many of them tended to

8. As one example, coal-laden lands in Puchoco (in present-day Coronel) were sold in 1850 by the cacique Ambrosio Requemilla and his wife, Santos Nequilpi, to two Chilean entrepreneurs. See Figueroa, *Historia de la fundación*, 70.

9. Darwin, *Beagle Diary*, 303. See also Darwin, *Geological Observations*, 398.

10. Zeitlin, *Civil Wars*, 23–24. Many excellent sources address the nineteenth-century development of the coal industry. Among primary sources, see del Barrio, *Noticia sobre el terreno* (1857); García, "Industria minera" (1861); Palma, *Un paseo a Lota* (1864); González, *El carbón* (1862); Figueroa, *Historia de la fundación* (1897). In English, see Bollaert, "Observations" (1855); and Alberdi, *Life and Industrial Labors* (1877). For excellent secondary analysis, see Ortega Martínez, "First Four Decades" (1982), *La industria del carbón* (1988), and "La frontera carbonífera" (1992); Mazzei de Grazia, "Los británicos" (1997), "Expansión de gestiones" (1998), and "Matías Cousiño" (1999); and Venegas Valdebenito, *El carbón de Lota* (2008).

11. Zeitlin, *Civil Wars*, 23–24.

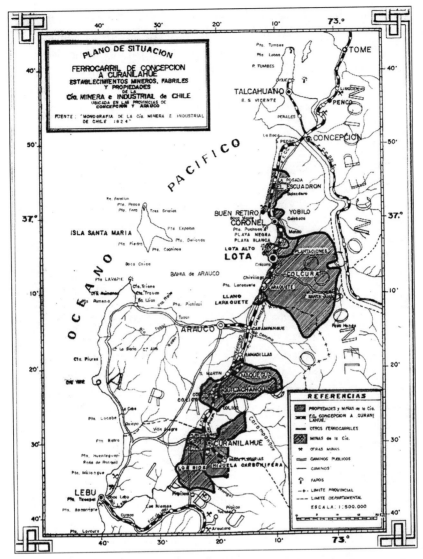

Map 1   CCIL map of the coal mining region. Reproduced from Octavio Astorquiza and Oscar Galleguillos V., *Cien años del carbón de Lota, 1852–1952*, Compañía Carbonífera e Industrial de Lota, 1952.

return to their land for the harvests. . . . With the passage of time, this migratory habit was lost; the workers who had brought their families and who were set up in good company housing preferred to stay at the mines, such that in a few years, there were already people who no longer thought about moving and who were recognized as permanent miners, who were trained on the job as drillers, haulers, etc.[12]

What early coal capitalists like Mackay did not foresee was that, as greater numbers of men became "permanent miners," an awareness of their collective identity would begin to emerge and thus also a growing sense of their rights and power. Difficult conditions in the mines and towns of the coal mining region soon gave rise to workers' organizations, which became increasingly radical over time and, by the turn of the century, joined the national labor movement, adopting its class-based politics. As Brian Loveman notes, "The mining proletariat created in the 1860s and 1870s would eventually make the coal mining region one of the most explosive areas of class conflict and union struggle in Chile."[13]

Less than a decade after Matías Cousiño founded the Lota company in 1852, coal workers staged several uprisings, including a rebellion in 1859 during the civil war of that year.[14] The next major upheaval occurred in 1875, when an economic crisis crippled the market for coal, forcing mines to reduce personnel, wages, and workdays, or, in some cases, to shut down entirely. In desperation, workers across the industry engaged in a series of spontaneous (or loosely organized) walkouts, to little or no avail.[15]

Over the next decades, many collective actions by coal town workers focused on the demand for payment in national currency rather than scrip (fichas), which could only be used in company stores. In 1885, moreover, three hundred Coronel workers protested to departmental authorities that they had not been paid wages of any kind for more than three months.[16] A few years later, in 1888, workers in Lota engaged in an "explosive, spontaneous, inchoate movement," aimed in part against the local

12. MacKay, Recuerdos, 57.
13. Loveman, Chile, 138.
14. Grez Toso, De la "regeneración," 418–22.
15. Ortega Martínez, La industria, 51–52, and "First Four Decades," 23–24.
16. La Esmeralda (Coronel), September 18, 1885, 3; Figueroa Ortiz and Sandoval Ambiado, Carbón, 51.

police, whose headquarters came under attack after several activist workers were arrested.[17] By this time, anarchists and members of the newly
founded Democrat Party had launched sustained efforts to organize
workers, as discussed below, first in mutual aid groups, then in resistance
societies and free unions, and later, after 1924, in legal unions.

As the coal industry developed, it became increasingly centralized. By
1914, the output of the Cousiño mines in Lota had surpassed that of the
Schwager Coal Mining and Foundry Company in neighboring Coronel. In
1919, the Cousiño company purchased all of the property of its competitor
in Curanilahue—Compañía de los Ríos—some 60 kilometers (about 40
miles) to the south. This purchase included the land, mines, steamships,
and railroad that the Compañía de los Ríos had recently acquired from
the British-owned Arauco Company, Ltd.—a highly significant acquisi-
tion since control of railroads and expansion of their routes were vital to
the continued growth of the coal mining industry. Moreover, after the
departure of the British company, Chile's coal industry was developed
exclusively with domestic capital, making its history quite different from
that of the copper industry, with its abundant foreign investment and
control.[18] By 1936, the Cousiño and Schwager companies together accounted for 90 percent of the nation's coal production.[19] Operating as a
monopoly, they created problems for labor and consumers alike—as well
as for the region's small and medium mines, principally in the province
of Arauco, which extracted lower-grade coal on a precarious footing,
under the constant threat of mass reductions and shutdowns.[20]

The coal mining operations of the Cousiño and Schwager companies
also provided the foundation for a variety of linked industrial, agricultural, forestry, and service activities, which strengthened the dominant
role of these two companies in the region. By the end of the 1920s, the
Cousiño company alone ran what Stephen Bosworth aptly described as "a
small empire . . . with a hydroelectric plant, a railroad, a fleet of ships,
tree plantations, machine shops, warehouses, a ceramics factory, and a

17. See Ortiz Letelier, El movimiento, 128. For other accounts of the September 1888
incidents, see Astorquiza, Lota (1929), 27; Molina Urra, Condición económico, 106; and Grez
Toso, De la "regeneración," 582.

18. Recent English-language studies of Chile's copper mines include Klubock, Contested
Communities; Finn, Tracing the Veins; and Vergara, Copper Workers. No comparable study has
been published on Chilean coal mines.

19. Fenner, Situación actual, 8.

20. According to Ricardo Fenner, another 1.25 percent of national coal production was
by the Coal Mining Company of Lebu, and the rest was divided among six companies that
primarily produced lignite coal, including Lirquén, Cosmito, Plegarias, and Colico Sur.
Small mines also operated in Magallanes and Valdivia. Fenner, Situación actual, 8.

chemical laboratory."[21] To this list should be added a sawmill, a crate factory, agricultural estates, port facilities, and company restaurants, stores, hospitals, schools, worker and employee swimming pools, social clubs, libraries, and sports arenas. Although the Schwager company also owned vast expanses of rural and urban property and operated diverse agricultural, industrial, transportation, and service enterprises, unlike the Cousiño company, it never acquired a major railroad or hydroelectric plant. Moreover, Schwager's mining operations were confined to the Coronel area, whereas those of the Cousiño company extended as far as the Plegarias mine, south of Curanilahue.

As Juan MacKay observed in the quotation above, for many families in the smaller mines, fishing villages, and countryside around the region and farther south, the possibility of employment in Lota or Coronel was enticing, even though it often required difficult sacrifices, such as living away from one's family.[22] In a sample of more than three hundred personnel files of Lota workers in the 1930s and 1940s, only 23 percent of the workers were born in Lota or Coronel. Another 25 percent had arrived from beyond the provinces of Concepción and Arauco, while most, 52 percent, were internal migrants from smaller coal mining towns, such as Lebu, or from the surrounding countryside. Lota and Coronel also developed as a regional hub of labor and political activism, with frequent visits from national and international figures, robust exchange of news and information, and continual mass gatherings.[23]

As mining and industrial enterprises consolidated and workforces grew larger and more stable, capitalist efforts to maintain worker passivity and compliance, in part by recruiting from the countryside, became ever more difficult. Beginning in northern nitrate mines and ports, mutual aid societies of the late nineteenth century, often led by the artisanal sectors, gave rise to more radical "resistance societies" known as "mancomunales," which engaged in class analysis in pamphlets and newspapers and carried out direct actions such as strikes.[24] Leftist labor politics

21. Bosworth, "True State," 15.

22. On internal migration, see Dirección General de Estadísticas, Census data, 1920, 1930, 1940, 1952, and 1960; Instituto de Economía, *La migración interna*; Vivallos Espinoza and Brita Peña, "Inmigración y sectores populares."

23. As described in later chapters, Lota and Coronel received visits from national candidates, presidents, ministers, senators and national deputies, investigative commissions, and even foreign dignitaries, such as U.S. Vice President Henry Wallace, who visited the region in May 1943.

24. Many diverse studies have been done on late nineteenth- and early twentieth-century labor organizations in Chile. Among the more classic works, see those listed in the bibliography by Barrera, Barría Serón, Bergquist, Breslin, DeShazo, Garcés Durán, Grez Toso, Jobet, Ortiz Letelier, Ramírez Necochea, Salazar, Segall, and Vitale.

quickly spread from the north to the rest of the country. By the early twentieth century, Chile, as elsewhere in Latin America and around the globe, was racked by the "social question."[25] Compared to their counterparts in many neighboring countries, Chilean workers soon emerged as a highly visible, organized force.[26]

One of the most significant early political voices for Chilean workers was the Democrat Party (Partido Demócrata; PD), founded in 1887, which had a strong following in the Concepción region. The Democrats, and the various political groups that developed from them, would play a crucial role in the labor politics of the next century. At the same time, workers of the coal mining zone were heavily influenced by anarchists and anarcho-syndicalists, such as Santiago shoemaker Luis Morales y Morales, who traveled south at the turn of the century to help organize the miners. In 1902, Morales was instrumental in founding the largest mancomunal in the area, the Lota and Coronel Workers' Federation (Federación de Trabajadores de Lota y Coronel; FTLC). Two years later, at the first national meeting of mancomunales, the coal mining zone was represented not only by the FTLC but also by the mancomunal of Lebu and the maritime guild of Coronel.[27] Under their leadership, workers in the coal region entered an explosive period of mobilization from 1902 to 1907, with waves of mass strikes and violent confrontations, although none as brutal as the 1907 massacre of nitrate workers at Santa María de Iquique.[28]

When class conflict intensified around the country, dissidents within the Democrat Party, led by an artisan printer from the north named Luis Emilio Recabarren, took issue with what they saw as the party's excessively reformist positions. Making good use of the printing press and his skill with words, Recabarren, who became known to workers around the country as "don Reca," advocated more explicitly class-based politics and more aggressive tactics. By 1912, Recabarren's writings and leadership, together with the work of thousands of his compatriots, led to the creation of a national Socialist Workers' Party (POS), which drew many dissident Democrats, anarchists, and independent Socialists. Five years later,

25. See Garcés Durán, *Crisis social*; Grez Toso, *La "cuestión social."*

26. For different analyses of the emergence of organized labor in Chile, see, for example, Bergquist, *Labor in Latin America*; DeShazo, *Urban Workers*; and Collier and Collier, *Shaping the Political Arena*.

27. Barría Serón, *El movimiento obrero*, 27–28; Escobar Zenteno, *Compendio*, 188–30, 201; Bosworth, "True State," 104–11.

28. On workers' consciousness, organization, and politics in the coal mining zone in the early twentieth century, see, for example, Bosworth, "True State"; Breslin, "Development"; Reynolds Neira, "Movimiento"; and Venegas Valdebenito, "Crisis económico." On the 1907 massacre of nitrate workers in Santa María Iquique, see especially Devés, *Los que van a morir.*

in 1917, Recabarren and his followers gained control of the national Federation of Chilean Workers (Federación de Obreros de Chile; FOCh), formed
back in 1909 under more moderate leadership. In 1921, in the wake of the
Bolshevik Revolution, the FOCh joined the Red International of Unions
and, in 1922, the Socialist Workers' Party became the Communist Party of
Chile (PCCh). This international alignment prompted many within the
labor movement (especially anarchists and reformists) to leave both the
POS and the FOCh, eventually giving rise to the Socialist Party (Partido
Socialista; PS) in 1932.[29]

During these years, Recabarren visited the coal mining region on several occasions, as did many other PD, FOCh, POS, and anarchist activists,
all working toward different forms of political organization along class
lines.[30] Some militants from the north even volunteered to move south
and work in the coal mines in order to help with organizing efforts. One
such volunteer was Armando González Uribe, who was born in 1890 to a
campesino family in the Andean region of Chillán, 150 kilometers (about
90 miles) inland from Lota. As one of Chile's many rural youths searching
for a way out of insecurity and poverty, González Uribe left home when
he was fifteen years old. Migrating north, he found work in the port of
Tocopilla, where he met Recabarren and soon joined the FOCh and the
POS. In 1918, when the FOCh sent a group of northern labor activists to
the coal mining region, Armando González Uribe was among them.[31]

The Great Strike of 1920: Worker Contention
and New Modes of Company Control

While working at the Schwager mines, González Uribe became a leader
of the FOCh's local council, and was active in organizing the "Great Strike
of 1920," widely referred to as "the first significant strike in the coal mining zone."[32] Starting in Curanilahue on March 8, 1920, this FOCh–led

29. Loveman, *Chile*, 164, 171–73.
30. Interview with Luis Corvalán Lépez. Meeting Recabarren was a recurrent theme in
many coal miners' testimonies. For published accounts, see Alcalde, *Reportaje al carbón*, 24,
25, 78.
31. Interview with Julia González Figueroa, daughter of Armando González Uribe, who
died in the late 1970s, at age eighty-seven.
32. The identical phrase "the first significant strike [*la primera huelga de importancia*]"
is found Astorquiza, *Lota* (1929), 107, and in *El Sur*, September 12, 1942, 3. The strike of 1920
is the most studied episode in Chilean coal mining history. See Pedreros, *La huelga grande*;
Fernández Darraz, "Carbón y sociedad"; Bosworth, "Impact of Coal Strikes," and "True
State"; Venegas Valdebenito, "La huelga grande" and "Crisis económica." Specifically regarding the role of women in this strike, see Figueroa Garavagno, *Revelación del subsole*, esp.
chap. 3, and Corvalán B., *El papel de la mujer*.

strike quickly spread throughout the region to involve nearly nine thousand people in a total work stoppage that lasted almost two months. Foremost among the miners' demands were wage and salary increases commensurate with the cost of living, a reduction in work hours, improvements in health and safety, greater shop floor control by unions, and greater respect for union delegates, all of which would repeatedly appear as points of contention in labor-company negotiations over the next several decades.

The government responded to the strike by placing the entire region under siege. Military squadrons, acting together with local police and company security forces, violently evicted the families of striking workers from their homes. The military also requisitioned collective and individual food supplies, prompting sharp protests from public figures such as Juan Pradenas Muñoz, a young leader of the southern FOCh and the Democrat Party, who would play a significant role in the labor politics of the 1930s and 1940s.[33] The residents of both Lota and Coronel fled to the seemingly safe terrain of Playa Blanca and Playa Negra, adjacent beaches between the two towns, where they set up makeshift shelters and collective cooking facilities.[34] This beach camp, however, proved to be an ideal setting for the military to exercise its control over the strikers and their families, who soon found themselves surrounded.[35]

The conflict in the coal mining zone was a prominent episode in the wave of social upheaval that swept Chile following World War I. In the year 1920 alone, an estimated fifty thousand Chilean workers went on strike—"an unusually high number," historian Jorge Rojas Flores tells us, and a calamity in "the absence . . . of legal mechanisms to resolve those conflicts."[36] Early in 1920, the last year of his presidency, the hard line taken by Juan Luis Sanfuentes (1915–20) against FOCh–led strikes in the coal mining region and around the country became a key factor shaping political alliances and platforms for the upcoming presidential elections. As coal miners collected scarce funds from around the country to bolster their strike reserves, an electoral coalition known as the "Liberal Alliance" met in Santiago in March and chose Arturo Alessandri Palma as their candidate. Alessandri ran as a liberal reformer with deep concern for the

33. Lagos Valenzuela, Bosquejo histórico, 34–36.

34. The names "Playa Blanca" (White Beach) and "Playa Negra" (Black Beach) derive from the fact that the sand on the northern half of the shore is notably darker than on the southern stretch, for geological reasons unrelated to the location of coal deposits.

35. See, for example, Lagos Valenzuela, Bosquejo histórico, 35n57, and the recollections of Lota miner Luis Alberto Barra Faúndez, in Alcalde, Reportaje al carbón, 8.

36. Rojas Flores, La dictadura de Ibáñez, 13.

plight of the working man; he pledged to "solve immediately economic and social problems through the creation of a Ministry of Labor and Social Security, and the passage of laws on the labor contract, social security, health and safety in the workplace, and labor dispute settlement."[37] Back in 1905, Alessandri had served on the first Board of Directors of the Lota and Coronel company, but now, in April 1920, as the standard-bearer for pro-labor reform, he "contributed $10,000 to maintain the strike of the coal miners."[38]

The Great Strike ended on April 30, when the parties agreed at last to submit the conflict to third-party arbitration and the workers returned to their jobs.[39] The final settlement provided for wage and salary increases of 10–30 percent, depending on occupation and also included a number of gains for the workers on key issues of community and workplace control. One of its most radical stipulations was to transfer responsibility for policing the mining areas from company security forces to the carabineros, or national police. The coal companies continued, however, to use their own corps of guards and spies, while also fostering patron-client relations with the carabineros stationed in their towns.[40] A 1928 publication promoting the Lota company claimed that there were "no private

37. Morris, *Elites*, 162.
38. DeShazo, *Urban Workers*, 176; see also Bosworth, "Impact of Coal Strikes," 34.
Founded by Matías Cousiño in 1852, the Coal Mining Company of Lota (Compañía Carbonífera de Lota), would change names and corporate structure several times in the twentieth century. Between 1905 and 1921, it was the Compañía Carbonífera de Lota y Coronel (CCLC; Coal Mining Company of Lota and Coronel), headed by Matías Cousiño's grandson, Carlos. In 1921, after acquiring the Curanilahue properties, the company was reorganized as the Compañía Minera e Industrial de Chile (CMIC; Mining and Industrial Company of Chile). In 1933, it went public and was renamed the Compañía Carbonífera e Industrial de Lota (CCIL; Coal Mining and Industrial Company of Lota), which would dominate the Chilean coal industry for the next thirty years. In 1963, the CCIL merged with the Schwager company in neighboring Coronel, to become the Compañía Carbonífera Lota-Schwager (Lota-Schwager Coal Mining Company). Then, in early 1971, the Popular Unity government of Salvador Allende nationalized all of Chile's coal mines and created the Empresa Nacional del Carbón (ENACAR; National Coal Mining Company). In 1994, ENACAR shut down its Schwager mines; in 1997, it closed down the Lota mines as well, thus bringing to an end a century and a half of large-scale coal extraction in Chile.
39. Héctor Humeres Magnan erroneously states in *La huelga*, 40, that this was the first case of third-party arbitration of a labor conflict in Chile. As Brian Loveman explains in *Chile*, 179, the interior minister during World War I "decreed the creation of a *voluntary* conciliation and arbitration system," and several strikes were resolved by meditation in 1918 and 1919.
40. In 1906, the Army Police (Regimiento de Gendarmes del Ejército) was transformed into the Carabineros Regiment, charged with the security of roads and fields in the frontier region of Concepción and Arauco, precisely where the coal mines were located. Beginning in 1924, this body was united with other security forces operating in the country, and in 1927, dictator Carlos Ibáñez del Campo created a single national police called the "Cuerpo de Carabineros," under the authority of the Ministry of the Interior. Always a highly central-

police operating on the Establishment," but did note the company's patronage of the national police: "In the service of order, the company provides large facilities for the carabineros' forces, to whose command it submits completely."[41]

Control of the use of force in the coal towns involved a power struggle between capitalists and the state, the resolution of which was crucial to the rights and protections that would be accorded to workers in their own power struggle with their bosses. The carabineros were charged with law enforcement throughout the communities, on both public and private property, including that of the coal mining companies. Carabineros were therefore called on to notify the companies' personnel departments when they picked up drunken workers; to quell skirmishes between workers and foremen; and to monitor and, at times, intervene in union and political gatherings. It was thus highly significant that, when the carabineros replaced private security forces in the coal towns, the companies moved quickly to exercise patronage by providing them headquarters, housing, coal, and other perquisites.

The 1920 arbitration settlement contained two other clauses that represented major victories for the workers. First, the companies were explicitly forbidden from interfering with the workers' freedom of assembly, although this stipulation would be egregiously violated many times in the coming years, when the companies used their private ownership of town property to control public meetings. And second, the settlement, which officially went into effect on January 1, 1921, mandated an eight-hour workday for most jobs in the mines.[42] This provision would also be violated or simply ignored many times in the ensuing years.[43] Indeed, few terms of the arbitration settlement were effectively implemented and enforced; they would remain points of contention for decades to come.

One settlement term, however, clearly played into the hands of capitalists desiring to cripple the FOCh. It stated that the companies had no

ized, militaristic body, the carabineros were placed under control of the Ministry of Defense after the military coup of 1973. See Loveman, *Chile*, 183; Rojas Flores, *La dictadura de Ibáñez*, 27; Valdés Urrutia, "Notas para la historia"; Peri Fagerstrom, *Apuntes*, vols. 3 and 4; and the Carabineros de Chile Web site: http://www.carabineros.cl/sitioweb/web/verSeccion.do?cod=121/ (accessed June 2009).

41. Rokha, *Monografía*, 56.

42. Part of the arbitration settlement is reprinted in Astorquiza, *Lota* (1929), 108–10. The effective implementation of an eight-hour workday was not actually achieved until the 1960s, when the workers won the "lamp-to-lamp policy," meaning that their shifts began when they first entered the mine, not when they arrived at the coal face up to two hours later.

43. See, for example, the discussion of the violent October 1942 conflict in Lota in chapter 5.

obligation to negotiate with any representatives of the workers who did not have active employment contracts.[44] In effect, this prevented full-time labor organizers and union leaders from delivering on promises to the workers. The Great Strike of 1920 thus marked the highpoint of the federation's organizing efforts in the coal mining region. Over the next several years, FOCh–led strikes continued with diminishing success, with a total of eight in 1920, five in 1921, and six in 1922, including a total regional stoppage in March. The strikes of 1922 were particularly difficult and disappointing for the workers, and mobilizations declined in their wake, with only four strikes in the coal mines in both 1923 and 1924.[45] Most of these "slowdowns, stoppages, strikes, and invectives" were motivated by distress in the face of rising inflation and ire at the companies' noncompliance with previous agreements and arbitration settlements.[46]

Political wrangling and shifting positions over how to resolve "the social question" in Chile would continue with great intensity over the next several decades. The Lota company's response to the upheaval of the early 1920s was to modernize its system of employee relations, adapting existing modes of discipline and control to make them compatible with ascendant reformist and populist views. On March 23, 1923, one year to the day since the end of the major 1922 strike, the Lota company, now called the Coal Mining and Industrial Company of Lota (Compáñia Carbonífera e Industrial de Lota; CCIL), created a powerful new administrative division—the Welfare Department.[47] This office was headed from the beginning by Octavio Astorquiza, a formidable man who would provoke the animosity of thousands of workers in the coming decades.[48] The first of its kind in the region, the Welfare Department was responsible for hiring workers and giving them sector and job assignments. For the first time, the company began to keep detailed intake records for each worker, which included a medical exam, a photograph, and information about the worker's past employment and family situation (fig. 5).

"The Welfare Department makes a moral assessment of the workers who join the Company," Astorquiza wrote twenty years later, "and the technical departments judge their competence. Then Welfare continues

44. Bosworth, "True State," 131.
45. Pizarro, La huelga obrera, 63, table 8.
46. Bosworth, "Impact of Coal Strikes," 40.
47. Astorquiza, in Lota (1942), 123, says March 23, 1923, whereas Astorquiza and Galleguillos V., in Cien años, 212, say March 23, 1922. Other sources use one or the other of the two dates.
48. Octavio Astorquiza was an agronomy engineer by training and a member of the Conservative Party, who had previously served as a national deputy.

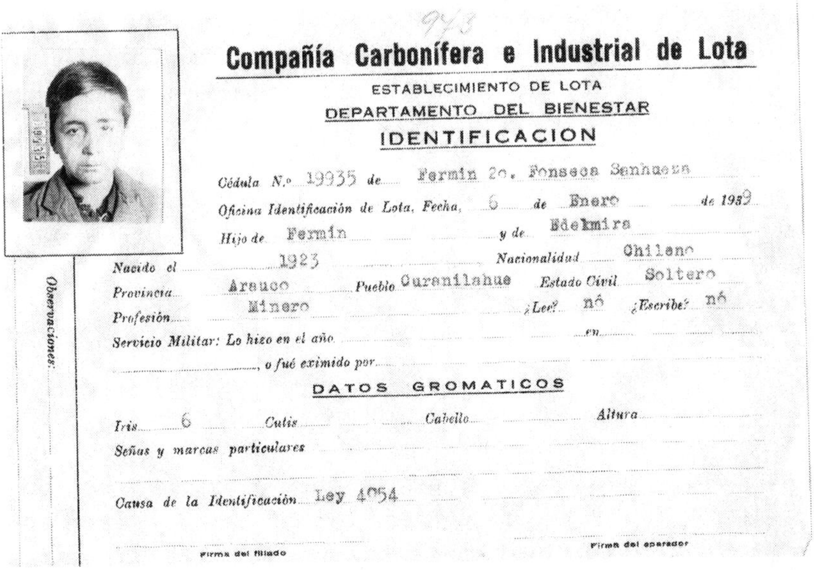

943

Compañía Carbonífera e Industrial de Lota

ESTABLECIMIENTO DE LOTA

DEPARTAMENTO DEL BIENESTAR

IDENTIFICACION

Cédula N.º 19935 *de* Fermin 2o. Fonseca Sanhueza

Oficina Identificación de Lota, Fecha, 6 *de* Enero *de* 1939

Hijo de Fermin *y de* Edelmira

Nacido el 1923 *Nacionalidad* Chileno

Provincia Arauco *Pueblo* Curanilahue *Estado Civil* Soltero

Profesión Minero *¿Lee?* nó *¿Escribe?* nó

Servicio Militar: Lo hizo en el año .... *en* ....

........, *o fué eximido por* ....

DATOS GROMATICOS

Iris 6 *Cutis* .... *Cabello* .... *Altura* ....

Señas y marcas particulares ....

Causa de la Identificación Ley 4054

Firma del filiado

Firma del operador

Observaciones:

Fig. 5 Worker intake record of the CCIL Welfare Department, 1939. Reproduced from CCIL personnel files, consulted at ENACAR, Lota Alto.

attending to them, and the merits and faults of each are noted in meticulously kept files [*prontuarios*]. This system has brought about a very favorable selection of worker personnel, and it can be said that today the Company has in its operations workers whose culture and efficiency is above the average observed in the country."[49] The moral culture of the workers, as assessed by company agents, was thus given equal weight with competency and efficiency in shaping their careers. Meritorious moral character, in the view of Astorquiza and his staff, was demonstrated by a respectful, subservient, apolitical attitude toward superiors and a willingness to work diligently under any conditions for any length of time. With these characteristics in mind, the hiring department showed a clear preference for recent rural migrants, and, for some positions, they particularly favored women. After assigning a hired worker to a particular sector, Astorquiza continued to wield vast influence over all aspects of that person's work life, including promotions, demotions, and section and shift transfers. The Welfare Department also maintained attendance records, controlled sick leave and vacation time, and selectively meted out both punishment and reward—all in an ongoing effort to create a stable, productive, and docile labor force. A word from Astorquiza

49. Astorquiza, *Lota* (1942), 123.

to a section boss could make all the difference in a worker's career with the company. And, given the Lota company's hegemonic position in the region, a negative "moral assessment" from its Welfare Department could effectively blacklist a worker throughout the coal industry and even farther afield.

Beyond the workplace, the greatest changes in the company's relations with its workforce were the ways its new Welfare Department entered workers' personal lives through the control of housing, coal allotments, health care, education, sports, and cultural activities. The CCIL's Welfare Department consisted of nine divisions: Employment; Neighborhood; Provisioning; Medical Service; Instruction; Publications; Worker Sociability; and Social Work, Nursing, and Sanitation.[50] The agents of all these divisions played significant roles in the lives of Lota residents. Provisioning officials, for example, had the power to choose which workers would receive allotments of coal as reward for their service and loyalty to the company. With the southern coast's long, wet winters, coal, used for cooking, bathing, sanitizing water, and heating, was vital for a family's survival.

To the company, the value of coal purchased by railroads, public utilities, foundries, and factories far surpassed any price its black gold could fetch on the local consumer market. This created a relative scarcity of coal in the very towns that were covered with soot from its mines. The company also withheld supplies of coal needed to run its own operations, including its ceramics factory, sawmill, trains, and steamships, and to heat the homes and offices of its administrators and employees and the Cousiño palace, as well as its hospital, schools, stores, and social centers. For its workers, the company set aside only a small amount of often damaged or low-grade coal.

Families who did not receive company patronage struggled to acquire enough dregs of coal simply to survive. On the fringe of the region's formal economy, hundreds of men, women, and children spent hours a day waist-deep in the Pacific Ocean swirling heavy nets to catch fragments of coal washing ashore from barge spills and sorting house discards. Known as "chinchorreros," or coal catchers, these poor residents then bartered their sacks of coal at the local market.[51] The demand for coal in the very region from which it was extracted also made it lucrative to steal, and regional newspapers frequently reported assaults on coal trains and storage facilities.

50. Ibid., 166–68.
51. See Salazar Hermosilla, "Los chinchorreros."

New perspectives on "the social question" that emerged from the turmoil of the early 1920s, together with the growing power of the Democrat Party and Alessandri's liberal reformism, all contributed to substantive changes in the coal companies' dealings with their workforces. Although the companies had been disciplining their workers in the private sphere long before the 1920s, the creation of the Lota Welfare Department brought new, more institutionalized modes of vigilance, punishment, and reward to the fore. In line with the populist upsurge of the era, the companies couched new social regulation in modern paternalist discourse; they inundated their towns with company-sponsored dances, parades, movies, and sports events.

At the same time, the companies' promotion of alcohol consumption in the mid-nineteenth century, which had lured many rural migrants into the mine camps, gave way to company sobriety campaigns and advocacy of regional dry laws. Also, despite periodic complaints from municipal councils, the companies often allowed, or even encouraged, their workers to farm small plots and to raise livestock within city limits, even on company property.[52] This not only improved the workers' nutrition at no cost to the companies, but also deepened workers' roots in their communities and served as a powerful incentive for workers to stay in their employers' good graces. Thus, beginning in the 1920s, the formidable gaze of the bronze Matías Cousiño was joined by that of Octavio Astorquiza and the officers of his multiarmed Welfare Department, as they filled out personnel records, signed hiring and firing forms, and distributed housing and coal allotments.

In this new mode of company paternalism, the line was thin, if it existed at all, between company actions to improve workers' lives and company efforts to control them. Juan Osvaldo Ramírez Flores was two years old in 1928, when his family was photographed next to a modern coal-burning stove, which they had won as a prize for having the tidiest house and best job attendance. Looking at the old photo, Ramírez Flores nostalgically recalled the Lota company's practice of rewarding workers not only for doing their jobs, but also for maintaining clean houses and well-adorned balconies. His family's prize stove, which "had a roaster on the side and a great chimney," became the centerpiece of his childhood home and the envy of his neighbors. Such prizes served as incentives for

---

52. See, for example, "Reglamento interno de Compáñia Carbonífera de Lebu para los establecimientos de Lebu y Manto Grande" (1934), BNCh; Lota Municipal Acts, June 5, 1941, vol. 1, 4/33–3/43, 313, BML; and interviews with Raquel del Carmen Padilla Vergara, Emelina Araneda, Juan Alarcón, and Julia González Figueroa.

"proper conduct," as defined by the company, not only on the job but also in the domestic sphere.[53] They promoted benign patriarchy at home, civil obedience in the community, and loyal submission in the workplace.

What Ramírez Flores downplayed in his recollections was the company's increased intrusiveness into the lives of its workers that went along with its distribution of prizes. As he explained, a social worker (*visitadora*) from the Lota Welfare Department made monthly visits to miners' houses, usually without prior notice, to take notes on all aspects of family and home life. Based on these reports, certain families were awarded prizes, such as a sewing machine, a child's bicycle, or a coal-burning stove.[54] For all families, these reports strongly influenced Welfare Department decisions about housing, coal allotments, and other benefits.

In preparing their reports, the social workers gathered information about intimate family matters, including alcoholism, gambling, indebtedness, marital infidelities, and domestic violence. They also accumulated evidence about workers' union and political involvements, all of which went into permanent files and often resulted in disciplinary action. The Welfare Department's vigilance and control of the company workforce, as well as the community more broadly, was aided by a cadre of informers (*soplones*), many of whom regularly received bonuses or extra deliveries of coal. More often, however, social workers gathered information in casual conversations on the street or in workers' homes, where someone appealing for a larger company house might let it slip that their Communist neighbors had mentioned an upcoming meeting.

Ramírez Flores's fond recollection of his childhood stove reflects more than just nostalgia; for many residents of the coal towns, the company welfare departments formed in the 1920s appeared as a potential source of assistance or even as kind benefactors. Families who won prizes, workers who were promoted or who were granted their housing requests or other benefits, had reason to look to the companies with hope and gratitude. Other people also turned to the companies with hope, but of a more desperate sort. This was the case of many women in the countryside who wrote to company welfare departments trying to locate the fathers of their children. Social workers would write back confirming or denying the men's employment; sometimes a social worker would visit a miner to find out more why he had abandoned his family and perhaps to issue a

---

53. Interview with Juan Osvaldo Ramírez Flores, whose father worked for the CCIL as a site-level construction supervisor (*contratista albañil*) in the Architecture Department, and thus was considered a white-collar *empleado*, rather than a blue-collar *obrero*.

54. Ibid.

warning.[55] In cases of domestic violence or abandonment involving women and children in company towns, social workers often took a more proactive stance. As recorded in personnel files, the men deemed responsible usually received several warnings, followed by punitive job transfers or other disciplinary measures.

Forging a New Industrial Relations System

The coal companies' heightened intervention in the homes and community spaces of their workers was paralleled by the increased involvement of the Arturo Alessandri Palma administration (1920–24) in both the economy and labor-capital relations. In the case of the coal industry, one of the most significant outcomes of the early 1920s labor agitation, as Stephen Bosworth argues, was that it brought an end to "decades of government indifference."[56] During the presidential campaign, when Alessandri had supported the striking coal miners, Chilean "workers thought that they might have found a champion for their cause."[57] Shortly after the October election, when another labor dispute erupted in the coal mines, President-elect Alessandri even invited a delegation of strike leaders to lunch at his home in Santiago. Showing their trust in his reformist pledges, the miners agreed to end the strike based on Alessandri's promises of "future government action."[58]

Alessandri's concerns about the coal industry were based not only on the conflictive social relations in the region, but also on the Lota company's moves to streamline operations. Just before the Great Strike of 1920, it had acquired the properties of the Curanilahue company, whose small and medium mines it soon closed down, causing layoffs and declines in production.[59] After conducting a number of economic and technical studies, the government gradually developed a more systematic

55. See, for example, Santos V. Chandia Vejar, Prontuario no. 968, and Ricardo Gajardo Fernández, Prontuario no. 1350, CCIL personnel files, consulted at ENACAR, Lota Alto. The three hundred and fifty personnel files that I consulted in 1997–98 were housed along with thousands of others in a dynamite bunker (polvorín enterrado) on the surface of the Lota mines. I was provided access to these files by ENACAR Personnel Director Bernardo Alarcón Rojas and his assistant Juan Venegas. I do not know the subsequent fate of these files.

56. Bosworth, "True State," 8.

57. Bosworth, "Impact of Coal Strikes," 34.

58. Ibid., 34–35.

59. Between 1921 and 1929, the following mines (among others) were shut down: Colico (1921), Playa Negra (1922), Nivel (1924), Quilachanquín (1924), Buen Retiro (1926), El Nueve (1926), Chilita (1927), and Plegarias (1929). See Mella, "Curanilahue," 28; and Silva Torres, "Impacto de la actividad," 39.

energy policy, which included taxes on imported fuels. While Congress hotly debated legislation to structure a modern industrial relations system, the government continued to arbitrate labor disputes on a case-by-case basis. Finally, in the wake of a strike in 1923, Alessandri established the National Coal Commission, whose findings would provide the basis for the first comprehensive coal mining law, passed in 1928.[60]

As Alessandri was emerging as a liberal reformer during the social unrest of the early 1920s, the consolidation of the Bolshevik Revolution ushered in changes for Chile's leftist forces. The FOCh joined the Red International of Labor Unions in 1921, and in December of that year, delegates of the Socialist Workers' Party (POS) voted to become the Communist Party of Chile (PCCh). Accepting the stringent twenty-one conditions of affiliation, the PCCh joined the Moscow-based Third International (Comintern).[61] Under Recabarren's leadership, and long after its birth, the new party would maintain the tight weave of radical politics and labor militancy that had characterized the FOCh and the POS.[62]

During the period of growing Communist strength and labor agitation between 1921 and 1924, members of the FOCh held all nine seats on the Lota Municipal Council. Company spokesman Octavio Astorquiza denounced the leftist councilmen for the "notable decline in municipal services, disorder in local finances, [and] lack of cleanliness in the city." He further claimed that the leftists had unleashed such terror and violence that two consecutive right-wing mayors "were assassinated in the course of their duties."[63] After this brief heyday of governance, however, Communist and FOCh politicians lost elections across the country in 1924. Astorquiza rejoiced that "elements of order" had regained control in Lota and begun to "correct the errors of the previous administration."[64] Also in 1924, as discussed below in greater detail, the military responded to years of mounting social conflict and political impasse by ousting President Alessandri and pushing through a new labor relations system. The social upheaval of the early 1920s thus gave way to a period of both repression and incorporation of Chile's working-class sectors. Not until the end of the World War II, from 1945 to 1947, "would there again be produced a climate of similar strike agitation," though, as Jorge Rojas Flores

60. Bosworth, "Impact of Coal Strikes," 35.
61. Barnard, "Chilean Communist Party," 57.
62. Angell, *Politics*, 128.
63. Astorquiza, *Lota* (1942), 200.
64. Ibid., 200–201.

notes, the battles of the mid-1940s would be waged "in a quite different political and social environment."[65]

In addition to the Federation of Chilean Workers and the Socialist Workers' Party, both of which had opposed Alessandri's Liberal Alliance, another significant political force among the coal miners in the 1920s was the Democrat Party (PD). Founded in 1887 as "a mildly socialistic party of the lower middle class and artisan groups," the Democrat Party had long been calling for social legislation.[66] Most Democrats thus rallied behind Alessandri's bid for the presidency. Soon, however, many became disenchanted and worked to block his legislative agenda.[67] The sharp division that developed in the Democrat Party came to the fore at its March 1920 national convention, when those who favored remaining in the Liberal Alliance narrowly defeated those who favored withdrawal.[68]

The head of the Democrat Party for the Concepción region, which included Lota, Coronel, and smaller coal mining towns, was Juan Pradenas Muñoz, a man with strong working-class support, who was elected national deputy from 1920 to 1924.[69] As a leader of the left wing of the PD, Pradenas Muñoz condemned government repression of striking workers, distrusted Alessandri's reformist promises, and strongly advocated pulling out of the Liberal Alliance.[70] Also representing the coal mining region in the Chamber of Deputies, however, was Robinson Paredes Pacheco (1915–22), a leader of the PD's right wing, who fully supported the Liberal Alliance and was subsequently named by Alessandri to a series of cabinet posts. A third national representative of the coal mining zone was a leading politician of the Radical Party, Pedro Aguirre Cerda, who, in 1920, at age forty-one, was elected senator for the province of Concepción. A strong advocate of the Liberal Alliance, Aguirre Cerda became Alessandri's interior minister in 1924; fourteen years later, he would be elected

65. Rojas Flores, *La dictadura de Ibáñez*, 13.
66. Morris, *Elites*, 157.
67. Ibid., 217–18.
68. Ibid., 218.
69. In the early 1930s, the Democrat Party split over the questioning of supporting Alessandri in his second bid for the presidency. Pradenas Muñoz led the left-wing faction that became known as the "Democratic Party" (Partido Democrático; PD-co), while the pro-Alessandri right wing kept the name "Democrat Party" (Partido Demócrata; PD). These two parties remained split through the Aguirre Cerda presidency, with the PD-co supporting the Popular Front and the PD opposing it. They reunited in November 1941. See, for example, Stevenson, *Chilean Popular Front*, 62, 113; and Cortés and Fuentes, *Diccionario político*, 142–43, 152–53.
70. Morris, *Elites*, 217.

president of Chile at the head of the nation's first Popular Front coalition.[71]

During the early 1920s, many actors across the political spectrum became convinced of the need for some form of legislation to control or reduce class conflict. For several years, Congress hotly debated different bills submitted by the Liberal Alliance and the Conservatives. Leftist leaders—including anarchists, FOCh and PCCh members, and many Democrats—were sharply divided over whether there should be a state-regulated system of social relations.[72] Opponents argued that any such system would primarily serve the elites' interests in containing and "depoliticizing" labor disputes. Proponents countered, however, that social legislation represented a signal victory in the relatively short, but passionate history of Chile's populist and Marxist political movements.

Prominent Communist leader Luis Emilio Recabarren was extremely wary of a legislatively controlled system for addressing labor-capital relations, even though he had long embraced participation in Chilean electoral democracy. After an unsuccessful bid for the presidency in 1920, Recabarren ran for (and won) a seat in the Chamber of Deputies in 1921. During the campaign, he declared, "We the workers now know that the social problem cannot be resolved by laws, for the bourgeoisie will never permit laws benefiting the people and if any were passed, they would not respect them. [Such laws] contribute instead to strengthening the capitalist system and they postpone and retard genuine popular emancipation, because they arouse hopes in the people that can never be translated into social welfare."[73]

What Recabarren and other opponents of the legislation foresaw was that a legalistic modern industrial relations system would limit the tactics available to leftist parties and labor groups and undermine their ability to fight for the interests of their constituents and social bases. As debates about social legislation raged on over the next three years, the political fortunes of the FOCh and the PCCh sharply declined. In the municipal elections of 1924, they lost control of city councils throughout the

71. Loveman and Lira, *Las ardientes cenizas*, 63–64. As president, Aguirre Cerda signaled the importance of coal mining to his national project by appointing politicians experienced in the region to key labor relations positions. In a strategic move to bolster working-class support for the fledgling Popular Front government, he named his former rival Pradenas Muñoz labor minister, while Paredes Pacheco served as deputy chief of the General Labor Office (Dirección General del Trabajo), which he then headed under Aguirre Cerda's successor, Ríos Morales.

72. Morris, *Elites*, 205–47.

73. Luis Emilio Recabarren, as quoted in Morris, *Elites*, 205.

coal mining zone and in other working-class regions around the country. In the congressional elections of that year, Luis Emilio Recabarren was one of many incumbent Communists who were defeated.

Meanwhile, the continued impasse between Alessandri and the Liberals, on the one hand, and a Conservative-controlled Congress, on the other, was blocking "urgent legislation for creation of a national bank, for social welfare laws, for military appropriations, and for other pressing matters."[74] Dismayed at the state of the country and concerned about the Alessandri administration, in September 1924, a group of military officers ousted the president and forced Congress to pass a comprehensive set of laws, including the labor code that Alessandri had been supporting. Among the most progressive social legislation in Latin America at the time, the laws provided for an eight-hour workday, substantial suppression of child labor, and numerous improvements in occupational health and safety.

They also created a host of institutions, such as conciliation boards and arbitration tribunals, that would henceforth regulate and mediate Chilean social relations, particularly the perennial disputes between workers and capitalists. Workers' rights to form trade unions and to bargain collectively were now legally recognized, subject to the sometimes byzantine requirements and procedures set forth in law.[75] Union activities would be tightly monitored by Ministry of Labor officials, who became a large, professional cadre over the next decades. The new system also included a workers' insurance and pension fund, the Caja de Seguro Obrero, to be run as a semiautonomous state agency with employer, worker, and government contributions.[76]

---

74. Loveman, *Chile*, 180.

75. As consolidated in the 1931 Labor Code, Chilean laws provided for the formation of two distinct types of unions: the *sindicato industrial* and the *sindicato profesional*. The sindicato industrial consisted of manual or blue-collar workers (obreros) in a given company with at least twenty-five eligible workers. Each company could have only one legally recognized industrial union, to which all workers were required to pay dues and with which the company was legally bound to negotiate. The second type of union, the sindicato profesional, could consist either of skilled, white-collar employees (empleados) in one company, which could also have a sindicato industrial, *or* of white-collar workers or manual workers in several companies in the same industry when there were not the requisite twenty-five workers to form an industrial union. Laws governing each type of union differed considerably, as for example, regarding profit sharing. The new laws required companies to distribute a certain percentage of their annual profits directly to workers and to give another percentage to their workers' industrial unions, but not to professional unions.

76. For a recent work on Chile's social security system from the 1920s to the 1970s, see Borzutsky, *Vital Connections*.

The legislation of September 1924 (and subsequent laws consolidated in the 1931 Labor Code) set the framework for a modern system of social and industrial relations that would endure in its essential features for the next four decades.[77] State institutions and actors now had increased formal power and jurisdiction, which, ideally, would make brute confrontations between labor and capital a thing of past. National laws and government mediation would allow both sides sufficient and equal opportunity in the public sphere for their interests to be recognized and contested. This, at least, was the liberal ideal behind the move to create legal and democratic modes to control class conflict and thus to promote capitalist development.

In the months following the passage of Chile's first major labor laws, the faction within the Chilean Communist Party that favored compliance with the new system began to gain the upper hand, eclipsing opponents such as Recabarren, who committed suicide in December 1924.[78] Just two weeks before Recabarren's death, Communist Deputy Luis Cruz published the first in a series of seven articles entitled "Must We Ask for the Repeal of the Recently Enacted Labor Code?"—to which his answer was no. Advocating a "qualified acceptance of the labor laws," Cruz argued that he and his comrades "must squeeze from the laws the greatest benefits possible, so as to build up superior revolutionary potential."[79] Carlos Contreras Labarca, who would serve as secretary-general of the Communist Party throughout the Popular Front period (1931–46), agreed with Cruz. As James Morris explains, "In [Contreras Labarca's] opinion, the FOCh should not reject the laws out of hand but rather should study them closely and 'to the extent they agree with some of our aspirations and immediate demands, we should take advantage of them IN ORDER TO PERSEVERE IN THE CLASS STRUGGLE.'"[80]

In 1925, a year after Recabarren's death, the FOCh convention affirmed the position that Cruz and Contreras Labarca had been advocating: strategic acceptance of the new social legislation. "The winning policy stated

77. Loveman, *Chile*, 184.

78. A number of different factors may have figured into Recabarren's decision to take his own life, including his disappointment with the Soviet Union, his frustration with Chilean Communist decline and factionalism, and his own personal, psychological problems. See Morris, *Elites*, 244.

79. Luis Cruz, as quoted from *La Justicia* (Santiago), November 24 and 26, 1924, in ibid., 244–45.

80. Morris, *Elites*, 245, quoting Carlos Contreras Labarca from *La Justicia*, April 5, 8, and 9, 1925; emphasis in original. Contreras Labarca received his law degree in 1924, just before these laws were passed. He was elected national deputy for the Pisagua and Tarapacá region (1926–30; 1937–41) and then senator for Santiago (1941–49). In November 1946, Contreras

that the FOCh would not allow itself to be deceived either by the mirage of reformism or by the intransigence of an antipolitical stand which could only serve the interests of the employer. The FOCh must, without losing sight of the ultimate goal of achieving power for the working class, 'use all the social legislation of the capitalist state to fight capitalism itself.'"[81] By 1925, however, military leader Carlos Ibáñez del Campo was wielding de facto power over the nation, and in this context, the federation's new strategy proved exceedingly difficult.[82] "The actual experiences of trying to organize plant unions during the politically unstable years of 1925–1927," Morris notes, "undoubtedly dampened rather than stimulated the ardor of those who sought to use the labor laws within the larger framework of their revolutionary aims."[83]

Despite the challenges they faced, Communists in the coal mining zone remained active, and in early 1927, the regional labor inspector for Concepción warned of their resurgent influence. The number of their followers increased daily, he said, as did the seditious orientation of their activities. In the inspector's estimation, the coal mining town of Coronel was "the principal Communist center in the country because of its high concentration of workers, between eighteen and twenty thousand."[84] Trying to thwart the politicization of its workforce, in early 1927, the Schwager company fired ten employees for their allegedly subversive ideas and activities. When the miners retaliated with a strike in March, the government sent troops to occupy the region, resulting in massive arrests.[85] According to estimates by historian Jorge Rojas Flores, in just two months, from February to March, over three hundred people across the nation were arrested or forced into internal exile (*relegación*), while countless others were fired from their jobs, placed under close surveillance, or forced into hiding.[86]

After May 1927, when Carlos Ibáñez del Campo became president in an uncontested election, thus formalizing his control of the state apparatus,

---

Labarca stepped down as head of the party and was named one of the three Communist ministers to serve in González Videla's first cabinet, as further discussed in chapter 8.

81. Morris, *Elites*, 246, quoting Contreras Labarca, from *La Justicia*, December 23, 24, 27, and 29, 1925.

82. Right-wing politician Emiliano Figueroa Larraín was formally the president of Chile, having won the 1925 elections held after the military intervention against Alessandri. Ibáñez, however, wielded the real power, and soon Figueroa Larraín took a leave of absence. In May 1927, he resigned and Ibáñez won the carefully controlled elections that followed.

83. Morris, *Elites*, 247.

84. Rojas Flores, *La dictadura de Ibáñez*, 133.

85. Ibid., 71.

86. Ibid., 35.

he continued his campaign of persecution against the mobilized working class and, in particular, militants of the Chilean Communist Party and the Federation of Chilean Workers. A few months later, when a group of workers at the Schwager coal mines walked off the job, Ibáñez again dispatched military forces; at least forty workers were arrested in the course of putting down the strike. A year later, when rumors circulated that "Communists and rebels" were yet again planning a strike in Schwager, the government renewed its repression.[87] Between 1927 and 1931, almost every leftist labor and political leader in the region spent some time in jail, exile, or hiding. Indeed, many repressive tactics that would be used in coming decades, such as infiltrating labor organizations and exiling political and labor leaders to islands and far reaches of the country, had roots in this period.[88] This political persecution, together with economic dislocations, caused a dramatic decline in the number of workers in the coal industry, from seventeen thousand to eleven thousand in just three years.[89]

Notwithstanding the stated concern of certain Ibáñez officials about a resurgence of revolutionary militancy in the coal mines, the FOCh did not respond to state and capitalist aggression by adopting more confrontational positions, although they did support the workers' use of strikes. Rather, the ascendant voices among leftist labor and political leaders continued to urge workers to accept the emerging legal industrial relations system—to negotiate and battle within the system, and even to use it to preserve FOCh's very existence. That Chile's organized workers did so was a key juncture in moving from their notable radicalism in the early 1920s to their embrace of the Popular Front project in the mid-1930s. With its cadres dispersed, in prison, underground, or under surveillance, the FOCh's "hostility," as described by Morris, "was not so much an expression of opposition to the labor laws as much as it was an expression of anger that the laws were being used to destroy FOCh organization and membership."[90]

In the coal mining region, only younger and less prominent activists were able to stay in the towns and pursue a degree of underground activity, although many were fired from their jobs and blacklisted from further

87. Ibid., 71–73.
88. A commission charged with investigating the repressive acts of the Ibáñez regime was formed just a week after his overthrow in 1931. For a collection of documents compiled in the investigation, see Loveman and Lira, Los actos.
89. Rojas Flores, La dictadura de Ibáñez, 133n120.
90. Morris, Elites, 247.

employment.[91] More notorious leaders of the old guard, such as Armando González Uribe, were forced to leave the region to escape arrest. With a young wife, whom he had met and married in Lota, González Uribe fled to the countryside around the small town of Nueva Imperial, where he worked at various jobs—digging canals, building bridges, and laboring at a mill. Not until after the Popular Front coalition was forged in 1936 and its candidates gained seats in local government did González Uribe consider it safe to return to Coronel, where he would regain his job in the Schwager mines and renew his work as a Communist labor activist.[92]

Even as it repressed leftist political and labor leaders, the Ibáñez dictatorship (1927–31) also made use of the new labor laws to reduce social conflicts, or at least to control their political ramifications, trying to channel them into narrow legal bounds. "The content of labor confrontations," Rojas Flores tells us, "came to be exclusively about immediate economic concerns; destabilizing orientations would not be permitted within the unions, nor would any intent to alter public order, 'discipline,' or 'social harmony.' State vigilance of the union organizations complemented the confidence deposited in its moderating action. This impulse toward social legislation and anti-oligarchic language (elements also present in Alessandri) gave Ibáñez quite broad social support among workers." Thus, although Ibáñez's ample use of state intelligence and security forces was critical in eliminating public opposition to his rule, the workers' "massive support of the government cannot be denied."[93]

Even the coal mining region, one of the first strongholds of the PCCh and the FOCh, quickly emerged as a key sector in Ibáñez's efforts to create a controlled labor movement. By at least one account, the coal miners' union of Lota (Sindicato Industrial de la Compañía Minera e Industrial de Chile) was the very first in the country to be legally recognized under the new social legislation.[94] From 1926 to early 1930, it was followed by three

91. One such young activist, fired from the Lota company in 1930, was Santos Leoncio Medel Basualto, who would serve as Lota's mayor throughout most of the 1940s, and who is discussed in greater detail in later chapters; see esp. chapter 2.

92. As we shall see in chapter 9, Armando González Uribe was among those who took over the Schwager mine during the strike of October 1947; after being detained for several days on a naval vessel, he was exiled from the region.

93. Rojas Flores, *La dictadura de Ibáñez*, 14.

94. In their 1962 study, James Morris and Roberto Oyaneder write, "The history of the establishment of legal unions in Chile begins in 1926, only two years after the union law was passed, when the industrial union of the coal mining workers of Lota obtained recognition as an organization from the Government." Morris, Oyaneder, and INSORA, *Afiliación y finanzas*, 17. Other evidence confirms that the Lota miners' union was founded on October 6, 1926, and granted legal recognition on December 17, 1926, but because the employees' union of the Valparaíso electrical company had been granted legal standing on September 30, 1926, this made it the second, not the first, union established in the country. All dates

other unions in Concepción and one in the neighboring port town of Talcahuano, though none of these (bakers, millwrights, and brewery workers) was directly related to the coal mining industry. The next coal miners' union to gain legal recognition was the Schwager workers' union (Sindicato Industrial de la Compañía Carbonífera y de Fundición Schwager), founded on July 7, 1929, and granted legal standing (*personalidad jurídica*) less than a year later. According to Rojas Flores, the Schwager miners' union was the most important at the time in terms of size, with more than three thousand members by 1930. As with the Lota union, the organized Schwager workers affiliated with the Republican Confederation of Civic Action (Confederación Republicana de Acción Cívica; CRAC), the apparatus designed by Ibáñez to control labor politics; both miners' unions "offered frequent words of respect and admiration for President Ibáñez."[95]

The repression unleashed by Ibáñez and the allure of his social policies were not the only reasons the Chilean Communist Party lost popular support in these years. In 1928, the party was accepted as a full member of the Communist International (Comintern), having been affiliated as a "sympathizer" since 1922, the year the POS became the PCCh. With their fortified commitment after 1928, Chilean Communists initiated a process often described as the "Bolshevization" of the party, which involved tighter and more centralized structuring of cells, as well as more formal lines of communication and decision making, from the local level to the national committee and on to Moscow. By restructuring its cadres, the Chilean Communist Party sought not only to strengthen its international ties, but also to eliminate the anarchist and reformist influences that had endured since its founding as the Socialist Worker's Party, which broke away from the Democrat Party five years before the 1917 Russian revolution.[96]

Also in 1928, the same year the PCCh drew closer to Moscow, the Sixth Congress of the Comintern set forth what became known as the "Third Period" policy of class warfare, with sharp antagonism to democratic bourgeois parties. The Comintern advocated United Fronts (Frentes Unicos) of Socialist workers, but Chilean Communists found themselves adapting the policy to refer to "a broad front that included middle[-class]

---

of the founding of legal unions come from the Registro Nacional de Sindicatos, Social Organizations Division, General Labor Office.

95. Rojas Flores, *La dictadura de Ibáñez*, 133.

96. See for example, Rojas Flores, "Historia," esp. 17; and Arrate and Rojas, *Memoria*, 1:134–36.

sectors" in their effort to survive and eventually defeat Ibáñez.[97] Still, from 1928 through 1931, the Communists' identification with revolutionary anti-statism and their extreme circumspection toward other political forces contributed to their isolation and dwindling base of support.

At the same time, the global depression of the early 1930s was wreaking havoc with the Chilean economy and devastating the coal mining communities. Many smaller and medium mining enterprises shut down entirely, casting thousands of workers into unemployment. Even the more heavily capitalized companies such as the Coal Mining and Industrial Company of Lota (CCIL) and Schwager cut back operations dramatically. Miners who managed to keep their jobs struggled to survive on paychecks from only two, three, or four days of work a week.[98] In 1930, the CCIL closed down all of its Curanilahue operations, causing "an exodus of families, [while] those that remain are going through very difficult times."[99] As described by the Methodist pastor for the Concepción district in 1934, "The Coal Mining Zone has lived hours of true anguish in recent times, and many are the sufferings and miseries that families in that region have endured. The situation has now partly normalized and hopes of better days are being reborn."[100] Despite this cautious optimism, mining operations in places such as Curanilahue and Plegarias did not reopen until 1938.

Precisely in 1931, as economic crisis put tens of thousands of people out of work, President Ibáñez secured the passage of Chile's first national Labor Code, a compilation of laws passed over the preceding decade, together with new articles, especially dealing with rural and domestic workers. Among its key features, as described by Brian Loveman, the code "established a national system of labor courts, as well as institutions to administer mandatory collective bargaining and arbitration [juntas de conciliación]." Firmly ensconcing the role of the state, the code "created a highly paternalistic and authoritarian system of government-worker relations." As Loveman explains,

> The code limited worker petitions and strikes to individual firms and restricted severely the activity of union federations. It gave authority to the government to order a "return to work" whenever a

97. See Gómez, "Factores," esp. 67. See also Ramírez Necochea, *Orígen*, 270–74.

98. For vivid descriptions of workers' lives in this period, see Acts of the Thirty-first Conferencia Anual de la Iglesia Metodista Episcopal, Concepción, January 6–12, 1931, 174, CDIME.

99. Ibid.

100. Acts of the Thirty-fourth Conferencia Anual de la Iglesia Metodista Episcopal, Concepción, January 23–29, 1934, 117–18, CDIME.

strike or lockout endangered public health or the economic or social life of the nation. Any labor conflict that failed to meet the rigorous requirements specified in the code could be declared illegal, and the unions were liable for any damages or losses under such circumstances. In practice these restrictive regulations meant that from 1932 on, illegal strikes outnumbered legal ones by a wide margin.[101]

Although the new Labor Code, which consolidated laws passed in 1924 and subsequent years, would strongly shape Chilean history for the next four decades, its immediate progenitor, Carlos Ibáñez del Campo, was forced from power shortly after its passage. In July 1931, in the face of extreme popular protest, the dictator resigned. His departure, James Morris explains, created space for "the rebirth of competition in the labor movement. The FOCh emerged from the underground and rapidly regained membership strength, although it . . . never recovered the prestige or the following it had enjoyed before Ibáñez."[102]

Differing from their position in the mid-1920s, when they had come to "qualified acceptance" of social legislation, "many FOCh leaders (the followers of Elías Lafertte) were now wary of the legal system and of the government."[103] This was due both to their recent experiences with legal unions, most of which had joined Ibáñez's Republican Confederation of Civic Action (CRAC), and to the PCCh's endeavor to follow the anti-statist policies of the Comintern. Newly reconstituted local and regional FOCh councils set out to reinvigorate "the free union as their organizing unit," and they enjoyed a brief resurgence, particularly in nitrate, copper, and coal mining areas.[104] In the coal mines, FOCh activists engaged in harsh and embittered battles for the hearts and minds of the workers, frequently clashing with existing legal unions as they sought to replace them with their own "free" (illegal) unions. Both the coal companies and the state moved quickly to halt the federation's revival. In August 1931, for example, in a blatant act of persecution, the top leader of the FOCh council in Lota was both arrested by the carabineros and fired by the CCIL.[105]

---

101. Loveman, *Chile*, 184–85. For a well-grounded assessment of problems in Chilean legislation regarding strikes, see Camu Veloso, *Estudio crítica*. See also Humeres Magnan, *La huelga*; and, for a summary less focused on the legislation, Barrera, "Perspectiva histórica," 119–55.
102. Morris, *Elites*, 158.
103. Ibid.
104. Ibid.
105. Rojas Flores, *La dictadura de Ibáñez*, 156.

Yet, as FOCh and PCCh leaders struggled to rebuild their working-class base, they increasingly questioned the hard-line policies of the Comintern's Third Period (1928–33). Taking a critical and pragmatic view, leaders such as Elías Lafertte began to reconsider the advisability, in the current Chilean context, of insisting on revolutionary militancy and shunning compromise with the more reformist social and political sectors.[106] Such policies were undermining the Communists' ability to gain a truly mass following, and only through popular strength, Lafertte and others became convinced, could they wield influence in the emergent model of state-mediated social relations.[107]

Even as the dominant faction within the Chilean Communist Party began to advocate working within the state system, other ideological and political forces maintained their opposition. Anarchists and Trotskyists (as well as some Communists) continued to reject legislated industrial relations, insisting instead on "free unions," with unfettered options for confronting capitalist exploitation. In 1931, the very year the Chilean Labor Code was adopted, a Trotskyist dissident group led by Manuel Hidalgo, Emilio Zapata, and others who had worked their way up through the Democrat Party and then the POS and the FOCh, broke away from the PCCh to form what would become known as the "Communist Left." Within a few years, Zapata would lead the formation of the country's first National Peasant League; he would also strongly oppose the Popular Front as a form of "class collaboration," particularly because it "sold out" the interests of rural workers.[108]

106. See Gómez, "Factores nacionales," 69; Galo González, "La lucha por la formación del Partido Comunista de Chile," *Principios* (July 1951): 4–9.

107. In hindsight, many analysts see stringent Third Period policies to have undermined the strength of the Chilean Communist Party by limiting its mass appeal. Some scholars argue that it was the PCCh's internal critique of these hard-line policies that compelled them to embrace the Popular Front strategy. Others recognize the shortcomings of the Communists' Third Period line, but argue that their adoption of the Popular Front strategy had more to do with external factors, such as the orders coming from the Comintern's Seventh Congress, or the maneuverings of Peruvian Communist Eudocio Ravines, who was sent to Chile by the Comintern in 1935 to promote the new anti-Fascist agenda. In the former group, see Gómez, "Factores nacionales," and Blasier, "Chile," 361–62. In the latter, see Faúndez, *Marxism*, esp. 25, 40–41; Halperin, *Nationalism*, 43; and Alexander, *Communism*.

108. In 1937, Zapata, Hidalgo and other dissident Communists joined the Socialist Party (PS) and brought many organized rural workers with them. In 1940–41, however, still opposed to Popular Front compromises, they left the Socialist Party and were joined by dissident Communists, to form the Workers' Socialist Party (Partido Socialista de los Trabajadores; PST). In 1944, when the PST dissolved, many of its members, including Carlos Rosales Gutierrez, Natalio Berman, and César Godoy Urrutia, returned to the fold of the Chilean Communist Party. Zapata and Hidalgo refused to do so. For excerpts and analysis of Brian Loveman's 1971 interview with Zapata, see Loveman, *Chile*, and *Struggle*; see also

Just as the Chilean Communists were contemplating major shifts in their domestic policies, across the Atlantic, a reveille sounded in the thunderous stomp of Nazi boots. When Hitler rose to power in March 1933, the Comintern executive committee publicly endorsed the new directions pursued by the PCCh, encouraging its affiliates around the world to enlist Socialist and even progressive pro-capitalist parties in collaborative action against Fascism. The Chilean Communist Party had already begun to "soften" its policies, and, as former national leader Galo González recalled, they were quick to embrace the Comintern's new mandates, setting out to become "a true party of the masses."[109]

Because their strategic position in the mining communities enabled them to bridge the political and the social, coal company workers would play a significant role in this project. While learning to battle for their own interests in the new industrial relations system, the coal miners became a significant electoral force and were able to bring diverse local and regional issues into public forums. The years of underground life in the 1920s and 1930s had trained Communist activists to build local networks of support out of personal connections. After the Ibáñez dictatorship, the advance of the Communist Party took place through conversations and small actions, not only in the mines but also on the beaches and soccer fields and in neighborhood bars of the coal mining region. Local activists of a new generation embraced the challenge of broadening and deepening the Communists' base of support, as they represented the coal mining region at the PCCh National Congress in 1933, "which proclaimed for the first time the character of the Chilean revolution as bourgeois-democratic, agrarian, and anti-imperialist."[110]

Yet Arturo Alessandri Palma, the "lion" of Chilean politics, who was just beginning the second year of his second (nonconsecutive) term as president (1932–38), was unwilling to countenance a public resurgence of the Communist Party, regardless of its growing embrace of bourgeois democracy. He sent national security forces to break up the 1933 PCCh National Congress. Many local militants from the coal mining region were arrested, together with prominent national leaders, who staged a hunger strike inside the Santiago jail.[111] Over the next several years, Alessandri would strive to consolidate his support among centrist and right-wing sectors by attacking Communists with only slightly less fervor than

---

Robert J. Alexander's December 17, 1946, interview with Hidalgo, RJAIC; and Olga Ulianova's essay, "La figura de Manuel Hidalgo."

109. Galo González, as quoted in Gómez, "Factores nacionales," 72.

110. Gómez, "Factores nacionales," 72, 74. See also Pizarro, La huelga obrera, 122.

111. Interview with Luis Corvalán Lépez.

Ibáñez had. Yet, unlike Ibáñez, Alessandri was a civilian president who extolled liberal democracy and sought to capitalize on his previously won reputation as a reformer, particularly among anti-Communist centrist democrats. Thus, despite its repressive measures, Alessandri's administration, at least in principle, offered greater democratic space for leftist labor and political organizing than the brutal Ibáñez regime had.

As the Communists and their allied labor forces emerged from underground to pursue strategies of mass mobilization and democratic participation, a new political force, the Socialist Party, appeared on the scene. Coming out of the short-lived Socialist Republic led by Marmaduke Grove and Carlos Dávila in 1932, this new party, based in the middle class, would become both a formidable rival and, at times, an invaluable ally of the Communists throughout the rest of the twentieth century. In 1935, under the growing threat of global Fascism, the Comintern held its momentous Seventh Congress. It was here that Bulgarian delegate Georgi Dimitrov carried the day with his advocacy of anti-Fascist Popular Front alliances; from this moment on, Communists around the world were called on to coordinate their efforts with Socialists and even certain Social Democrats.[112] Because the Chilean Communist Party had already undertaken fundamental shifts in this direction, it was quick to embrace the new Comintern strategy. As Tomás Moulian explains, "It was only left for them to complement the thesis of bourgeois-democratic revolution with a short-term government program and a scheme of alliances."[113]

Meanwhile, also at the time of the 1935 Comintern Congress, the Concepción-Arauco regional committee of the PCCh sent party activist Aniceto Martínez González—a former Lota coal miner—"to direct the reorganization of the Communists of Lebu."[114] Martínez González's affiliation with the Communist Party stemmed from his activism as a CCIL worker in the late 1920s and early 1930s. In 1931, when a commission of workers "accompanied by some Communists" appeared at the administration building to file a list of grievances, Martínez González was among them.[115] Though it is not clear whether he was a union delegate or PCCh

112. See Dimitrov, "Fascist Offensive" and "Unity of the Working Class," his main speeches at the Seventh Comintern Congress, on August 2 and 13, 1935. For versions circulating in Chile at the time, see Dimitrov, La unidad (Santiago and Madrid, 1935).

113. Moulian, "Desarrollo político chileno," 16–17.

114. Pizarro Soto, Lebu, 337.

115. Note in Miguel Provoste Flores, Prontuario no. 945, CCIL personnel files, consulted at ENACAR. Lota Alto. The note seems to have been misfiled since no. 945 was not on the list, whereas no. 845 was.

member at this time, he was soon fired from the CCIL, which made him available for organizing workers in other coal mining towns.

Arriving in Lebu in mid-1935, Martínez González began to recruit a leadership cadre of young men with wide appeal in local society. These included a schoolteacher, two civil servants of the labor and treasury offices, the owner of a pastry factory, and a railroad machinist. Several of the new directors of the Lebu PCCh would become key actors in the local Popular Front, effectively bridging working-class and community politics. The railroad machinist Victorino Monsálvez, for example, was one of the first two Communists voted onto the Lebu City Council in 1938. "Within a few years," as historian J. Alejandro Pizarro Soto observes, "the PCCh in Lebu would show such "great political and leadership capability" that they would come "to control the municipal majority."[116] When Martínez González was satisfied with his organizing efforts in Lebu, he moved back north to Coronel, where he, too, won a city council seat in the 1938 elections. By May 1940, Martínez González was secretary-general of the Coronel PCCh, and, from May 1941 through mid-1944, he served as mayor of the city.[117] The meteoric rise of Communist workers such as Victorino Monsálvez and Martínez González to elected and appointed leadership positions would powerfully shape the politics of the coal mining region in the 1940s—bringing to the fore a model of citizen workers who would vigorously assert their rights.

Notwithstanding the efforts of dissident groups, what transpired at the national level from the 1920s to the 1930s was essentially the defeat and marginalization of anarchist, Trotskyist, and other "far Left" currents by the ever more powerful Chilean Communist Party (PCCh) and, after 1933, the Socialist Party (PS). In the coal mining towns, the ascent of Communists promoting broad alliances and legal paths of conflict resolution meant the eclipse of Armando González Uribe's generation, reared on Recabarren's anti-statist ideology, and the rise of a generation whose political ideas were formed during the tumultuous birth of a state-centered model of social relations. How this new generation consolidated power at the local level during the Popular Front era of Chilean politics is the subject of chapter 2.

116. Pizarro Soto, *Lebu*, 337.

117. Aniceto Martínez González seems to have left the coal mining region in 1944, but he continued to work for the Communist Party, possibly in Santiago. His name did not appear on any lists of persons arrested or exiled from the coal mining zone in 1947–48, nor was it removed from the region's electoral registers under the Law for the Permanent Defense of Democracy (LDPD). It did appear, however, on a list of "dangerous agitators" who were detained at a military camp in the northern port town of Pisagua.

CHALLENGING EXCLUSION:
THE BIRTH OF THE POPULAR FRONT IN THE COAL REGION

As the Popular Front project took shape in Moscow and Santiago, local identities and politics influenced the way it was enacted and experienced in different Chilean communities and regions. Studies of Chile's international relations and congressional wrangling do not adequately capture the significant changes that transpired in the lives of working-class Chileans beginning in the mid-1930s. In the coal mining towns, the Popular Front gave rise to new divisions and new alliances, and to new hopes, expectations, and demands. At the heart of the contest between pro- and anti-Front forces in the coal mining towns was the very definition of democracy—who could and could not participate, and who would wield the power to define the terms of inclusion and exclusion.

In May 1938, just one month after a national Popular Front convention launched the presidential candidacy of Pedro Aguirre Cerda, the Lota City Council held its annual inaugural meeting in the municipal building—"a little wooden house with scarcely three narrow, unsuitable rooms," on the edge of the main plaza in Lota Bajo.[1] As soon as the meeting was called to order, a newly elected Communist councilman named Santos Leoncio Medel Basualto rose from his seat to challenge the exclusion of certain members of the public from council sessions. A recent ordinance mandated that all persons seeking to enter the building obtain "cleanliness certificates" attesting to their having recently bathed. Medel Basualto

---

1. *El Sur*, September 12, 1942, 4.

assailed this requirement as a political move to keep out the working-class supporters of the Popular Front. Opposing Councilman Luis Segundo Muñoz Solar countered that the ordinance was necessary "due to the manifest filthiness of many who had been attending, and of the women who brought babies that cried inside." Concurring with Muñoz Solar, the mayor and other municipal officials declared that "they had no objection to allowing people to attend the sessions . . . as long as they came clean, no women or children came, and order and respect were maintained."[2]

The Lived Contours of Exclusion

Requiring cleanliness certificates was a thorny policy in a city where buildings, beaches, faces, and lungs were shrouded in ever-present coal smoke and dust. In the mid-1930s, approximately eight thousand people, or about one-quarter of the population of Lota, worked directly for the Coal Mining and Industrial Company (CCIL), which, in most cases, meant direct, continual contact with coal or its by-products.[3] Because there were no bathing

2. Acts of Lota Municipal Sessions (henceforth "Lota Municipal Acts"), May 15, 1938, in vol. 1, 4/33–3/43, 196, BML. The procedure for obtaining "cleanliness certificates" was not clear in my sources. Several people I interviewed said they had to sign in to use company bathing facilities, so this may have been where documentation was obtained. As Juan Alarcón recalled of the showers at Schwager, "They inscribed the names of everyone who went there. Why? Probably to keep statistics about whether the people maintained good habits or not, I don't know, but I remember that they had a book and they inscribed us in it, and also sometimes we had to carry our beds there, the mattresses . . . because they put them in hot steam to disinfect them." Interview with Juan Alarcón; see also interview with Raquel del Carmen Padilla Vergara.

3. CCIL employment figures vary widely depending on whether they include operations outside the mines, such as forestry, plantations, shipping, and railroads, and whether they refer only to those employed in Lota or include those working in the CCIL mines in Curanilahue and Plegarias. Engineer Ricardo Fenner said that the CCIL mines had 6,529 workers and 294 white-collar employees in 1935, which seems to include all three of the company's mine sites. Octavio Astorquiza gives a larger total of 9,604 workers in 1935, which he says included 4,986 in the mines and 4,618 in the company's other operations. An internal company document refers to 8,045 workers in 1935. Fenner, Situación actual, 8; Astorquiza, Lota (1942), 132–33; CCIL, "Cuadro comparativo de las inversiones hechas por la Compañía en los años que se indican, comparadas con las de Schwager," December 1939, in folder titled "Administración General, Lota Alto, 1930–194–," Coal company records, consulted at ENACAR, Lota Alto. The diverse company records that I consulted in 1997–98 were housed in the basement of ENACAR's Casa de Cultura in Lota Alto. I was provided access to these records by Enso La Mura and Marcos Risetti, who were in charge of early efforts to organize a museum and library. I do not know the subsequent fate of these records.

Some women and girls worked in the company's restaurants and stores, while others worked in the ceramics factory or the coal sorting and cleaning facilities at each mine head. No women or girls worked inside the mines, and the male miners' strong belief that the mines were a jealous woman long kept women from descending into the pits. Several

facilities at the mine heads in the mid-1930s, after emerging from their shifts, workers remained covered in soot until they reached their homes or the common showers at the company hospital in Lota Alto. One lifelong resident recalled that when she was a child playing in the streets of Lota, the sight of the filthy, black-faced miners returning home so terrified her she would run away to hide.[4] Once the miners reached their homes, some would bathe in tubs filled by wives or daughters with water carried in from neighborhood taps, while others would simply wash up outside the best they could. As Emelina Araneda recalled of her childhood in Lota in the 1930s, the miners "arrived, but with faces like monkeys, so they'd go outside to the spigots, because it wasn't like now when there are faucets everywhere, they'd go outside naked like that to the spigots to wash themselves."[5] That women and children were repeatedly exposed to naked or half-naked men at public washing facilities was one of the pressing moral issues raised by life in the coal mining towns.

People working directly in the mines were not the only ones who had difficulty keeping clean. After workers brought coal up from deep beneath the Pacific Ocean, it was hauled to sorting facilities and onto the main rail line by trains that hurled smoke into the air and scattered coal dust behind them.[6] Coal was also transported onto steamships by small barges, with so much falling into the ocean that men, women, and children known as "chinchorreros" eked out a minimal subsistence gathering the black chunks that washed ashore.[7] For heating in the winter and for

sources address women's employment issues, such as the 1939 Schwager contract petition, which included a special demand for increased wages of female coal washers. June 1939, FIC, vol. 2184, ANCh. The 1942 copy of the Internal Statutes of the Schwager Company actually contains a section on "Protection for Workers' Maternity." Letter from Schwager Company to IDT (Inspector Departamental del Trabajo; Departmental Labor Inspector), Oficio no. 186, February 28, 1942, FDGT, 1942 Oficios, vol. 33, ARNAD.

Approximately thirty thousand residents lived in the greater Lota area in 1935, about one-quarter of whom worked for the mining company. This does not include people working in the informal economy around the mines, such as women and children who carried food products to sell at the mine heads; the chinchorreros, who collected the coal that washed ashore on Lota's beaches; or the *fletadores*, who transported wood and coal in their own carts.

4. Sra. María, Centro de Adultos Mayores de Lota Bajo (Lota Senior Citizens' Center) interview.

5. Interview with Emelina Araneda.

6. The CCIL had an internal railroad, which connected all of the mines and surface infrastructure in Lota Alto. Tracks also ran through the station in Lota Bajo, which were used by the state-owned railroad and by the CCIL-owned Concepción-to-Curanilahue railroad.

7. For a glimpse at the lives and work of the chinchorreros, based on their own testimony, see Salazar Hermosilla, "Los chinchorreros." On the coal miners themselves, see Montecinos, "Los mineros."

cooking all year round, Lota residents relied on a steady supply of coal pushed through city streets in open carts. In the entrails of brick and iron ovens, it was transformed into the noxious black billows that perennially covered the city. Coal was also used in many local industries, including the brewery and the CCIL's metalworking and ceramics factories, adding to the pollution of air and water. Everyone in Lota's middle- and working-class sectors came into daily contact with coal, as they worked, played, and walked on Lota's largely unpaved streets, which produced clouds of dust in the summer breezes and turned to heavy mud in the winter rains. Keeping clean in this environment was indeed no easy task.

The city of Lota consisted of two distinct districts. Upper Lota, or Lota Alto, was the exclusive domain of the CCIL, essentially controlled as a "company town" even though it was situated within the larger city. This area began at the shore, where the docks and mine shafts were located, and extended up to a coastal ridge, where the main street was lined with the company's administrative buildings, hospital, schools, rows of workers' houses, and even an electric stoplight, installed in the early 1940s. To the east of the main street, the ridge sloped down into Lota Bajo, the "public town," which contained the municipal government, public schools, independent businesses, and public and private housing of all sorts. As the head of the CCIL's Welfare Department, Octavio Astorquiza, put it, the life of Lota Bajo and its various activities were "born under the cover of, and as a consequence of, the coal mines.[8]

The notion of separate geographic spheres of company versus civil control was complicated by the fact that the de facto "private area" of the CCIL was formally under the jurisdiction of Chile's constitutional government. At the same time, the "public city" was built largely on company property since the CCIL owned the vast majority of land in both districts of Lota, as well as the surrounding fields and forests. Although the company directly occupied or managed all of its property in Lota Alto, it lent or leased out most of its holdings in Lota Bajo. These arrangements often gave the CCIL the upper hand in dealings with civic authorities because the company could block efforts to build public housing or to make other infrastructural improvements simply by refusing to lend or lease the necessary land.

On the winding hillside road between Lota Alto and Lota Bajo, the company installed a large iron gate, which towered as a symbol of division between the two realms of the city, although it was kept open most

8. Astorquiza, Lota (1942), 197.

of the time. The spatial demarcation was reinforced by differences in the quality of urban infrastructure and standards of living. Though it provoked sharp debate, company spokespersons and other supporters of Chile's bourgeoisie often referred to Lota Alto as a "model industrial city," noting that the CCIL had pioneered not only in a range of extractive and productive enterprises, but also in facilities for its workforce, including housing, health clinics, schools, theaters, sports arenas, restaurants, stores, and even a swimming pool.[9] Workers and their leaders contended that many of these alleged "benefits," such as the company restaurant and store, actually served the company's interests more than the workers'. They also questioned the company's claim of enlightened magnanimity, arguing instead that most community resources had been hard won through the workers' long and persistent struggle.

Company propagandists certainly tended toward both hyperbole and Europhilia when describing Lota Alto, as in the following description by Octavio Astorquiza: "Crossed by innumerable railroad lines, perforated by multiple tunnels, adorned by the multicolored streaks of the buildings, the gardens and the forests, filled with activity and effort, the area in which the principal operations of the Coal Mining and Industrial Company of Lota are carried out is a touch of Europe in the long belt of territory that makes up the nation."[10] Such images contrasted sharply with the poor conditions in Lota Bajo, as described in an article in El Sur which followed the view of a person emerging from the train station, a few blocks from the central plaza where the municipal house was located: "The first thing the traveler sees is an open canal of putrid water, then dirty alleys with wooden buildings as old as the town itself, [and] farther on, a working-class neighborhood abandoned to its misery . . . there is no architectural order nor the least concern in building for ornamental or hygienic issues."[11]

Notwithstanding the company's self-aggrandizement in its portrayals of Lota Alto, workers who were granted housing and access to other facilities there did tend to live better than those who did not receive such

9. On the differences between Lota Alto and Lota Bajo, see, for example, El Sur, September 12, 1942, 4, 7; Astorquiza, Lota (1942), 197; Astorquiza and Galleguillos V., Cien años, 118, 211. See also Pradenas Muñoz's intervention, Senate Session, July 4, 1938, 755–57, BCNCh; and Endlicher, "Lota," 3–19.

10. Astorquiza and Galleguillos V., Cien años, 118. As discussed in chapter 1, coal mining capitalists were all Chilean, but with Europhile tendencies, as reflected in their architecture, company operations, and employment of Europeans as engineers andmanagers. Workers' representatives in the 1940s used the European orientation of the Chilean coal capitalists to undermine the capitalists' claim that they constituted a patriotic national bourgeoisie.

11. El Sur, September 18, 1941, 48.

favors. As with other mining companies throughout the country, the CCIL had for decades used the provision of housing and other perquisites in its efforts to develop a stable, dependent, and docile workforce.[12] The best houses in Lota Alto to which workers might aspire were the cement and wood row houses that lined the main streets; in less desirable areas, company houses were made entirely of wood (figs. 6 and 7). Yet, even by the mid-1940s, the CCIL still fell far short of its repeated promises to provide sufficient and adequate housing for all its workers and their families. Decisions about workers' accommodations and benefits were determined by the company's Welfare and Housing Departments, headed by Octavio Astorquiza and Carlos Duarte, respectively. These administrators wielded such power over people's lives that they were described by the Communist newspaper *Frente Popular* as "petty and ridiculous dictators" and "minuscule Chilean czars."[13]

In both company and private housing, space was tight and overcrowding severe, with many more families residing in each block than was originally intended. After a long work shift a miner would come home to "a

Fig. 6 Company row houses (*pabellones*) in Lota Alto, 1996. Photo by Jody Pavilack.

12. On the Braden copper company's promotion of domesticity to build a stable workforce, see Klubock, *Contested Communities*, esp. chap. 2.
13. *Frente Popular*, October 16, 1937, 2.

Fig. 7   Company pabellones in Lota Alto, 1996. Photo by Jody Pavilack.

cage of 4 × 4 meters [13 × 13 feet], with a terrible stench," young Communist leader Volodia Teitelboim wrote in 1946, "where the dining room, kitchen, hall, bedroom, oven, and drying clothes are all merged together."[14] To help make ends meet, families in both company and private housing often took in pensioners, single miners or couples who paid monthly room and board. Moreover, due to the chronic shortage of company housing, often two different families would be assigned to the same dwelling, one as the main occupants and the other as the *agregados*, or "add-ons." A sample survey of the CCIL's personnel files of the 1930s and 1940s indicates that an average of two families, with a total of ten to twelve people, resided in each single-family dwelling.[15]

With the overcrowding caused both by voluntary rental arrangements and forced company assignments, children and adults of all ages and both sexes slept together in the same room, and often in the same bed. Problems associated with overcrowding were made worse by the fact that unrelated men were sharing the intimate spaces of the home. Women in such complicated domestic situations at times had to battle unwanted advances by these men, the suspicions of their spouses, and even their

14. Teitelboim, "Lota aguerrida," 23.
15. CCIL personnel files, 1930s–1940s, consulted at ENACAR, Lota Alto.

own desires. As the national Investigations Service noted in a 1942 report, "In the existing houses several families must reside together, obliging them, given the scarcity of rooms, to give lodging to other couples and to some single workers, which morally prejudices the very constitution of the original family occupying the house."[16]

At the front line of dealing with the difficult and often violent domestic situations engendered by scarce and inadequate housing were company social workers; they provided assistance to miners' wives and children who would otherwise have had no recourse. Despite the social workers' often heartfelt efforts, multiple families living together in cramped quarters undermined the company's long-standing project of fostering domestic stability as a way to keep its workers reliable and docile. Overcrowding also undercut the company's efforts to present Lota as a "model industrial town." Even a coal face supervisor, who enjoyed greater housing privileges than other workers, felt compelled to file a complaint in May 1938 against the agregado who had been assigned to live in his company house. The supervisor was in good standing with the company, having worked "since 1928 with good conduct and attendance, [and] having come to occupy a post of confidence." But the conduct of the agregado was "making life impossible with his wife inside the home," the complaint record reads, "obliging [her] to move back to Curanilahue. He requests that he be given a smaller house or that the agregado be moved, so that he can have peace with his wife."[17]

Another complicated domestic situation occurred in the life of Julio Lagos Peña, who began to work for the company as a general coal face assistant (*apir*) in 1934.[18] As a widower with three young children under the care of other relatives, Lagos Peña was assigned to be an agregado in the household of Joaquín Marín Azocar, who lived with his mother and five siblings. In the same household there lived another agregado family, consisting of a carpenter in the machine shop, Humberto Arellano Arellano, together with his wife and their two children.[19] This meant that a

16. Report of the Comisión de Servicio Encomendada, Sección Sindical de la Dirección General de Investigaciones e Identificación, Santiago, "en ocasión de la visita del Presidente Ríos," Oficio no. 16, September 14, 1942, FMI, vol. 10788, ARNAD.

17. Note from CCIL Jefe de Población, May 1938, in Liborio Quijada Sobarzo, Prontuario no. 1053, CCIL personnel files, consulted at ENACAR, Lota Alto.

18. Julio Lagos Peña, Prontuario no. 1045, CCIL personnel files, consulted at ENACAR, Lota Alto.

19. In Chile, a person born out of wedlock and not recognized by at least one parent was sometimes identified by repetition of a single known last name, as in "Humberto Arellano Arellano." This status was also often indicated, especially in official records, by the designation "(N)," for "natural," after the person's single last name, as in "Humberto Arellano (N)."

total of twelve people from three separate families were living in the same confined space. In June 1939, Lagos Peña legally married Marín Azocar's forty-two-year-old mother, Etevelina Azocar. When Marín Azocar left the employment of the company to join the carabineros, he recommended that the house be formally assigned to Lagos Peña.

Exactly one year later, the newlywed Etevelina filed complaints with the company Welfare Department against her husband, claiming that he was abusive and had thrown her out of the house together with her children. She also denounced the agregado Arellano for abuse, though the record does not specify whether verbal, physical, or sexual. A note from the social worker suggested that the house be put in the name of the next eldest of Etevelina's sons, who was working as a day laborer (jornalero) in the company's ceramics factory. As of October 1942, however, the house was still assigned to Lagos Peña, who was in fact awarded a 10-peso prize for having the tidiest home. Some domestic reconciliation seems to have taken place, and by 1944, Lagos Peña and Etevelina had two children together.

The struggle to keep their families in company housing or to improve their living situation was a key factor pressing women and children into the workforce. In 1930, for example, José Florentino Orellana Suazo, the fourteen-year-old son of a miner, began work as a child apprentice in the company ceramics factory, earning 3 pesos per month. Three years later, seventeen-year-old José Florentino was working as a "trapper" (portero) in the mine galleries when his father died and he became the head of the household. Though he was granted his father's monthly ration of coal, his lowly position did not give him sufficient bargaining power to get his mother and siblings out of their "extremely tight" situation as agregados in a tiny row house. The family's plight was so desperate that it provoked sympathetic reports from the social workers of the Welfare Department: "This worker is the only breadwinner for his mother and six siblings. . . . It is recommended that his job position be improved at the first opportunity in light of the afflicted situation in which the family finds itself."[20]

When neither José Florentino's efforts nor the social workers' appeals produced results, the family made the difficult decision to offer the company the labor of their next oldest boy, Juan de Dios, who had just turned fourteen. The Welfare Department hired the young boy at a meager wage but refused to change the family's housing situation. A note in José Florentino's personnel file read, "What this family wants is to be given a house

20. Note from CCIL Social Worker, September 1935, in José Florentino Orellana Suazo, Prontuario no. 1022, CCIL personnel files, consulted at ENACAR, Lota Alto.

to themselves (now they are agregados), for which I don't see any possibility, given the scarcity of houses; those which might become vacant are destined for the very meritorious workers or for specialists in some job—according to the orders of the Welfare Chief."[21] Over the next seven years, the family's fortunes did not improve, and whether out of resentment, frustration, or for some other reason, in 1943, José Florentino attacked the foreman of the Pique Grande mine. He was sentenced to thirty days in the Coronel jail and was barred from ever again working for the CCIL. The Welfare Department then designated Juan de Dios head of household, but the now twenty-one-year-old miner did not have enough seniority or standing with the company to get the family's housing situation improved.

From the Mines to the Municipal Hall:
The Rise of a Communist Mayor

Though they were fully aware of workers' complaints, the overcrowding and squalor in which the workers lived did not induce the Lota city councilmen of the mid-1930s to press for improvements. Any move to question or improve the workers' living conditions meant confronting the CCIL, which was the implicit patron, and often the explicit employer, of almost all local public officials at the time. This was also the case in other coal mining towns: Curanilahue was dominated by both the CCIL and the Colico Sur company; Coronel, by Schwager; and Lirquén and Lebu, by separate companies. Instead of taking the coal mining companies to task for providing grossly inadequate housing, the city councilmen blamed the workers for their plight, calling them "brutes steeped in immorality and filth." Because their identities and fortunes were tied to the coal mining bourgeoisie, the councilmen made every effort to keep clear the distinction between "respectable people" and "degenerate workers."[22]

City officials thus banned from council sessions not only "unbathed" (working-class) men but also "women with babies that cried," indeed, all

---

21. Note from CCIL Jefe de Población, January 28, 1936, in ibid.

22. The middle class in Lota included small business owners and merchants, service professionals, and upper-level company employees (beneath the top administrators, who for the most part, lived in Santiago or Valparaíso). The Lota company clearly sought to promote a middle-class model for the comportment of "decent people" as a way of instilling discipline and docility in upwardly mobile workers who strove to join this small group. On the construction of cultural divisions in Mexican mining communities between "decent people" (gente decente) and the workers, see William French, Peaceful and Working People, and "Progreso Forzado." See also Smith, "Tonypandy 1910."

women and children. Mothers unable to quiet their babies or control their children perfectly fit middle-class images of the uncivilized state in which most of Lota's residents were seen to live. Yet the ban on women attending municipal sessions directly contravened (and was likely a response to) the fact that women had been granted suffrage for municipal elections in 1934 and had thus been formally incorporated into the democratic polity. Although Chilean women tended to favor conservative candidates when they voted in 1935, for the first time in Chile's history, it was precisely these representatives of the old order who sought to bar them from attending sessions. In their view, having deposited the proper ballot in the proper box, women should return home and refrain from further participation in public life.

What were the city councilmen in Lota saying with their exclusionary actions in the mid-1930s, as the Popular Front coalition gained force and launched its national presidential campaign? The broadest statement in this regard was that only those who "maintained order and respect" were to be admitted to council sessions. This was a defense of hierarchical notions of culture and class, in which these self-appointed guardians of privilege and property insisted that, even though filthy workers and fecund women had been granted formal democratic rights, they were not equal citizens. Participation was a fundamental step in any contest for power, and it was thus to be vigorously controlled. Members of the working class were to indicate their acceptance of this order of things by showing the utmost deference to their betters.

Since most elected officials had a symbiotic relationship with the coal mining companies, they refused to make even the slightest gesture to ameliorate the worst conditions of exclusion and to stave off mass frustration and mobilization. David Robertson Stuart, Lota's mayor in 1935–36, held numerous high company positions over several decades, including general manager of all CCIL operations in Curanilahue and Colcura. Born in Chile to parents of mixed Anglo and Hispanic ancestry, Robertson studied at the American School and the British Institute before gaining employment in 1912 at the British-owned railroad, steamship, and coal mining enterprise Arauco Company, Ltd. When the Lota company acquired the assets of the Arauco Company in 1919, Robertson continued what would be a long career as a top CCIL executive there.[23] Likewise,

---

23. Robertson Stuart was born in Traiguén, Chile, in 1894. His parents were Juan Robertson and Catalina Stuart, suggesting that his grandparents may have emigrated from Britain. *Diccionario biográfico* (1967), 1331.

Robertson's successor as mayor in 1936, Juan Bull Sanhueza, also of mixed Anglo and Hispanic ancestry, headed the CCIL's Wages and Salaries Division at least through 1942, when a company publication written by Astorquiza praised him as "a worthy collaborator."[24] Both men brandished notions derived from traditional class- and gender-based hierarchies—notions of natural difference, decency, and deference. They tried to block public challenges to the company's exercise of power and to prevent working-class men and women from encroaching on their world of privilege.[25]

Santos Leoncio Medel Basualto was the only city council member who challenged this exclusionary order in the mid-1930s. He was also the only elected official who had ever worked in the coal mines—and the only Communist on any city council or other government institution in the region. Born on November 10, 1905, to a large working-class family in the coastal mining town of Lebu, in the province of Arauco, Santos Medel had experienced firsthand a brutal capitalist response to working-class mobilization. As a young boy, he had stood beside his mother and siblings in Lebu's central plaza watching as his father, a young coal miner, received fifty lashes for his role in the first workers' mancomunal. According to Medel's nephew, "The lashes hit my grandfather in the head so many times, they left him deaf."[26] Though Medel was too young to do anything to stop the flogging, he had several older brothers. When one of them, Esteban, a sailor away at the time of the incident on a company ship transporting coal from Lebu to Cauquenes, returned home to find his father bedridden and deaf, he vowed revenge. On his next voyage, Esteban led a mutiny. Adding to Santos Medel's formative afflictions, when the mutiny was suppressed, Esteban was thrown into the sea and left to drown.[27]

With the household in emotional grief and financial strife, Santos Medel, then five years old, accompanied another of his older brothers into the depths of Lebu's Junquillos mine, "to become a man and to learn a

24. El Sur, September 12, 1942, 2; Astorquiza, Lota (1942), 138; and Astorquiza and Galleguillos V., Cien años, 173.

25. Just a few years after Robertson Stuart stepped down as mayor, the Communist newspaper Frente Popular denounced him as the "feudal lord" who, while representing the CCIL, ordered a tenant farmer's house to be burned down since the land belonged to the company and the farmer was behind on his payments. Robertson thus revealed his "anti-worker hatred," the paper declared, as he moved to "revive medieval times." Frente Popular, February 29, 1940, 7.

26. Interview with Evaristo Azócar Medel. Evaristo is the son of Santos Medel's sister Rosa, who was also present at her father's beating.

27. Ibid.

trade."[28] When he turned eight, Medel got a paid job with the company, leading blind and weary horses as they pulled coal cars through dank, narrow passages winding for miles beneath the floor of the Pacific Ocean.[29] By the time he turned fifteen, Medel's family had moved to Lota, 100 kilometers (about 60 miles) to the north, where he secured a job with the Coal Mining Company of Lota and Coronel, then headed by Carlos Cousiño, grandson of Matías, the company founder.[30] With the legacy of his militant father and brother, and a desire to avenge the crimes against them, Medel soon became involved in workers' politics, serving as a youth delegate of the FOCh–led Lota Miners' Council in the early 1920s. In 1926, as Carlos Ibáñez emerged as Chile's new right-wing strongman, twenty-one-year-old Medel Basualto joined the then-illegal Chilean Communist Party (PCCh).[31]

Santos Medel was part of a new generation of local activists who embraced the challenge of broadening and deepening the Communists' base of support. He had represented the coal mining zone at the 1933 national PCCh Congress, when the party had moved toward a strategy of democratic participation and promotion of capitalist development. Two years later, in April 1935, in the first municipal elections in which women were permitted to vote, Medel became the only Communist elected to the Lota City Council since the tumultuous and violent period of the early 1920s.

Working to rebuild mass support for the party since its decline in the years of clandestine militancy, Medel Basualto quickly demonstrated the will and ability to challenge the elitist practices of his political opponents. In April 1937, he brought the problems of marginalized sectors of the Lota community inside the walls of municipal government, inviting a group of renters living in abysmal conditions to present their case at a council session. Though one of the group's key complaints was precisely inadequate hygiene facilities, Medel's fellow council members condemned

28. Interview with Luis Corvalán Lépez. From my study of 320 CCIL personnel files from the 1930s and 1940s, approximately 30 percent of company workers began employment before age eighteen. Young boys might work as trappers inside the mines, opening and closing the ventilations doors, or outside planting tree seedlings in the company's forests. Or they might do even more grueling work as "salt pickers" (*pica-sals*), submerging in the icy waters of the Pacific to scrape the sides of company ships. On child labor in Chilean mines, see Rojas Flores, "Trabajo infantil."

29. Although the Lebu and Curanilahue coal mines lay inland, the galleries of the Lota and Coronel mines stretched up to 12 kilometers (about 7.5 miles) from the shore, at depths of up to 800 meters (about 2,600 feet) beneath the Pacific Ocean.

30. On the Lota company's name (and structural) changes, see chapter 1, note 38.

31. Interviews with Luis Corvalán López and Evaristo Azócar Medel.

these working-class residents for their uncleanliness, complaining that, just after they left, bugs were found in the municipal building.

Shortly after this session, the police arrested Santos Medel, not for the first time, on charges of violating internal state security laws. While he was in jail, the rest of the council passed the ordinance requiring "cleanliness certificates" discussed above. When he returned to the municipal fray, Medel denounced this move as a ruse for "keeping out the people who accompanied me." The mayor, Juan Bull Sanhueza, a CCIL white-collar employee, claimed that it was nothing more than "an indispensable hygienic measure."[32] But Medel insisted that his opponents' complaints about hygiene were politically motivated, with the ultimate aim of exclusion: "Not even the cleanest [working-class] people have the right to enter. I'm sure that all of this is nothing more than a pretext to prevent the people from finding out what goes on in the Municipal Council."[33] Medel's effort to address problems faced by a group of Lota residents had thus become a battle over inclusion in a fundamental forum of local democracy.

Standing up for the rights and vital needs of people who had long been marginalized and ignored, Santos Medel quickly achieved unsurpassed popularity in Lota and the surrounding region, coming to be seen as a hero, while remaining "one of us." This growing public esteem would soon win him the position of mayor—Lota's first and only mayor elected by the Popular Front coalition, who was repeatedly reelected until the repression of 1947. As longtime Communist leader Luis Corvalán Lépez recalled, Santos Medel came to be seen as "both father and brother to the miners. . . . Thousands and thousands of people went to see him, to listen to his advice, his inspiring voice, and even to ask him to arbitrate household disagreements or disputes among neighbors or fellow workers [compañeros]."[34]

This drive to intervene personally to improve the lives of Lota's workers and to expand their participation in local democracy did not exhaust the meaning of Santos Medel's politics, nor the reactions he provoked in his fellow council members. In the mid-1930s, as the lone representative of both the working class and the Communist Party on the Lota City Council, Medel faced not only the CCIL's economic and social domination of the region, but also the moves by President Arturo Alessandri Palma

32. Lota Municipal Acts, April 16, 1937, vol. 1, 4/33–3/43, 162, BML.
33. *Frente Popular*, October 10, 1937, 5.
34. Interview with Luis Corvalán Lépez. See also Corvalán Lépez's eulogy on Santos Medel in *El Siglo*, May 3, 1967.

and the national right-wing parties to maintain the status quo by force. Local issues raised on the city council were strongly affected by the broader discord between supporters and opponents of the government's efforts to suppress popular mobilization and labor agitation.

The battle lines of political and social conflict were indistinguishable in Chile. In January 1935, a national railroad workers' strike sparked mass opposition to the Alessandri government, which would eventually bring the Center and Left parties into alliance. Santos Medel had first been elected to the Lota City Council in March 1935, in the immediate aftermath of the strike. Less than five months later, the Comintern held its Seventh Congress, at which Bulgarian delegate Georgi Dimitrov put forth the Popular Front strategy. Thus, while Medel was pushing for respect of the socioeconomic and political rights of Lota's working-class majority, the Communists were trying to persuade the Socialist, Democratic, and Radical parties, as well as their own cadres at all levels, to join forces to uphold democracy. The language of "Fascism and anti-Fascism" quickly supplanted that of "Communism and anti-Communism" as a key discursive framework for interpreting local, national, and international conflicts.

As Communists and the "Bloc of the Left" worked to expand opposition to Alessandri, elite sectors responded with unmitigated hostility, refusing any moves toward greater democratization.[35] In January 1936, another railroad workers' strike threatened to turn into a national general strike when it was joined by tens of thousands of other workers, including bakers, carpenters, electricians, weavers, seamen, and miners.[36] In the coal region, workers of the CCIL–owned Concepción-to-Curanilahue railroad participated, as did the Schwager miners. Though the Lota miners did not achieve a full strike, their alleged acts of sabotage and indiscipline were severe enough to provoke a twelve-hour company lockout. Octavio Astorquiza declared that this was "the first time in fourteen years" that "lamentable acts" had "interrupted the social tranquility reigning in the

35. The Bloc of the Left was a coalition organized in 1934, primarily for municipal and congressional elections. Paul Drake summarizes it as follows: "Dominated by the Socialists, the Bloc included the Democratics (the more reformist half of the divided Democrat Party), the Communist Left, and a splinter group from the left wing of the Radicals and had hopes of winning whole Democrat and Radical parties away from the Alessandri government." Drake, *Socialism and Populism*, 171. The Bloc of the Left was a precursor to the Popular Front, which also included the Communists.

36. For an excellent analysis of the 1935 and 1936 national railroad workers' strikes and their role in the formation of the Popular Front, see Garcés Durán, *Movimiento obrero*, chap. 2.

Lota Establishment."[37] On February 4, the second day of the strike, the government sent military forces to occupy the most conflictive areas in the country, chief among which were the coal mining region, Concepción, Santiago, San Rosendo, and Temuco.[38] Four days later, President Alessandri placed the entire country under a state of siege (*estado de sitio*), dissolved Congress, and moved against leftist political and labor leaders, forcing many of them into internal exile (*relegación*).[39]

Communist Councilman Santos Medel was among the first "agitators" arrested in Lota. While he was in jail this time, the rest of the city council voted unanimously to send a telegram to President Alessandri expressing their "support and approval . . . of [the president's] patriotic attitude in the face of the Communist activities recently carried out in the country."[40] Alessandri's claim that Communists were plotting to usurp control of the state confirmed the conviction of Lota's right-wing leaders that Medel's gestures in defense of the workers were only a ruse. He was a Communist agent, they said, who manipulated local realities and used workers and poor women and children as pawns in a foreign game. That Medel was a second- or third-generation coal miner undercut the legitimacy of these accusations, but in no way lessened his opponents' attacks.

Yet the incident in question—a workers' strike—had broad social support and the political backing not only of the Communists, but also of Socialists, Democratics, and most members of the centrist Radical Party. Indeed, it was growing concern about the antidemocratic nature of the repression unleashed against strikers and agitators that finally gave the upper hand to the left wing of this middle-class party. After months of intense internal debate, ten days after the national strike ended, the Radical Party Assembly voted to forge electoral alliances with the Marxist parties.[41] The resultant Popular Front coalition, formally constituted at the

37. Astorquiza, *Lota* (1942), 124. Astorquiza's statement is incorrect: Lota saw several episodes of labor conflict between 1922 and 1936, though most strikes of the period were at Schwager in Coronel.

38. Garcés Durán, "Movimiento obrero," 125.

39. Alessandri's measures were carried out under Decree Law no. 50, of June 24, 1932, which was essentially Chile's first internal state security law; Decree Law no. 343, of July 30, 1932, by which Alessandri was able to bring the railroads under military control; and Law no. 5163, of April 28, 1933, which granted the president extraordinary powers at his request for periods of up to six months. See Loveman and Lira, *Las ardientes cenizas*, 17, 27–28, 30, 44; Alessandri Palma, *Recuerdos*, 3:61–66.

40. Lota Municipal Acts, February 15, 1936, vol. 1, 4/33–3/43, 126, BML.

41. Many scholars along with Garcés Durán note the key role of the railroad workers' strike in consolidating new political and labor alliances. See, for example, Morris, *Elites*, 261; and Faúndez, *Marxism and Democracy*, 40.

national level in March and April 1936, included the Communists, left-wing Radicals, Democrats, Socialists, and Radical Socialists.[42] The railroad workers' strike and its repression also paved the way for unity among Socialist and Communist labor sectors, and when the Confederation of Chilean Workers (CTCh) was created in December of that year, it, too, joined the Popular Front coalition.[43]

Marxists, Centrists, and Pentecostals: Battling Company Resistance

Santos Medel was not alone in the resurgent combativeness that marked these years. Among those with whom he shared a cell in the Coronel jail in 1936 was Víctor Manuel Mora Mora, a Mason, Evangelical pastor, and Socialist leader, who had also been arrested for "defending the rights of the coal miners."[44] A decade earlier, in 1926, the same year that Medel joined the Communist Party, Víctor Mora had arrived in Lota from Talcahuano to assume his post as the new pastor of the Episcopal Methodist Church. With Methodist membership small and static, a few lay believers had begun to feel that the church was no longer in touch with the needs and sensibilities of local working-class men and women. Pastor Mora brought a new proselytizing zeal to the Lota Methodists. As membership grew, Pastor Moisés Torregrosa, head of the Methodists' Concepción region and Mora's superior, commended him for his "unusual fervor, enthusiasm, and spirit of prayer. The youth league, the ladies' [group], and the local missionary society have been powerful vehicles pushing the work forward. . . . For thirty consecutive nights, the evangelization campaign has been held at seven different locations, [and] the people have not shown the least signs of tiring. All this very intense labor has brought about the conversion of numerous sinners."[45]

This spirit of membership renewal coincided with efforts by church dissidents to connect more closely with the needs and desires of the people. Rather than discourage these efforts, the new pastor tried to create

42. The most detailed English-language work on the day-to-day political intrigues of this period is still Stevenson's *Chilean Popular Front* (1942). See also Drake, *Socialism and Populism* (1978). In Spanish, see Aguirre Cerda, *Epistolario* (2001); and Milos, *Frente Popular* (2008).

43. At its founding convention, the Confederation of Chilean Workers (CTCh) accepted both free and legal unions, and the Communist-led Federation of Chilean Workers (FOCh) agreed to fold itself into it. The anarchist-led General Confederation of Workers (Confederación General de Trabajadores; CGT) maintained its separate identity.

44. Ossa, *Espiritualidad popular*, 89, 90.

45. Acts of the Episcopal Methodist Church, 1927, 50, as cited in ibid., 32.

even greater space for popular expression within local Methodist activities. When members of his flock began to engage in Pentecostal practices such as spirit possession, prophetic visions, and speaking in tongues, the mother church in Santiago censured Pastor Mora, transferring him to Curacautín in 1927. This did not halt the burgeoning movement.[46] During Mora's two-year absence from Lota, the dissident group, now with about forty members, began to meet in a house apart from the rest of the Methodists. When he returned in 1929, Pastor Mora headed up the new group, which took the name "Wesleyan Mission" to evoke images of Methodist founder John Wesley preaching to common folk in the fields, just as Mora and his followers now preached to townsfolk in the plazas of Lota and Coronel.

The new church, with its Pentecostal leanings, staked out a place in opposition not only to the Methodists, but also, and even more acutely, to the Catholic Church.[47] As Wesleyan youths preached in the central square of Lota Bajo, they were often confronted by Catholic youths. When their arguments grew more heated, a public debate arose between Pastor Mora and the Lota parish priest. Chilean sociologist Manuel Ossa sees a process of empowerment in these confrontations, as people previously belittled by their supposed superiors developed a collective identity to challenge dominant social hierarchies. Feeling victorious in their debates with the Catholics, the Wesleyans "acquire[d] a new consciousness of themselves; they [were] no longer culturally inferior beings . . . but now they themselves participate[d] in the power of discourse. Proof in action: they were listened to by some three thousand people gathered in the plaza."[48]

Protestants of both traditional and Pentecostal denominations were well aware of the formidable connection between the Catholic Church and the coal mining companies.[49] Ossa interprets the Wesleyans' ardent

---

46. Interview with Pastor Roberto Garrido Riquelme, December 5, 1997.

47. In 1935–36, the national Episcopal Methodists sent numerous telegrams to President Alessandri denouncing his government for collusion with Catholics and persecution of Protestants. See, for example, Acts of the Thirty-sixth Annual Conference of the Episcopal Methodist Church, Angol, January 7–13, 1936, published in El Cristiano 42 (March 1, 1936).

48. Ossa, Espiritualidad popular, 43.

49. Though it took place later in time, one of the most extreme instances of the connection between the Catholic Church and the CCIL was that of the Campos Menchaca brothers. When, in 1948, the chapel (capela) in Lota Alto became the parochial church San Matías Apóstol, the first priest named to it by the Archbishop of Concepción was thirty-year-old Pedro Campos Menchaca, whose brother, Mariano Campos Menchaca, was a Navy captain and instructor at the School of Anti-Submarine Warfare, until 1952, when he replaced Octavio Astorquiza as the head of the CCIL's Welfare Department. See Astorquiza and Galleguillos V., Cien años, 97, 146, 213; and Diccionario biográfico (1967), 262.

defiance as "the conquest of a parcel of power," which "even in the symbolic domain of religion, could have . . . great social, and even political, importance."[50] After describing the coal companies' persecution of Wesleyan miners, who were frequently suspended, demoted, or laid off, he concludes that "in reality, in the Lota fiefdom, the resolute and conscious attitude of Pastor Mora and his group must have been seen as an unprecedented and dangerous provocation."[51]

Two of the forces against which the Wesleyans positioned themselves—the Catholic Church and the coal mining bourgeoisie—were key actors in the *dominant* structure of economic and cultural power. Yet they soon found themselves crossing paths with the *emergent* force in the region, the Communists.[52] These distinct sociocultural movements, Communism and Pentecostalism—one political and atheistic, the other apolitical and fervently deistic—developed concurrently in the 1920s–1940s throughout the dozens of communities tied in varying ways to the production of coal. Social conditions and daily struggles in the coal region shaped the local development of these national and international movements, pushing an often quiescent form of ecstatic Protestantism in a leftist direction, much as they would Catholic liberation theology in other regions of Latin America several decades later. Conversely, the ascendance of Pentecostal and Communist activities in the coal towns influenced the way they acted in national and international arenas.

Like the Communists, the Wesleyans were also questioning, defying, and transforming the old order, marked by the Catholic-company nexus of power. Pastor Roberto Garrido, one of Mora's successors at the head of the Wesleyan Mission, explained that the Wesleyans' battles against both the coal mining companies and the Communists developed because "this movement was not just about religious instruction." Rather, Pastor Mora "was making the members of the Church understand the rights that corresponded to them by virtue of their work." One of the pastor's favorite mottos, inscribed on a Wesleyan crest, was "One God, One Country, and One Social Class."[53]

In their effort to mobilize the men and women of the coal mines around a new faith, Mora and his Wesleyan followers found themselves

50. Ossa, *Espiritualidad popular*, 43.
51. Ibid., 44.
52. The terms "dominant" and "emergent" are meant as Raymond Williams defines them in *Marxism and Literature*. By at least 1936, the Methodist Youth League in Lota was explicitly addressing themes of "Christianity, Communism, Socialism, and Theosophy." See *El Cristiano* 42 (March 21, 1937): 83.
53. Interview with Pastor Roberto Garrido Riquelme, September 15, 1997.

in competition with the Communists. After coal miner Baltasar Rodríguez joined the Wesleyan Mission in Lota in 1939, he became active in trade union politics. He later recalled "episodes of heavy fighting with Communist compañeros in the depths of the mine."[54] By Rodríguez's own account, it was when he stood his ground against the Communists by refusing to attend their meetings that he was approached by a group of fellow workers who asked him to run as their section delegate. Before agreeing, Rodríguez consulted with Pastor Mora: "Well, do something there if you can help—he told me—before the Communist Party devours everyone."[55]

After Mora was expelled from the Methodists, one of his Wesleyan brothers taught him the trade of shoemaker,[56] and he began to move among the local artisans. When the Socialist Party emerged in Chile in 1933, Pastor Mora co-founded its Coronel branch, which he headed for many years. The party had a strong base in precisely the social and cultural groups represented by Mora—artisans, merchants, midlevel civil servants, Masons, and Protestants. Politics now shaped Mora's relations with the Communists at least as much as religious, cultural, and union issues did.

Antagonism between Socialists and Communists was one of the critical barriers to the formation of Popular Front coalitions, both nationally and locally. When, in the face of right-wing opponents, the two parties began to reach tentative accords at the national level, Mora's own position toward the Communists took a new turn. In 1937, as head of the Coronel Socialist Party, he proposed a tactical alliance with his erstwhile enemies the Communists. At the end of the year, a group of local politicians met and chose Mora to serve as the first president of the Coronel Popular Front.[57] A few months later, in a leadership shuffle, Mora was demoted to vice president, and Communists were promoted to the two top positions,

---

54. Baltasar Rodríguez, as quoted in Ossa, *Espiritualidad popular*, 192–93. The link between Evangelicals and labor politics was also seen in the person of Higinio Monsálvez Peña, the first president of the Curanilahue miners' union, elected in 1926. By 1930, he was pastor of the Universal Church of Curanilahue and president of the National Christian Mission. The latter was either an alternate name for the Wesleyan Mission or a closely related organization. Astorquiza, *Lota* (1929), 180, and *Lota* (1942), 183; Ossa, *Espiritualidad popular*, 63.

55. Baltasar Rodríguez, as quoted in Ossa, *Espiritualidad popular*, 193. Rodríguez did become a leader in the miners' union and was later president of a neighborhood council, founder of a local sports club, a candidate for the Lota City Council and for the Chamber of Deputies, and a militant in the Socialist Party.

56. Ossa, *Espiritualidad popular*, 80.

57. *El Obrero* (Coronel), December 31, 1937, 6; and Ossa, *Espiritualidad popular*, 103.

secretary-general and president. This reflected both the ascendance of the Chilean Communist Party in the community and the crucial role of the coal miners: the new secretary-general, Florencio H. García, was a leader of the Schwager industrial union.[58]

With a member of the Unified Democratic Party (Partido Democrático Unificado; PDU) as treasurer and a Socialist as press and propaganda secretary, the newly formed Coronel Popular Front committee was notably lacking Radicals. An article announcing the constitution of the Front explained, "The Radicals were not represented [because] they were awaiting the resolutions of their directorate." The committee "agreed to hold a position open on the Directive Council for the Radicals of Coronel, *but not to admit anyone as delegate or candidate for City Council who is an employee, or in the service of, the Schwager Company.*"[59]

The Radicals' refusal to join the local Popular Front committee occurred not only in Coronel, but in many other coal mining towns as well. In Lebu, for example, the Front committee was headed by a Communist, a Radical Socialist, and a Democrat, while the deeply divided Radical Party withheld its support.[60] Although advocates of the Front had gained control of the party at the national level, anti-Front forces still prevailed in the coal mining zone. Indeed, Concepción and Arauco were two of the six provinces whose representatives voted against joining the Popular Front coalition at the PR's National Congress in 1936.[61] Moreover, one of Concepción's national deputies, Lionel Edwards Atherton, was an anti-Communist Radical who fervently opposed the alliance.[62]

As noted above, one of the first accords reached by the Coronel Popular Front committee was "to not admit anyone . . . who is an employee, or in the service of, the Schwager Company," which made clear the Front's opposition to the coal companies' long-standing control of municipal and

58. Oficio no. 419, September 24, 1936, FMI, vol. 9250, ARNAD; Oficio no. 144, June 1, 1937, from Coronel IDT to the IGT (Inspector General de Trabajo; Inspector General of Labor), and Oficio no. 565, May 12, 1937, from Labor Minister to IGT, both in FDGT, 1937 Oficios, vol. 20, ARNAD.

59. *El Obrero*, February 12, 1938, 2; emphasis in original.

60. The Communist on the first Lebu Popular Front committee was a railroad machinist who would win a seat on the Lebu City Council in the 1938 elections discussed later in the chapter. Pizarro Soto, *Lebu*, 337, 339. On the Radical Socialist Party, John Stevenson observes, in *Chilean Popular Front*, 113n4, that "its some five thousand members were almost all concentrated in Santiago, and it was little more than the personal political machine of Deputy Juan Bautista Rossetti."

61. Urzúa Valenzuela, *Historia política de Chile*, 492. The six provinces whose delegates opposed the Popular Front were countered by twelve provinces whose delegates voted in favor of it, with delegates from one province abstaining.

62. Ibid., 492–93.

community affairs. Throughout the coal mining zone, many right-wing Radicals opposed to the Front were employees or tacit collaborators of the companies. Having expressly excluded this group, local Popular Front committees held open positions for the Radical Party, hoping that the more progressive faction might eventually prevail. In the end, however, right-wing Radicals held the upper hand throughout the region, and local branches defied the pro-Front position adopted by the national party.[63]

Local Popular Front committees were formed in 1937–38 with an eye to the upcoming municipal elections, scheduled for April 1938, as well as to various union elections in the region to be held in May. In Coronel, Pastor Victor Mora became one of two Socialist candidates running for a seat on the city council, together with a schoolteacher named Carlos Rosales Gutierrez. Since the municipal elections were to take place in the midst of the presidential campaign, they became an important occasion for the parties and coalitions to test their strength in different regions. Top national politicians thus traveled the country to mobilize support for their candidates in local contests. Socialist Deputy Natalio Berman, for example, spoke in Coronel on behalf of Mora and Rosales, explaining to a crowd of three hundred people that "it is necessary for the Popular Front to win the municipal elections, in order to be in position to triumph in the elections for President of the Republic."[64] For nearly two months beginning in February 1938, the Coronel Socialist paper *El Obrero* teemed with articles promoting Mora and Rosales. Mora was hailed as a longtime defender of the working class; his position as pastor and founder of the Wesleyan Mission was never mentioned.

Company Resistance to the Popular Front Advance

While Communists worked to build strong, organized bases at the local level, the coal mining companies did not sit idly by. They increased their disciplinary mechanisms, including the use of spies and agents to control not only their workers, but also community life more broadly. Social and political battles took shape on the streets of the coal towns, where people

63. For more on the Coronel Front committee, see *El Obrero*, March 26, 1938, 3.

64. Providencia Confidencial no. 67, March 26, 1938, from Carabineros Director General to Interior Minister, FMI, vol. 9787, ARNAD. In 1933, Natalio Berman co-founded the Socialist Party in Concepción, the district that elected him national deputy. In 1939–40, he led a dissident faction, known as the "Nonconformists," that became the Workers' Socialist Party (PST), which both Mora and Rosales would soon join. By 1944, Berman and about two-thirds of the PST membership had joined the Chilean Communist Party (PCCh).

from opposing camps often interacted on a first-name basis. Company agents and Communist militants might well meet up on the soccer field or in a corner tavern; and administrators and workers, though largely occupying different parts of town, would still pass one another on the street or while strolling in Lota Alto Park.

To become a "party of the masses," the Communists tried to connect the problems felt most immediately and intimately by the residents of the coal mining zone—those for which they consistently mobilized—with the party's national and global objectives. For the Chilean Communist Party, linking the local with the national and international (the present with the future and the particular with the abstract) was a central means of developing ideologically committed militants. For the residents of the coal mining zone, the connections drawn between their pressing material concerns and more distant social and political issues gave greater meaning and a sense of importance to their everyday lives and activities.

As civil war raged in Spain, in October 1937, the Communists in Chile's coal mining region staged a large rally on Playa Blanca—the stretch of beach between Lota and Coronel—to pay homage the Spanish Republican forces. Playa Blanca lay outside the proprietary reach of the Lota and Schwager companies, but was still accessible from both towns; it was thus often used for large public rallies, as during the strikes of the early 1920s. The companies, however, were in no mood to tolerate boisterous rallies in support of Spanish Republicans, especially since the Popular Front in Chile had gained ground in the congressional elections earlier that year.[65] The Communist newspaper *Frente Popular* reported that Carlos Duarte, the Lota company's chief housing officer, together with other, unnamed authorities, set up blockades to prevent people from arriving at the October rally site. Those who did attend were subject to being identified and reported by company spies, and in the days that followed, many

65. In the March 1937 congressional elections, the Right held on to a majority in both the Senate and the Chamber of Deputies, but "certain electoral trends encouraged supporters of the popular front." Loveman, *Chile*, 207. Together, the Popular Front parties won 10 out of 25 seats in the Senate and 66 out of 146 in the Chamber of Deputies. Baeza Flores, *Radiografía política*, 219. The Communists only won six national deputy seats, compared to three won by the Nazi Party (Movimiento Nacional Socialista; MNS), and fifteen by the Socialists. One major consequence, as Loveman observes, was that the "significant gains by the Socialist Party helped persuade many Radicals to maintain the popular front for the upcoming presidential elections of 1938." Loveman, *Chile*, 207. On the March 1937 election, see also Urzúa Valenzuela, *Historia política de Chile*, 492–93; Stevenson, *Chilean Popular Front*, 97–98; Lafertte Gaviño, *Vida de un comunista*, 295–97; Loveman and Lira, *Las ardientes cenizas*, 55; and Pizarro Soto, *Lebu*, 339. See also Jobet, *Ensayo crítico*, 199–200; and Ortega Martínez et al., *Corporación de Fomento*, 40.

workers in Lota and Coronel "were . . . told to vacate their houses or [were] expelled from work."[66] More than simply responding to the miners' support for the Spanish Republicans, the companies were determined to preempt further leftist gains in local and national politics. Highlighting the companies' hostility to Communist political advances, one article claimed that "when they fire the workers, they tell them to go ask Medel or Pairoa to give them a job," referring to Santos Medel and to Communist Deputy Amador Pairoa Trujillo, who had traveled to the region to participate in the rally.[67]

Company harassment of the workers continued unabated in the ensuing months. When Lota worker Zoilo Villablanca went to the Welfare Office to try to get his job back after being fired and evicted, he was told that "they would gladly give it back to him if he would bring them 'a little information' on the Communists, or if he would give a beating to Councilman Medel."[68] The Communist newspaper *Frente Popular* called on civic authorities to defend the rights of constitutional government against usurpation by the feudal powers of the Lota company. One article blamed the extralegal persecution of workers on "Carlos Duarte, advised by Sr. Octavio Astorquiza, the true kings of Lota Alto."[69] The Communists also denounced the local labor inspector for failing to defend the rule of law—the hard-won Labor Code of 1931—against flagrant company violations. The inspector, they said, ignored the situation of the fired and evicted workers, many of whom were left in the streets for five, eight, or ten days. Recognizing that the company's legal exercise of power did not extend beyond its property, the article emphasized the illegality of company actions on public land: "The local authorities should get involved in this matter since Eulogio Sandoval exercises his profession as a spy outside of the company domain, always lurking around the workers' locale, the ex-FOCh [hall]."[70]

Such occurrences were not limited to Lota and Coronel. In Curanilahue, in early November 1937, three men—a barber, a farmhand, and a shoemaker—were "taken by surprise" and found to be in possession of "subversive proclamations, identity cards, and stamps corresponding to

66. *Frente Popular*, October 16, 1937, 5.

67. Pairoa was a national deputy for Santiago in 1937–41 and was then elected senator for the region of Curicó, Talca, Linares, and Maule. Pairoa died "prematurely" in 1944, and the bitterly fought election to replace him in the Senate was won by Arturo Alessandri Palma. Millas, *En tiempos*, 349.

68. *Frente Popular*, November 20, 1937, 4.

69. *Frente Popular*, October 16, 1937, 5.

70. *Frente Popular*, November 20, 1937, 4.

the Communist Party and the International Red Aid Committee." All three men were charged with violating Internal State Security Law no. 6026.[71] Later the same month, two more Curanilahue workers were arrested "for the 'crime' of belonging to the Communist Party."[72]

As the companies increased their efforts to halt the Communists' advance, *Frente Popular* repeatedly referred to the head of the Schwager Welfare Office, Alfredo Betteley, as "the Pirate of Schwager" and "the worst enemy of the workers."[73] Indeed, the general sentiment among workers was that the offices run by Astorquiza and Betteley were departments of harassment (*malestar*), rather than of welfare (*bienestar*).[74] Both offices maintained a network of spies "who sell out compañeros of their own class for a few miserable privileges." One Schwager miner sent a letter to the paper accusing company agents of "doing everything possible to pull the workers into a strike, in order to get those who most strongly defend their interests to come out into the streets" so they could be readily identified and suppressed.[75] Such preemptive action against future mobilizations indicates that the companies viewed the momentum of leftist organizing among the workers as a significant threat.

Throughout 1938, but especially in the months leading up to the May union elections, the Coronel Socialist newspaper *El Obrero* joined its Communist counterpart in publicly denouncing Schwager Welfare Officer Betteley. Among other transgressions, they claimed, Betteley had denied the miners' representatives leave from work to attend the National Miners' Federation (Federación Nacional Minera; FNM) Congress in March.[76] And he had obstructed the work of Popular Front council members both by denying them access to company-controlled areas of Coronel and by refusing to negotiate fairly on public issues.[77] In the Schwager union elections of May 1938, the company went to great lengths to prevent Communist labor leaders from winning control.[78] When company candidates prevailed, *El Obrero* accused Betteley, "the Pirate of Schwager," of having

71. Oficio Confidencial no. 9, from Arauco Departmental Governor to Arauco Intendant, November 9, 1937, FMI, vol. 9787, ARNAD.

72. *Frente Popular*, November 20, 1937, 4.

73. The two expressions come from *El Obrero*, May 14, 1938, 3; and *Frente Popular*, November 27, 1937, 5, respectively.

74. Interview with Pastor Roberto Garrido Riquelme, December 5, 1997.

75. *Frente Popular*, November 27, 1937, 5.

76. *El Obrero*, March 5, 1938, 6.

77. *El Obrero*, April 16, 1938, 1.

78. *El Obrero*, May 7, 1938, 3. Although the company was still trying to keep its hand-picked leaders in office, it soon began to support Socialist candidates as a way of defeating the Communists.

rigged the elections by persecuting, bribing, or otherwise manipulating the workers.[79]

The coal miners were a strong force in the social, political, and cultural dynamics of the region, and control over their unions was crucial in any struggle for power. Yet, even as local Popular Front committees were formed and pro-Front candidates won seats on municipal councils, the unions remained almost entirely controlled by leaders in the pocket of the companies (*líderes amarillos*). Thus few strikes were called in these years, most notably, one at Schwager in March–April 1936[80] and another in May 1937, to defend the right of the workers to freely elect their own leaders. During the fifteen days of the May strike, the police wielded a heavy hand, forcefully intervening in rallies and arresting at least eight workers, who were charged with violating internal state security laws.[81]

At play here was a battle between the Communists and the company for control of the Schwager miners' union. Unlike the Lota union, where Communists did not win leadership positions until 1939, the Schwager union had a Communist president and most likely also a Communist treasurer as early as 1936. Going into the 1937 union elections, however, the Schwager company fought back, firing more than a dozen workers, four of whom were candidates in the union elections.[82] When the incumbent Communist leaders protested the layoffs, labor officials ruled that, since the company had fired the workers two days before the union's primary elections, the candidates did not have immunity. The final elections went forward, with mixed results. The incumbent Communist president was elected director, whereas the new president and secretary were "company men" (*apatronados*). Overall, the company was pleased with this director-ate and "strongly deplore[d]" its ouster after 1939.[83]

These early struggles for municipal and union control were hard fought and seldom won by pro-Front candidates, but through them, a new kind of militancy developed around the Popular Front project. A collective enthusiasm began to emerge, with growing insistence on politi-cal participation and socioeconomic justice. The gains made at the local

---

79. *El Obrero*, May 14, 1938, 3.

80. Letter from Schwager Administrator to Union President, June 26, 1939, FIC, vol. 2184, ANCh.

81. *Frente Popular*, September 18, 1937, 6.

82. Oficio no. 565, May 12, 1937, transcribing telegram from Schwager Miners' Union, and Oficio no. 144, June 1, 1937, from Coronel IDT to Concepción IPT, FDGT, 1937 Oficios, vol. 20, ARNAD. One *oficio* says twelve workers were laid off, whereas the other says it was eighteen.

83. Letter from Schwager Administrator to Schwager Miners' Union President, June 26, 1939, FIC, vol. 2184, ANCh.

level opened a path to victory in the upcoming presidential elections, to be held in October 1938. In winning there, the Popular Front coalition might be able to generate new possibilities for Chilean democracy.

The 1938 Municipal Elections and Turmoil on the Coronel City Council

On April 3, 1938, when municipal ballots were tallied across the nation, the anti-Front governing bloc won by a broad margin over the Popular Front parties, the independent sectors (including the National Socialists), and the Ibáñez supporters.[84] These results held throughout the province of Arauco, including the coal mining towns there. In Curanilahue, for example, the electorate chose four anti-Front politicians (two right-wing Radicals, an Independent, and a Democrat), and only one Popular Front representative—Communist José Cruz Delgado Espinoza.[85] "This result demonstrated that the dissident Radicals were a majority in the province of Arauco," historian Jaime Etchepare explains, "due to the greater rightist inclination of the Araucanian Radicals, who were primarily landowners and members of the upper middle class."[86] The three Radicals elected in the coal mining town of Lebu also strongly opposed alliance with the Communists. They were joined on the Lebu City Council by two Conservatives, a Liberal, and a Democrat. Against these seven anti-Front council members, two Communists stood alone.

In Coronel, home of the Schwager company, the sweep of anti-Front forces was not as clear. Socialist Carlos Rosales Gutierrez received the most votes of all the candidates, but his fellow party member Mora was not elected.[87] Two of the three Communist candidates won seats, including a woman, for the first time in Coronel history. Marking another shift from the preceding era, neither the Liberal nor the Conservative candidate was elected. The Radical Party emerged as the dominant electoral

84. During these elections, the governing bloc consisted of the Liberal, Conservative, Agrarian, Democrat, and Republican Action parties. For municipal election results around the country, see Urzúa Valenzuela, *Historia política de Chile*, 498.

85. Delgado Espinoza was treasurer of the local Communist Party in 1937, when he was arrested for allegedly violating the Internal State Security Law. In 1941, he would be elected national deputy from the Arauco region, joining coal miner Damián Uribe Cárdenas from Lota on the Communist bench in Santiago.

86. Etchepare Jensen, García Valenzuela, and Valdés Urrutia, *Historia de Curanilahue*, 31. See also Mella, "Curanilahue," 30.

87. In addition to the official results, see also Acts of Coronel Municipal Sessions (henceforth "Coronel Municipal Acts"), May 14, 1938, 765–68, consulted at Mayor's Office, Coronel; and *El Obrero*, April 9, 1938, 1.

force, winning seats for three of its seven candidates. As in the rest of the region, these Radicals represented the right wing of the party and opposed joining forces with the Marxists. With seven seats on the Coronel City Council, the three–three split (two Communist seats; one Socialist seat versus three Radical seats) was broken by the election of Simón Salazar Castillo, a member of the Unified Democratic Party (Partido Democrático Unido; PDU), the leftist breakaway faction of the Democrat Party (Partido Demócrata; PD) led by Juan Pradenas Muñoz.[88]

The new Coronel council held its inaugural meeting on May 14, 1938, just one day before Santos Medel would challenge the exclusion of "unclean" residents from Lota City Council sessions. As the Coronel council members began to vote on which of them would serve as mayor, the newly elected Socialist, schoolteacher Carlos Rosales Gutierrez, requested permission to speak. When he was informed that the Organic Law of Municipalities did not allow for open debate at that time, "Sr. Rosales, nonetheless, rose from his seat and began his speech . . . in the name of the Popular Front." Those in attendance cheered with such fervor that Rosales himself "asked them for their attention and patience [and] not to interrupt."[89]

Rosales bitterly condemned the adversaries of the Popular Front for their corrupt campaign activities and "moral poverty." He accused the incumbents of using municipal employees to distribute anti-Front campaign posters, of buying votes, and of trying to bribe candidates. Rosales claimed that he himself had been offered a promotion if he would move to Santiago; when he refused, he was involuntarily transferred to a school in Yungay (more than a thousand miles from Coronel), just three days before the election. His opponents "sustained the ridiculous and strange theory" that, through such measures, "a schoolteacher could become disloyal and traitorous to those who had supported him." Instead of selling out, Rosales had resigned, proclaiming that "from now on, there would be a gap in the teaching field, but there would be one more soldier in the trenches fighting with flag held high for social demands [reivindicaciones]." Rosales also claimed that the anti-Front forces had arranged for the detention of key figures in the Popular Front campaign, who, tellingly, were released the day after the election.

---

88. Two of the three Radicals (Arturo Hughes Cerna and Florencio Fuentes Fuentes), as well as the Unified Democratic candidate (Simón Salazar Castillo) were incumbents, having first joined the Coronel City Council after the June 1935 elections. All three of the Communists and Socialists were elected for the first time.

89. Coronel Municipal Acts, May 14, 1938, 765–68, consulted at Mayor's Office, Coronel.

His denunciations became ever more vehement, until finally Rosales turned his attention to newly elected Councilman Simón Salazar Castillo, whom he accused of "committing a triple betrayal: of his Party, of his class, and of the Popular Front." When asked by the acting council president to change his tone, Rosales responded, "We Socialists take it as a matter of course to tell truths and to denounce betrayals like the one about to be committed." The Unified Democratic Party (PDU)—"a party of the people," Rosales proclaimed—had chosen to ally itself with the Popular Front.[90] Campaigning under the banner of the Front, Salazar had thus enjoyed the full support of the Communists and Socialists.[91] Immediately following his election, however, he announced that henceforth he would be siding with the Radicals. According the Socialist paper *El Obrero*, the Radical Party had cut a "dirty deal" with him to give the anti-Front forces a majority on the Coronel City Council.[92] Salazar claimed that he was only following the directives of the PDU, but Rosales insisted that the Unified Democrats had not abandoned the Popular Front. Eventually, the debate gave way to the vote for mayor and for each position in its order of precedence. As Rosales had feared, the Popular Front lost every position by four votes to three, which resulted in a council controlled by the anti-Front members and led by Radical Mayor Arturo Hughes Cerna.

The Popular Front council members were deeply disappointed at having come so close to winning control of the council, but this did not undermine their sense that history was now moving in their favor. Socialist Councilman Rosales declared that, even as a minority, "we will control the direction of the new Municipality with the cleanness of our procedures and our moral uprightness." Using a biblical metaphor to convey the Marxists' political aspirations, Rosales continued, "We clothe ourselves in the hope that some day the people will be witnesses when we throw the dealers out of this house, just as Jesus Christ threw them out of the Temple."[93]

One reason the Popular Front council members in Coronel believed they would be able to achieve advances from their minority position was their favorable estimation of Mayor Arturo Hughes Cerna, even though

90. Ibid.

91. Contrary to Rosales's claim that Salazar's treachery occurred after the election, a local Socialist newspaper claimed he was an "anti-Front Democrat, current councilman, ambitious and incompetent" the day before the election. See *El Obrero*, April 2, 1938, 6.

92. *El Obrero*, April 6, 1938, 2.

93. Coronel Municipal Acts, May 14, 1938, 765–68, consulted at Mayor's Office, Coronel.

he had opposed the Popular Front during the campaign and was exposed as an "ex-[white-collar]employee of the Schwager Company."[94] In Rosales's harangue against the anti-Front politicians, he had been careful to make an exception for Hughes Cerna, "of whom he had a high opinion."[95] When the next council session was held four days later, tempers had cooled, and Communist Councilman Aniceto Martínez González took the floor to proclaim that he and his Popular Front colleagues would give their full support to the new mayor for the benefit of the people (el pueblo), noting that "until now the municipalities have been in the hands of small circles of people who, in general, have been in the service of the companies."[96] All the council members, across the political spectrum, then chimed in, declaring their desire to work together for the progress of the city and the well-being of its people.

Just two months later, however, Radical Councilman Florencio Fuentes noted his confusion at the eruption of a new round of infighting: "I thought all this had ended and that a compañerismo existed in our municipal activities." What shattered the fragile peace was Mayor Hughes Cerna's absence from the council due to ill health. This left control in the hands of Simón Salazar Castillo, the PDU councilman who had inspired such animosity among the Popular Front politicians when he was elected with their support, but then switched sides. "Mayor don Arturo Hughes deserves our fullest confidence," Rosales told the council, "because he brings with him a guarantee of honor and uprightness, for the positive advance of the Municipality." Salazar Castillo, by contrast, did not merit their support in the least "for not having sufficient moral uprightness or character. For being a traitor to his Party, to his class, and to the people."[97]

The Popular Front council members stood firm, refusing to attend any future meetings chaired by "the traitor" Salazar Castillo. At the next meeting, on August 17, 1938, the pending implosion was forestalled by the reappearance of Mayor Hughes Cerna, to whom all the parties again pledged their cooperation. When, however, Hughes Cerna again fell ill in the coming months, the Coronel municipality was once more racked by conflict, which became increasingly heated as the parties mounted forces for the October 1938 presidential elections.[98]

94. El Obrero, April 2, 1938, 6.
95. Coronel Municipal Acts, May 14, 1938, 765–68, consulted at Mayor's Office, Coronel.
96. Coronel Municipal Acts, May 18, 1938, 769, consulted at Mayor's Office, Coronel.
97. Coronel Municipal Acts, July 20, 1938, 793–95, consulted at Mayor's Office, Coronel.
98. El Obrero, October 10, 1938, 3.

FROM TREMORS TO QUAKES:
THE POPULAR FRONT WINS THE PRESIDENCY IN 1938

Beginning in the mid-1930s, Popular Front committees were formed at local, regional, and national levels, and these Center-Left voting blocs showed growing success in municipal and congressional elections. Going into the presidential campaign of 1938, however, political dissension among the Front parties seemed an insurmountable obstacle to victory. The Socialists rallied behind their leader, Marmaduke Grove; the Democratic Party put forward Juan Pradenas Muñoz, a pro-labor stalwart from the Concepción region; and the Radicals nominated Pedro Aguirre Cerda, a former lawyer and educator from the right wing of their party, referred to as "don Tinto" (literally "Mr. Red Wine") for his extensive vineyards. The Communists' initial response was to refrain from endorsing any of the candidates, in the hope that they might still garner sufficient Radical and Socialist support for a single, more Left-leaning populist figure. But when Radical Senator Gabriel González Videla declined their appeals to run without his party's nomination, the Communists put forward their own candidate, Elías Lafertte Gaviño.

Also entering the fray was former dictator Carlos Ibáñez del Campo, whose presidential bid was backed by Chile's small Nazi Party (MNS) and a diverse group of Ibañistas, including dissidents from the Popular Front parties. Against this diffusion of forces, the Liberals and the Conservatives, Chile's traditional right-wing parties, rallied around the candidacy of Gustavo Ross Santa María, a man who had earned the ardent animosity of the Left during his years as an "arch-conservative" finance minister in the Alessandri administration (1932–38), where he "represented the interests of the propertied classes."[1] Yet, as long as centrist and leftist forces remained divided, Ross's victory seemed assured.

Well aware of the cost of disunity, the diverse opponents of Gustavo Ross entered into intense negotiations about conditions and procedures for a Popular Front convention. Finally, in mid-April 1938, representatives of the nation's centrist and leftist parties, together with the Confederation of Chilean Workers (CTCh), gathered in Santiago to try to reach a consensus around a single candidate. After several days of heated debate, discord began to subside, especially through the diplomatic efforts of two key left-wing Radicals: Deputy Justiniano Sotomayor and Senator González Videla. Sotomayor had traveled across the political spectrum, from drafting the Republican Militia (Milicia Republicana) bylaws in the early 1930s to fervently supporting the Popular Front by 1938.[2] González Videla, on the other hand, had long maintained close ties with the Chilean Left, especially the Communists. He now worked to persuade the Communists and the Socialists that an Aguirre Cerda administration would open new opportunities for political advances and social reform. One by one, the parties withdrew their candidates and pledged their support for Aguirre Cerda, who emerged as the standard-bearer of the Popular Front coalition.[3]

In the coal mining town of Coronel, the local Socialist paper, El Obrero, lauded the contributions of Sotomayor and González Videla to the Popular Front Convention, which "gave life to the candidacy [of Aguirre Cerda, a candidacy] with the greatest intellectual prestige and the widest doctrinal content that has ever been seen in Chilean political history."[4] Praising Sotomayor and González Videla for "hav[ing] gone beyond the limits of their party," El Obrero proclaimed that it was they, not the Right-leaning Radicals, who "legitimately embody the true sense of the hour that Chilean radicalism is living since it placed itself at the vanguard of the Frontist movement." Having thus "acquire[d] the stature of indisputable representatives of the people," González Videla and Sotomayor became key figures in the Popular Front's presidential campaign.

With the national electoral alliance thus tenuously in place, the ailing fifty-nine-year-old Aguirre Cerda began to tour the country, accompanied

---

1. Loveman, Chile, 203, 208.
2. Urzúa Valenzuela, Historia política electoral, 26, and Historia política de Chile, 488. See also Laferrte Gaviño, Vida de un comunista, 303, and El Obrero, October 1, 1938, 4.
3. El Obrero, April 30, 1938, 1. See also Loveman, Chile, 208–9; and Jobet, Ensayo crítico, 200.
4. El Obrero, October 1, 1938, 4.

by González Videla, Sotomayor, and other leading politicians of the Popular Front parties. As they moved from city to city, they realized that achieving unified action at the local level would be no easy task. In the recent municipal elections in the coal mining zone, for example, Socialists and Communists had been unable to reach agreement and each ran their own lists of candidates. Moreover, the local Radicals had deviated from the national party line to oppose the Popular Front, and members of the local Unified Democratic Party (PDU) had vacillated in their positions. On campaign visits to the coal region, it became clear that the fragility of local Popular Front alliances was making it difficult to garner mass support for Aguirre Cerda's candidacy. Elías Lafertte Gaviño, a top Communist leader who accompanied Aguirre Cerda on the campaign trail, described the candidate's visit to Lota as a near-disaster, with the speakers packed "on the back of a truck sunk in the mud," trying desperately to elicit enthusiasm from a small crowd. Indeed, nowhere on the southern tour did Aguirre Cerda draw large, impassioned crowds. "Little by little, through patient work, he did gain ground and votes," Lafertte observed, but "it would have been much easier and better if the Popular Front had a strong and monolithic organization." Analyzing the political discord, Lafertte noted that "Socialists in the provinces followed the same line as they did in Santiago, of aversion and animosity toward the Communists. The Radicals, for their part, were linked to the workers' parties only in a very superficial and occasional way."[5]

Lafertte's assessment notwithstanding, in the coal communities, local Socialists, such as Coronel Councilman Carlos Rosales Gutierrez, did ally with Communists to defend the Front, while local Radicals opposed any alliance with the Marxists. Why did the Socialists and Radicals of the coal mining provinces follow a different line than their Santiago counterparts? As Wesleyan pastor and Socialist Councilman Víctor Mora clearly found, the sharp class divides in the coal mining communities—between *obreros* (blue-collar workers), *empleados* (white-collar employees), and *jefes* (executives), as well as great differences in the size of each group—gave the Socialist Party in the region more of a working-class base than it had at the national level, where the party's strength lay among artisans, state functionaries, and other middle-class sectors.

The southern Radicals, for their part, were led by landed interests, including future President Juan Antonio Ríos Morales (1942–46), who were intensely hostile to any organizing efforts among rural workers or

---

5. Lafertte Gaviño, *Vida de un comunista*, 313, 314.

tenant farmers. These men thus wanted no part in the Popular Front alliance promoted by the Communists, which threatened to disrupt the old order in the countryside. At various points during World War II, however, after securing prohibitions on rural organizing, even these right-wing Radicals would accede to fleeting alliances with both the Socialists and the Communists.[6]

Despite the Popular Front's fragile unity at the base, throughout the winter of 1938—June, July, and August in the Southern Hemisphere—local Popular Front forces in the coal mining zone persevered in their campaign for Aguirre Cerda. Miner and musician Luis Alberto Barra Faúndez recalled how Communist Councilman Santos Medel put together a youth band for don Tinto's visit to Lota and Coronel "to go out and play in the rallies, in the 'uprisings' as we called them."[7] After his mid-June visit to Lota, Aguirre Cerda traveled on to mining and agricultural communities farther south, where local organizers struggled to mobilize the small crowds that came to see the Popular Front candidate. In Arauco, about sixty people had gathered at the station, and together with "some horsemen . . . from the neighboring countryside," they marched to the municipal theater, where another two hundred people waited, "among them, a great number of women and many children." The mayor of Arauco, Manuel Rioseco Espinoza, president of the local Unified Democratic Party (PDU), opened the rally, followed by the president and vice president of the local Radical Party (PR).[8] The prominence of these PDU and PR politicians at the rally signaled that both of these party branches were now supporting the Popular Front, which they had not done, at least not consistently, in the municipal and union elections of the previous months.

Reinforcing the PDU's endorsement of Aguirre Cerda, national Democratic leader Juan Pradenas Muñoz, a longtime defender of the working class with a strong following in the coal mining zone, also appeared on the stage. So did Senator Marmaduke Grove, who conveyed to Socialist militants their national party's support of the Popular Front candidate. The appearance of these two politicians at the rally was especially important since, as late as mid-April, they had both been presidential candidates.[9]

---

6. Ministerial Order no. 34 of 1939 and Law no. 8811 of 1947 effectively prevented rural unionization, as discussed briefly in the introduction. See also Loveman, *Struggle*, esp. 118–19, 124–32; and Loveman, *Documentary Supplement*, 102–15, 138–58.

7. Luis Alberto Barra Faúndez, as quoted in Alcalde, *Reportaje al carbón*, 7.

8. Providencia Confidencial no. 9, June 18, 1938, from Eduardo Agrela Guevara, Arauco Departmental Governor, to Interior Minister, FMI, vol. 9788 (2 of 5), ARNAD.

9. *El Obrero*, April 16, 1938, 1.

While eulogizing Aguirre Cerda, the speakers denounced the "mistakes of the current government," especially its violations of "the freedom of the press, of assembly, [and its] abuses of members of [Congress]." They held right-wing candidate Gustavo Ross, Alessandri's finance minister, largely responsible for "the bad situation of the country."[10]

Police observers at the rally, both uniformed and undercover, reported that all but one of the speakers performed "calmly, without fiery passion and without directly attacking functionaries of the current Government." The only exception was Senator González Videla, who accused Alessandri of having "betrayed the Radical Party . . . allowing himself to be carried away by the Right and especially by Sr. Ross."[11] A few months later, when the coal mining town of Lebu launched its Popular Front electoral campaign, González Videla was the keynote speaker. With Communist, Socialist, and Radical banners flying high, he again boldly assailed the president, calling him a traitor to those who had put him into office and condemning him for "going over to the side of the aristocracy and foreign capitalism."[12]

Although Gustavo Ross made no campaign visits to the coal mines, he did venture to the neighboring city of Concepción in late July 1938. Three thousand supporters turned out to greet him, an impressive number for a damp, wintry day, but so did a "large group of opposing forces," waving banners and chanting, "Death to Ross!" Throughout the afternoon, the police broke up "various marches and sudden gatherings of opposition forces, consisting of Nazis, university students, and elements of the Popular Front."[13] In one incident, protestors threw rocks at the local Conservative Club, breaking several windows.[14] Ross averted another clash when he canceled a meeting at the University of Concepción Law School after receiving word that hundreds of student protestors were blocking the entrance.[15]

10. Providencia Confidencial no. 9, June 18, 1938, from Arauco Departmental Governor to Interior Minister, FMI, vol. 9788 (2 of 5), ARNAD.

11. Ibid.

12. Oficio Confidencial no. 451, September 5, 1938, from Interim Arauco Intendant to Interior Minister, FMI, vol. 9788 (2 of 5), ARNAD. As González Videla denounced Alessandri for "betrayal," he likely never imagined that he would face the same charge less than a decade later. See chapter 9.

13. Providencia Reservada no. 178, August 6, 1938, from Humberto Arriagada Valdivieso, Carabineros Director General, to Interior Minister, FMI, vol. 9788 (2 of 5), ARNAD.

14. Ibid. For a fascinating look at the significance of place in popular protest action, see James, "October 17th."

15. Providencia Reservada no. 178, August 6, 1938, from Carabineros Director General, to Interior Minister, FMI, vol. 9788 (2 of 5), ARNAD.

102 HOPES AND PROMISES

Although both Ibañistas and Popular Front supporters rallied in opposition to Ross, neither had the numbers to defeat him on their own. But the situation was soon to change. On September 5, 1938, an estimated thirty-two armed young men affiliated with the Chilean National Socialist, or Nazi, Party (MNS) occupied the building of the Workers' Insurance Fund (Caja de Seguro Obrero), located across the street from the presidential palace. At the same time, another thirty-two youths took over a building at the University of Chile in an ill-conceived attempt to overthrow the government and place Ibáñez in power. President Alessandri ordered the carabineros to dislodge the youths at any cost. After raiding both buildings, with heavy exchanges of gunfire and several deaths, the police led the surviving occupiers from the university to the Workers' Insurance Fund building, where they summarily shot nearly sixty of the young Nazis. The government implicated both Carlos Ibáñez del Campo and Nazi leader Jorge González von Marées in the attempted coup and charged them with conspiracy. From his jail cell, Ibáñez withdrew from the presidential race and pledged to support Aguirre Cerda, a bizarre twist by which the Chilean anti-Fascist Popular Front gained the votes of the National Socialists.[16]

On October 25, 1938, when roughly 88 percent of Chile's registered voters (limited to literate, adult males) went to the polls, Pedro Aguirre Cerda won 50.2 percent of the vote, while right-wing candidate Gustavo Ross Santa María came in a close second, with 49.2 percent.[17] Indeed, in this "bitter, violent, shrill electoral contest," the margin of victory was so narrow that Ross would not concede until he was sure he could not get military backing to assume the presidency by force.[18] Under a different electoral system, such as that of the United States, where all the electoral college votes of a given state go to the candidate receiving the most votes there, Ross might well have been Chile's next president since he won thirteen of the country's provinces to Aguirre Cerda's eleven.

Concepción and Arauco, the provinces containing the coal mines, were among those giving a majority of their votes to the Popular Front candidate.[19] In Concepción, Aguirre Cerda garnered 63.9 percent of the vote,

16. See Jobet, *Ensayo crítico*, 200. For Alessandri's account of these events, see Alessandri Palma, *Recuerdos*, vol. 3, chap. 11.

17. Dirección del Registro Electoral, presidential election results, 1938, SERCh. Electoral laws passed in the 1870s and 1880s "removed property qualifications and extended the vote to [all] adult, literate males." These requirements were confirmed in the 1925 Constitution, which included other significant electoral reforms. Loveman, *Chile*, 164–65, 182. By the 1930 Census, according to Paul Drake in *Socialism and Populism*, 203, "12% of the population was registered." Thus, in 1938, "about 5% of all Chileans elected Aguirre Cerda president," which was "a higher turnout than in 1932."

18. Loveman, *Chile*, 208.

19. Election results by province are in Urzúa Valenzuela, *Historia política de Chile*, 500–501.

compared to Ross's 35.7 percent, whereas in Arauco the margin of victory was much closer, 51.5 percent to 48.1 percent. These results were consistent with the greater degree of industrial development and urbanization in Concepción, and its much larger coal mining workforce. As Paul Drake wrote of the 1938 election results, "The Front . . . won the heavily populated urban provinces of Santiago, Valparaíso, and Concepción. High provincial votes for Aguirre Cerda coincided with indices of modernity, such as urbanization, unionization, higher average wages paid to workers, and low religiosity."[20] Although the province of Arauco remained predominantly agricultural, its coal mining operations, railroads, and related industries would have provided a large enough urban working-class vote to give the provincial majority to Aguirre Cerda.[21]

Yet what is surprising is that, in both Concepción and Arauco Provinces, it was votes from the rural areas—and not from the coal mining communities—that put Aguirre Cerda over the top. Despite the resurgent influence of the Communist Party in the coal towns, Aguirre Cerda fared well above his national average only in Coronel (59.9 percent) and Penco (65.7 percent).[22] In Lota, on the other hand, the 50.4 percent vote for Aguirre Cerda was 10 percent lower than in the province as a whole, and almost 5 percent lower than the neighboring agricultural community of Santa Juana (55.8 percent).[23] Moreover, despite his slim victory in the province of Arauco, Aguirre Cerda lost by a large margin in that province's two principal coal mining towns, Curanilahue, where he garnered only 29.1 percent of the vote, and Lebu, which gave him only 39.7 percent (table 1).[24]

20. Drake, *Socialism and Populism*, 204. See also Loveman, *Chile*, 208–9.

21. In the 1930 Census, the percentages of urban population in the three departments constituting the province of Arauco were Arauco: 27 percent; Lebu: 24 percent; and Cañete: 11.5 percent, giving a provincial average of slightly more than 20 percent. See Silva Torres's discussion of these results in "Impacto de la actividad," 93–94. By 1952, the province of Concepción was 76.1 percent urban and 23.9 percent rural, but the province of Arauco was just the reverse, 28.6 percent urban and 71.4 percent rural. Dirección General de Estadísticas, *Censo de 1952*, 151, BNCh.

22. Penco itself was not a coal mining town, but the *comuna* included the Lirquén mines. Penco was home to several other industrial operations, including a major sugar refinery and a ceramics factory.

23. The comuna of Lota was 89 percent urban, whereas the comuna of Santa Juana was only 17 percent urban, according to the 1952 Census. Dirección General de Estadísticas, *Censo de 1952*, 3, BNCh. The official 1938 election results in the coal mining zone contrast sharply with the summary provided by Paul Drake, who noted that "Ross had scored nearly twice as well in the rural *comunas* . . . as in the urban ones: 61.5% to 37.5%. Aguirre Cerda had recorded the opposite pattern: 38.2% in the rural communities and 61.5% in the urban." Drake, *Socialism and Populism*, 259 and 204, table 13.

24. In addition to official election results, see also Pizarro Soto, *Lebu*, 340, who says that in Lebu, Ross received 731 votes to Aguirre Cerda's 502.

Table 1 Results of 1938 presidential election in coal mining communities

Location	Estimated Population	Registered voters	For Pedro Aguirre Cerda	%[a]	For Gustavo Ross	%[a]	For Carlos Ibáñez	Blank votes	Invalid, annulled votes	Totals	%[b]
							Votes cast				
Coronel	27,000	3,063	1,634	59.9	1,083	39.7	0	11	0	2,728	89.1
Lota	32,000	3,156	1,410	50.4	1,384	49.5	0	3	0	2,797	88.6
Santa Juana	—	566	325	63.6	172	33.7	0	0	14	511	90.3
Department of Coronel	70,000	6,785	3,369	55.8	2,639	43.7	0	14	14	6,036	89.0
Penco	6,700	1,225	722	65.7	374	34.0	1	2	0	1,099	89.7
Department of Concepción	—	12,927	7,538	66.5	3,741	33.0	1	44	5	11,329	87.6
Province of Concepción	300,000	31,173	17,417	63.9	9,734	35.7	1	75	24	27,251	87.4
Curanilahue	13,000	931	248	29.1	604	70.9	0	0	0	852	91.5
Department of Arauco	28,000	2,229	1,024	50.6	998	49.4	0	0	0	2,022	90.7
Lebu	8,000	955	324	39.7	493	60.3	0	0	0	817	85.5
Los Alamos	6,000	473	178	42.8	238	57.2	0	0	0	416	87.9
Department of Lebu	14,000	1,428	502	40.7	731	59.3	0	0	0	1,233	86.3
Province of Arauco	65,000	5,382	2,481	51.5	2,318	48.1	0	0	18	4,817	89.5
National totals	4,800,000[c]	503,871	222,720	50.2	218,609	49.2	112	1,523	924	443,888	88.1

SOURCE: Dirección del Registro Electoral, presidential election results, 1938, SERCh. See also Urzúa Valenzuela, *Historia política electoral*, 33–38, and *Historia política de Chile*, 501–4.

[a]Percentage of votes cast.

[b]Percentage of registered voters who voted in this election.

[c]Estimate based on national population as reported in the 1930 and 1940 Censuses: 4,287,445 and 5,025,539, respectively.

The remarkably small numbers of votes Aguirre Cerda received in the coal mining towns might be explained in several ways. First, as discussed in previous chapters, the coal mining companies maintained diverse modes of vigilance over their workers beyond the confines of the mines, and the companies' powers of retribution may have intimidated some workers into staying home or even voting for the bosses' candidate. Company control of voting, whether by force, enticement, or outright bribery (vote buying, or *cohecho*), marked Chilean political cultural throughout the nineteenth century and well into the twentieth, particularly for local contests. Second, as seen in the municipal elections of 1938 and the ensuing internecine battles on city councils, neither the Radicals nor the Unified Democrats in the coal communities wholeheartedly supported the Front; indeed, some may well have viewed the decision by their national leaders to join forces with the Marxists as unconscionable. And third, it is also likely that some militant leftist workers continued to distrust estate-owning Aguirre Cerda, despite efforts by national leaders to assuage their doubts.

When Aguirre Cerda assumed office on December 24, he was joined by a cabinet that included all the major Popular Front parties except the Communists.[25] Some sources indicate that he had offered them posts, but that the Communists had refused for "tactical reasons related to the image of the government": they were determined not to jeopardize the fragile opening for a leftward shift in the Chilean state.[26]

"A Crusade of Equality, Justice, and Welfare for All": Methodist Support for the Popular Front

Despite the relatively narrow margin of victory for the Popular Front candidate and the volatile political arrangements sustaining his presidency,

25. The political configuration of Aguirre Cerda's initial cabinet—six Radicals, three Socialists, and two Democrats—was maintained until June 1941, albeit with some changes from the right to left wing of the same party, and vice versa. Stevenson says that Aguirre Cerda also sought to include members of the Alianza Popular Libertadora, the coalition formed around Ibáñez in 1938, but they declined. Stevenson, *Chilean Popular Front*, 94–95.

26. Pizarro, *La huelga obrera*, 107–8. See also Cortés and Fuentes, *Diccionario político*, 101. In his memoirs, however, González Videla says the Communists actively sought control of the Labor Ministry and other top posts. When the Socialists opposed such a move, Aguirre Cerda asked him to "convince [his] Communist friends" to withdraw their request. González Videla, *Memorias*, 1:297.

diverse sectors of society felt new currents of possibility and quickly conveyed their excitement at the change in government.[27] The Episcopal Methodists, for example, had been highly critical of the Alessandri administration, particularly its social policies. They decried inadequate wages and deplorable living conditions, which they saw as largely responsible for the working classes' moral degradation. In this regard, they even coined a new term: the *economic-moral level of the people*. The Methodists also insisted that the government fully respect democratic institutions and practices. In a 1935 telegram to President Alessandri, they argued that

> the economic-moral level of the people of Chile will never rise if the nation remains strangled by alcohol and unchecked gambling. Lotteries [and] prostitution undermine virtues [such as] honesty and turn Chileans to vice. We reiterate [our] strong desire for absolute respect for the freedom of the press, speech, and assembly. We are in favor of liberty for all who suffer imprisonment for this reason. We suggest that the best way to halt typhus and other scourges afflicting Chile is to dress, feed, and house the people, giving them [adequate] wages to raise their miserable standard of living and to replace the unhealthy dwellings that so abound in the Republic.[28]

Finding these ideals unfulfilled by the Alessandri administration, the Methodists emerged as vocal champions of the Popular Front. The telegram they sent to newly inaugurated Aguirre Cerda from their January 1939 annual conference differed notably in tone from their communications to Alessandri: "We fraternally and respectfully greet you and fervently express our support so that the work of your Government may effectively benefit the people," and be the work "of progressive governance [and] of eminent social justice." Holding out the promise of bountiful enthusiasm and cooperation, on the one hand, the Methodists also made clear the conditions for their support, on the other: the Aguirre Cerda administration was to "comply strictly with the Program of the Popular Front, to which we loyally adhere."[29] The Methodists favored the redistribution of wealth and privileges called for in the Popular Front

27. "A crusade of equality, justice, and welfare for all" is taken from Acts of the Thirty-ninth Annual Conference of the Episcopal Methodist Church of Chile, held in Santiago, January 7–12, 1939, 118.

28. Acts of the Thirty-fifth Annual Conference of the Episcopal Methodist Church of Chile, held in El Vergel, January 7–15, 1935, 141, CDIME.

29. Acts of the Thirty-ninth Annual Conference, 103, CDIME.

project, and they also hoped to achieve greater social mobility, free from the discrimination and persecution to which they had so often been subjected. Their approval of the new government was contingent on its fulfillment of the promise to deepen democracy by overcoming exclusionary practices—precisely the kind of practices Santos Medel was fighting in the Lota City Council. In hopeful terms, the Episcopal Methodists' annual conference celebrated the Popular Front victory: "The Chilean citizens, through the legal procedures of suffrage, free of the demeaning and demoralizing buying of votes [cohecho], have made possible the installation of a government that reflects the transcendent desire for social justice, human dignity, and economic and cultural well-being for the vast numbers of our fellow citizens who were excluded for so many years from the marvelous banquet of life."[30]

The Methodists' optimism in the political realm coincided with a movement of spiritual renewal within the Church, a decade after the Wesleyans broke away from what they perceived as the Church's theological and social ossification. In mid-1938, as the Chilean Methodists celebrated the 200th anniversary of the sect's founding in London, they were moved by the spirit of change sweeping the nation. The report coming from the Concepción district was particularly clear in this regard, explaining that "in the midst of the chaos and confusion that the world and our own country have been living in recent years," the Methodist Church had moved its preaching into the streets, "as did its founder Mr. John Wesley," in order to avoid becoming "cold, mechanical, and routine" and to reach the people with "a new baptism of the Holy Spirit." These changes in the theological and spiritual orientation of the Methodists were directly linked to material conditions and relations of production, with explicit language demanding social justice. "We have to seek out the sacred fire," the report continued. "With a Church like that we will show the world new and better paths; we will preach brotherhood and love among all people; we will fight against the misery, hatred, and egoism of men; we will offer a Gospel that transforms, strengthens, and elevates life; we will begin a crusade of equality, justice, and welfare for all, in the name of Our Lord Jesus Christ."[31]

Coming out of the brutal years of the Great Depression, when they, along with so many others, had struggled to survive and to help those in need, the Methodists of Chile seemed to be moving toward a "preferential

30. Ibid., 124–25.
31. Ibid., 115–18.

option for the poor," akin to that of Catholic liberation theology of later decades. Again contrasting their experiences of the Depression under the Alessandri administration with the new hopes raised by the Popular Front, the Methodists wrote,

> Such compassion on a day when poverty was inevitable is transformed for us, on a day when poverty can be abolished, into a demand for justice in the distribution of the fruits of industry and the earth. From the perspective of Evangelical Christianity, it is intolerable that multitudes of men, women, and children live without opportunities that well-off people consider prime necessities for themselves. God did not create workers to be mere instruments to the end that others make money. The well-being of all should be the fundamental objective of all processes of production and distribution.[32]

Radical transformations within the Church were especially pursued by its younger members, and all the more so by those who grew up in working-class communities, such as the coal mining town of Lota, where, in the early years of the Popular Front, the Methodist Youth published their own local paper, *Nueva Alborada* (New Dawn).[33] On the front page of the first issue, in October 1939, the young Lota Methodists proclaimed, "Those who believe that Christianity is a narcotic are no longer tooting their horn: [The light of] new reform shines through in the ranks."[34] After strongly condemning Marxism, despite the Marxist tone of many of their own proclamations, the editors of the paper regretted that some Christians "in certain epochs, and for lack of understanding . . . did not urge church members to affiliate with unions or to fight for their economic demands [*reivindicaciones*]." These Lota youths appreciated their Church's efforts to help individuals liberate themselves from vice and depravity largely because this made them better able to participate in collective battles for economic and social justice.

The most ardent and disciplined militants of all political parties and social movements were Christians, these young Lota Methodists argued,

32. Ibid., 124–25.
33. What little information I could find about the editors of *Nueva Alborada: Un Vocero de la Juventud Metodista* (Lota) indicates strong ties between the Methodists of Lota and those of Curanilahue. One editor was a "close collaborator" of the Curanilahue church back in 1930, while another had started a new youth league in Curanilahue in late 1939. The second and, I believe, last edition of the newspaper was published in September 1940.
34. *Nueva Alborada* 1 (October 1939): 1, 4.

since the Church had "polished them" to serve humanity. They referred especially to Luis Emilio Recabarren, founder of the modern Chilean labor movement and Communist Party, claiming that his ideals had come directly from the Methodist Church "because it was she who, in his infancy and adolescence, knew how to fill him with love toward the needy classes." Recabarren "always used quotes from [the Bible] to speak to the masses," and though the working class "at [other] times denies the Bible and Christianity," when Recabarren spoke, the workers "applauded those same passages with true enthusiasm."[35]

The young Methodists of Lota praised their elders for "comprehending better than anyone the suffering of the exploited masses" and for helping to build the kind of individual moral character that might contribute to greater socioeconomic justice. They were not content, however, with liberal notions of individual mobility and morality, and they advocated a greater role for the institutions of a democratic state and civil society: "A more direct intervention in [social] problems is necessary. This is already being understood by all sincere and honorable Christians, and movements of a political-social character are thus emerging, although we still don't know where they will lead." However cautious and conditional their support for the Popular Front, the young Methodists were certainly exuberant in their hopes about where the new current *might* lead. As the last line of the *Nueva Alborada* article proclaimed, "The tremendous turn [of events] taking place . . . will culminate in an era of true justice, peace, and happiness in our land."

The 1939 Earthquake and Its Aftermath: A New Day amid the Rubble

After his June 1938 campaign visit to Lota (during which young Luis Barra Faúndez played the trombone in the municipal band), Aguirre Cerda's next trips to the coal mining zone would be as president on occasions of death and destruction. On January 24, 1939, just one month after his inauguration, forty minutes before midnight, a devastating earthquake razed fifty thousand square miles in southern Chile, from Concepción to Talca. Registering 8.3 on the Richter scale, the quake was centered on the town of Chillán, in the foothills of the Andes, 150 kilometers (about 90 miles) inland from Lota. As many as fifty thousand people died in this

35. Ibid.

natural disaster, with property damage estimated between 30 and 40 million dollars.[36]

Up and down the long coastal strip of the coal mining region, the people of Lota, Coronel, Lebu, and smaller towns stood in their streets in utter shock, fearful of further tremors, tidal waves, and flooding. When they began to clear away the rubble and to find their missing loved ones, however, they were relieved to discover that the number of deaths was remarkably low. Grave injuries to people and severe damage to property, businesses, and infrastructure, however, were extensive, as was the displacement of people from their homes. In Lota, for example, though only ten people died, hundreds were severely injured and thousands more thrown into unemployment and homelessness. Of the 2,205 company houses at the time, all but 130 sustained serious damage.[37] Company houses (pabellones) were sturdier than the makeshift dwellings occupied by the town's less privileged workers, which collapsed in catastrophic proportions. The quake also demolished the municipal building in Lota Bajo, that "little wooden house" where City Councilman Santos Medel had delivered his fiery speeches, together with the fire station, police headquarters, schools, commercial houses, market stalls, and the parish church.

The Methodists' temple in Concepción was completely destroyed and their meeting house in Curanilahue severely damaged. Even more devastating to the Methodists' efforts to reinvigorate and expand their following in the region was the mass exodus of people who had lost their homes and jobs as businesses were forced to shut down. In the Concepción district alone, which included the coal mining towns of Lota, Coronel, and Curanilahue, the Methodist Church lost more than two hundred members.[38]

The extent of damage wrought by the 1939 earthquake in southern Chile has never been thoroughly studied, nor have the sociopolitical dimensions of the reconstruction that followed.[39] John Reese Stevenson

36. Stevenson, *Chilean Popular Front*, 131; Loveman, *Chile*, 211; *New York Times*, January 26, 1939, 5, January 27, 1939, 1, and February 1, 1939, 3; *Times* (London), January 26, 1939, 10, January 27, 1939, 13, and February 3, 1939, 16; "Chile: Worst Shake," *Time* magazine, February 6, 1939.

37. Endlicher, "Lota," 10; and Pereira Gigogne, "Lota," 6–8.

38. Concepción District Report, Forty-first Annual Conference of the Episcopal Methodist Church of Chile, held in El Vergel, January 9–14, 1941, n.p., CDIME

39. A 2007 documentary film entitled *1939: Chillán desaparace* shows original footage of the damage. For decrees, letters, reports, and other documents, see FIC, vols. 2153, 2154, 2163, 2164, and 2168, ANCh. For an innovative study of the 1944 quake in Argentina, see Healey, *Ruins of the New Argentina*.

briefly discusses national political responses to the quake in his 1942 book *The Chilean Popular Front*, while Wilfried Endlicher provides a few comments on its effects in Lota in his 1986 article about that city. Highlighting the benefits that came from reconstruction, Endlicher writes, "Just a few months later, not only were [the damaged houses] repaired, but also, 1,000 new houses were built. Moreover, these new concrete buildings were clearly different from the old wooden block houses."[40] The challenge of reconstruction was not quite as simple as Endlicher's remarks make it sound, however. Existing lines of political debate took new turns as the nation searched for the most effective means to address the emergency in the South.

Although the proportions of the crisis were similar to those of the worst Depression years (1930–34), the social, political, and economic tides had begun to turn. The way houses, schools, roads, businesses, and mines were rebuilt in the wake of the 1939 earthquake would prove to be a cornerstone of the Popular Front's national industrialization program. Dating back to debates in the 1920s over social legislation, many forces that would come to constitute the Popular Front had long sought ways to strengthen the state's ability to regulate and invest in the national economy. Even after Aguirre Cerda won the presidency, however, attempts to create a state development agency were repeatedly stymied by the "Liberal-Conservative congressional majority [who] were bitterly hostile to the creation of such [an agency]."[41] Now, in the aftermath of the 1939 earthquake, as people throughout the country in all walks of life gathered around their radios listening to news from the ravaged zone, advocates of increased state intervention found a window of opportunity.

In close dialogue with the Aguirre Cerda administration, Popular Front congressional leaders proposed an earthquake reconstruction bill that included the creation and funding of the new Chilean Economic Development Agency (CORFO).[42] Under the jurisdiction of the Ministry of Public Works, this agency was designed to function as a critical tool for heightened state involvement in the economy. Capitalizing on human sympathy for the earthquake victims, CORFO proponents also drew on widespread concern about possible disruptions of coal production. Their proposals finally gained congressional approval in April 1939. "The nation," Stevenson explains, "would not have countenanced parliamentary obstruction

40. Endlicher, "Lota," 10.
41. Stevenson, *Chilean Popular Front*, 131–32.
42. On the CORFO, see Bulnes Aldunate, "La Corporación"; Sarasin, "La Corporación"; CORFO, *Cinco años*, and CORFO, *veinte años*; Finer, *Chilean Development Corporation*; Silvert, "Chilean Development Corporation"; and Ortega Martínez et al., *Corporación*.

of the necessary reconstruction legislation."[43] Popular Front politicians finally had the institutional vehicle they desperately needed if their national industrialization plans were to come to fruition. As Chilean historian Luis Ortega Martínez aptly notes, "The creation and development of the CORFO represented a historic reorientation of the Chilean State."[44]

Summarizing the initial mandate and priorities of the CORFO, the U.S. Tariff Commission wrote that it was "formed with the stated objectives of increasing national production, raising standards of living, lowering costs of production, improving the financial situation of the nation, and seeing that all productive enterprises are supplied with needed materials and capital."[45] Even though concerns about coal production were instrumental in the agency's creation, the coal mining industry never became a key area of CORFO investment, largely because of the control wielded by the Lota and Schwager companies over the country's major mines. In the province of Arauco, and particularly in the Lebu area, however, the CORFO did salvage a number of small and medium mines that had declared bankruptcy after struggling since the Depression.

In March 1939, less than two months after the great earthquake and just before Aguirre Cerda signed the CORFO bill into law, the coal mining zone suffered yet another major disaster—an explosion of methane gas in the Schwager mines, described by one publication as "the most horrifying tragedy ever registered in the mining history of Coronel."[46] As emergency sirens wailed from the company bell tower, miners' families dropped their daily activities in schools, houses, and market stalls and ran in panic-stricken crowds toward the mine. Carabineros and company security forces cordoned off access to the mines, but many people, including immediate family, found a way in. The Schwager rescue brigade also rushed to the scene, where they determined, in the words of one account, that "to have arrived at the burning area would have been suicide."[47] Many

43. Stevenson, *Chilean Popular Front*, 131–32. Many works highlight the importance of the 1939 earthquake for the passage of the CORFO legislation. See, for example, Muñoz Goma, *Chile*; Finer, *Chilean Development Corporation*; and Ortega Martínez et al., *Corporación*. See also Loveman, *Chile*, 211–12.

44. Ortega Martínez et al., *Corporación*, 110.

45. U.S. Tariff Commission, *Mining*, 19.

46. *Centenario de Coronel*.

47. Ibid. Many interviewed residents recalled this explosion. Raquel Padilla, for example, conveyed the horror she experienced as a young girl when the men emerging from the mine were given brandy. This, her mother told her, was to determine whether they were "already on fire inside," in which case "the brandy would burn their innards." If they did not die immediately upon drinking, they could still be saved. Interview with Raquel del Carmen Padilla Vergara.

miners were still alive, struggling toward the exit through flames, smoke, and collapsing timbers; yet the decision was made to seal the burning coal face with dynamite explosions to prevent the spread of the fire. Of the two hundred men working that face, only one hundred and forty survived, many of whom were covered by third-degree burns. Twenty-three corpses, charred almost beyond recognition, were dug from the ruins, while another thirty-seven miners' bodies were never found. The Communists denounced the Schwager company's disregard for worker safety, and almost immediately Aguirre Cerda traveled to the mines to express his condolences to the families who had lost their husbands, sons, fathers, and brothers.

Although support for Aguirre Cerda in the coal mining zone was growing, so was political factionalism in the national Popular Front. Less than six months after his return from the heartrending scene at the Schwager mines, the president faced his most difficult challenge to date: a "bitter rivalry between the principal government parties, the Radicals and the Socialists."[48] This political conflict, which threatened to break up the Popular Front coalition, involved both competition for administrative posts, and more substantive points of disagreement about government policies and ideological principles. The Socialists had been given three posts in Aguirre Cerda's first cabinet, but in September 1939, the party replaced all their original ministers with more leftist and more powerful figures—Oscar Schnake Vergara, Rolando Merino Reyes, and Salvador Allende Gossens. By this move, they sought to push the government toward more radical and rapid change and, in particular, to counterbalance what they deemed to be the undue economic conservatism of Radical Finance Minister Roberto Wachholtz Araya.[49]

Because all three of the new Socialist ministers came directly from Congress, special elections were held in October 1939 to fill their seats. The new minister of land and colonization, Rolando Merino Reyes, was from the Concepción region. A lawyer, professor, and owner of a medium-size agricultural estate, Merino had previously served as intendant of Concepción (1931–32), leader in the Socialist Republic (1932), and national deputy (1933–39). Elected to replace him in Congress was the fiery councilman from Coronel, Carlos Rosales Gutierrez.

48. Stevenson, *Chilean Popular Front*, 99.

49. The Socialists' strategy succeeded: on December 26, 1939, Wachholtz Araya resigned and was replaced by the more Left-leaning Radical Pedro Alfonso Barrios. Relations between the two parties immediately improved, but not until two months later did Marmaduke Grove, leader of the Socialist Party and the national Popular Front, announce "that the misunderstandings between the Radicals and the Socialists had been ironed out and that relative harmony reigned within government circles." Stevenson, *Chilean Popular Front*, 100.

When special municipal elections were held in February 1940 to replace Rosales on the Coronel City Council, the sole candidate was Rosales's old friend Víctor Mora, who had run unsuccessfully in 1938.[50] From
the moment he joined the city council, Mora followed in Rosales's footsteps, showing himself to be a strong supporter of the Popular Front. In
June 1940, only four months after Mora took office, the man who had
been holding together the Front and anti-Front forces on the city council,
Mayor Arturo Hughes Cerna, resigned, "for personal reasons."[51] When the
council met to select a new mayor, Socialist Councilman Víctor Mora proclaimed that "being a member of a truly class-based party, he would vote
for Sr. Martínez, a representative of the people," referring to Communist
Aniceto Martínez González. With the Radicals on the council still in opposition to the Front, however, Martínez González lost by four votes to
three. The winner, Florencio Fuentes, was a Radical whom the Popular
Front had denounced in the bitterly fought 1938 elections as a "lackey of
the [Schwager] Company, and the most incompetent political leader that
Coronel has seen."[52] Martínez González also accused the new mayor of
doing "whatever the imperialist company of Coronel orders [him] to do."[53]

Víctor Mora would also soon follow Rosales in a new direction. In late
1939, a group emerged within the Socialist Party, known as the "Nonconformists," who opposed what they deemed to be their party's insuffi-
ciently critical stance toward the Popular Front government. These
Socialist dissidents were led by Natalio Berman Berman, who, born in
Russia in 1908, had become a Chilean citizen in 1929. Berman's political
influence was particularly strong in the Concepción region, where he
worked as a medical doctor in the early 1930s, and helped to found the
regional branch of the Socialist Party (PS). Elected as a national deputy
for the region in 1937, Berman had strong support in the coal mining
towns, and many local Socialists followed him into the Nonconformist
faction, including Carlos Rosales Gutierrez and Víctor Mora. In mid-1940,
the Socialist Party expelled Berman and his followers, who then formed

---

50. Document no. 1239, October 11, 1939, from Ramón Zañartu, Electoral Registry Director, to Concepción Intendant, FIC, vol. 2181, ANCh.

51. *Centenario de Coronel*. More specifically, the *revista* mentions the mayor's need "to
attend to his businesses outside the locality." It is likely, however, that ill health was also a
factor. After serving as mayor two consecutive terms, Hughes Cerna died "in the prime of
youth" in Concepción, on June 15, 1948. Sometime after his death, the city of Coronel honored Arturo Hughes Cerna by naming a local elementary school after him.

52. *El Obrero*, April 2, 1938, 6. On the contest for mayor, see Coronel Municipal Acts,
July 19, 1940, cited in Ossa, *Espiritualidad popular*, 111.

53. Coronel Municipal Acts, vol. 1929–40, July 20, 1938, 793–95, consulted at Coronel
Mayor's Office.

the Workers' Socialist Party (PST). Just a few months later, the PS did break with the Popular Front coalition, though its members remained in the cabinet. By 1944, about two-thirds of the PST's members, including Berman and Rosales, as well as César Godoy and Orlando Millas, had joined the Communist Party. Another third, including Víctor Mora, had returned to the PS.

As Aguirre Cerda weathered his first six months in office, local Popular Front forces in the coal towns moved to transform the institutions of power that had long favored the economic elite and right-wing parties. In May 1939, for example, the Popular Front committee of Penco, where the Lirquén coal mines were located, wrote to the intendant (*intendente*) of Concepción demanding removal of a local judge, Adrian Henry, who was a member of the Conservative Party. The Popular Front committee argued that it reflected poorly on the present government to have "an active agent of the Right" remain in such a position—"engaged as we are in purging the public administration of rightist elements."[54]

In the coming years, representatives of the Popular Front parties would come to win leadership positions throughout the coal mining region, radically shifting the balance of power at the local level. In 1941, for example, Communist Santos Medel would move from his beleaguered minority position on the Lota City Council into the more prominent and powerful position of mayor. Just as the first local Popular Front committee in Coronel had censured Schwager lackeys, so, too, did the new Lota mayor immediately take the Lota company to task for its hostile obstructionism: "I regret that the Mining Company has been discourteous toward this new Municipality: I have addressed myself to them in official correspondence, in accordance with the law, to request compliance with certain stipulations, but to date, these notes have not been answered in official form. The most we have achieved is, at times, a spoken reply on the part of subaltern employees."[55] Perhaps recalling the childhood nightmare of his father's beating, the new Communist mayor of Lota set the tone for a period of intense struggle against company control of the region—albeit struggle within the legalistic framework and tempered language of the day. Part II of *Mining for the Nation* explores the nature and outcomes of sociopolitical contests that took place in the coal mining zone during World War II.

54. Letter from Simón Pino B., President, and José Rivera R., Secretary, Popular Front of Penco, to Concepción Intendant, May 26, 1939, FIC, vol. 2184, ANCh.

55. *El Sur*, September 2, 1941, 9.

PART II

COLLABORATION AND CONFLICT

WORKERS CONTEND WITH THE COMPANIES AND
THE POPULAR FRONT GOVERNMENT, 1940–1942

By the early 1940s, the balance of power at the local level had shifted dramatically in favor of the Popular Front parties, especially the Communists, throughout the coal mining region. Communists won the mayoralty and city council seats not only in Lota, where Santos Medel was elected mayor, but also in Coronel, Curanilahue, Lebu, and other towns. From the first year of Pedro Aguirre Cerda's presidency, they began to sweep union elections as well. In May 1939, Communists won all five leadership positions in the Lota coal miners' union. Despite fierce opposition by the companies and competition from the Socialists, they would retain these positions in every annual election through 1947.

Similarly dramatic shifts in leadership occurred in the miners' unions of Coronel, Curanilahue, Colico, Lebu, and Plegarias, and in unions of metalworkers, sailors, port workers, and railway workers throughout the coal mining region. At the same time, the unions of the region began to more effectively coordinate their efforts across companies, localities, and occupations, with heightened integration of labor and community issues. As organized workers pressed the state to intervene on their behalf in industrial disputes, they were increasingly empowered to speak out about broader problems in the region and to raise national and even international political issues.

In the coal towns, unions took up with fervor not only wages and working conditions, but also living conditions, social and cultural life, and moral responsibility. Problems such as housing shortages, domestic violence, and alcohol abuse were of great concern to diverse sectors of society—from organized Communist workers to middle-class Methodists and even capitalist bosses. Popular Front politicians and government officials thus devoted considerable attention both to investigating such areas of public welfare and to proposing reforms. But even as they introduced new populist language and practices of inclusion, conciliation, and social reform, many of these same political actors mobilized state power in more traditional ways to exclude popular sectors from national economic and political life and to repress leftist labor and political leaders who promoted working-class interests. The Popular Front thus operated like a hydra whose two most prominent heads worked at cross-purposes.

Both facets of the Popular Front appeared in the government's multiple interventions in labor-management conflicts and community issues in the coal mining zone in the early 1940s. This chapter addresses the mixed content of a series of tripartite labor agreements reached in 1941 among organized workers, capitalists, and the state and the equally mixed recommendations of a 1941 report on the coal mining zone written by General Jorge Berguño Meneses at the behest of the nation's president. It shows how the government's response to "the coal problem," an oft-used phrase during the war years, consisted of two intertwined strands: traditional modes of control, on the one hand, and new promises that the state would address at least some of the workers' grievances, on the other. Workers and their leaders construed such promises as public affirmations of the justness of their positions. And, indeed, in both local and national arenas, labor and political leaders periodically achieved contracts, decrees, laws, and policies favorable to the workers, often highly so.

Thus, even though powerful sectors of society, including forces within the Popular Front itself, worked zealously to block or undermine the more profound reforms of the project, the organized popular sectors still experienced new space to voice their demands and aspirations. Campaign promises and subsequent agreements were repeatedly taken back, minimally fulfilled, or honored only after many delays, but the very fact that national politicians, including the head of state, were making such pledges served as public affirmation of the nonpartisan, just, and urgent nature of the coal miners' demands. Calling on the government to honor its progressive promises thus became a crucial battle strategy for workers and their leaders, as they linked local material issues with broader debates about social justice, democracy, and the industrial advance of the nation.

New Modes of State Conciliation:
From Dry Laws to Tripartite Agreements

Twice a month, long lines of anxious men and women formed in front of the Lota company payroll windows, amid swarms of vendors of all sorts. While wives tried to secure the miners' wages to maintain their households, bodega owners throughout town replenished their liquor stocks and prepared their establishments for long hours of drinking and gambling. Following these bacchanal nights of release from the drudgery of the mines, worker attendance dropped so significantly that the Monday after payday came to be called "San Lunes," or Saint Monday, a popular workers' "holiday" dating back to the Industrial Revolution in Europe. Since the birth of the coal mining towns in the mid-nineteenth century, alcohol abuse had become an endemic problem, and diverse actors in civil society voiced great concern about its consequences—from absenteeism to delinquency, domestic violence, and cirrhosis.

By the time the first Popular Front standard-bearer, Pedro Aguirre Cerda, donned the presidential sash, wartime concern over coal production had provoked an explosion of national debate about living and working conditions in the region and especially about the high incidence of alcoholism among coal miners. All of the diverse voices weighing in— Methodists, Catholics, Communists, mining capitalists, labor leaders, press editors, and government agents—agreed on the extent of the problem. Where they disagreed, sometimes fundamentally, was over what caused workers to abuse alcohol and how best to remedy the problem. According to one widespread view, the miners were driven to alcohol by the miserable conditions in which they lived and worked. In a 1941 report on the coal mining zone, further discussed in a section to come, Army General Jorge Berguño, put forward this view: "The miner, constantly malnourished, who works at a depth of hundreds of meters, where there is no life-giving air for his lungs to take in, returns out of breath to the surface and tries to recover, even if artificially, his sense of vitality. How to recover it? Only with alcohol. And so, this sad picture gets worse."[1]

Whereas Berguño put the blame on a general state of affairs, leftist labor and political leaders indicted the capitalists for exploiting the workers with callous disregard for their well-being. Going a step further, Communist labor leaders directly accused the coal companies of supplying

1. Berguño Report, as reprinted in El Sur, August 29, 1941, 8.

workers with alcohol to keep them submissive and compliant. This accusation was out of date and largely unfounded. Indeed, company bosses
constantly complained about the effects of drinking on workers' attendance and job performance. In their view, however, alcohol abuse was
not related to poor nutrition or debilitating work conditions, as both the
Communists and Berguño alleged. Rather, they saw the workers' excessive
drinking as a moral failing, encouraged by the climate of decadence and
indiscipline created by political agitators, especially the Communists.

Unable to reconcile these opposing views on the causes of alcohol
abuse, but pressed to intervene in the problem, President Aguirre Cerda
traveled to Lota and Coronel in November 1939. There, with the express
support of both workers and bosses, he declared the region a "semi-dry
zone." Henceforth, the sale and consumption of different types of alcohol
would be severely restricted. Enforcing the restrictions proved virtually
impossible, however, and complaints flooded in from diverse sectors of
society.[2] By March 1940, just months after the president's decree, the Second Congress of the National Miners' Federation (FNM) was one among
many voices calling for the coal region to be declared a "fully dry zone."[3]
When the Senate took up the issue a few months later, Liberal Party
leader Alvaro Santa María, a member of the CCIL's Board of Directors,
complained that the semi-dry zone decree had clearly not reduced alcohol
consumption in the coal towns. Virgilio Morales, a Democratic senator
from Lebu, went even further, claiming that wine consumption had actually increased from the previous year, as had public drunkenness and
delinquency.[4]

Concerns about drinking were integrally tied to debates about productivity. Thus, when the workers' collective contracts expired in early 1941,
alcohol consumption emerged as a prominent issue. Over the next several
months, representatives of the national government, the coal mining
companies, and different unions in the industry engaged in tough negotiations over diverse aspects of working and living conditions in the region.
On May 15, "by mutual agreement with the mine owners and the labor
unions," the Aguirre Cerda administration finally decreed that Lota and
Coronel be made fully dry zones, "prohibiting under heavy penalty the

2. *Boletín Minero* (December 1939): 1365–75; *El Obrero*, November 25, 1939, 1; Astorquiza
and Galleguillos V., *Cien años*, 137; *Frente Popular*, January 18, 1940, 4.
3. *El Chiflón*, June 1942, 36.
4. Senate Session, June 17, 1940, 478, 482, BCNCh.

manufacture, transportation, sale, or consumption of any alcoholic beverage whatsoever in these areas."[5]

This dry zone decree was one of many significant points of agreement reached that May, as company, union, and government representatives endeavored to resolve not only immediate wage disputes but also broader issues affecting coal production. Indeed, the May 1941 tripartite accords highlight the government's tendency in these years to operate well beyond passive mediation of labor-capital issues. Thus, for example, the government agreed to pay miners a 35-peso bonus for each ton of coal extracted over the average of the previous three months.[6] Because the state-owned railroad and public utilities were the largest consumers of Chilean coal, the promised bonus amounted to a peculiar type of subsidy: the buyer was now rebating the seller with the stipulation that the rebates flow directly to the workers.[7] Moreover, the state had become the major investor in a number of small and medium mines in the province of Arauco through the national development agency, CORFO, created in the aftermath of the devastating 1939 earthquake.

Even though the main objective of the May accords was to increase coal production, tellingly, most of its clauses dealt with living conditions in the mining towns. Progressive forces in the administration were convinced both that the miners' well-being was crucial to their productivity and that the coal companies would not invest sufficient resources to this end. The government thus promised to allocate 4.5 million pesos "for the improvement of the sanitary conditions of the coal mining establishments, housing, the installation of sports fields, cultural centers, technical and vocational schools, for the improvement of the nourishment and clothing of schoolchildren, and other ends described in the accord[s]."[8]

5. "New Wage Scale and Working Conditions in Chilean Coal Mines, 1941," *Monthly Labor Review* 53 (July 1941): 221–22, citing information from the commercial attaché at the U.S. Embassy.

6. *El Chiflón*, July 1942, 6, 8. See also *El Sur*, September 3, 1942, 7.

7. According to the U.S. Tariff Commission, the breakdown of Chilean coal consumption in 1938 was as follows: "railroad and steamship transportation accounted for 43 percent; public utilities, 20 percent; industrial plants (excluding mines and smelters), 18 percent; and domestic use, 11 percent." The report further explained that "the large power plants of the copper mines and smelters and the nitrate industry in northern Chile use imported crude oil exclusively, while the Braden Copper Co., south of Santiago, utilizes hydroelectric power. The use of coal by these large enterprises is confined principally to their railroads." U.S. Tariff Commission, *Mining*, 27.

8. *El Sur*, September 3, 1942, 7. Other sources indicate that the community improvement accord was signed in mid-June, not mid-May. See, for example, *El Siglo*, June 18, 1941, 4.

Such state-funded projects appealed to broad sectors of the electorate, from workers to municipal politicians to company shareholders, albeit for different reasons. They fit comfortably within the framework of social welfare policies promoted by President Aguirre Cerda, as he strove to fulfill his campaign slogans of "Bread, Roof, Overcoat!" and "To Govern Is to Educate!" In the specific context of the coal mining communities, these projects also represented an effort by ascendant leftist and centrist politicians to utilize state resources to compensate for private capital's failure to meet the basic needs of its workforce. In this sense, the Popular Front government's move beyond a neutral role of mediator stemmed from its incapacity, or reluctance, to fundamentally alter the social struc-ture. If it could sufficiently offset the devastating consequences of exces-sive profit taking, the Aguirre Cerda administration could avoid the radical measures required to make relations between labor and capital truly just and equal. Navigating between Scylla and Charybdis, the Popu-lar Front government also sought to avoid overt repression as a means of keeping the demands of organized workers in check.

Another key point of contention between the unions and the compa-nies in the early 1940s was over lines of authority and control in the pro-duction process. In mining operations, decisions made at the point of production always involved balancing maximum extraction with reason-able safety measures. The miners believed they knew as much as their supervisors, if not more, about work in the mines. And because it was their lives on the line, they had long demanded respect for their input on shop floor decisions. Workers also insisted that section and job assign-ments be based on qualifications and merit rather than politics, favorit-ism, or personal vendettas. In the labor-management agreements signed on May 17, 1941, however, the unions compromised greatly on these issues in return for a raise in the minimum daily wage to 15 pesos for most workers in the mines. "In return for wage concessions," the U.S. journal *Monthly Labor Review* reported, "the unions agree to discipline their mem-bers, to desist from interfering in any way with the orders issued by the working bosses, and to see to it that workers report for their shifts on time and in fit condition."[9]

Liberal Senator Hernán Videla Lira, president of the National Mining Society (Sociedad Nacional de Minería; SONAMI) as well as former gen-eral manager of and major shareholder in the Lota company, saw the accords in much the same way. "Sr. Videla believes that the agreements

9. "New Wage Scale," *Monthly Labor Review*, July 1941, 221–22.

reached with the workers have translated into considerable wage increases," the *Boletín Minero* explained, "and that, once a better understanding of discipline and the execution of the bosses' technical orders in the workplace are achieved, it will be possible to increase production in the large mines."[10] In the progressive climate of the Popular Front era, Videla Lira shrewdly refrained from criticizing the workers' demands or the government's intervention and instead focused on the central goal subscribed to by all the parties—increased coal production—while emphasizing the responsibility of the workers.

"To Stem the Flood of Popular Movements": Continuing Modes of State Persecution

The companies' drive to reassert their control over the production process was an indicator of how powerful the Communist unions had become.[11] Even as the Popular Front government increasingly intervened in the social and economic problems of the region—through the dry zone decree, the payment of production bonuses, and investment in community welfare and infrastructure, for example—it sought to prevent workers organized under Communist leadership from exercising the kind of power that would radically transform the status quo.

Shortly before the May 1941 accords were signed, President Aguirre Cerda commissioned Brigadier General Jorge Berguño Meneses to investigate declines in coal production. More specifically, Berguño was to assess the "extent of coercive activity" and the risk of a strike movement in the coal mining region.[12] His report would be submitted to the staunchly anti-Communist interior minister, Arturo Olavarría Bravo, who had

10. "Actas del Consejo General de la SONAMI, Sesión no. 993, el 15 de mayo de 1941," *Boletín Minero* (June 1941): 600. Hernán Videla Lira was president of the SONAMI from at least 1938 to 1948; he was also a Liberal senator for the Atacama-Coquimbo region, from 1941 to 1965. Hernán Videla Lira had close ties to the Lota company, serving as its general manager for several years, until 1928, when his brother, Guillermo, became vice manager and, in 1946, general manager. As of 1952, Hernán was still connected to the CCIL, both as a shareholder and as one of the company's "agents for the sale of coal." Astorquiza and Galleguillos V., *Cien años,* 149.

11. "To stem the flood of popular movements" is taken from Loveman and Lira, *Las ardientes cenizas,* 95.

12. On Berguño's commission, see *El Sur,* August 24, 1941, 7–8. Excerpts of the Berguño Report were published in *El Sur* over the following weeks, and in *El Mercurio* from July 25 to July 31.

joined Aguirre Cerda's cabinet in December 1940.[13] Olavarría Bravo's appointment reflected the government's "commitment to protect private property and to repress 'professional agitators.'"[14] His repression of a railroad workers' strike in May 1941, precisely when General Berguño was traveling to the coal mines, left "no room for doubt that the other side of the Popular Front coin was that of a dam designed to stem the flood of popular movements."[15]

The state's main keepers of this metaphoric dam were the local and regional officials of the Ministry of Labor, who shaped, reflected, and carried out changes in the government's position toward labor and capital. It was thus significant that, in June 1941, the Coronel departmental labor inspector, Adolfo López Brandt, accused the five outgoing officers of the Schwager miners' union—all Communists—of misusing union funds.[16] After several months of investigation, Coronel Criminal Court Judge Jorge Cerrutti ordered the arrest of four of the five officers, exonerating only the union president.[17]

The range of possibilities under "misuse of funds" was vast since Chilean labor law severely regulated both the collection and use of union dues and provided ample supervisory powers to government labor officials. "The annual budgets of unions must be approved by a government labor inspector," the U.S. Embassy labor attaché noted in a 1944 report, "and all expenditures of 2,000 pesos or more must be authorized by a labor inspector. No funds may be used for political or 'resistance' purposes, nor may contributions be made to the C.T.Ch., which is not legally recognized." Furthermore, funds paid to the unions by the companies, as required by hard-won profit-sharing laws, were particularly restricted and could only be spent under a budget approved by a special tripartite commission. In reality, such strict control over union dealings proved impossible to maintain, and most unions were able to send their dues to the

13. *El Sur*, July 11, 1941, 5. Olavarría Bravo left Aguirre Cerda's cabinet in October 1941, but he continued to play an active role in national politics. When President González Videla named Communist ministers in 1946, Olavarría Bravo reacted by founding the Chilean Anti-Communist Action League (Acción Chilena Anticomunista; AChA; see chapter 8).

14. Loveman and Lira, *Las ardientes cenizas*, 95.

15. Ibid. While the Ministry of the Interior did greatly influence the direction of government policy, Olavarría Bravo's reactionary orientation was somewhat offset by other members of the cabinet, including Democratic Labor Minister Pradenas Muñoz, Socialist Public Works Minister Oscar Schnake; and Socialist Health Minister Salvador Allende.

16. *El Sur*, July 3, 1941, 13. Before being sent to Coronel, López Brandt was a labor official in the nitrate mines. He may also have been a Socialist: in February 1943, Coronel's Socialist newspaper described him as "a functionary of recognized decency in the service of the workers." *La Trinchera*, February 1, 1943, 1. Both *El Siglo* and the Communist-led Coronel CTCh, on the other hand, constantly denounced him.

17. *El Sur*, August 28, 1941, 8, 9; *El Siglo*, August 28, 1941, 7.

Confederation of Chilean Workers (CTCh) and to industry-specific federations, such as the National Miners' Federation (FNM), on a regular basis. They were also able to build up moderate strike and solidarity funds. Such technical violations, though unseen or overlooked by the government, were no secret: anti-labor politicians and the conservative press made "frequent accusations . . . that [union] funds are being used for purposes prohibited by [law]."[18]

In the case of the detained Schwager leaders, Communist Deputy and Undersecretary of the CTCh Reinaldo Núñez Alvarez, a close ally of the coal miners, quickly traveled to Coronel to defend them, claiming that they were being harassed primarily for paying dues to the CTCh and its affiliated industrial federations.[19] Núñez was careful to condemn only particular individuals and not state intervention per se: "The fact that Labor Services seeks to exercise greater vigilance over the financial activities of the unions has been distorted and arbitrarily interpreted by some of the Labor Inspectors who, in this way, reveal their hatred of the organized working class." Then, situating the case in the broader context of political conflict, Núñez claimed that the current detention of union leaders "forms part of the plan organized by the enemies of the working class . . . who strive, by all possible means, to create a climate propitious for them to move against democratic liberties and against the government, in order to replace it with a Fascist dictatorship."[20] Among these enemies, he especially lambasted the Conservative representatives in Congress, claiming that it was they who led certain local and provincial officials down an errant path.

This strategy of creating space between administration policy and its local enactment often served the interests of the government. Labor inspectors at times became henchmen enforcing unpopular policies, from which the president and labor minister could distance themselves. As seen here, the strategy could also be used by working-class spokesmen to criticize state actions without directly antagonizing the government, from which organized labor still sought concessions in return for its loyalty.[21] Thus, according to Núñez's crafty argument, by defending their

18. Labor Attaché Report, 9/15–10/15, 1944, 11, USNA, RG 59. On union fund regulations, see also Angell, *Politics*, 62.

19. Communist Deputy Delgado Espinoza made the same allegation in Congress: because workers paid dues to the CTCh and the FNM voluntarily, he said, their contributions were not illegal. "Situación de la industria carbonífera," Chamber of Deputies Session, August 27, 1941, 2512, BCNCh.

20. Reinaldo Núñez, statement on arrest of Schwager union leaders, *El Sur*, August 28, 1941, 8.

21. The argument that organized labor sought to avoid reproach from the national government at this time is complicated by a letter from the Regional Union of Coal Mining

elected Communist officials and labor federations, union members were actually protecting President Aguirre Cerda from treacherous right-wing forces making headway within his own governing apparatus. Núñez made this link even more explicit when he proclaimed that "in defense of the interests of the unions we represent . . . we will fight with the same firmness as we did on the 25th of October 1938," referring to the day Aguirre Cerda was elected president, with Communist and CTCh support.[22] Reaffirming their resolve, coordination, and sense of power, nine unions in the coal mining region decided jointly to continue sending dues to the CTCh, agreeing that "if one of the unions or leaders were threatened, the other coal industry unions, from Lirquén to Lebu, would respond decidedly."[23]

Another union *was* soon threatened, when the communal labor inspector (ICT) for Lota scrutinized the account books of the miners' union there. Although protests erupted against both the Lota and Coronel labor officials, a decisive regional response failed to materialize. In Lota, each different section and mine shaft sent commissions of five workers to the ICT to demand the return of the union books. When this tactic proved unsuccessful, on August 26, about three hundred people gathered in the street outside the ICT's office in Lota Bajo, which turned out to be closed since the inspector was in Concepción. The group took advantage of the situation to hold a meeting. While workers were making impromptu speeches, the police arrived under the command of Lieutenant Saa Sánchez, who "proceeded to peacefully dissolve the gathering." After the police left the scene, part of the crowd reassembled in front of the office, "believing that the [inspector] was hiding inside," but soon dispersed voluntarily.[24] In the pattern of appealing directly to national government officials, the Lota CTCh quickly sent a telegram to the interior minister, "energetically protesting the crushing of democratic liberties" since the subdelegate of the Concepción Intendancy had denied workers the right to meet in the public plaza. The telegram called on the government to

---

Syndicates (URSC) to CTCh Secretary-General Bernardo Ibáñez, which blamed the director general of labor for ordering inspectors in the coal towns to prohibit contributions to the CTCh. *El Sur*, August 29, 1941, 7.

22. Reinaldo Núñez, statement on arrest of Schwager union leaders, *El Sur*, August 28, 1941, 8.

23. URSC letter to Bernardo Ibáñez, as reprinted in *El Sur*, August 29, 1941, 7.

24. *El Sur*, August 30, 1941, n.p., and August 28, 1941, 8; *El Siglo*, August 27, 1941, 8. A year later, on October 4, Lieutenant Saa Sánchez would again be called in to break up a public gathering, at which time three workers would be killed and dozens seriously injured. See chapter 5.

comply with the Popular Front electoral program and to respect the hard-won victories of the working class.[25] In the case of the Lota union, the accounts seem to have been in proper order: none of the leaders was charged with misuse of funds.

General Berguño Denounces the "Unchecked Dictatorship" of Communist Unions

It was in the context of this growing tension between the unions and the government that the Berguño Report was prepared.[26] Most observers expected the findings to serve the interests of those seeking to curb the power of labor and to destroy the Communist Party. On June 29, 1941, one week after Soviet Union declared war on Germany, Lota miners gathered for a meeting, at which Union President Lorenzo Gallardo Gallardo noted the workers' near-palpable apprehension about the forthcoming report. Union Treasurer Juan Lorenzo Córdova added, "We must not let down our guard since it is known that the coal mining zone is liable to be militarized by the Supreme Government, an occurrence [we] could not accept since under such a measure [we] would be obliged to work by force."[27] At the same meeting, the head of the Lota CTCh, Pablo Labraña, who was "esteemed as the greatest leader of the workers," also referred to the possible militarization of the mines, noting that this had already happened in the United States.[28]

When excerpts were finally published in the national press in July and August, the Berguño Report prompted heated debate in the coal mining region, the Congress, and union halls and political party offices throughout the country.[29] The report began by declaring that "today the production of coal is as necessary to the national economy as air is to life."[30] The

25. Telegram from Deputy Interior Minister to Concepción Intendant, August 28, 1942, FIC, vol. 2255, ANCh.

26. The phrase "unchecked dictatorship" is taken from the Berguño Report, as quoted by Socialist Deputy Bernardo Ibáñez, Chamber of Deputies Session, August 6, 1941, 1659, BCNCh.

27. Juan Lorenzo Córdova, as quoted in El Sur, July 3, 1941, 13.

28. A few months later, Pablo Labraña was dead. News reports at the time said he committed suicide after killing a young girl with whom he was allegedly having an affair. Many people I interviewed in Lota, however, claimed that the police assassinated Labraña just outside the union office. El Sur, September 24, 1941, 11, September 25, 1941, 11, and September 27, 1941, n.p.; interviews with Fresia Vidal Ojarse (September 15, 1997), Omar Sanhueza Segunda (September 10 and October 13, 1997), and Emelina Araneda.

29. See, for example, Chamber of Deputies Sessions, July 29, 1941, 1317–58, July 30 1941, 1525–38, August 6, 1941, 1653–64, and August 11, 1941, 1773–1808, BCNCh.

30. Berguño Report, as reprinted in El Sur, August 24, 1941, 7–8.

ensuing two hundred and fifty pages covered a wide range of topics, from technical and human factors in the production process to wages, living and working conditions, unions, and politics. The report discussed quality of life issues, many of which had also been raised in the May accords—housing, education, health and safety, athletic and cultural facilities—in each of the coal mining communities.

As a surprise to many readers, Berguño criticized a number of company practices and policies about which workers had long complained. By taking the workers' position on certain issues, Berguño demonstrated his independence and enhanced the credibility of the overarching anti-Communist message of his report.[31] Thus he deplored the "extremely unhygienic" collective latrines in the coal towns and deemed worker housing inadequate in both quality and quantity, noting that "it is regrettable to us to be in disagreement with the Compan[ies] on this subject since, with rare exceptions, one cannot speak of 'comfort' in the workers' homes, due to overcrowding."[32] Berguño also decried the state of medical care, noting the insufficiency of home visits by doctors or nurses in Lota and Coronel and the lack of any hospital facility within a reasonable distance from the Plegarias and Curanilahue mines. Where the report affirmed the workers' position on such grievances, they would be able to invoke it to their advantage in future battles.

Berguño also censured the companies for turning their stores and restaurants over to private concessionaires, who assured themselves of "appreciable profit margins" by selling well above the prices established by the General Commissariat of Subsistence and Prices.[33] Moreover, the concessionaires refused to sell on credit, which forced workers to borrow against their future paychecks at high interest rates in order buy basic goods for their families.[34] Historically, the companies themselves had monopolized the sale of goods to their workers, so as to enmesh them in debt or recoup a portion of the wages paid out. But, with the abolition of company scrip and the passage of labor laws in the 1920s, this practice

31. Both General Berguño and the report's backers stressed the "objectivity" of the investigation. Berguño even claimed that he was "incognito" during much of his visit to the coal mining zone, though it is not clear how this would have been possible since the brigadier general's visit was widely publicized. El Sur, August 24, 1941, 7–8.

32. Berguño Report, as reprinted in El Sur, September 7, 1941, 7–8.

33. Created during the brief Socialist Republic of 1932, the General Commissariat of Subsistence and Prices (Comisariat General de Subsistencia y Precios) was charged with regulating the production, distribution, and pricing of basic consumer goods; it remained in service until the 1970s. Loveman, Chile, 203. See also chapter 8.

34. El Sur, September 7, 1941, 7–8.

became both illegal and untenable from a public relations perspective. As the government increased its regulation of the prices of basic goods, the companies found it more profitable, and politically more expedient, to contract out the provisioning of their workforces.

When the report moved from living conditions in the community to issues of workplace discipline and organization—the heart of company control of the coal industry—its criticisms became fewer and more equivocal, though with notable exceptions. In no uncertain terms, Berguño condemned the company practice of beginning a miner's eight-hour work shift only when the miner reached the coal face to which he was assigned. As the report explained, "If you consider that [the miners] must cover 2 or 3 (at times up to 4) kilometers underground, they must leave their homes 1½ or 2 hours early."[35] Added to this was the problem of transportation from the workers' homes to the mine shafts, even before the additional underground travel, most of which was on foot.[36] Berguño recommended that a system of four six-hour shifts replace the current system of three eight-hour ones. He further recommended that shift assignments be rotated so that no miners would work exclusively at night "since it is not the same sleeping by day as by night, especially in houses with an excessive number of inhabitants." Then, in his most direct criticism of company methods of social control, Berguño argued that "the fact that an unexcused absence constitutes sufficient cause for the firing of an employee implies an excessively strict criterion, in the human sense of things." He recommended that the companies use the more reasonable Army system for classifying and penalizing absences.[37]

These points of "regrettable disagreement" with the coal company executives undermined their claim to be progressive capitalists who provided humanitarian living and working conditions for their workers. Yet, notwithstanding its criticisms of company policies, the crux of the Berguño Report was its unequivocal condemnation of the advances made by

35. Ibid.
36. As laid out in company statutes, the first shift worked from 7 A.M. to 3 P.M., the second from 3 P.M. to 11 P.M., and the third from 11 P.M. to 7 A.M. Due to lack of transportation between the coal faces and the surface, however, the actual time spent underground per shift was not the stipulated eight hours—a hard-won victory of the miners' 1920 strike—but closer to ten or eleven hours. This did not include the time workers spent dressing and preparing their equipment on the surface before and after their shifts. Nor did it include the time workers spent traveling between their homes and the mines, in most cases, on foot. Not until the 1960 strike did the workers win "lamp-to-lamp" work shifts, meaning that their eight hours began when they first entered the mine shaft, rather than when they reached their assigned coal face or section. El Sur, August 29, 1941, 7–8; and interviews with Omar Sanhueza Segunda (September 10 and October 13, 1997).
37. Berguño Report, as reprinted in El Sur, September 7, 1941, 7–8.

the Communists in organizing and mobilizing the coal workers.[38] "Political forces external to the region," the general declared, were inciting "labor indiscipline," which he deemed the number-one barrier to increased coal production. The hold of the Communist-controlled unions over the workers created a "climate [that] was becoming more suffocating [for production] each day," especially with "the multiplication of public gatherings [and] an appreciable increase in absenteeism at work."

Grievances about workplace and community problems had to be taken seriously, Berguño believed, principally because they could be so easily manipulated by the Communists to increase worker militancy for political ends.

In many memoranda prepared by unions throughout the region, General Berguño saw "unusual uniformity," which "indicated to me . . . constant communication between the respective union leaderships." The growing coordination of the regional labor movement, however, was not a positive development in Berguño's view, but rather a threat to existing power relations. Discussing the 1941 contract negotiations, the general observed with alarm that "all the [working] masses of the coal mining zone were . . . given over, in a single bundle, to the union organizations, which maintained a perfect bond of unity and understanding among themselves." The coal miners, he warned, played a strategic role in pulling together other unions in the region.[39]

Berguño levied his sharpest attack against the section delegates, who "unconditionally served the Communist Party" while establishing themselves as a parallel line of control to company supervisors at all points in the production process, and even in the community.[40] These agitators,

38. An official Army history published in 1985, at the height of the Pinochet regime, highlighted the 1941 Berguño Report. The caption under a full-page photo of Berguño proclaims him a hero, who had "unmasked the action of Marxism against the most profound values of the Nation [Patria]." According to this Army history, Berguño's investigation had been necessary because "the coal sector was strategic for the country's economy and for national security. It provided the principal source of energy and constituted the basis for all national development and for transport. Precisely because of this strategic importance, the Communist Party fixed upon the unions of the coalfields as one of the objects of its control . . . a virtual duplication of command was created between the company, on one hand, and the union leaders and delegates, on the other. . . . [The] notorious drop in production could not be attributed to technical reasons in the extractive process since the companies had been making investments that should have increased it." Estado Mayor General del Ejército de Chile, Historia, 36–37.

39. Berguño Report, as reprinted in El Sur, August 24, 1941, 7–8.

40. Contention over control of production was as old as the unions themselves, and respect for mine floor delegates had been one of the coal miners' key demands in the strikes of the early 1920s. In the Popular Front era, industry spokesmen continually denounced the unions for maintaining a parallel structure of authority in the mines, especially after the Communists gained control of the unions in the mid-1930s. For a moderate version of this

according to Berguño, were "delegates in a foreign house," who took it upon themselves to investigate "the slightest orders of the foremen and engineers, and even to reach agreements directly with them when it [came] to applying disciplinary measures to a worker." Thus, Berguño claimed, "when a worker is summoned [by his boss] on the job, he goes immediately to protest to his 'delegate,' who will quickly move in his defense, whether or not the case is just." In this way, the section delegates acted "as a brake on the oversight of the foremen and engineers since their intervention neutralizes or undermines the orders of the latter." Moreover, Berguño charged, the delegates were not purely or primarily motivated by concerns about production and safety, but, "named by the unions, that is to say, by the Communist Party," they pursued "intransigent and passionate ideological activity." Promoting a revolutionary Communist agenda, they "periodically force[d] the workers to attend political meetings, to the detriment of the number of hours worked."[41]

Berguño's anti-Communist language echoed that of other government officials, including Concepcion Intendant Desiderio González and Director General of Labor Mariano Bustos Lagos, who had long been denounced by the coal unions for favoring the bosses (see below).[42] Berguño relied heavily on information from these officials, especially in his discussion of violence meted out in the depths of the mines against workers who dissented from the "acting union regime." As recounted to him by the intendant, such violence ranged from mild threats to deadly retribution, often made to look like common work accidents to avoid criminal charges. "Despite [their] apparent form," Berguño wrote, "such misfortunes almost always befell elements known as 'nonconformists' or 'traitors to the cause.'"[43]

Two instances of political violence cited by Berguño also speak to the use of government spies inside the mines. In the first, an undercover agent employed by the intendant of Concepción took a job with the Lota company in order to report on the workers' activities. When the agent was run over by a coal car that had jumped the tracks—a quite common occurrence in the mines—both the intendant and General Berguño alleged that the Communists had killed him. The second instance involved

charge, see the 1936 report by coal mining engineer Ricardo Fenner, "Análisis de los factores."

41. Berguño Report, as quoted by Conservative Deputy Sergio Fernández Larraín in El problema del carbón, 10.

42. See, for example, Letter to Concepción Intendant from Regional CTCh Leaders, April 3, 1939, FIC, vol. 2184, ANCh.

43. Berguño Report, as reprinted in El Sur, August 26, 1941, 11.

the death of a national investigations agent who was also working under-cover in the mines. Disputing Berguño's claim that the agent was assassi-nated, Communist Deputy Uribe said that he had committed suicide after a drinking spree, noting that the courts had confirmed this account.[44]

Berguño also cited a well-known instance of violence perpetrated against a Schwager miner, Homero Madrigal Miranda, who belonged to the Nonconformist faction of the Socialist Party. While fighting against Communist control of the union, Madrigal Miranda stood up at a general assembly in August 1940 to denounce the leadership for mismanagement of funds.[45] When the meeting was over, a group of workers surrounded him, hitting him on the head and stabbing him in the stomach and legs. Madrigal survived the attack, and the police arrested several Communist workers for the crime.[46] The assault reflected the strong animosity felt by Communist loyalists toward those who sought to challenge the party's hold in the region—though few dared to do so quite as openly as Madri-gal. The incident in the Schwager union was certainly not the only case of politically inspired local brawling, but such spontaneous outbursts did not reflect an orchestrated campaign of violence, as Berguño asserted.

Right-wing political and economic actors hailed the Berguño Report as a paragon of "fidelity, independence, and honor" and as "entirely em-pirical," without "a single assertion in it that was not irrefutably docu-mented." After thus exalting Berguño's credibility, Conservative Deputy Sergio Fernández Larraín insisted that "even read superficially, [the re-port] leaves a clear and precise impression on us: The Communist Party dominates the coal mining zone in a totalitarian fashion, through the union organizations, spreading a climate of war, using all means, includ-ing political terrorism."[47]

Police agents in the field supported these allegations. Shortly after re-lease of Berguño's findings, for example, a police colonel in Curanilahue reported on a speech made by Communist Deputy for Arauco José Cruz Delgado Espinoza at a local union assembly. Echoing language used by Berguño and his right-wing allies, the police colonel claimed that Deputy

44. Ibid.; and Berguño Report as quoted by Damián Uribe Cárdenas, Chamber of Depu-ties Session, July 29, 1941, 1353, BCNCh.

45. Telegram no. 116, from Concepción Intendant to Interior Minister, August 6, 1940, FIC, vol. 2212, ANCh.

46. Telegram no. 709, from Interior Minister to Concepción Intendant, August 6, 1940, FIC, vol. 2212, ANCh; Chamber of Deputies Session, August 7, 1940, 1874, BCNCh; Fernández Larraín, El problema del carbón, 12, citing the Berguño Report; Ossa, Espiritualidad popular, 114, citing Coronel Municipal Acts, August 21, 1940.

47. Fernández Larraín, El problema del carbón, 6.

Delgado had exhorted the workers "to counteract the report," calling on the unions and the party to

> keep ironclad unity in the ranks, maintaining the people's intense revolutionary spirit at all times, staying ever alert to defend their threatened rights, with arms if necessary, which is why the organization and training of the people's militias should not be neglected for any reason. In this sense, I recommend to the Communist delegates inside the mines that they maintain close contact with their people and with the leadership, and also that they keep a close watch on suspicious elements, to avoid any attempt at betrayal and to give them what they deserve.[48]

With the Communists vehemently denying Berguño's charge that they engaged in acts of political violence, it is unlikely that one of their top national politicians—himself from the coal mining zone—would have called the workers to arms at a public rally attended by police agents and journalists. It is more likely that Delgado had "referred to [General Berguño] in harsh and deprecating words," as the police colonel also noted, "adding that his entire report was the product of false data and information provided by the administrators of the interested mining companies." These were the true "reactionary forces," Delgado claimed, who had "induced" General Berguño "to slander the working masses."[49] The First Congress of the Regional Union of Coal Mining Syndicates (Unión Regional de Sindicatos Carboníferos; URSC) went a step further, publicly condemning Berguño for having drafted "a Fascist report . . . lacking truth and favoring the companies."[50]

The Berguño Report also prompted heated debate in Congress, where one of the Communists' main strategies was to counter its claims by providing alternative assessments of the same issues. Communist Senator Elías Lafertte, for example, made a long speech on working conditions in the mines in which he refuted the assertion, made in the annual stockholder reports of both the Lota and Schwager companies, that "the coal shortage is due to the laziness of the workers, who refuse to work; to the vice of alcoholism that has preyed upon them; to the 'pernicious' influence

---

48. Document no. 11, August 11, 1941, from Arauco Carabineros Prefect to Arauco Intendant, FMI, vol. 10788, ARNAD.

49. Ibid.

50. First Congress of the Regional Union of Coal Mining Syndicates (URSC), September 1941, as quoted in *El Sur*, October 16, 1941, 10.

of the union delegates inside the mine; and to other factors for which the workers always turn out to be responsible." Even though the Communists had discredited the Berguño Report as based on false information, Lafertte strategically invoked it throughout his speech, noting that its recommendations for improvements in the coal miners' living and working conditions seemed to be "already forgotten." To bolster his own account of the appalling conditions in the mines, Lafertte would proclaim that, as "General Berguño himself . . . says, word for word," and then quote at length from the report.[51]

Union, Company, and State Maneuvers in the Wake of the Berguño Report

Debates among Santiago policy makers about coal mining problems took place against the backdrop of heightened tension in the mines themselves. On September 9, the same day Elías Lafertte spoke on the Senate floor, a violent altercation broke out between foremen and workers in the depths of the Pique Alberto mine shaft in Lota. This "riot" or "uprising," as it was described in company documents, occurred during the change from the second to the third work shift, when several people, listed by the company as "general delegates of the union," blocked a second-shift foreman from leaving the mine. According to the company account, one third-shift driller punched a foreman named Ramírez in the face, while another hit him from behind. Several other foremen were also attacked.[52]

The clash in the Pique Alberto was likely related to indignation stirred up the Berguño Report: workers felt the need to defend themselves against what they saw as false accusations and continued injustices. Such violent altercations, however, were not part of the labor strategy of the Communist Party. Keeping a large force of cadres in a state of readiness for planned collective actions, such as work stoppages or marches, would enhance the power of the workers' representatives in legal and institutional proceedings. Outbursts of violence by individuals or small groups of workers, on the other hand, forced the delegates into a difficult dilemma: if they did not back the workers, the delegates

51. Elías Lafertte, "Condiciones del trabajo en las minas de carbón," Senate Session, September 9, 1942, pp. 1972, 1973, 1976, BCNCh.
52. "Nomina de los obreros en——[?] el motín del día 9 de septiembre de 1941——[?] en el——[?] tercer turno." This is a single loose page found in José O. Aravena Muñoz, Prontuario no. 689, CCIL personnel files, consulted at ENACAR, Lota Alto. The dashes and question marks indicate illegible portions of the original.

would lose their standing, but, if they did back them, they would fuel the violent conflict between labor and management and lend credence to right-wing charges that union delegates promoted obstructionism, sabotage, and delinquency.

In the case of the Pique Alberto altercation, the Lota company fired seven of the twelve workers named as the principal perpetrators of the assault, including all five known to be union delegates or leaders. Shortly after the firings, on September 22, Director General of the Carabineros Oscar Reeves Leiva submitted a report on the incident, in which he stressed that "a marked discontent among the working masses of the coal mining zone" had resulted in "confrontations with . . . the Coal Mining Company and strike threats." "This turmoil," according to the director general, "is due to the workers' desire to get the Company to introduce improvements in actual working conditions. . . . The small disputes provoked by this situation occur on a daily basis, and are aggravated by the Company's intransigent refusal to look for a solution. This becomes a permanent theme for the workers' orators and agitators, who take advantage of the situation and add fuel to the prevailing discontent."[53] Directly contradicting the thrust of the Berguño Report, Director General Reeves placed underlying responsibility for the confrontations on the company, rather than on union delegates or the Communist Party.

As the director general delved further into the incidents in Lota, he implicitly accused the company of provocation. He noted that CTCh leader Bernardo Ibáñez Aguila had intervened in the case, trying to convince the company not to fire the workers, but "instead to punish them for their error by transferring them to a different work section or mine shaft." Much to Reeves's frustration, the company refused these appeals and proclaimed, through its administrator, that it "would not back down, even if this were to provoke a strike."[54] As General Berguño had done in his own report, Reeves conveyed his irritation with company officials, whose refusal to compromise made it more difficult for the government to keep the peace and maintain law and order.

These indictments of the company were coming from the chief of the national police, a man who was far from soft on labor. Indeed, it was Reeves who had executed Interior Minister Olavarría Bravo's harsh program against militant workers, which, in the countryside, he described

53. Providencia Confidencial no. 92, October 4, 1941, from Carabineros Director General to Interior Minister, FMI, vol. 10456, ARNAD.
54. Ibid.

as "the final judgment."[55] Reeves's report had no effect on the Lota company's position, however, and, several months later, the miners voted to denounce the handling of the Pique Alberto incident. After exhausting other legal and political avenues, on December 15, the miners sent an ambiguously worded ultimatum both to the company and to a number of government officials. They insisted that the fired workers be rehired within five days, but refrained from using the word "strike."[56]

During contract talks in these same months, by contrast, labor leaders repeatedly used the word "strike" as an imminent threat. The different language used in each of these situations reflected the unions' awareness of the distinction the public drew between legal and illegal strikes, with the latter to be avoided whenever possible. The unions were engaged in a delicate balancing act: while trying to push the companies to get what they needed, they could not push so hard as to lose legitimacy in the public eye and thereby lose their chance for favorable government intervention. A legal strike over a contract petition, which by definition had been sanctioned by government labor authorities, would be far easier to defend as part of the workers' collaboration with national development than a strike on behalf of workers who had violently attacked their supervisors.[57]

The labor-management talks under way at the time were exceptional since contracts had been signed back in August and September. The companies had failed to comply with many stipulations of those agreements, however, and the workers were also raising other issues, which the agreements had not covered. In November 1941, the Schwager miners' union submitted "a partial contract petition," which, though it did not explicitly refer to wages, raised issues such as family allowances, fines and pay docking, the calculation of coal loads, safety helmets and waterproof clothing, and rules for missed work, especially due to military service.[58] Drawing where possible on recommendations made in the Berguño Report, the petition also demanded improvements in housing, collective washing areas, and other community facilities.

55. On repression of rural labor movements and Director General Reeves Leiva's role in it, see Olavarría Bravo, *Chile entre dos Alessandri*, 1:452–53. See also discussions in Loveman, *Chile*, 212, and *Struggle*, 163; and Loveman and Lira, *Las ardientes cenizas*, 96–97.

56. Circular letter from Industrial Union of Lota Miners to CCIL Administrator, Lota Labor Inspector, Coronel Departmental Governor, Concepción Provincial Labor Inspector, Concepción Intendant, and CTCh National Directorate, "Solicitamos reincorporación de los 7 obreros despedidos Sec. 'P[ique] Alberto,'" December 15, 1941, FIC, vol. 2238, ANCh.

57. Communist labor leaders would stress the legality of the coal miners' strike of October 1947 (see chapter 8).

58. *El Chiflón*, June 1942, 26. Chilean labor law required companies to pay allowances for their employees' family members, thus raising the overall wage bill.

Touching on a contentious national issue, the petition also questioned the Schwager company's right to control the lives of workers and other community residents by virtue of its extensive ownership of urban property. Effective state jurisdiction over its citizens in a democratic republic was being challenged by the company's de facto local authority. The miners' petition demanded therefore that the Schwager company "open the gates to provide access to the Puchoco and Colonia neighborhoods [of Coronel]." Otherwise, they argued, the company was illegally blocking the free movement of citizens through their own community. Also in a bid for greater control over their jobs and lives, the workers again insisted on special rights for section delegates: they should be allowed to leave their work areas when necessary to handle problems elsewhere and should enjoy immunity from unwarranted suspensions and undesired transfers.[59] Far from making concessions on these points, both the Schwager company and the CCIL quickly initiated a wave of reprisals, including layoffs, fines, suspensions, and section and shift transfers. The newly elected Schwager union treasurer was suspended, for example, for allegedly attacking a mine foreman, and at least three other workers were arrested by the police on charges of impeding the freedom to work.[60]

Local judges were complicit in the companies' campaigns against their workers, at least in the eyes of coal miners and other community residents. Singled out as targets for special indignation were Judge Jorge Cerruti, who served as both Labor and Criminal Court judge for Lota and Coronel and had convicted the Schwager union leaders for misuse of funds just a few months earlier, and his secretary, Reinalda Pino.[61] The miners were so indignant that they sent a letter directly to the acting head of state, Vice President Jerónimo Méndez Arancibia, demanding Cerrutti's removal.[62] As for the judge's secretary, "with her despotic and haughty temperament," they claimed, Señorita Pino "abuses everyone who comes to the court with threats and shouting." Indeed, "the residents of the [coal mining] zone dread going to this court because of their fear of this

59. Unnumbered document, November 3, 1941, "Da cuenta de asamblea extraordinaria del Sindicato Obrero de Schwager y pliego de peticiones aprobados," FMI, vol. 10456, ARNAD.

60. El Chiflón, June 1942, 26. These Schwager workers were still in jail as of June 1942.

61. El Chiflón, June 1942, 26. Back in early 1940, however, the Concepción-based Communist newspaper Frente Popular had described Cerrutti as "a distinguished magistrate . . . a correct and efficient authority, [who] is loved and respected in all union, political, and social circles." Frente Popular, January 20, 1940, 4.

62. Aguirre Cerda temporarily stepped down in October 1941 due to rapidly failing health; according to the 1925 Chilean Constitution, Interior Minister Méndez Arancibia automatically became vice president and acting president.

secretary." In the same letter, the miners also complained about hostile elements within the local police force.[63] Thus, in the workers' view, the companies' arbitrary actions and their refusal to fairly negotiate contract petitions combined with the apparent complicity of certain state representatives to create a climate of deepening conflict in the closing months of 1941.

The Death of President Aguirre Cerda and the Miners' Conditional Support of His Successor

Precisely at this most unpropitious time, on November 25, 1941, President Pedro Aguirre Cerda ("don Tinto"), the unlikely champion of the Popular Front, died of tuberculosis. Two weeks later, while Chilean political parties were wrangling over Aguirre Cerda's successor, the Japanese bombed Pearl Harbor, and on December 8, the United States of America entered World War II. Less than a month later, twenty-six countries signed the Declaration of the United Nations, by virtue of which their governments would adhere to the principles of the Atlantic Charter and would commit their military and economic resources to the Allied cause. These international developments strongly informed electoral politics in Chile at both local and national levels. "Probably more than any other campaign in Chilean history," John Stevenson observes, the 1942 presidential elections "emphasized foreign affairs."[64]

In the Radical Party primary, held in mid-December, the staunchly anti-Communist Juan Antonio Ríos Morales had defeated the party's left-wing leader, Gabriel González Videla, in a vote "so close that it had to be decided by the party's electoral tribunal."[65] In the wake of the primary, Socialists backed their own candidate, Oscar Schnake Vergara, while the Communists tried "to persuade González Videla to reject the decision of

---

63. Letter from Schwager Miners' Union to Vice President Méndez Arancibia, as reprinted in El Siglo, January 2, 1942, 6, and January 4, 1942, 10.

64. Stevenson, Chilean Popular Front, 119.

65. Ibid. 118, citing El Mercurio, December 18, 1941, 23. According to Stevenson, the nationwide vote was 14,953 to 14,222. In the coal mining region, the department of Coronel, which included the towns of Lota and Coronel, gave 227 votes to Ríos Morales and 153 to González Videla. In the province of Concepción, Ríos Morales received 1,661 votes, González Videla 1,048, and Florencio Duran Bernales 69. Telegrams no. 115, from Coronal Departmental Governor, and no. 347, from Concepción Intendant, both to Interior Minister, [December 1941], FMI, vol. 10456, ARNAD.

the Radical primary and run as an independent candidate."[66] Rallies were held around the country, and especially in Communist strongholds such as the coal mining region, workers enthusiastically endorsed González Videla, calling for "the withdrawal of Ríos and Schnake" and "the designation of a single anti-Fascist candidate."[67]

In this political context, the coal mining companies began to warn that an illegal strike was imminent, and carabineros in the region were put on alert. In January 1942, top CCIL administrator Isidro Wilson informed the Lota chief of police that the miners' union had held a secret meeting on January 2 to plan a general strike for the next day in both Lota and Coronel, a strike that he thought was only partly related to contract disputes. "Above all," Wilson claimed, the union's actions were "intended to pressure the political parties to ensure the selection of a single candidate acceptable to the Communist Party for the upcoming presidential elections." Section delegates, he said, were inciting the workers to "prepare for an indefinite strike . . . according to instructions they have received from Communist Party leaders in Santiago." He added that workers were being ordered to accumulate weapons, including unused explosives from inside the mines.

Wilson's statement was replete with dubious allegations. Though dynamite was frequently stolen from the mines, it had never been used for acts of terror or sabotage, as he implied. Even Judge Cerrutti and CCIL Welfare Chief Astorquiza had observed that the economics of survival, not politics, motivated such thefts.[68] Moreover, it is unlikely that the Communists would have thought an illegal strike or revolt in the coal mines was a smart way to convince a centrist politician to run as their presidential candidate. Nonetheless, Wilson sought to spread fears of an uprising of Communist workers, primarily to influence the outcome of internal disputes in the Radical Party—making it more difficult for the party's left wing to gain ground. On Wilson's advice, the carabineros of

66. Stevenson, *Chilean Popular Front*, 118.
67. *El Siglo*, January 2, 1942, 6; see also *El Siglo*, January 14, 1942, 3.
68. In November 1936, police carried out surprise inspections at mine exits, arresting eighteen workers at Lota and nineteen at Schwager for theft of explosives. Judge Cerrutti, who tried the cases, agreed with CCIL Welfare Chief Astorquiza that "these explosives were stolen for commercial ends and not for use in any revolutionary plot." Providencia Confidencial no. 430, December 10, 1936, from National Director of Investigations, Identification, and Passports to Interior Minister; see also Providencia Confidencial no. 530, November 13, 1936, and no. 534, November 14, 1936, both from Carabineros Director General to Interior Minister, all in FMI, vol. 9250, ARNAD.

the Lota and Coronel precincts were placed on barracks alert, ready to move at any moment. The police also intensified their watch over essential infrastructure in the region, including mines, electrical plants, water pipelines, dock facilities, and railroads.[69]

No general strike took place on January 3, as Wilson had warned, but the miners did continue to appeal for favorable government intervention. On that very day in Santiago, the president of the Lota union, Juan Lorenzo Córdova Beltrán, presented Labor Minister Juan Pradenas Muñoz with a memorandum containing the workers' principal demands. First and foremost, they called for the reinstatement of the seven workers who had been fired in September for the clash in the Pique Alberto. Second, they called for automatic payroll deductions for special contributions agreed to in union assemblies, such as money for the wartime groups "Wings for Chile" and "Aid to Democracies," as well as contributions to the Confederation of Chilean Workers (CTCh). The memorandum also insisted that company administrators and section foremen fully recognize the rights of union delegates "as a means of generating harmony and facilitating the resolution of small difficulties." Finally, the government was called on to fulfill the promises it made in the May 1941 agreements.[70]

After presenting their memorandum to officials in Santiago, the union leaders returned to Lota and held a public rally to discuss their trip. Police forces quickly arrived, however, and arrested several labor and political leaders, including visiting Deputy Damián Uribe and Lota Mayor Santos Medel. The next morning, about fourteen thousand people staged a protest in the CCIL stadium in Lota Alto, where the miners and port workers declared themselves on strike. To the demands in the memorandum, the workers now added a new one: the immediate dismissal of the police lieutenant responsible for the previous day's arrests, a man accused by El Siglo of showing "overt Fascist tendencies."[71] On January 8, Schwager workers joined the strike, and on the same day, Labor Minister Pradenas Muñoz and almost the entire national leadership of the CTCh traveled by plane to the region. This intervention resolved the immediate crisis, but on the conciliation board, where the contract petitions were being negotiated, company representatives remained intransigent.[72]

69. Providencia Reservada no. 5, January 6, 1942, from Carabineros Director General to Interior Minister, FMI, vol. 10787 (1 of 2), ARNAD.

70. El Siglo, January 4, 1942, 13, and January 6, 1942, 6. The demand for reinstatement of the seven Lota workers had become a rallying cry. See El Siglo, January 2, 1942, 7, and September 8, 1942, 3.

71. El Siglo, January 9, 1942, 6, and January 8, 1942, 6.

72. El Siglo, January 8, 1942, 6; El Chiflón, June 1942, 26.

The swift high-level government response to the situation stemmed partly from the wartime priority given to coal production and partly from political interests on the eve of the presidential election. It also reflected Pradenas Muñoz's personal commitment to the workers of the region. Born in the coal mining town of Lebu, in the province of Arauco, Pradenas Muñoz had been a revered leader of both the Democratic Party and the Federation of Chilean Workers (FOCh), the precursor to the CTCh, throughout the 1910s and 1920s. He had also been a maritime worker in the port city of Talcahuano, some 15 kilometers (10 miles) northwest of Concepción, where he edited the FOCh's regional journal.[73] Between 1921 and 1924, at the height of FOCh–led strikes in the coal mines, Pradenas Muñoz was a national deputy representing the workers of the region, and, as senator for Santiago from 1933 to 1940, he continued to defend their interests.[74] In March 1940, Aguirre Cerda's appointment of Pradenas Muñoz as labor minister raised great hopes among popular sectors around the country, as would his reappointment to that post in President González Videla's first cabinet in January 1947. People in Concepción and Arauco particularly trusted Pradenas Muñoz because "in his youth, he had lived with the workers of the zone and was himself a worker, which is why he understands the anguish of the working class and their constant battle against the companies' arrogance and antisocial, inhuman treatment of the miners."[75]

The Democratic Party, which Pradenas Muñoz co-founded, was one of the centrist forces that immediately supported the candidacy of Juan Antonio Ríos Morales, even as the Communists and Socialists were pursuing other options. As soon as he won the Radical Party nomination, Ríos Morales "called for the formation of a 'powerful democratic and progressive bloc,' and asserted that 'democracy must be preserved by a government founded on public order, authority, and discipline.'"[76] Like Pradenas Muñoz, Ríos Morales was also a son of the coal mining region, yet he was far from having been a worker himself. Born to a landowning

73. On the life of Pradenas Muñoz, see Pedreros, *Huelga grande*, 8; Campos Harriet, *Historia*, 270; Cortés and Fuentes, *Diccionario político*, 391.

74. In July 1938, for example, Pradenas Muñoz spoke out against an article in *El Mercurio* that described Lota Alto as "a model town of its kind," based on its infant mortality rate of 26 percent compared to 31 percent for Lota Bajo. How could this be construed as "a marvel," asked Pradenas Muñoz, when the national infant mortality rate was 24 percent? "Mortalidad Infantil en Lota," Senate Session, July 4, 1938, 755–57, BCNCh.

75. *El Siglo*, September 29, 1947, 1. *El Chiflón*, July 1942, 10, also strongly hails Pradenas Muñoz.

76. Stevenson, *Chilean Popular Front*, 118, quoting from *El Mercurio*, January 2, 1942, 13, and *Pan-American*, January 1942, n.p.

family in Cañete, just to the south of Lebu, he represented the right wing of the Radical Party. Though he participated in early efforts to organize the Popular Front, Ríos Morales subsequently opposed President Aguirre Cerda's collaboration with the Communists, and even co-sponsored a bill to outlaw the party, which Aguirre Cerda vetoed in mid-1941.[77]

Although the Marxists had serious misgivings about Ríos Morales's candidacy, they were more concerned about the possible victory of former dictator Carlos Ibáñez del Campo, who had secured the backing of Conservatives and most Liberals. The Socialists therefore withdrew their candidate, Oscar Schnake, and, when it became clear that Gabriel González Videla would not break with his party to run as an independent, the Communists also gave their support to Ríos Morales, however reluctantly. His electoral coalition, the Democratic Alliance, thus came to include all the Center and Left parties of the previous Popular Front, which had been torn asunder in November 1940.[78] Near the end of January, after Pradenas Muñoz had calmed the region's labor unrest, Ríos Morales made a campaign tour throughout the coal mining towns. He was greeted by "great shows of sympathy," especially in Lebu, where he had attended primary school, and in other towns around in the province of Arauco, where he was born, and which he had represented as both national deputy and senator.[79]

On February 1, 1942, 56 percent of Chilean voters chose Juan Antonio Ríos Morales as their new president; Carlos Ibáñez, supported by the right-wing parties, received 44 percent of the vote.[80] In the coal mining region, the contest was not nearly as close, with the provinces of Concepción and Arauco voting 70 percent and 95 percent, respectively, in favor of Ríos Morales. In the coal mining communities themselves, the vote for

77. Several political memoirs discuss Ríos Morales's role in early efforts to forge the Popular Front. Communist leader Elías Lafertte, for example, recalled that many clandestine meetings in 1935 "took place in the automobile of Juan Antonio Ríos, driven by him." Lafertte Gaviño, *Vida de un comunista*, 303. Another Communist leader, Orlando Millas, noted that Ríos Morales's possible candidacy pushed Aguirre Cerda to embrace the Front. Millas, *En tiempos*, 256.

78. Interpretations vary about the degree of continuity between the Democratic Alliance and the Popular Front. See, for example, Stevenson, *Chilean Popular Front*, 120; Drake, *Socialism and Populism*, 268; and Loveman and Lira, *Las ardientes cenizas*, 112.

79. Pizarro Soto, *Lebu*, 351.

80. At the national level, fewer than 12 percent of all Chileans, including women and children, were registered to vote, and of these, 80 percent actually voted. This means that that less than 10 percent of the total population participated in the selection of the new president. In the presidential elections of 1938, which Drake described as a "more ideologically defined and heated contest," 88 percent of the registered voters cast ballots. Drake, *Socialism and Populism*, 269n6.

Ríos Morales was even more favorable: 87 percent in Coronel, 91 percent in Lota, and 95 percent in both Curanilahue and Lebu.[81] These percentages were well above those won by Aguirre Cerda less than four years earlier, although esteem for him had grown greatly among working-class residents of the coal mining zone, who now deeply grieved his untimely death.

Assuming office in March 1942, at the height of World War II, Ríos Morales transformed his predecessor's slogan "To Govern Is to Educate" into "To Govern Is to Produce." His administration nominally continued to pursue the Popular Front ideal of industrial development in which labor-capital relations would be harmonized through the just mediation and appropriate intervention of the state. Yet, as Paul Drake explains, "Aguirre Cerda's successor perpetuated the late president's emphasis on industrialization but downplayed his accompanying concern with reforms for urban labor."[82] Thus, when Ríos Morales's first cabinet was sworn in on April 2, 1942, Labor Minister Pradenas Muñoz—the workers' strongest ally in the previous government—had been replaced by a far more conservative member of the Democratic Party, Leonidas Leyton. Then, in late October, just after the police shootings in Lota, Leyton himself was replaced with an even more controversial Democratic, Mariano Bustos Lagos.[83]

A paragon of the developing "technical-professional" bureaucracy associated with the Ministry of Labor, Bustos Lagos had significant experience, came from a "good" social and political background, and believed in the effectiveness of the new industrial relations system. As early as 1925, he had been named to the Extraordinary Commission of Labor Inspectors charged with implementing the country's first major social legislation. Complying with the 1931 Labor Code and subsequent laws, however, often meant that he had to reject the illegal activities of unions and political parties.[84] Thus, in his capacity as director general of labor

---

81. Dirección del Registro Electoral, presidential election results, 1942, SERCh. Ríos Morales's higher returns in the more rural province of Arauco than in the province of Concepción may have been due, in part, to his being a landowner from Cañete, in the heart of Arauco.

82. Drake, *Socialism and Populism*, 267–68.

83. Leyton's replacement was part of a larger cabinet shakeup on October 20, which began with "the collective resignation of all the Ministers . . . based on the desire to give the President of the Republic complete freedom to resolve the recently developing situation." *El Sur*, October 21, 1942, 1. Socialist Public Works Minister Oscar Schnake had presented his resignation back in early September, in opposition to Law no. 7200, which granted the Executive extraordinary powers. Schnake remained in his post, however, until the October crisis.

84. Rojas Flores, *La dictadura de Ibáñez*, 64.

under Aguirre Cerda, Bustos Lagos incited great animosity among workers in the province of Concepcion. The regional CTCh even wrote to the president insisting that he be dismissed "for his nefarious work carried out against the working class of the country" and his "defense of the great industrialists and landowners."[85]

The appointment of someone like Bustos Lagos to a post recently held by worker advocate Pradenas Muñoz indicated Ríos Morales's continued adherence to the model of bureaucratic social intervention. But it also signaled a change in the government's favored political and class alliances. As Brian Loveman explains, "Ríos renewed Radical contacts with Conservatives and some Liberals as the Right recognized the benefits of state support for *private* industrial enterprise. They also appreciated Ríos' order against rural unionization. Rapprochement between moderate Radical party factions and the Right coincided with a growing middle-class conservatism."[86] The presumably "Center-Left" coalition government of Ríos Morales was thus actually based on a loose and shifting alliance of diverse political and socioeconomic sectors. His first cabinet included not only right-wing members of the Radical and Democratic Parties, but also Socialists, side by side with aristocratic Liberals. As Julio Faúndez has observed, "Not surprisingly, this unlikely coalition—which was typical of the period 1942–52—soon broke up, leading to permanent cabinet instability."[87]

The paradox of the period was that the Ríos Morales administration maintained the Popular Front rhetoric of state intervention to promote social justice, even as it used state institutions to keep labor in check. To this end, Ríos Morales also took advantage of the widespread discourse—propagated more by the Communists than by the parties in government—of patriotic cooperation of both capital and labor with the state in the interests of national industrialization, progress, and the defense of democracy against the threat of Fascism.

Yet, while reaping benefits from the workers' anti-Fascism and their support of Chile's democratic government and its model of social relations for increasing production, the Ríos Morales administration repeatedly refused to break diplomatic ties with the Axis powers. Communist

85. Letter from Regional CTCh to Concepción Intendant, April 3, 1939, FIC, vol. 2184, ANCh.

86. Loveman, *Chile*, 215. In essence, President Ríos Morales continued his predecessors' policy of enforcing ministerial order no. 34, which effectively blocked the formation of rural unions; this is discussed in a bit more detail in the introduction.

87. Faúndez, *Marxism and Democracy*, 69.

labor sectors thus offered the president only tentative support, continually trying to push him toward more radical reforms on the home front and toward more decisive anti-Fascist positions internationally. "President Ríos," Loveman and Lira explain, "felt identified with the program of economic modernization begun by the Popular Front and with its rhetoric of social justice. . . . Challenged by the context of World War II and by the task of recomposing the party system, Ríos vacillated between an authoritarian discourse and one which maintained reminiscences of Aguirre Cerda."[88] This tendency of the government to "vacillate" only increased the intensity with which different sectors tried to push and pull it in different directions.

Back in January, CCIL administrator Isidro Wilson had construed the threat of strikes as part of a Communist campaign to influence the upcoming presidential elections. Now, as soon as the elections were over, the coal capitalists again accused labor of politically motivated unrest. On March 30, 1942, for example, top Schwager administrator Harry Cahill informed the Concepción intendant that union leaders had "ordered the workers to begin preparing for a strike," to be held between April 6 and 10, just days after Ríos Morales's inauguration. According to Cahill, the company's noncompliance with a workers' petition submitted back in September was only a pretext for the strike: the real motives were political. Just after the presidential election, Cahill claimed, the coal mining zone was racked by agitation, "provoked and sustained by its union leaders, who, obeying orders from the capital, were preparing to put the new President to the test." Administrators at both the Schwager and Lota companies were nervous about these stirrings, which Cahill described as "unjustified" since collective contracts would not expire for another five months.[89] When the police investigated the situation, they found that "strike false alarms are very common among the workers and are especially spread by Communist leaders, who try to keep the workers whipped up in a state of courage and expectation." Operations continued normally, the police reported, and they did not anticipate a strike.[90]

A few months after Cahill issued his alarmist allegations, in the midst of the Chilean winter of 1942, President Ríos Morales gained a significant weapon against both real and perceived threats to national stability,

88. Loveman and Lira, Las ardientes cenizas, 112.

89. Providencia Confidencial no. 3, transmitting text of Oficio Confidencial no. 3, March 30, 1942, from Concepción Intendant, FMI, vol. 10787, ARNAD.

90. Providencia Confidencial no. 76, from Carabineros Director General to Interior Minister, May 7, 1942, FMI, vol. 10787, ARNAD.

whether from the Right or the Left. In July of that year, Congress passed Internal State Security Law no. 7200, a piece of war-footing legislation that gave the Executive a variety of "special powers," including increased control of wages and prices to combat speculation and sabotage. Law no. 7200 fundamentally "reordered the administration of the state, internal and external security, and the management of the national economy, significantly expanding the attributions of the president."[91]

Over the coming years, Article 23 of this law, which authorized the president to declare areas of national territory to be "emergency zones," would assume particular significance. According to a November 1942 supreme decree regulating the emergency zones, "civil authorities were to be replaced by military 'Jefes de Plaza,' virtually establishing martial law and submitting civilians to military jurisdiction."[92] As Loveman and Lira explain, Law no. 7200 "was a measure determined by the immediate situation of the Second World War." Yet, "despite the debatable constitutionality [of its provisions], they would serve the two succeeding governments as routine elements for the repression of political and union movements."[93] In this vein, the law strengthened what Loveman and Lira refer to as "the legal basis for restricted democracy in Chile."[94]

Just as Congress was passing Law no. 7200, Communists and labor leaders began lobbying for legislation to increase wartime coal production by reducing the number of miners' holidays, but paying double time for work on Sundays and the remaining holidays.[95] Congressional debates over this new bill were as polarizing and hostile as those surrounding the Berguño Report a year earlier, and they covered many of the same issues. Conservative Senator Maximiliano Errázuriz Valdés, for example, cited labor indiscipline provoked by union delegates as the single greatest cause of production shortfalls. Arguing that new wage incentives would only worsen the situation, he openly blamed the now-deceased Pedro Aguirre Cerda for breaking down lines of control at Schwager. According to Errázuriz, when the president visited the Coronel mines, he had personally persuaded Schwager administrators to allow mine floor delegates to intervene directly in worksite problems, which was not the norm in the industry. By contrast, Errázuriz claimed, at Lota, Lirquén, and other mines, delegates merely reported back to the union, but did not, on their

91. Loveman and Lira, *Las ardientes cenizas*, 112.
92. Ibid.
93. Ibid. 113. Loveman and Lira make a similar point on p. 28.
94. Ibid. 113.
95. *El Chiflón*, July 1942, 20, 22.

own initiative, promote section work stoppages or other obstructionist acts. Expressing contempt for what he perceived as the Popular Front's undue advocacy of labor rights, Errázuriz declared that "this calamity of union delegates [at the Schwager company] is due exclusively to the personal work of President Aguirre Cerda, whose lack of vision as a head of state was revealed in this, as in everything else."[96]

Despite such openly hostile opposition, on October 2, 1942, Congress did pass Law no. 7289, suspending a number of holidays in the coal mining zone for the duration of the war but establishing double pay for work on Sundays and the remaining holidays. Less than a week later, on October 7, Communist Deputy Damián Uribe traveled to the coal mines to explain the terms of the new law to his former workmates. In Lota, Uribe would witness far more violent opposition to the workers' gains than the vitriolic words of Senator Errázuriz, as we shall see in chapter 5.

96. "Situación de los obreros en las minas de carbón," Senate Session, August 18, 1942, 1358–59, BCNCh.

5

"WITH A BULLET IN HIS HEART AND THE CHILEAN FLAG IN HIS HAND": POLICE SHOOTINGS IN LOTA, OCTOBER 1942

On an early evening in October 1942, springtime in southern Chile, a group of coal miners and their leaders found themselves quarreling inside the cramped quarters of a two-story company row house in Lota Alto that served as union headquarters. Outside, a tumult raged in the plaza and street, with national police (carabinero) troops wielding sabers, firing rifles, and charging their horses into a large crowd of miners and community residents. The police had been called in by the Coal Mining Company of Lota to disperse an unauthorized union assembly being held on company property. When the troops attacked, men, women, and children fled in all directions, with many scrambling into the parochial church, which towered just across the street.

Those who found refuge inside the union office were arguing over who would have the honor of carrying the Chilean flag when the group marched back outside to try to stop the violence. A few minutes later, former union secretary Carlos Silva Torres emerged from the building draped in the Chilean red, white, and blue. As he stepped into the street, a bullet ripped through the chest of this young Communist coal miner, knocking him to the ground. His blood spilled across the flag, "dyeing red the land of black gold."[1] The Communist newspaper *El Siglo* proclaimed, "As a symbol of those heroic miners who sacrifice their lives in superhuman labor, in order to give momentum and progress to the country's industries, to the economic development of the entire nation, and

1. *El Siglo*, October 8, 1942, 3.

unfortunately, also to fill the pockets of the businessmen and their lack-eys, who have no conscience, the worker leader Silva fell mortally wounded, with a bullet in his heart and the Chilean flag in his hand."[2] Silva Torres's corpse was soon joined by two others, raising the death toll in this police attack to three, with dozens critically injured.

The slaying of these coal miners by the national police in the company town of Lota Alto occurred on October 7, 1942, a crucial year in World War II, when the United States achieved a major victory over Japan at the Battle of Midway, and the Red Army struggled tenaciously to repel the Nazi assault on Stalingrad. Chilean workers of all political hues mobilized to defend democracy against Fascism in its multiple forms and to increase production for the war effort. The political elite in Chile were losing control over the language of patriotism, which acquired new dimensions as leaders of the popular sectors embraced it. The decision by a group of unionists in a vital industry to unfurl the Chilean flag as they faced fire from the national police speaks to the complex developments in relations among labor, capital, and the state in the preceding years.

A closer look at the October 1942 violence in Lota and the responses it generated raises at least three points central to understanding the entire Popular Front era. First, these events reflect a historic convergence—dramatically embodied in Carlos Silva Torres's dying embrace of the Chilean flag—when Communist internationalism merged with its putative opposite, patriotic nationalism. At a strategic level, this convergence was based on Marxist-Leninist two-stage theory, revived by Stalin, in which a bourgeois-democratic revolution was held to be a necessary precursor to a Socialist revolution. The workers were to see their labor as a contribution to national industrial development and, concomitantly, to the cause of democracy, both at home and abroad. It was with these larger goals in mind that Communist-led workers participated in a tripartite industrial relations model (labor-capital-state) aimed at alleviating class conflict, and even agreed to "no strike" pledges throughout the war years. Yet, as the events of October 1942 demonstrate, the workers' patriotism in no way diminished their sense of class-based rights or quelled their leaders' efforts to battle tenaciously for them, though they now did so more through political negotiation and appeal to national sentiment than through direct confrontation with capitalists or the state.

Second, the events of October 1942 expose contradictions between the tripartite model for harmonious industrial relations and the reality of

2. Ibid.

class conflict, contradictions that simmered menacingly, and periodically erupted, throughout the Popular Front decade. The union assembly so brutally broken up by the carabineros had been called to discuss the annual contract negotiations, during which company administrators had refused almost all of the workers' petitions. The well-organized and disciplined coal workers insisted that their rights not be forsaken under the Communist Party's National Unity strategy, which urged them to continue to support the Ríos Morales administration. Communist union leaders thus had to find ways to rein in the workers' potentially explosive indignation, while still defending their rights within the framework of cross-class cooperation. And, as with other sectors of society, they now employed strategic discourses about patriotism to advance their interests.

From the perspective of the unions, the Lota company's refusal of the workers' just demands undermined possibilities for increasing the extraction of coal, a commodity vital to Chilean industrialization in the early 1940s. With that in mind, Communist labor leaders directly accused the coal capitalists of economic and political sabotage—of subverting through their intransigence not only the industrial development project of the Popular Front, but also Chilean democracy itself. Caught up in the international political fervor of the day, they denounced the coal capitalists not merely as unpatriotic but as "Fascists." For the miners themselves, the notion of the coal companies as a fifth column was personified in the company administrators and their henchmen, particularly the much-loathed Welfare Department chiefs, as well as mine shaft overseers and section supervisors. The coal miners saw these company men as the most immediate manifestations of Fascism, which they could therefore directly and legitimately combat.

The unions' complex efforts to reconcile class conflict with Popular Front, or cross-class, politics also raise questions about the forms of confrontation adopted in these years. Class warfare was de-emphasized; perennial conflicts between labor and capital were now situated in debates about national progress, and especially about the importance of substantive democratization to the process of industrialization. In their new role as citizen workers, the coal miners had a growing sense of their power and the rightness of their positions vis-à-vis their capitalist employers. The government's recognition of social justice as an element of the Popular Front development model reinforced the workers' convictions and raised their expectations. The strategic battles waged by labor leaders were now more about securing public sympathy and favorable state intervention than about confronting the companies directly. The state

emerged as an arena of maneuvering between Right and Left, where agricultural, mining, and industrial interests constantly struggled with
working-class interests to push and pull centrist governing forces to their
respective sides.

The killing of workers by the national police on company property and
at the company's behest also raises critical questions about jurisdiction,
in terms of the spatial, symbolic, and legal dimensions of class and citizenship. How did property define literal and symbolic boundaries between workers and citizens in the coal mining communities? How did
the ownership of property translate into authority over citizen workers?
Did the private jurisdiction claimed by the coal mining companies by
virtue of their property ownership override the public jurisdiction accorded the state? And, if so, how could the government muster the political will and power to challenge such claims?[3]

And third, the events of October 1942 highlight the sense of possibilities engendered in this period in Chilean history. Even though the governments of the Popular Front era often moved to curb workers' challenges
to their capitalist employers, they did so without relinquishing a discourse of justice and harmony in industrial relations. Acknowledging the
legitimacy of many of the workers' grievances and promising to intervene
on their behalf, government actors appeared to take the workers' side, at
least on some issues. This was a powerful basis from which workers could
continue to confront their employers. And occasionally, as in the aftermath of the October 1942 killings, representatives of the government even
censured the coal mining companies directly. At least to some extent, the
workers believed in the Center-Left governments' intentions to fulfill the
promises of a progressive modernizing democracy, and they believed that
by battling reactionary capitalists, they were assisting the state in its capacity to do so.

Mobilization in these years generated a collective fervor, and the story
of October 1942 indicates how this influenced subsequent developments.
Although the intent of anti-labor repression is to intimidate workers and
to weaken their will to resist, in this situation, it served to reinforce the
workers' sense of the rightness of their position and raised hopes that the
government would increase its direct intervention on their behalf. The
miners had long desired the transformation of the capitalist coal mining
industry into a public utility under the just management of the state;

---

3. The Lota killings raised fundamental questions about the meaning of "private property," a highly political issue with a long history in Chile. See Loveman, *Struggle*, 3–11.

anger and indignation over the October 1942 killings served to rally support for nationalization.

"Bloody Nazi Provocation in Lota": The Police Assault on a Public Gathering

Throughout September 1942, diverse unions in the coal mining industry were embroiled in their annual contract negotiations. Early in October, the companies put forth counterproposals regarding wages, but refused to consider any of the workers' other petitions. The union leaders engaged in the negotiations in Santiago responded unanimously that the "counterproposals" had so little relation to the workers' demands they could not be taken seriously. In their statement, widely published on October 7, the union leaders added, "We are hoping for a firm attitude on the part of the Government in order to obtain legitimate proposals from the companies."[4]

A firm attitude would indeed be shown by the Lota-based carabineros, who, at least nominally, represented the national government.[5] On Wednesday, October 7, the same day its leaders' rejection of the company counterproposals was published, the Lota union moved to update its members on the state of the negotiations.[6] Following long-established procedures, the union scheduled two different assemblies, one in the morning and another in the evening, to ensure that members from all three work shifts could attend. It requested permission from the company to hold these meetings in the small plaza in front of the union headquarters, a two-story corner house in one of the residential blocks known as "pabellones." This permission was necessary since, as with all property in Lota Alto, both the building and the plaza belonged to the Coal Mining and Industrial Company of Lota (CCIL). Although the union often held its assemblies in this plaza, on this occasion, the head of the CCIL's Welfare Department, Octavio Astorquiza, announced the company's new policy: collective gatherings would no longer be permitted there. He told the union leaders to use an alternative site, the company stadium, which was

---

4. *El Sur*, October 7, 1942, 5. *El Sur* was Concepción's major independent newspaper. The same article under a different headline appeared in *El Siglo* on the same day.

5. On the history of the carabineros, see chapter 1, note 40.

6. Sources on the October 7, 1942, incident in Lota differ in many details. I have relied especially on the official Rettig-Pazols Report, as reprinted in *El Sur*, October 18, 1942, 4, discussed later in this chapter.

closer to the mines but much farther from the residential area of Lota Alto.

The union leaders agreed to hold the morning assembly in the stadium, but the workers who attended expressed outrage at the company's telling them where they could and could not meet. It would be impossible to hold the evening assembly in the stadium, they shouted, since it had no electric lights and they would not be finished by nightfall. The union members therefore decided to hold the evening assembly in the more centrally located plaza, the customary site for such gatherings. According to El Chiflón, the newspaper of the National Miners' Federation (FNM), the union leaders did not perceive this collective decision as an act of open defiance of the company that could provoke violent confrontation. Rather, they assumed "the Company would realize that the second meeting could not be held in the Stadium for the reasons given," and based on this assumption, "they took no further steps."[7]

The second work shift at the mines ended at 3 P.M., but given the lack of transportation, it took the workers more than an hour to reach their homes from the coal faces. It was not until after 5 P.M. that people slowly began to gather in the plaza outside the union headquarters in anticipation of the meeting, which was scheduled to begin there at 7 P.M. By 6:30 P.M., more than a thousand people had crowded into the plaza and filled much of the street between the union office and the parochial church directly across from it.[8] As was usually the case in such union assemblies, many workers were joined by their wives and children. Moreover, many Lota community residents who did not work directly for the Lota company, such as bakers, merchants, and fishermen, also attended these meetings, knowing that their own lives were intimately tied to the outcome of the miners' contract negotiations, known in Chile as "collective disputes" (conflictos colectivos).[9] Union meetings were significant social happenings in the coal mining communities, and virtually anyone, regardless of age, gender, or occupation, might be found in attendance.

Shortly before the evening assembly was to begin, the chief of the carabineros' Lota Alto precinct, Lieutenant Roberto Saa Sánchez, appeared on the scene accompanied by between ten and twenty officers on

7. El Chiflón, November 1942, 2–3. The National Miners' Federation (FNM), then solidly under Communist leadership, published El Chiflón monthly, beginning in May 1942.

8. Estimates of people in the plaza vary between 1,000 and 4,000. See, for example, El Sur, October 9, 1942, 9, and October 10, 1942, 12.

9. "Collective dispute" (conflicto colectivo) is the term used both in the Chilean Labor Code and colloquially to refer to the gamut of proceedings set in motion by a union's submission of contract petitions.

horseback. He informed the union leaders who were gathered at the podium in front of the union entrance that, by orders of the company, the assembly could not be held there. Although there is no record of the conversation that may have taken place, the union leaders did use their loudspeaker to tell the workers they had been ordered to leave. By all accounts, this announcement angered the workers, who began to shout that it was too late in the evening to go to the stadium. Then, before any collective decision could be made about how to respond to the situation, Lieutenant Saa ordered his forces to break up the gathering.

The Rettig-Pazols Report, commissioned by the government in the wake of the incident, confirmed that the police moved in prior to any acts of violence on the part of the workers, who then "made the first demonstrations of active resistance."[10] "Some of those gathered," the official report explained, "began to throw rocks at the troops, especially at the lieutenant, who was successively hit by several of these projectiles. Lieutenant Saa lost control of himself and had to be led out of the plaza."[11] With his removal from the scene, the troops fell under the command of Sergeant Galindo Zambrano, who, according to the report "ordered them to proceed more energetically."[12] When the police began to wield their clubs and sabers and direct their horses into the crowd, mayhem ensued, with men, women, and children running in all directions, some to find shelter inside the small union office and the parish church across the street, while others "tried to defend themselves with clods and bits of wood."[13] Damián Uribe Cárdenas, a Communist national deputy present during the events, affirmed that "the victims of this aggression reacted in one way or another to defend their lives," but, he added, they were "quickly defeated since they lacked any type of weapons."[14]

At some point, the police began to fire their rifles, but here the various accounts disagree. According to both the FNM's *El Chiflón* and the independent Concepción newspaper *El Sur*, it was Lieutenant Roberto Saa Sánchez who gave the order and who fired the first shot.[15] This would have been impossible according to the government-commissioned account, in which Lieutenant Saa had already been "led out of the plaza." Without specifying who issued the command, the official report states that the

10. Rettig-Pazols Report, as reprinted in *El Sur*, October 18, 1942, 4.
11. Ibid.
12. Ibid.
13. *El Chiflón*, November 1942, 2–3.
14. Damián Uribe Cárdenas, as quoted in *El Siglo*, October 14, 1942, 3.
15. *El Chiflón*, November 1942, 2–3; and *El Sur*, October 8, 1942, 7.

first shot was fired into the air and that the police only aimed at the crowd when the stone throwing intensified. An article in the Communist newspaper *El Siglo*, on the other hand, states that it was Lieutenant Osvaldo Cerpa who gave the order to fire, and that he did so in the midst of "great panic among the women and children."[16]

Where all accounts agree is that when a group of people stepped out the front door of the union office, they were immediately fired upon. At the head of this group were Roberto Gómez Sandoval, the current union secretary, and Carlos Silva Torres, a former union secretary, both of whom were hit, indicating that at least some of the police had their sights trained on the entrance. Gómez Sandoval sustained only a moderate injury to his left leg, but Silva Torres was carried out of the plaza with a gaping hole in his chest. When he died in the hospital the next morning, he became an instant and powerful martyr, not least of all because he was bearing the Chilean flag when he was shot. According to a later account in *El Chiflón*, Silva Torres was not simply holding the flag, but had wrapped himself in it:

> In view of the seriousness of the situation, they agreed to get out the Chilean flag, and, with it, head toward the Stadium, as a means of drawing the people away from that place [the plaza and union office], and ensuring that, out of respect for the national flag, the police would stop firing. But it didn't turn out like that. And they shot the bearer of the national tricolor. We must point out that there was a real battle among the workers over who would carry the national flag since everyone wanted the honor of carrying it, as a symbol of peace. The honor and the misfortune went to our comrade [*compañero*], felled before his time, the young union leader Carlos Silva T., who was shot wrapped in the folds of our Chilean flag.[17]

Such patriotic hyperbole was an overt appeal to the Ríos Morales administration to uphold the alliance between the state and its citizen workers called for in the nation's new industrial relations model. Yet from the deep contradictions in the model came the government's response—at least one military regiment was readied for immediate transport to Lota. Manuel Basa Ramírez, a twenty-one-year-old Lota native, was completing his mandatory military service in Concepción, 65 kilometers (40 miles)

16. *El Siglo*, October 8, 1942, 1.
17. *El Chiflón*, November 1942, 2–3.

to the north of Lota, when he was ordered to return to his hometown as part of a repressive force. "They brought us from the Chacabuco regiment," he recalled, "to inside the station to wait for the train, to come to put down the riot, that's what we were doing, waiting there . . . when a new order arrived, that everything had been brought under control, so they returned us to the regiment, we never did come here, but we had already been given the orders [to shoot] anyone [who] moved against us."[18]

A few minutes after the initial shooting stopped and the situation had calmed down, a new group of carabineros arrived, under the command of Police Captain Domingo Márquez Castillo, to arrest those responsible for the incident. At the center of the commotion inside the union office, Captain Márquez found Deputy Damián Uribe Cárdenas, a Communist Party militant and former coal miner who had served as secretary of the Lota union before being elected to Congress. Uribe had arrived from Santiago that afternoon to explain to the workers the terms of Law no. 7289, passed five days earlier, which reduced the number of holidays in the coal mining zone as part of the wartime production effort, while granting miners double pay for work on Sundays and the remaining holidays.

In a move that would incite almost as much controversy as the killings themselves, Captain Márquez ignored Uribe Cárdenas's congressional immunity and had him arrested. The police also detained between fifty and seventy other leaders, workers, and community residents, including more than a dozen women, all of whom were taken to the Lota police station.[19] All of the leaders of the miners' union were arrested, with the exception of Roberto Gómez Sandoval, the secretary, who was hospitalized with a gunshot wound, and Alberto Sandoval Alvárez, the president, who was away at the time of the incident. Also jailed was Marcelino Gajardo, the head of the Lota section of the national Confederation of Chilean Workers (CTCh), a key actor in the Popular Front coalition. Deputy Uribe was released later that same evening, whereupon he reported that he had been "assaulted" by Police Lieutenant Cerpa.[20] The other detainees remained in custody and were soon transported to the departmental jail in neighboring Coronel.

18. Interview with Manuel Basa Ramírez.
19. *El Sur*, October 8, 1942, 7; and *El Siglo*, October 8, 1942, 1.
20. On the front page of its October 8, 1942, edition, *El Siglo* reported that Deputy Uribe had been "savagely beaten" by Lieutenant Cerpa. In his own statement about the "bloody events" in Lota, published both in *El Sur*, October 10, 1942, 12, and in *El Siglo*, October 14, 1942, 3, Uribe described being punched several times by Cerpa.

While these arrests were under way, dozens of people were carried by their companions to the nearby company hospital, the only medical facility in Lota at the time. Among the hospitalized were four police officers who had sustained injuries when the crowd hurled stones, including Lieutenant Saa, who had suffered serious facial and cranial contusions. Most, however, were workers and labor leaders wounded by police bullets, rifle butts, clubs, sabers, and even by the trampling hooves of police horses.

One miner taken to the hospital in critical condition was Pantoleón Zambrano, a member of the Communist Party, who had been shot in the gut. Whereas Silva Torres's patriotic martyrdom came to represent the sense of the massacre as a national tragedy, Zambrano's killing represented the personal tragedy of the many people affected in some way by the violence of October 7. Suffering from a mortal wound, but still conscious, Zambrano and his girlfriend, Doralisa Lagos, convinced the hospital chaplain to marry them. Shortly after uttering his vows and kissing his new wife, Zambrano died at 3:45 P.M. on October 8; the following day, both Communist and independent newspapers published photos of his bedside wedding.[21]

The Communist and labor press sought to emphasize the humanity of the coal miners in an appeal for national public sympathy. Zambrano's deathbed marriage vividly portrayed human beings who lived, loved, and died just as did the progressive middle class whose support was crucial for radicalizing the Center-Left project. By drawing attention to the miners' home and family lives and the implications of the killings for wives and children, Zambrano's story made it more difficult for the incident to be justified or written off simply as another conflict between rebellious Communist workers and their bosses, with the police caught in the middle.

Together with Silva Torres and Zambrano, the third victim in this "treacherous triple assassination" was a twenty-two-year-old miner named Juan Antipil Maurelia, whose body was found just outside the union office with a bullet hole in his temple.[22] All sources mentioning the death of this young man highlighted his identity as a Mapuche, a member of an indigenous people with a long history of resistance in Chile, although many omitted the fact that Antipil was also a Communist Party

21. *El Siglo*, October 9, 1942, 1; and *El Sur*, October 9, 1942, 9.
22. *El Sur*, October 8, 1942, 7. Antipil Maurilia's age comes from *El Siglo*, October 8, 1942, 1. His name is spelled differently in different sources.

militant.[23] Another injured Mapuche miner was Pedro Huenchún, who was shot in the thighs and lost the use of his legs. The identity of these victims as both miners and Mapuches was invoked as symbolic capital in the Communist effort to reconcile the workers' grievances against capitalist exploitation with the cross-class nationalist project of the era.

One of the key developments of the Popular Front decade was that direct action to debilitate capitalism and the bourgeois democracy it engendered was replaced by political battles against socioeconomic, political, and cultural exclusion within the nation. The Communist strategy was now to push for the expansion and deepening of democracy to ensure that the popular sectors could fully participate in the bourgeois revolution, defend their interests, and be ready for the Socialist revolution when conditions were right. Communist activists among the coal miners thus concentrated their efforts on organizing and mobilizing "weaker" sectors of the working class, such as tenant farmers, rural workers, women, and the original inhabitants of the territory eventually conquered by the Chilean nation—the Mapuches.

Weeks before the massacre in Lota Alto, diverse unions in the coal mining industry had issued a united manifesto, addressed to the Confederation of Chilean Workers (CTCh), the National Miners' Federation (FNM), and the nation, which conveyed the core aims of their mobilizing efforts in these years: "The unity of the proletariat and the people [el pueblo] and active and strong national solidarity, in the end, conquer egoism, introducing new advances in the principles of social justice and [toward] the right of every worker to live and to be respected as a citizen, as a patriot, and as a member of civilized human society."[24] With this discursive strategy, the Communist Party sought to join its ideological mandate as the promoter of international working-class unity with its nationalist project of the war years. Indeed, "the unity of the proletariat and the people" was at the heart of the project pursued by the Communist coal miners in these years, and it was precisely as the embodiment of this unity that the victims of October 7 were portrayed: Silva Torres was a patriot worker; Zambrano, a husband worker; and Antipil, a Mapuche worker. Together they evoked the image of citizen workers, whose right to justice and respect as members of civilized human society had been

23. Even fifty years after the slayings, several of the people I interviewed emphasized that one of the victims was a Mapuche, and one person even recalled his name. Interviews with Omar Sanhueza Segunda (October 13, 1997), Fresia Vidal Ojarse (September 15, 1997), Manuel Basa Ramírez, and Evaristo Azócar Medel.

24. El Sur, September 12, 1942, 6.

betrayed by the egoism of the coal mining bourgeoisie, which provoked the "barbarous bloodbath" on October 7, a harbinger of the violent reactions to come.[25] In the Communist schema, in other words, coal workers were the strategic starting point for a broader popular democratic movement in the region.

"Choking Back Their Feelings in the National Interest": The Patriotic Decision Not to Strike

Anger and confusion raged in the immediate wake of the shootings.[26] While the bodies of the slain and injured workers were being carried to the hospital, the police transported their detainees to the Coronel jail. The rest of the local population, including thousands of people who were not even present at the initial meeting, began to gather outside the union office in Lota Alto, seeking information, solace, and some concrete way to deal with their rage. When the miners' assembly came under attack, the residents of the community set their individual and sectarian differences aside and united around a sense of shared identity. Despite the threat that they might again be violently dispersed, the men and women of Lota refused to retreat to the privacy of their homes.

"Among the workers and the general population," *El Siglo* reported, "a profound indignation reigns. The streets have been taken over by the residents who are demanding immediate freedom for the detained and punishment of the Fascist provocateurs. The union building is full of workers and women demanding . . . the immediate departure from Lota of those responsible."[27] The phrases "workers and the general population" and "workers and women" were part of the Communists' rhetorical strategy to portray the miners as an integral part of the community, and yet somehow also distinct from it. The workers could thus draw strength from their position in relation to production—from their class-based interests—while at the same time invoking the ascendant spirit of democratic nationalism, which legitimized their cause with a broader segment of Chilean society.

The extreme volatility of the situation was not lost on the leaders and militants who met in the Lota Bajo office of the Confederation of Chilean

25. *El Siglo*, October 8, 1942, 3.
26. "Choking back their feelings in the national interest" is taken from *El Chiflón*, November 1942, 2–3.
27. *El Siglo*, October 8, 1942, 1.

Workers (CTCh) to discuss what actions to take. In keeping with the legal, democratic strategies that the Chilean Communist Party (PCCh) had embraced, their first move was to send a telegram of protest to the president and the interior minister. The acting leaders then faced a difficult decision at a time when the jailing or hospitalization of the union's elected leaders had wreaked havoc with its normal decision making. Should they declare a strike, which seemed to be the prevailing sentiment of the outraged workers who filled the streets, and risk a backlash from the general public for disrupting vital coal production? Or should they ask the miners to head back into the tunnels to extract coal for a company that had just spilled workers' blood—not during an illegal strike or heated protest, but at a simple union assembly? The fundamental legal right to assemble, for which Chilean workers had fought long and hard, was now placed in jeopardy by the companies' refusal to cooperate.

Leaders and workers thus had to weigh the justice of a strike against the symbolic capital of not striking. They also had to consider how this decision would be viewed in terms of national and international Communist Party objectives and strategies. As a bastion of working-class support for the party, the coal miners had some say in adapting national party mandates to local circumstances. Indeed, throughout the latter half of 1942, the Lota Communists had come under criticism by the PCCh Central Committee for their reluctance to collaborate with "intermediary sectors" or with certain, supposedly progressive, "elements" within the company.[28] The Chilean Communist Party had been moving toward a new wartime strategy known as "National Unity," which aimed at forging the broadest possible anti-Fascist alliances. The party's affiliated workers were expected to fully participate, but in the midst of acute conflict and continual provocation by company administrators, workers of the coal region found it difficult to perceive them as allies. In the words of the Central Committee, "the Lota comrades [compañeros] . . . believed for many months that the National Unity [strategy] could not be applied in the coal mining zone since there, in the opinion of some, only two forces exist: the Company and the Communist Party, and whoever is not of the Party is classified as belonging to the Company camp." Citing their Lota cadres as one of the sectors of the party that did "not sufficiently comprehend" the National Unity strategy, the Santiago leadership set out to convince them that "there exist intermediary sectors that should not be undervalued, since without them, it is not possible to realize National Unity." Even

28. PCCh Central Committee Resolutions (1943), 50.

more difficult for the coal miners to accept was the idea that "even in the Company itself, there are elements interested in National Unity, [and] that, in general, certain common interests exist between the workers and the Company, which can serve as the basis for the formation of National Unity."[29]

Caught between party pressure and the throngs of angry people milling in the streets around the CTCh and union offices for hours after the bloodshed, the acting leaders in Lota decided at last that a strike should be averted. They immediately set out to spread the word, trying to convince the miners that returning to work was the best way to serve both their own interests and those of their nation. These efforts were successful, and at 11 P.M. that same day, the 2,500 men of the third shift entered the mines, as did all miners the following day.[30] In the ensuing weeks, the labor and leftist press played up the miners' voluntary return to work, citing it as a powerful demonstration of their patriotism and their cooperation with the Ríos Morales administration in its efforts, through increased coal production, to contribute both to national development and to the Allied struggle against Fascism. As argued in the FNM newspaper, El Chiflón,

> The workers' patriotism, so slandered by the press of the oligarchy, was seen not only in their dying with their arms around the Chilean flag and their defense of Constitutional Rights. It was also seen in . . . their having continued to work, not interrupting the job of extracting coal. As a protest, the [miners] did not want to go down in the coal pits. But they went down [anyway], choking back their feelings in the national interest so that coal production would not slacken. In light of this singular gesture, the nation [patria] should pay homage to the miners, and the Government should reward them [by] obligating the Companies to accept the contract petitions that their workers have submitted to them.[31]

This was the language of reciprocity: the miners sacrificed for the nation by working despite the outrage committed against them, and, in return, the government was to intervene to "obligate" the companies to make concessions. Workers expected both that the guilty would be punished and that their socioeconomic demands would be met—and they backed

29. Ibid.
30. El Sur, "October 8, 1942, 7.
31. El Chiflón, November 1942, 2–3.

up this expectation with the threat that a strike could still be called at any moment.

Labor organizations and media repeatedly emphasized that the workers' cooperation was contingent on the government's just intervention, and that they remained in a powerful bargaining position, with their capacity to halt coal production at any time. The leadership had managed to convince the miners to return to the coal pits, *El Siglo* explained, "but if energetic measures are not taken against the provocateurs on the Company payroll, it is going to be very difficult for operations to continue normally since the workers demand the immediate punishment of the guilty."[32] Similarly, a telegram sent from the Lota miners' union to the president, the interior minister, and other national figures demanded a full investigation into the incidents and punishment for those found guilty: "Otherwise, the stability of operations [is] in jeopardy."[33] This, then, was the two-edged sword of "conditional collaboration," a strategic position adopted by labor leaders as they struggled to advance the workers' interests in the Popular Front years.

Though the immediate threat of a strike had passed, the workers' anger had not, and the situation remained highly volatile. Late in the day on October 8, "with the objective of quelling, in part, the great unrest," the national police prosecutor's office (Fiscalía de Carabineros) ordered the release of forty of the men and thirteen women who had been arrested. Public indignation was not assuaged by this gesture, however, particularly since the union's acting president, Abraham Lara Astorga, remained in the Coronel jail, and, by some accounts, was being held "incommunicado."[34]

Meanwhile, in the days following the October 7 incident, top government officials met dozens of times with labor, political, and industry leaders in Lota, Concepción, and Santiago. On the afternoon of October 9, leaders from the Confederation of Chilean Workers and the coal mining unions met in Santiago with President Ríos Morales himself, who informed them that he had already named a two-man commission to investigate the incident. Director General of Information and Culture Raúl Rettig Guissen and Carabineros Director General Osvaldo Pazols Alfaro had departed for Lota the previous day, less than twenty-four hours after

32. *El Siglo*, October 8, 1942, 1.
33. *El Sur*, October 10, 1942, 12.
34. *El Siglo*, October 9, 1942, 4. See also *El Sur*, October 9, 1942, 9.

the shootings occurred.[35] Ríos Morales's rapid response reflected his desire to avoid an outright break between leftist labor sectors and his government.

During the second half of 1942, the Communists and the Confederation of Chilean Workers had been trying to strengthen the Center-Left coalition around the president. At the time of the violence in Lota Alto, organizations affiliated with the Democratic Alliance were preparing to hold large rallies around the country on October 13, to show of support for President Ríos as he set off on a trip through both South and North America.[36] In the wake of the Lota killings, they were thus careful not to indict the national government itself. To the contrary, the CTCh publicly declared "the Coal Mining and Industrial Company of Lota [to be] the only entity responsible for this criminal attack against the working class."[37] In one editorial, *El Siglo* even made excuses for Ríos Morales's cordial interactions with company officials during his September visit, describing the latter as "Nazi spies" who had deceived the president: "This barbarous bloodbath by the enemies of the workers and the nation [*patria*] . . . has occurred just days after the visit of His Excellency the President of the Republic [when] beneath the words and pledges of collaboration with which some company leaders received the President was the hypocritical anti-Chilean attitude of Nazi spies, of those who detest the democratic way of life [and] seek to carry out grave provocations to cause the ruin of the country and to open the door to bandits of the fifth column."[38]

Acting as their patron, the company provided the carabineros with housing, coal, and other perquisites; it was therefore, *El Siglo* and *El Sur* argued, directly responsible for their actions.[39] Company patronage did indeed appear to make the carabineros at least as responsive to the orders of the company as to those of the government and gave rise to the charge

---

35. *El Siglo*, October 10, 1942, 4. The Rettig-Pazols commission was formally decreed by the interior minister on October 8, 1942. See Ministerial Order no. 129, as transcribed in Oficio no. 2246, October 9, 1942, FIC, vol. 2255, ANCh. Raúl Rettig Guissen, a lawyer and militant of the Radical Party, would head the 1990–91 Commission for Truth and Reconciliation, which investigated the disappearance of persons during the 1973–89 military dictatorship of Augusto Pinochet. Rettig died in May 2000. For an extended interview with this fascinating historical figure, see Rettig Guissen, *La historia*.

36. Newspaper articles mobilizing support for Ríos Morales appeared side by side with those denouncing the Lota killings. See, for example, *El Siglo*'s front page on October 9, 1942.

37. *El Siglo*, October 9, 1942, 4.

38. *El Siglo*, October 8, 1942, 3.

39. *El Siglo*, October 9, 1942, 4; and *El Sur*, October 9, 1942, 9.

that the CCIL was, in fact, controlling the zone as a "feudal fiefdom." Outrage at this arrangement was provoked not only by the October police attack, but also by many previous instances of extralegal connections, as when company administrators were able to put the police on barracks alert simply by calling the local chief, or when they called the police out in force for union elections, as in May 1942. Having many times witnessed the carabineros acting in "a spirit of provocation toward the workers" in the coal mining towns, the Confederation of Chilean Workers called for "the total change of personnel in the carabineros' garrison."[40]

Capitalist co-optation of the national police was in violation of the Constitution. It had also been so, of course, under Carlos Ibáñez and Arturo Alessandri in the 1920s and 1930s, but these administrations were more focused on controlling popular sectors than on enforcing the legal limits of the rights of capital. Now, in late 1942, such reactionary social practices were seen to clash sharply with the Popular Front's progressive, modernizing project. Much more decisive intervention was thus required by the state to curb capitalist abuses, an essential step in making "harmoniously mediated" industrial relations truly viable.

On October 8, while the government-appointed investigative commission was en route to the region, the open caskets of the three victims were laid out for public viewing at the Communist Party office in Lota Bajo. The following day, a funeral procession made its way from there to the union office and then on to the cemetery, where thousands of people from around the region, as well as from Concepción and Santiago, gathered to eulogize the martyred workers and to assail the reactionary forces threatening the democratic promise of the Popular Front era.[41] At a moment when the Communist Party was steadfastly pursuing its strategy of National Unity, El Siglo sought to chase away the specter of class conflict. In both its editorials and news coverage, it emphasized the difficult struggle for harmony, reporting that "in the meetings where workers have voted to protest the criminal attack against the miners of Lota, they have understood that it is more urgent than ever to go out and establish powerful organizations for anti-Fascist democratic unity, thus permitting the development throughout the country of a vast movement to combat the Fascists so as to end the constant provocations against the working class and the democratic sectors of the population."[42]

40. El Siglo, October 9, 1942, 4.
41. El Sur, October 9, 1942, 9, and October 10, 1942, 12.
42. El Siglo, October 10, 1942, 4.

Telegrams of support for the Lota miners, demanding investigation of the police attack and punishment for the guilty, poured in from almost all labor sectors in the region—miners, bay and dock workers, sailors, railroad men, bakers, the workers of the CCIL's ceramics factory—and from hundreds of different political and social organizations around the country, including the Democratic Alliance of Santiago and the Directive Committee of Radical (Party) Workers.[43] Many of these expressions of solidarity, particularly as reported by El Siglo, linked "the treacherous triple assassination committed in Lota" to a series of other violent incidents, most notably the killing of a group of campesinos in the south and the murder of a local CTCh secretary. Together, these were seen as clear evidence of systematic persecution of the popular sectors by Fascist segments of society, which the government of the Center-Left Democratic Alliance was called on to stop. Again emphasizing the reciprocity owed to the Lota workers for their show of loyalty, one article in El Siglo claimed that these repressive incidents served "to deepen the sentiment of all democratic sectors across the nation that the Government should, once and for all, proceed to end [relations with] the Fascist elements causing these crimes, and that it should end the policy of interaction with those elements which sacrifice the workers who, as in the case of Lota, were a bastion of the electoral forces that contributed to the defeat of the candidate of the Axis embassies, Carlos Ibáñez, and the triumph of the current President of the Republic."

Another article on the same page added to the list of attacks one "committed against the Mapuches in San Juan de la Costa."[44] As with the leftist press's emphasis on the Mapuche identity of slain coal miner Juan Antipil, this was part of a strategy to build from localized labor conflicts to the idea of a movement of "all democratic sectors," based on cooperation and solidarity among miners, campesinos, rural workers, and the Mapuches. Not only was the national coal mining bourgeoisie excluded from this grouping of democratic sectors, but it was also seen as one of the "Fascist elements causing these crimes."

Women also played a significant role in the development of this regional popular movement. In addition to their direct activism, women of the coal mining zone generated a kind of symbolic capital that served efforts to transform the male miners' industrial conflict into a popular struggle for democratization. Communist press accounts of the October

43. El Siglo, October 9, 1942, 1, 4, and October 10, 1942, 4.
44. El Siglo, October 10, 1942, 4.

7 police attack thus highlighted the key roles played by women and children. One *El Siglo* article, for example, stated that, even as miners were being "savagely beaten" by the police, they remained calm, trying only to disperse as quickly as possible. The violence, however, "produced a great panic among the women and children," and it was "when this panic broke out that [Lieutenant] Cerpa ordered the troops to fire."[45] Although the miners were portrayed here as peaceable and innocent, they still readily appeared as aggressors in the national imagination. By focusing on "women and children" as quintessential helpless victims, the article sought to elicit indignation and greater sympathy for the workers' cause.

A few days after the violent confrontation in Lota, the first Departmental Women's Convention took place in the neighboring town of Coronel. Formally aspiring "to raise a great women's movement [from within] all the progressive sectors of the Chilean population," the convention focused more on class-based socioeconomic battles and international politics than on gender-specific issues. At the closing session on October 11, Eva Rivas, a leader of the local branch of the Movement for the Emancipation of the Chilean Woman (MEMCh), noted that the convention had thoroughly studied the contract petitions of the unions and fully supported them. Then, turning to the recent massacre in Lota, Rivas stated that the slain workers "died for demanding more food for their children, more well-being for their wives [*compañeras*], and more security for themselves on the job." This portrayal of the miners as family men and providers again served to "humanize" what opposition forces presented as brute male workers stirred to violence by Communist agitators. Rivas called on all women to unite "in defense of our home and our nation [*patria*], today under the threat of falling into the clutches of the Fascists." "Mothers, sisters, wives, and daughters," she went on to say, "the pain of millions of women who today wail under the boot of Fascism obliges us to redouble our efforts in defense of our freedom. Thus we will contribute so that this war ends victoriously for the United Nations. In doing so, we will secure justice and liberty for ourselves and for our children."[46]

"The Undue Extension of Rights Accorded to Property": Conclusions of the Rettig-Pazols Report

On October 13, just after the close of the Departmental Women's Convention, while national attention was still riveted on Lota, a cable broke in

---

45. *El Siglo*, October 8, 1942, 1.

46. Eva Rivas, as quoted in *El Chiflón*, November 1942, 15. On Rivas's MEMCh membership, see Providencia Confidencial no. 22, January 31, 1941, FMI, vol. 10455, ARNAD.

the CCIL's Pique Grande mine shaft and coal cars hurtled off the tracks, leaving fourteen people injured, with five in grave condition. Workers insisted that the accident could have been avoided since union delegates had reported the poor condition of the cable several weeks earlier.[47] The accident reinforced the miners' claims about company disregard for health and safety, as conveyed in their August contract petitions, especially their insistence that greater worker control of the shop floor was a crucial part of the solution.

More than two months after the workers had submitted petitions, however, the parties still could not reach agreement. The day after the Pique Grande accident in Lota, union leaders from around the coal mining zone traveled to Santiago to meet with the labor minister and to negotiate with company officials through the mediation of the director general of labor (DGT). After several days of meetings, the union leaders concluded that company intransigence was making any immediate solution impossible and they prepared to return home. On the morning before they left Santiago, demonstrating the "high level of interest shown by the government in achieving a solution to this conflict," President Ríos Morales invited the delegation to meet with him personally.[48] Though described by *El Siglo* as "cordial," the meeting was more symbolic than substantive. The union leaders continued to stress the coal workers' "patriotic cooperation with the Government in its drive for increased national production and for strengthening of democracy in the fight against Fascism."[49] At the same time, the leaders insisted—in the name of the residents and workers of the coal mining zone—that Chile immediately break ties with the Axis powers and establish diplomatic relations with the Soviet Union. In response, the president "expressed his firm commitment to cooperate with the democratic countries," but did not address the issue of Chile's diplomatic ties with any greater specificity.

Shortly after meeting with the coal miners' delegation, President Ríos Morales received the final report on the October 7 violence in Lota, prepared by Director General of Information and Culture Raúl Rettig Guissen and Carabineros Director General Osvaldo Pazols.[50] Dated October 14, the Rettig-Pazols Report first presented a brief narrative of the events, then drew conclusions and made recommendations.[51] Declaring that the police

47. *El Sur*, October 14, 1942, 8. *El Siglo* says that seventeen people were injured, eleven critically. *El Siglo*, October 14, 1942, 1.
48. *El Siglo*, October 17, 1942, 6.
49. Ibid.
50. Ibid.
51. The Rettig-Pazols Report is reprinted in *El Sur*, October 18, 1942, 4.

had acted in response to the workers' disobedience and were justified in repelling their aggression, the report exonerated all of the officers, including Lieutenant Roberto Saa Sánchez. Regarding the violation of Deputy Uribe Cárdenas's congressional immunity and the claim that he was beaten in police custody, the report took note of the parties' different versions and then concluded that, in the authors' opinion, "the mistreatment did, unfortunately, occur."[52] As part of a deeper tradition of conciliatory politics in Chile, Rettig and Pazols were trying to straddle both sides of the situation, recognizing while also excusing abuses by national security forces.[53] Although they found no criminal wrongdoing by any police officers, they nonetheless highly commended the Zone 4 chief of police for quickly "adopt[ing] a measure that would signify the beginning of strict proceedings against the responsible official[s]": the transfer of Osvaldo Cerpa, the lieutenant who allegedly assaulted Deputy Uribe, from Lota to Concepción. Three days after the incident, Director General Pazols had also ordered the suspension of Captain Márquez.

Moving on from the responsibility of individual officers, the report turned to the issues underlying the incident, foremost among which was the conflict between the company's property rights as it exercised them and the rights of citizens as guaranteed by the Constitution, particularly the right of workers to freely assemble, not just in Lota but throughout the country:

> In fact, up to this point, it has been standard practice, in all mines in the country, to include among the rights enjoyed by the mining companies that of regulating many rights of citizenship, the full guarantee of which is found in our own political Constitution. Furthermore, the rights that correspond to individuals and to unions by virtue of the labor laws are exercised, in many respects, under the authority of the very same companies. . . . The mistake[n practice] stems from the undue extension of rights accorded to property.[54]

52. Rettig and Pazols also note that the final verdict rested with the "indictment prepared by the military courts." The carabineros had been under the Ministry of the Interior since 1927, so I do not know why this case would have come under military court jurisdiction.

53. On the deep patterns of conflict and conciliation in Chilean history, which assumed a particular form and rhetoric in the mid-1940s, see Loveman and Lira, *Las ardientes cenizas*; for their analysis of events between 1941 and 1943, see 105–15.

54. *El Sur*, October 18, 1942, 4.

The debate over rights to control different aspects of workers' lives was crucial in the midcentury struggle over different models of democracy. Which rights naturally attached to the ownership of property? Which to the state? And which to the workers themselves? The previous century of oligarchic dominance witnessed the consolidation and expansion of the rights of private property. Now representatives of both labor and the state were pushing to shift the balance, each in their own direction. Union and political leaders representing the coal miners made use of democratic avenues to press for state intervention as an intermediary step toward greater worker control. The Ríos Morales government, on the other hand, made use of worker support and leftist conciliation to bolster its own power over both workers and capitalists.

As indicated in the Rettig-Pazols Report, at the heart of the Popular Front project, a battle was being waged between the bosses' control of their workers and the state's jurisdiction over its citizens. This mode of contention played out not only in mining towns, but also on rural estates, where efforts by government officials to enforce labor laws were often seen as encroachments on the rights of private property. As in the situation in mining communities such as Lota in October 1942, Loveman explains, for rural landowners, "private property meant that governmental regulation did not extend into the territory of their proprietary domain. The use of force by landowners also indicated, however, that in some cases, despite all efforts to evade or subvert application of labor law, labor inspectors insisted on compliance. Physical force, the least subtle and, over the long run, the least effective manner of resistance to labor legislation in the Chilean context, represented an anachronistic response by landowners unable to otherwise impede the increasing restriction of proprietary authority contained in labor law."[55]

Thus in Lota, the CCIL had called on the carabineros, who were sanctioned to use state force, to counter efforts by workers and certain political and government actors to develop a more modern system of industrial relations. The Rettig-Pazols Report discussed the rights of property owners in mining communities based on legal opinion no. 208, of April 1942, issued by the State Defense Council (Consejo de Defensa Fiscal), which had "establish[ed] an essential distinction between what may be understood as the industrial sector within a 'camp [*campamento*]' of this nature, and the part that should be considered a 'town [*población*].'" This legal opinion argued that company statutes (*reglamentos*) and their enforcement had to reflect the limits of property rights vis-à-vis the authority of

55. Loveman, *Struggle*, 105.

the state: "In what exceeds the contractual obligations that the worker owes to the boss, the latter ceases to have jurisdiction, and the worker or employee—a citizen now—remains subject only to the authority of the State."[56]

Drawing on this opinion for its assessment of the situation in Lota, the Rettig-Pazols Report concluded that *only* the appropriate civil authority had the right to regulate public meetings "in that part of the camp [*campamento*] which is considered a town [*población*]," regardless of the company's ownership of the property in question. The report recommended that the president grant this regulatory power exclusively to intendants, governors, and subdelegates, all of whom were executive branch appointees. In following this recommendation, on October 21, President Ríos Morales and Interior Minister Raúl Morales Beltrami would issue a supreme decree that made it illegal for mining companies to restrict the time or location of workers' meetings. Provincial governors were to promptly submit a "regulatory plan," listing appropriate sites for public meetings within each mining camp.[57]

To the surprise of many, the Rettig-Pazols report took an even more radically interventionist turn with regard to the internal affairs of the CCIL. It began by reflecting on the nature of social relations: "Experience indicates that the basic prerequisite for harmony between workers and owners is the courtesy that the bosses show their subordinates. This is a human factor, whose importance is beyond discussion because it has been proven that the arbitrary or rude attitudes of the bosses or administrators of industries multiply labor conflicts or make their resolution more difficult." Rettig and Pazols then referred directly to the head of the CCIL Welfare Department, Octavio Astorquiza, sharply criticizing his prejudiced, inflexible, and arbitrary attitudes and actions toward the workers, which, they said, made him a serious impediment to harmonious relations between the company and its workforce. Rettig and Pazols were fully "convinced that Sr. Astorquiza must be relieved of his current post," and they recommended that the Executive intercede directly with the company to bring this about. Rettig and Pazols argued that "the Supreme Government and the Company have an interest in maintaining cordial relations. On the part of the Executive, this interest stems from, among other reasons, its desire to achieve greater social tranquility. The

56. *El Sur*, October 18, 1942, 4.

57. *El Sur*, October 22, 1942, 22. The question of state versus company jurisdiction over workers' assemblies subsequently played out in other mining areas, such as the Sewell camp of the El Teniente copper mines. See Klubock, *Contested Communities*, 252.

Company, in turn, requires the protection of its rights by the Government. In the name of this reciprocal need, the urgency of replacing its Welfare Chief should be made known to the Company in question."[58] This formulation of tripartite relations in the Popular Front era captured both its utopian dimensions and at least one of its tragic misconceptions—the premise that the capitalists needed the government as much as the government needed the capitalists.

CCIL Managing Director Juan Manuel Valle responded promptly and publicly to the Rettig-Pazols Report. In an open letter, Valle noted his surprise at its version of events. He strongly defended Octavio Astorquiza as an "employee who, after twenty years of service, has the full confidence of the Company; who possesses a calm and level-headed character; and who, we are certain, would never stray from the norms and traditions that the Company insists on at all times."[59] This was a bold position since Astorquiza's attitudes and actions were being criticized as arbitrary and abusive by a well-respected centrist lawyer and the chief of the national police, both of whom had been commissioned by the president. Yet, rather than offer any conciliatory gestures, Valle pointedly rejected the Rettig-Pazols assessment and, in doing so, rebuffed the government's efforts to harmonize industrial relations. Whatever steps the Ríos Morales administration took to curb "the undue extension of the rights accorded to property," it certainly did not succeed in removing Astorquiza, whose power in the company would only increase in the coming years.

"The Constant and Immediate Participation of the State"

The question of the government's mandate to intervene in the social relations of the coal industry went beyond the specific case of Astorquiza.[60] It also went beyond the Rettig-Pazols Report and became an issue for the progressive middle class, a key sector in the construction of "the people" (el pueblo) in the Popular Front era.[61] In an editorial that reflected wider public support for increased state intervention in the coal industry, the regional centrist newspaper El Sur proclaimed that, until the national

58. Rettig-Pazols Report, as reprinted in El Sur, October 18, 1942, 4.
59. Juan Manuel Valle, as quoted in El Sur, October 25, 1942, 3.
60. "The constant and immediate participation of the State" is taken from an editorial by Carlos González Utreras in El Sur, October 20, 1942, 3. As of October 1943, González Utreras was secretary of the Democratic Alliance Committee for the province of Concepción, but I do not know his party affiliation.
61. On the middle class during the Popular Front era, see Barr-Melej, Reforming Chile.

plan for electrification was implemented, "coal mining [would] continue to be an essential industry. That is why anything related to it should be given preferential treatment by the state. Removing obstacles to the production of the combustible fuel that, every day, is vital to the country means laying solid foundations for our economy, and, therefore, for our social organization."[62]

The editorial expanded from the case of Astorquiza to propose more generally that "one way to avoid the discord that, at times, develops among the principal participants in the settlement of socioeconomic differences would be for the Government to intervene more or less directly in the designation of the person who will head the Social Welfare Department of each company that hires more than a certain number of workers." Without specifying the legal basis for such overt public involvement in the operations of a private company, the *El Sur* editors insisted that "only the constant and immediate participation of the State will be able to prevent the continued recurrence of damaging and painful incidents in the coal mining zone." Though noting the great distances between the mines and the provincial capitals, where most government offices were headquartered, they still took the provincial governors of Concepción and Arauco to task for paying insufficient attention to the coal mining areas. Undue company control did indeed stem from extensive company ownership of property in the coal towns, the editors argued, but the problem was greatly exacerbated by the "relative absence of governmental authority in these centers of production."

As noted above, the Communist and labor press repeatedly argued that the government should ensure a favorable outcome for the workers in their contract disputes in light of their patriotic decision to maintain coal production despite the repression to which they had been subjected. The existing imbalance of social forces made it impossible, labor leaders argued, for the government's mediation to be both just and impartial: true justice required government intervention to strengthen the workers' position.

The October 1942 slaying of three unarmed workers had catapulted the coal mining region into the center of public attention, and in the ensuing month, the Ministry of Labor itself took the lead in the contract negotiations. After weeks of "exhausting sessions, sometimes for 7 or 8 continuous hours,"[63] on November 2, the parties finally reached agreement. A

---

62. González Utreras editorial in *El Sur*, October 20, 1942, 3.
63. *El Chiflón*, November 1942, 18–19. See also the front page editorial in the same issue.

minimum wage of 20 pesos per day would be established for all workers in the industry, with pay increases ranging from 4 to 6 pesos.[64] Though the workers' original petition had requested raises averaging 8 pesos, the final settlement was easily construed as victory by their leadership. Even more widely hailed as a positive outcome was the commitment of all parties to form permanent tripartite production committees at each mine, to be headed by a Ministry of Labor official. As reported in the centrist newspaper *La Epoca*, these committees would "work continuously" for "better understanding of the factors of production" and "possibilities for general improvement."[65]

The Chilean Communist Party (PCCh) maintained that the outcome of the 1942 collective disputes in the coal industry was highly favorable to the workers and that it was only possible because of their patriotic choice not to strike in the wake of the October shootings. In the January 1943 report of the PCCh's Central Committee, Juan Vargas Puebla praised the miners, who "did not allow themselves to be provoked and who, with their unity and firmness, achieved the signing of a contract that granted wage increases, respect for section delegates, and the commitment to organize Production Committees."[66]

Justifying the Communists' strategy of cross-class political alliances, Vargas argued that the peaceful and favorable resolution of the coal miners' disputes showed that broader national and international objectives could be achieved without sacrificing the interests of the workers. "The results obtained in these battles and others," he declared, "prove that the working class defends the interests of Chile and its own class interests with true patriotism, increasing production, defending the democratic regime and social gains, and strengthening the fight for National Unity against Fascism."[67] The Communists would soon claim another great victory for democracy in the wake of the Lota shootings: on January 20, 1943, the Ríos Morales administration finally severed diplomatic ties with the Axis powers.

64. *La Época* (Santiago) November 21, 1942, 5.

65. Ibid. See also Gallardo, "Problemas nacionales," 12–13. Lorenzo Gallardo was secretary of the regional council of the National Miners' Federation (FNM) and former president of the Lota miners' union.

66. Juan Vargas Puebla, "La clase obera en la lucha contra el fascismo," in PCCh Central Committee Resolutions (1943) 65–66.

67. Ibid., 67.

6

"SOLDIERS OF DEMOCRACY":
COLLABORATION AND CONFLICT DURING WORLD WAR II

On January 20, 1943, the Chilean government, under President Juan Antonio Ríos Morales, broke diplomatic ties with the Axis powers and joined forces with the Allies. Chile was the second-to-last-country in the Americas to do so, leaving only Argentina behind. Chilean Communists had been advocating this move for years, and they now claimed it as their victory. They played up the moral high road taken by Communist coal miners in the aftermath of the October 1942 shootings in Lota, which had won them favor with the public and the administration, and took full credit for the president's change of heart. Many factors, of course, played into the timing of Ríos Morales's decision, not least of which was the Soviet Union's clear progress toward a hard-won victory at Stalingrad, where the Red Army's killing of more than a half million German soldiers would lead General Friedrich Paulus to surrender on February 2, 1943, and mark a major turning point in the war. As the prospects of the Axis powers declined and the prestige of Stalinist parties rose, Ríos Morales began to reassess Chile's international alignments. Throughout most of 1942, the U.S. State Department had put strong pressure on Chile and Argentina to sever ties with Germany, Italy, and Japan. By the end of the year, Chile's reluctance to do so had reached what Michael Francis described as "the level of a major foreign policy controversy."[1] The president's decision, after ten months in office, to move into full alignment with the

1. Francis, "United States and Chile," 91.

United Nations was influenced by his desire to improve Chilean relations with the United States and to qualify for the Lend-Lease program.[2]

Communists throughout Chile were elated: they had finally achieved formal government and military backing for the anti-Fascist crusade that they had renewed with fervor after Nazi Germany invaded the Soviet Union back in June 1941.[3] The PCCh Central Committee called upon "the working class and all of the people [todo el pueblo]" to maintain "the strictest vigilance against the spies, saboteurs, and elements suspected to have relations with the fifth column."[4] People throughout the coal mining towns fully embraced this duty, organizing Civil Defense and "Unity for Victory" committees and moving into action.[5]

The Ríos Morales administration was also concerned about a possible backlash from pro-Axis forces in Chilean society and took measures to prevent industrial sabotage and to foil possible coup attempts. Under Article 23 of Internal State Security Law no. 7200, passed one year earlier, the president declared several emergency zones, foremost among which were the coal, nitrate, and copper mining regions and certain industrial centers. These decrees entailed a suspension of many civil liberties and the immediate transfer of governing power from civilian authorities to military officers known as "Jefes de la Plaza."[6] In the coal mining zone, the military implemented "tight surveillance of vitally important sites, such as the coal mines, electric power plants, drinking water facilities, machine shops, and others directly connected to the maintenance of our daily lives."[7] Not only Lota and Coronel, but even the smaller coastal town of Lebu became militarized when the designated emergency zone delegate arrived there with a large contingent of Navy troops aboard the battleship O'Higgins.[8] At the same time, the Chilean Congress approved wartime measures, similar to those in the United States, for detaining foreigners

2. The term "United Nations" was first used in the title of a declaration signed by twenty-six countries in January 1942; it became the formal term for the Allies and the basis for the organization created in June 1945. In March 1943, the United States did sign a Lend-Lease agreement with Chile and slowly began to supply it with some arms, but by the end of the war, "only 30% of the materials agreed upon had been transferred." Meneses Ciuffardi, El factor naval, 196, 197–98, 203–6.

3. Communists around the world pursued anti-Fascist campaigns at the Soviets' behest, beginning in early 1933, but suspended them in the period of the Nazi-Soviet Nonaggression Pact, from August 1939 to June 1941.

4. PCCh Central Committee Resolutions (1943), 65.

5. On the work of the Unity for Victory committees in Lebu, see Pizarro Soto, Lebu, 355.

6. La Opinión (Lota; CCIL publication), February 1943, 1.

7. La Trinchera (Coronel), January 23, 1943, 1.

8. Pizarro Soto, Lebu, 355.

from the Axis countries and other suspected Fascist agents.[9] The principal internment camp was located in the far north of the country, amid the arid nitrate pampas near the port of Pisagua.[10]

Workers and their political allies applauded the emergency measures, which, the government explained, were intended to prevent any disruptions of production or civil order that "might result from the break in relations with the Axis countries,"[11] But leftist leaders were also aware how readily these same measures could be turned against them, especially in light of the president's long history of anti-Communism, his close association with Chile's economic elite, and his resistance to major social reforms. They therefore warned their workers to remain on guard against not only fascistic capitalists and right-wing politicians, but also certain forces within the government, to which the leaders had given their conditional support, but which they still did not trust. The PCCh Central Committee called on its working-class followers "to defend with the utmost energy their democratic liberties and social victories and to denounce the functionaries and bosses who, under the influence of Axis agents, seek to pervert the intended purpose of the Emergency Zones, using them to attack the rights of workers."[12]

Concerns shared by the Communists and the Executive about possible sabotage and subversion provoked by the break with the Axis powers were not entirely unfounded. Segments of the Chilean Right perceived this move as a rapprochement between the Ríos Morales administration and the Communists and began mustering support for a coup to install a hard-line government that would reestablish relations with the Axis. In January 1944, British intelligence provided evidence that right-wing coup preparations were well advanced, and the United States sent a naval cruiser to the port of Valparaíso to forestall any such move, "as a demonstration of solidarity and friendship . . . with the Government of Chile."[13]

9. The Chilean Communist Party was a leading advocate of the emergency internment policy, though the same legal grounds used to imprison Fascists at the height of the war would be used repeatedly against Communists in the coming years. See Carlos Contreras Labarca's inaugural speech, "Chile Unido en el Frente de la Libertad," in PCCh Central Committee Resolutions (1943), 21–22.

10. The Pisagua military camp was also used as a prison during the Ibáñez regime of the 1920s. It would gain further notoriety during the González Videla repression of 1947–48 (see chapter 9), and again after 1973, under Augusto Pinochet. See Frazier, Salt in the Sand, chap. 5.

11. La Trinchera, January 23, 1943, 1.

12. PCCh Central Committee Resolutions (1943), 65.

13. Confidential urgent telegram from Secretary of State Cordell Hull to Ambassador Bowers, January 6, 1944; reproduced and discussed in Meneses Ciuffardi, El factor naval, 201–2.

Among the identified coup plotters was none other than Brigadier General Jorge Berguño Meneses, the staunch anti-Communist who had investigated the coal mining zone in 1941 at the behest of Popular Front President Aguirre Cerda.[14] Also named in the plot were other top military officers, the leader of the Chilean National Socialists, Jorge González von Marées, and former President Carlos Ibáñez del Campo, all of whom were allegedly backed by the government of Argentina.[15] General Berguño was forced to resign his commission and was kept under close surveillance by the secret police for at least the next year.[16] Berguño's exposure and ouster served to discredit key conclusions of his report, especially that it was the Communists, not the companies, who were to blame for low productivity in the mines. Although the downfall of General Berguño was a blow to the coal mining capitalists, the anti-Communist measures adopted or strengthened as a consequence of his report remained firmly in place.[17]

The government's break with the Axis and moves against the Chilean ultra-Right strengthened the position of the Chilean Communist Party, creating more favorable ground for it to work with broad segments of society in patriotic, anti-Fascist campaigns. The very day after the announcement of Chile's diplomatic shift in January 1943, the PCCh Central Committee opened its Twelfth Plenary Session, whose proceedings were published under the title "Chile United in the Global Anti-Nazi Coalition." The thrust of this meeting was to reaffirm and strengthen the party's pursuit of the policy line known as "National Unity," which aimed at replacing Ríos Morales's original Democratic Alliance with a broader and stronger coalition.[18] Local committees had formed in the coal mining region as early as April 1942, but it was not until the end of the year that

14. Loveman and Lira, *Las ardientes cenizas*, 115.

15. Meneses Ciuffardi, *El factor naval*, 199–202; Maldonado Prieto, "'La Prusia de América del Sur.'"

16. Police reports on Berguño's daily movements exist from January 1944 to January 1945. This is an incomplete collection, however, and it is possible that he was observed by the secret police before and after these dates. Servicio de Observación, Fondos Varios, vols. 669 and 670, ANCh.

17. The irony of police surveillance of Berguño is that it was his report on the coal mining zone that prompted the Army's secret police to step up its study of the members and activities of the Marxist parties. After the Berguño Report's release, "the Investigative Police started to check for and remove persons indoctrinated by the Communist Party from the lists of persons called for military service." Heinz and Fruehling, *Determinants*, 403–4; see also Estado Mayor General del Ejército de Chile, *Historia*, 47–48.

18. The National Unity policy was first promoted at the Chilean Communist Party's Eleventh Plenary Session in October 1941, four months after Nazi Germany invaded the Soviet Union. The faction of Socialists led by Marmaduke Grove gave the policy some support, but most of the Socialist Party strongly opposed it. Though the PCCh Central Committee reaffirmed its commitment to National Unity at its January 1943 session, the policy was

the PCCh began to pursue the National Unity strategy in earnest, and not until the January 1943 plenary session that it became official policy.

Using wartime rhetoric of good versus evil, the Chilean Communist Party sought to increase its network of political allies by embracing all sectors of Chilean society except those deemed to be Fascist. In theory, domestic allies could now include pro-democracy segments of the bourgeoisie and even the traditional aristocracy, represented politically in the Liberal and Conservative Parties. In reality, few of these Right-leaning elements were willing to join forces with the Communists, and the leftist press continued its harsh attacks against them. By contrast, the PCCh's relations with almost all Center and Left forces were notably strengthened. In remarkable testament to the greatly enhanced power and status of the Chilean Communist Party, its 1943 plenary session was launched with a flurry of written greetings and personal appearances by leaders of the Radical, Democratic, Socialist, and Workers' Socialist Parties, as well as the Confederation of Chilean Workers, all of whom praised the Communist Party for advancing both workers' interests and the cause of democracy. Thus, speaking for the Workers' Socialist Party, César Godoy Urrutia declared the Communist Party "to be the majority party of the working class, which in Chile, as in all the world, provides direction for the workers." And, speaking for the Radical Party, Héctor Arancibia Laso commended the Communists for "taking up the banner of the defense of the people and carrying it with honor and correctness."[19]

Although the U.S.–Soviet wartime alliance was certainly the immediate impetus for such gestures of respect and cooperation, looking toward the end of the war, many Left-leaning centrists in Chile hoped to continue friendly relations with the Communists in order to shape a postwar world of peace and social justice. This vision was also held by many New Deal advocates in the United States, one of the most powerful of whom was Vice President Henry Agard Wallace. In a lecture delivered at Ohio Wesleyan University in early March 1943, Wallace declared, "The future well-being of the world depends upon the extent to which Marxianism, as it

---

never really successful. See PCCh Central Committee Resolutions (1943); and Barnard, "Chilean Communist Party," chap. 6, esp. 288–89.

19. PCCh Central Committee Resolutions (1943), 3. As discussed in chapter 3, César Godoy Urrutia's decision to support the PCCh was an interesting turn of events since his dissident Nonconformist faction had split from the Socialist Party in mid-1940 due to its support of the Popular Front and especially its acquiescence to what the Nonconformists deemed the excessively reformist Communist line. Yet, by 1944, Godoy Urrutia, together with Orlando Millas, Natalio Berman, Carlos Rosales, and other leaders of the Workers Socialist Party (PST), moved to disband their party and join the PCCh. About two-thirds of the PST members became Communists, while others, such as Víctor Mora, returned to the Socialist Party.

is being progressively modified in Russia, and democracy, as we are adapting it to twentieth-century conditions, can live together in peace."[20]

Mr. New Deal Hails the Miners of Lota: The March 1943 Visit of U.S. Vice President Henry A. Wallace

Just days after his talk in Ohio and with the full support of President Roosevelt, on March 16, U.S. Vice President Henry Wallace boarded a Pan American–Grace Airways plane for a month-long goodwill tour of Latin America, to include stops in Costa Rica, Panama, Bolivia, Peru, Ecuador, Colombia, and Chile. The first U.S. vice president ever to visit South America, Wallace "insisted that protocol arrangements be kept simple by subordinating formal functions and official ceremonies to grass roots tours of farms and factories." Wallace sent word that, in lieu of "lavish ceremonial gifts" typically bestowed on foreign dignitaries, he would most appreciate Latin American folk music recordings.[21]

After visiting several other Latin American countries, on March 26, Wallace landed in Santiago, where nine of Chile's major political parties and labor organizations had published a joint manifesto encouraging all citizens "to render public homage to Vice President Wallace, to the people of the United States, and to President Roosevelt, who are defending the cause of freedom and democratic ideals."[22] Despite Wallace's request for simplicity, Ríos Morales received him with full state honors, and as Wallace's car traveled from the airport to downtown, nearly a hundred thousand people lined the streets, waving party banners and shouting, "Down with Fascism!"[23] Over the next several days, the vice president attended luncheons, dinners, military parades, and other events in his honor, including a ceremony at the National Stadium before an estimated eighty thousand people. In the halls of the Chilean Congress, he gave a powerful speech in Spanish, in which he declared that the "revolutionary march" of the people would bring about "peace based on social justice." Chile, he said, would have "a distinguished place" in this postwar order, "as a nation that showed the way."[24]

20. Henry A. Wallace, introductory address to the Merrick Lectures, in Wallace et al., *Christian Bases*, 15–16. See also Schapsmeier and Schapsmeier, *Prophet in Politics*, 34.

21. Schapsmeier and Schapsmeier, *Prophet in Politics*, 46.

22. *New York Times*, March 25, 1943, 7.

23. *New York Times*, March 27, 1943, 4. The official program for Wallace's visit was published as a two-page pamphlet, *Visita oficial del Excmo. Sr. Henry A. Wallace*.

24. Quotes from *New York Times*, March 28, 1943, 6; see also *New York Times*, March 29, 1943, 5, and March 30, 1943, 26. Copies of many of Wallace's addresses delivered in Chile are located in "Speeches by Wallace," Box 1943, in the Henry A. Wallace Papers.

Although he graciously acceded to such state-sponsored pomp and circumstance, Wallace also insisted on visiting Chile's farms, vineyards, ports, industrial centers, and the nitrate, copper, and coal mines so vital to the war effort. "I'm eager," he told reporters, "to meet and personally contact those associated with work production."[25] After four days in the capital, on March 30, Wallace flew to Concepción, and then traveled by car to Lota, where nearly ten thousand people of all classes and political persuasions lined the streets to greet him, with a preponderance of Communist and union banners waving amid Chilean and U.S. flags.[26]

Many of the region's top Communist leaders, including Lota Mayor Santos Medel, shared the stage with the illustrious U.S. Democrat—the vice president of the most powerful country in the United Nations—who addressed the crowd in Spanish, hailing the Chilean coal miners as "soldiers of democracy," as vital and valiant "as were those men in uniform fighting on the battlefields." Amid loud cheers of pride and approval, Wallace spoke to men who had come from long shifts of hard labor, to women who had lost their husbands or fathers in methane gas explosions, and to young boys who were already making the descent deep into the mines. Here in the heart of Chile's coal mining region, Wallace declared this to be the century of the common people, not the century of international monopolies, whose greed would be checked, or of imperialist forces in the United States. "In this century," Wallace proclaimed, "there will be no nation which will enjoy the divine power to exploit other nations." Again the crowd cheered enthusiastically, committed, as was Wallace, both to victory over the Fascists and to the social and economic changes necessary for just and lasting world peace.[27]

The tone and content of the vice president's speech in Lota, together with news of his face-to-face meetings with other Chilean workers, generated high expectations for his visit. Yet, despite Wallace's openness to common folk, CCIL administrators were able to control his activities to a large degree. Playing up their image as progressive capitalists, they showed Wallace the company restaurant, sports arena, swimming pool, hospital, and only the best housing. They also arranged for him to meet with workers and white-collar employees hand-picked for their loyalty to

25. New York Times, March 27, 1943, 4.
26. New York Times, March 31, 1943, 10. See also "Mr. Wallace Goes South," Time, April 5, 1943. The impressive turnout in the coal mining region testifies to Wallace's strong following among leftist working-class sectors. His largest turnouts in Santiago numbered between forty and eighty thousand.
27. New York Times, March 31, 1943, 10.

the Lota company and their anti-leftist sentiments. After Wallace's visit, the National Miners' Federation (FNM) denounced the CCIL for putting "a screen in front of his eyes . . . so that he could not see the horrible misery in which the miners live."[28]

Yet Henry Wallace did see the plight of the workers, and he deeply respected their aspirations for a better life and their commitment to just and sustainable democracy. His 1943 goodwill tour of Latin America, including his visit to the Chilean coal mines, was "an unqualified success in every way," according to two of his biographers. "The massive receptions accorded Wallace," they write, "were truly awe inspiring."[29] U.S. Ambassador to Chile Claude G. Bowers, whose invitation had prompted the Latin American tour, could not have been more pleased. "Never in Chilean history," he proclaimed, "has any foreigner been received with such extravagance and evidently sincere enthusiasm." In a separate report, he noted that "the enthusiastic reaction of the common people cannot be explained away by press preparations, party orders or anything else than the idea that here was a man representing the United States fresh from Washington who was their friend and deeply interested in their welfare."[30] After returning to the United States on April 24, Wallace gave several press conferences and public addresses about his Latin American experiences, again describing the coal miners as "the most solid soldiers of democracy that he had come across in Chile."[31]

As vice president and chairman of the Board of Economic Welfare (BEW), Wallace sought to renew Latin American confidence in the U.S. commitment to Good Neighbor policies, especially related to production and trade. Wallace's credibility among Latin American workers was high since one of his early victories as BEW chairman was the inclusion of mandatory "labor clauses" in contracts with Latin American producers. Designed to ensure adequate wages and working conditions while maximizing productivity for war needs, these labor clauses were virulently attacked by New Deal opponents. Senator Robert Taft, for example, accused Wallace of "setting up an international W.P.A."[32] Great numbers of

---

28. *El Chiflón*, May 1943, 17–18.

29. Schapsmeier and Schapsmeier, *Prophet in Politics*, 46–47.

30. Claude G. Bowers to Cordell Hull, March 29, 1943, as quoted in Schapsmeier and Schapsmeier, 47.

31. Henry A. Wallace, as quoted in Teitelboim, "Lota aguerrida," 21. Teitelboim offers a beautiful rendering of Wallace's speech about his visit to the coal mines, though he says it was given at the Lincoln Memorial. I believe, however, that the speech he refers to is "We Are All Americans," delivered on May 16 in Central Park, New York City. See Henry A. Wallace Papers; see also *New York Times*, December 21, 1943, 11.

32. Schapsmeier and Schapsmeier, *Prophet in Politics*, 44–45.

working-class Latin Americans, on the other hand, deeply appreciated the clauses, which set Henry Wallace on a path to become one of the most respected, even beloved, U.S. politicians in all of Latin America.

A devout internationalist, Wallace had long recognized the importance of strong and equitable relations with Latin American republics—not only with their statesmen and capitalists, but also with the continent's laboring masses. As early as the mid-1930s, he "initiated an intense program of self-education on Latin America," reading widely in history and politics, mastering the Spanish language, and listening to Latin America folk music, which he would collect and enjoy throughout his life.[33] From his insistence on labor clauses to his delivery of speeches in Spanish, Wallace's affinity with Latin Americans was far from one-sided. As Edward and Frederick Schapsmeier write, "Many Latins, particularly the poor, regarded him as their only spokesman. Knowledge of this trust spurred Wallace to promote the kind of foreign policy that would fulfill the hopes and aspirations of the common man everywhere."[34]

To his command of international relations, Wallace brought a sensitivity to class issues and a commitment to progressive socioeconomic reform. In one of his most famous speeches, delivered in New York City in May 1942, Wallace took issue with Henry Luce's notion of twentieth century as the "American century," proclaiming it instead to be "the century of the common man." Widely reported in the Chilean press and quickly published in Spanish, Wallace's ideals resonated with the political culture and social aspirations of many sectors of Chilean society, from the Wesleyan Socialists and Catholic Falange to the Communist miners.[35] Like the diverse forces in the ever-shifting Center-Left alliances in Chile, Wallace himself combined Social Gospel theology, Christian utopianism, Wilsonian democratic principles, and in general, a "strongly held conviction that capitalism was in need of reform and greater morality."[36]

As wartime needs grew, however, debates raged in the United States over the continued relevance of New Deal policies. Even President Roosevelt, striving for unity in the Democratic Party, claimed that the progressive New Deal causes he had championed so fervently in the 1930s were no longer national priorities. He nonetheless continued to support his

33. Ibid., 40.
34. Ibid., 44.
35. The English title of Wallace's May 1942 speech was "The Price of Free World Victory." For versions that might have circulated among Chilean workers, see Wallace, *Después de la guerra* and *El siglo del pueblo*.
36. Linus Pauling, foreword to Schapsmeier and Schapsmeier, *Prophet in Politics*, ix.

embattled vice president, one of the most ardent proponents of a radical social agenda, who "never relented in seeking to keep alive the New Deal philosophy."[37] As evident in many of Wallace's writings and speeches, he was also among the minority of politicians in the capitalist world who accepted international Communism's embrace of democratic institutions. Wallace supported alliances with the Soviet Union and Communist Parties as essential, not only for victory in the war, but also for any lasting postwar peace. He believed that, without full and equal collaboration between Marxists and Western democracies, capitalism and imperialism would run rampant, destroying the possibility for justice necessary to sustain peace. Wallace was thus quite pleased with the prominent role of the Communist Party in Chilean society and politics, particularly under the broad banner of National Unity.

In pursuing alliances across class and ideology, Chilean Communists were following the lead of Moscow. In May 1943, shortly after Wallace returned to the United States, the Comintern dissolved itself. Such a strictly class-based organization, Communist leaders explained, no longer served the interests of its member parties, which, in the context of the war, needed to devote all their energies to anti-Fascist coalitions. Looking toward the postwar era, moreover, many Communists around the world anticipated continued cooperation with progressive democratic forces. To Henry Wallace, the dissolution of the Comintern demonstrated that "Communism was no longer a revolutionary ideology to be used for subversive purposes."[38] From soldiers of revolution disclaiming nationalism, Communist workers were now to remake themselves into patriotic citizen workers, defending democracy at home and abroad. Led by the Communists, many Chilean workers became increasingly confident that a strategy of broad coalitions would bring about a leftward shift in national politics and usher in long-sought socioeconomic reforms.

Wallace was not the only U.S. government official contemplating the role that strong leftist labor movements in places such as Chile were likely to play in the postwar world. In 1943, the State Department developed a pilot project under which a corps of labor specialists would report from overseas embassies. In December 1943, the first ever U.S. labor attaché, Daniel L. Horowitz, took up his post at the U.S. Embassy in Santiago. Chile was chosen as the test country rather than Mexico, according to Horowitz, because Chile had "important trade unions [that] influenced

---

37. Schapsmeier and Schapsmeier, *Prophet in Politics*, 50.
38. Ibid., 34.

political party activity," and because its U.S. ambassador was enthusiastic about the idea, whereas Mexico's was not. With a master's degree in political science and labor economics from New York University and a doctorate in public administration from Harvard, Horowitz had previously taught both labor history and techniques of collective bargaining to U.S. trade unionists. In Chile from 1943 to 1946, he investigated all issues concerning labor relations and politics and reported back to the ambassador and the secretary of state. Valuing his detailed assessments, the State Department quickly expanded its Labor Attaché Corps, first in Latin America, and then, after the war, into Europe and around the world.[39]

While Horowitz immersed himself in Chilean labor politics, Communist leaders were debating how to strengthen their National Unity line of cross-class collaboration, particularly in light of recent moves by U.S. Communist Party (CPUSA), led by Secretary-General Earl R. Browder. Arguing that the advance of industrial capitalism was vital for the well-being of both democracy and the workers themselves, Browder called for full support of the bourgeoisie and renunciation of particular working-class interests. Thus virtually erasing the Marxist basis of the party's existence, he transformed the CPUSA into the Communist Political Association, which, on the eve of the 1944 campaign, "proclaimed its support of Franklin D. Roosevelt for President."[40] Beyond the immediate election, as Ernst Halperin explains, "Browder's entire policy [was] based on the assumption that Soviet-American wartime cooperation, and consequently also the extremely moderate wartime policies of the Western Communist parties, would continue in the postwar period."[41]

---

39. After leaving Chile, Daniel Horowitz continued a successful career as an international labor specialist, both in the State Department, with postings to France and India, and in scholarship, with his acclaimed monograph *The Italian Labor Movement* (Harvard University Press, 1963). The Labor Attaché Program also continued to develop, celebrating its fiftieth anniversary in 1993, with Horowitz as the keynote speaker. In 1994, Horowitz gave a lengthy interview as part of the Foreign Affairs Oral History Collection of the Association for Diplomatic Studies and Training; it is available through the Library of Congress at http://hdl.loc.gov/loc.mss/mfdip.2004horo3/ (accessed June 2009). See also Weisz, "Labor Diplomacy." In his 1994 interview, Horowitz refers to an anonymous accusation made against him in 1946 for fraternizing too closely with Chilean Communists. But Ambassador Bowers dismissed the charge as ludicrous since it would have been impossible for Horowitz to report on labor unions in Chile without meeting frequently with both Communists and Socialists. Horowitz was subsequently transferred from the U.S. Embassy in Chile to the State Department's International Labor Division. See also Hrenchir, "Claude G. Bowers," 261–62. Also in 1994, the 103rd Congress commended the Labor Attaché Corps for its fifty years of "nurturing freedom and assisting in the development of democratic values and processes throughout the world," noting that "throughout the Cold War [the Corps] played a crucial role in the struggle against Communism." See H. Con. Res. 257 (October 3, 1994), 103d Cong., sess. 2; *Congressional Record*, October 3, 1994, H27331.

40. Gaddis, *United States*, 57.

41. Halperin, *Nationalism and Communism*, vii–viii.

With the Soviet victory in the Battle of Stalingrad, the tides of war had turned in favor of the Allies, and in November 1943, in Teheran, Iran, Stalin met for the first time with Roosevelt and Churchill to iron out a strategy for final victory. Soon thereafter, Browder published his views on the peaceful coexistence of capitalism and Communism in a book he entitled *Teheran: Our Path in War and Peace*. The term "Browderism" began to circulate among Communist parties around the globe, including the Chilean Communist Party, which, throughout the first half of 1944, debated how best to adapt Browder's ideas to the particularities of Chilean politics and labor relations. Under a Browderist line, workers would be called on to increase production, as they had been doing since the rise of Fascism and the stirrings of war in the mid-1930s. Workers would also be asked to avoid strikes whenever possible, a policy first adopted after Nazi Germany invaded the Soviet Union, and upheld even under provocation such as the October 1942 shootings in Lota.

While agreeing with Browder that "the policy of national union against Fascism [was] in general a just policy," some Chilean Communists worried that such extreme collaboration as that shown by the CPUSA might engender "a certain weakening of the independent fight of the proletariat."[42] On the whole, however, PCCh leaders believed that conciliatory policies were necessary during the war, and most became convinced that conciliation could be a useful tactic for advancing workers' interests even after the war. In August 1944, the PCCh Central Committee thus "refashioned its policies and actions to make them consistent with Earl Browder's concept that class collaborationism rather than class conflict would be the motor force for fundamental change in the postwar world."[43] Yet, as Chilean Communists renewed their support of cross-class alliances to promote national industrial development, they struggled to keep their commitment to defend the interests of the workers.

A Walkout and a Resignation: Crisis on the Arbitration Tribunal

Widespread rhetoric of cooperation, patriotism, and national union did not eliminate social conflict or generate sustained harmony in labor relations. Both workers and capitalists developed new strategies to prevail in

42. Corvalán Lépez, *De lo vivido*, 46. On the PCCh's view of Browderism, see Neruda, "El marxismo." In later years, party leaders Luis Corvalán Lépez and Orlando Millas both claimed that the Chilean Communist Party was less swayed by the Browderist "deviation" than were many other Latin American Communist parties, though Corvalán Lépez did lament that they had sacrificed workers' interests. Corvalán Lépez, *De lo vivido*, 46; PCCh, *Ricardo Fonseca*, 131; Millas, *En tiempos*, 343.

43. Barnard, "Chile," 72.

the disputes that continued to erupt almost daily, from the shop floor to the national political arena. Both sides used speeches, pamphlets, and the press to elicit public sympathy for their positions and to increase their lobbying power with government officials and lawmakers. Appeals to progressive nationalist sentiment presented complications for pro-capital officials within the administration, who had to uphold the government's expressed commitment to labor rights in the Popular Front era. The capitalists themselves and right-wing politicians outside the government, however, showed little restraint in their moves to disarm organized labor.

In March 1944, just as the Chilean Communist Party was moving toward a fuller embrace of Browder's notion of class collaboration, the Labor Attaché at the U.S. Embassy, Daniel Horowitz, observed an increase in "sharp antagonism . . . between employers and labor unions," accompanied by "a strong and bitter campaign on the part of the conservative press against organized labor." Horowitz also noted "growing tension between the labor movement and the Government, with some indication that internal strife may develop among various officials of the labor movement itself.[44] From the workers' perspective, this "sharp antagonism" centered on a combination of social and political issues, including "low living standards, the rising cost of living, and the alleged large profits in industry." It also involved the status of the Chilean Workers' Confederation (CTCh), which, though still formally illegal, had been generally treated as a legitimate representative body throughout the Popular Front years.[45]

How would the politics of National Unity play out against the reality of such "sharp antagonism" between workers and their bosses? A test case arose in the coal mines in late 1943 when the collective contracts affecting over twenty thousand workers expired. Negotiations for new contracts took place among company, union, and government delegates on the Permanent Conciliation Board for Extractive Industries, in Concepción, beginning on November 1, 1943.[46] The negotiations were marked by explosive debates about productivity, with accusations of obstructionism and outright sabotage hurled from all sides. Company spokesmen and the conservative press repeated the same charges made in the 1941 Berguño report, blaming "the unquestionably high degree of absenteeism among

44. Labor Attaché Report, 2/15–3/15, 1944, 1, USNA, RG 59. This was likely Horowitz's first report from the field; he arrived in Santiago in December 1943.
45. Ibid.
46. The Permanent Conciliation Board was a different entity from the Tripartite Production Committees created by the November 1942 agreements.

the workers" on the control wielded by section delegates and Communist agents, who allegedly used their power for unpatriotic, partisan ends. Union representatives and the leftist press replied that the workers had elaborated clear, effective plans to increase coal extraction, including union-management productivity committees for each work section, but the companies had refused to consider their proposals.[47]

After nearly two months of fruitless negotiations on the conciliation board, Labor Minister Mariano Bustos Lagos directly intervened. Meeting personally with company and union officials in early February 1944, he proposed a graduated increase in wages averaging 18 percent, which was refused by both sides.[48] "The Companies claim[ed] that the eighteen per cent would wipe out all their profits," explained U.S. Labor Attaché Horo-witz, and the 10 percent increase they offered instead was flatly rejected by the unions.[49] According to the 1931 Chilean Labor Code, when negotia-tions on the conciliation board terminated without an accord, worker and employer representatives had the option of moving to voluntary arbitra-tion.[50] They had to agree not only to take this step, but also on who would be the presiding arbiter, usually selecting a government official whom both parties believed to be neutral. If either of the parties refused arbitra-tion, union representatives could seek authorization from the concilia-tion board to hold strike votes.

In the case of the coal disputes in late 1943 and early 1944, these stan-dard Labor Code proceedings were complemented by the direct involve-ment of top-level government officials, seeking to avoid an industry-wide strike. After his proposed wage settlement was rejected, Labor Minister Bustos Lagos again met with the parties in dispute and convinced them to accept voluntary arbitration with tripartite tribunals to be headed by his deputy minister, Claudio Aliaga Cobo, who was just then arbitrating a similar dispute in the Potrerillos copper mine.[51] In late February, Aliaga

---

47. Labor Attaché Report, 1/1–2/15, 1944, 6–7, USNA, RG 59.

48. As discussed in chapter 4, the Concepción CTCh had denounced Bustos Lagos as a "nefarious" anti-labor agent when he served as director general of labor (Director General del Trabajo). Letter from Regional CTCh to Concepción Intendant, April 3, 1939, FIC, vol. 2184, ANCh.

49. Labor Attaché Report, 1/1–2/15, 1944, 6–7, USNA, RG 59.

50. In certain sectors, such as state employees, arbitration was obligatory under the 1931 code.

51. A separate arbitration tribunal was created for each of the companies involved, but all the tribunals had the same labor representative and the same presiding arbiter. Labor Attaché Report, 2/15–3/15, 1944, 6, USNA, RG 59. The mine in Potrerillos was owned by the Anaconda Copper Company. See Klubock, *Contested Communities*, 27; and Vergara, *Copper Workers*.

Cobo announced a settlement decision that was so objectionable to the Potrerillos workers they immediately began an illegal strike rather than accept its terms. As later described by the CTCh's National Directorate (Consejo Directivo Nacional), "With audacity and by a stroke of the pen, [Sr. Aliaga] snatched away rights that the workers had previously achieved, by instituting a rationing system worthy of the times of the feudal lords."[52] Workers around the country bristled at the pro-capital bias of Aliaga's Portrerillos decision, and in anticipation of their own arbitration proceedings, the coal miners publicly declared that "they, too, would not accept an unjust award."[53]

For their part, the coal companies were also preparing for this new round of arbitration, and they sent out a variety of menacing signals. On February 28, for example, the Lirquén Coal Mining Company announced that "because of lack of markets for its coal," it would "reduce the work week of its 2,000 workers to three days." For older residents of the coal mining communities, this threat evoked the distress of the mid-1920s, when a diminished market for coal had pushed the companies to drastically reduce the workforce and limit workdays, or, as in the case of Curanilahue, to shut down the mines entirely. The extreme struggle for daily survival that took hold throughout the region had intensified with the Great Depression, leaving visceral memories of misery. Now, however, after nearly a decade of economic recovery, the claim of insufficient demand for coal caused Labor Attaché Horowitz to question the Lirquén company's motives and integrity: "In view of the existing coal shortage in the country, the Company's announcement would appear to have been prompted by an attempt to influence the outcome of the coal labor dispute."[54] The miners' unions protested vigorously, and again the government directly intervened, with the minister of economics and commerce offering the companies marketing assistance and purchase guarantees for their coal.

This direct intervention of top state officials beyond normal procedures reflected the importance of coal to the nation's economic development. Observers such as U.S. Labor Attaché Horowitz also saw "the activity in Government circles with respect to this dispute" as indicative

52. "Translation of Statement by Confederación de Trabajadores de Chile Issued after Resignation of Mr. Aliaga in Coal Dispute Arbitration," in Labor Attaché Report, 3/15–4/15, 1944, Appendix II, 2 (henceforth "CTCh Statement"), USNA, RG 59.
53. Labor Attaché Report, 2/15–3/15, 1944, 6, USNA, RG 59.
54. Ibid.

of a broader trend.[55] Throughout the ensuing months, the labor and interior ministers, and even the president himself, continued to show active interest in the outcome of the coal industry conflict, meeting repeatedly with union and company officials, as well as congressmen from the region.

When the coal arbitration meetings got under way in mid-February, tensions were high and debates heated. The miners' representative on the tripartite tribunal was Communist Deputy Reinaldo Núñez Alvarez, a former mechanic who had risen through the ranks of a metalworkers' union to become a national leader of the Confederation of Chilean Workers, before being elected to Congress in 1941 from the Santiago district.[56] On principle, Núñez Alvarez accepted government arbiter Aliaga Cobo's repeated insistence that any wage or benefit increases had to be within "the limited margin allowed by the companies' profits."[57] Yet he grew increasingly angry at what he perceived as Aliaga's collusion with the company representative to understate profits. After nearly a month of impassioned wrangling, the dispute came to a crisis at the March 20 meeting when Núñez was repeatedly called to order for what Aliaga described as his "aggressive and disrespectful attitude" toward both himself and the company representative. In his third outburst, Núñez openly accused Aliaga of conspiring with the companies to allow shareholders "to put thirty-four million pesos in profits into their pockets."[58] He then stormed out of the room, displaying what Aliaga described as a "violent and unusual attitude."

Infuriated and frustrated, Deputy Minister Aliaga remained seated for some time, and then he, too, left the ill-fated March 20 meeting. A Right-leaning Radical, Aliaga believed that his mandate from the Ríos Morales administration was to strengthen capitalist production, while offering social measures to assuage the workers' sense of injustice. As he endeavored to achieve these objectives, largely through traditional closed-door arrangements, Claudio Aliaga had come face to face with a new visage of workers' power, backed by the growing Communist Party, at the head of a broad popular movement for greater inclusiveness and transparency in Chilean democracy. By walking out of the meeting, Reinaldo Núñez defied

55. Ibid.
56. In the late 1940s, under repression unleashed by President González Videla, Nuñez would be imprisoned at the Pisagua military camp. See chapter 9.
57. Aliaga Cobo's resignation letter, March 20, 1944, in Labor Attaché Report, 3/15–4/15, 1944, Appendix I, 2 (henceforth "Aliaga Cobo's resignation letter"), USNA, RG 59.
58. Ibid., 4.

long-standing notions of appropriate deference in hierarchical power-sharing arrangements. He, an "uncultured" Communist worker, was challenging the rules of the political game by which Aliaga had risen through government ranks.

To convey his emphatic rejection of the Communist workers' newly claimed rights, Deputy Minister Aliaga immediately resigned as arbiter of the coal industry disputes. Key to the democratic potential and effective functioning of the tripartite labor relations system developed in Chile in the 1930s and 1940s was the neutrality of government labor officials, whose sole mandate was to work for the well-being of the nation. Aliaga Cobo thus began his resignation letter by refuting allegations of favoritism and complicity with the companies. He claimed that these attacks, spread through the leftist press, were politically motivated: "The atmosphere created through the press campaign, based on the personal efforts of political labor leaders, might lead public opinion to think that the Government is acting with partiality and is not maintaining the equitable balance that must control disagreements between Capital and Labor." In Aliaga's view, the problem was not that the government favored the capitalists, but rather that it was in danger of losing its independence because of the strong-arm tactics of leftist labor. Contrary to the Communists' National Unity rhetoric, Aliaga complained, Núñez and his constituents had refused to compromise, insisting that the arbitration decision grant all of the workers' demands. As U.S. Labor Attaché Horowitz reported, "Because of the pressure brought to bear upon the Government and upon him by labor and Leftist political elements," Aliaga claimed he was "'prevented . . . from making a decision freely and with dignity.'"[59]

Horowitz found Aliaga's resignation letter to be "phrased in less temperate language than is normally characteristic of Government officials," which reflected the high degree of personal animosity that had developed between the parties.[60] Aliaga described himself as "an official, [who] under no direct obligation, patriotically and [in a spirit of] self-denial," had agreed to preside over the tripartite tribunal. He bitterly denounced the "uncultured and arbitrary" attitude of labor representative Núñez. Tacitly upholding a model where agreements would be reached in gentlemanly closed-door sessions, Aliaga condemned Núñez for bringing public, political pressure to bear on labor contract negotiations: "The

59. Labor Attaché Report, 3/15–4/15, 1944, 1, USNA, RG 59; Aliaga Cobo's resignation letter, 4.
60. Labor Attaché Report, 3/15–4/15, 1944, 3 USNA, RG 59.

Arbitration Tribunals are lawful institutions even though, in some cases, as in the present, they are made up of uncultured persons. . . . This situation becomes more serious when one of the members of the Tripartite Arbitration Tribunal, [acting] in an uncultured manner, ignores the ethics governing the conduct of a lawful Tribunal and becomes a public leader of the interests he represents on the Tribunal."[61]

What seems to have been most threatening to Deputy Minister Aliaga was the degree of confidence shown by "a public leader" such as Deputy Núñez, who felt secure in the loyal support of his base and in his ability to mobilize public opinion and segments of the government on behalf of his positions. In the weeks before the fateful March 20 confrontation, Núñez had repeatedly accompanied leaders of the coal miners' unions in meetings with politicians and government officials in Santiago. Aliaga strongly condemned this as inappropriate lobbying, designed "to obtain the necessary support that will enable them to exert pressure on the arbitrator."[62]

Aliaga was certainly correct that the positions and attitudes adopted by Reinaldo Núñez on the arbitration tribunal reflected more than his own temper. Showing their support for Núñez after his walkout, the coal unions proclaimed their outrage at what they viewed as the government representative's insolence, now added to perennial company intransigence. The miners repeated their threat to go on strike if their demands were not met. At the same time, Núñez and his fellow labor leaders were quite effective at mobilizing public support for the workers, even among non-Communist and middle-class sectors. Aliaga complained that while arbitrating the coal disputes, he received "more than fifty telegrams pressing me to favor *all* of the workers' claims," which he cited as another of the Communists' pressure tactics, reinforcing the labor representative's alleged unwillingness to compromise. The telegrams of support for the miners, however, came not only from labor unions and leftist political organizations, but also from merchants and other middle-class residents of the coal towns, most of whom were not affiliated with the PCCh or the CTCh, but who tended to support the centrist Radical and Democratic Parties. These were precisely the sectors with which the Communists had been strengthening ties under the National Unity strategy.

In this sense, what government arbiter Aliaga opposed was not so much Deputy Núñez's deviation from the model for labor-capital-state

61. Aliaga Cobo's resignation letter, 2.
62. Ibid.

relations begun with the Popular Front, but rather the threat of the model's fruition under the presumably more cooperative National Unity line. His frustration was in direct proportion to the new possibilities generated since the mid-1930s for the forceful assertion of workers' demands in national policy-making forums. Aliaga had found himself confronted by an "uncultured" worker, backed by the powerful Chilean Communist Party, the Confederation of Chilean Workers, and a broad base of centrist allies. In this context, Aliaga believed that the coal miners' threat to strike was an egregious act "against the interests of the country"; their building of a broad support base for political ends worked "against the public peace"; and, their meetings with government officials, together with the barrage of telegrams on their behalf, established "a dangerous precedent."[63]

To expose the insidious motives driving Núñez's behavior, Aliaga focused his attack on the legally vulnerable CTCh, which, by law, could neither represent workers in collective disputes nor receive dues from them since unions were prohibited from political or "resistance" activities. With the ascent of the Popular Front, however, which the confederation had backed, government officials had ignored many of these restrictions, as had centrist politicians and the media. Notwithstanding complaints from the Right, the CTCh now enjoyed de facto, though still not de jure, standing. Simply denouncing the confederation for getting involved in labor disputes would thus not have served Aliaga's purpose. Instead, he charged that the CTCh, allied with the Communists, had *instigated* the labor disputes in the coal mining zone for purely political ends. As he wrote to the president in his resignation letter, "I believe, your Excellency, that the institution of arbitration is the only escape valve existing in our social legislation for avoiding damage to the country and to the national economy from the prolongation of irresolvable collective disputes generated by the Confederation, which manufactures labor demands."[64]

The CTCh's National Directorate immediately issued a strong response to the "innumerable falsehoods, inventions and slander" contained in Aliaga's letter, whose "essence serves to undermine order, democracy, and the tranquility of the country with tactics similar to those used by individuals who have always been greatly interested in stirring up warfare, not only of labor with capital, but also [of labor] with the Government

63. Ibid.
64. Ibid., 4.

which these workers themselves have put into power."[65] The language of potential or emerging warfare between labor and the government was a clear warning to the Ríos Morales administration of the danger of abandoning the Center-Left platform on which it was elected. Again, the strategy was to hold the government accountable in terms of its own professed model for harmonious industrial progress.

Thus the National Directorate took Aliaga to task for failing to uphold his own ideals: "The C.T.Ch. did not believe, until after Sr. Aliaga's declaration, that a man who calls himself a democrat could ridicule the just and legitimate claims of the workers." As further evidence of Aliaga's duplicity and hypocrisy, the directorate cited his claim to have made a "careful inspection" of all the coal companies' properties, when, in fact, he had refused to go down into the mines for health reasons. This was highly significant in the directorate's view since he therefore "did not see the inhuman conditions under which the miners work in order that the Companies may increase their capital and dividends by paying the workers starvation wages and depriving them of the means of attending to their meager needs." According to the CTCh leaders, this helped to explain why the arbitration tribunal ignored "the workers' requests for the adoption of measures [that would] improve working conditions and prevent accidents."

Denying the charge of undue pressure from leftist political and labor leaders, the National Directorate insisted that "if any pressure existed at all, it was exerted knowingly and shrewdly by the Companies on Sr. Aliaga." The directorate then cited Central Bank statistics showing that the general increase in living costs over the previous five years was 180 percent, whereas wages and salaries had risen by only 100 percent.[66] As U.S. Labor Attaché Horowitz also argued, these economic indicators undermined allegations that the workers' demands were "manufactured" by the CTCh or other labor or political leaders. Sidestepping the CTCh's role in coordinating the coal miners' campaign, the National Directorate appealed to the public for sympathy: "The workers' claims are the natural and logical consequence of the rise in the cost of living and the greed, monopoly, and usury of capitalists, and are not manufactured by the Confederation of Chilean Workers or by federations, but [rather] by HUNGER and MISERY."[67]

65. CTCh Statement, 1.
66. Ibid., 2.
67. Ibid.; emphatic capitalization in original.

The Disunity of National Unity: Strains in the
Tripartite Model of Labor Relations

Horowitz reported that the conservative press and politicians were using the controversy around Aliaga's resignation in their attack against organized labor, and particularly against the CTCh and its affiliated federations, which were illegal, and therefore, they said, should not be allowed to operate with such de facto legitimacy. They presented events in the coal industry as evidence that the CTCh was trying to undermine the institutions of arbitration, and by extension, the rule of law itself. Armed with this justification for moving against labor, the Chilean Right found a heady example in Venezuela, where the government had simply "dissolved all unions which had a political complexion," meaning specifically unions under Communist control.[68] In Chile, "some conservative newspapers pointed to the action in Venezuela as a model method of dealing with the Chilean labor movement." Horowitz thus concluded that, far from indicating aggression by the workers or their political allies, "the coal dispute, together with the Venezuelan developments, furnished an opportunity for increasing the press attacks upon organized labor."[69] What Horowitz did not explain was that the impetus to step up attacks on labor was related precisely to the success of its tactics over the preceding years, which had greatly strengthened the workers' ability to assert their interests in the national arena.

Less than a week after Aliaga Cobo's resignation, the tripartite tribunal was reconstituted, with Osvaldo Vergara Imas, chief of the Production Department of the Ministry of Economics and Commerce, presiding. On April 4, Vergara issued a settlement decision for the Lota dispute that included wage raises of 20–22 percent, which was slightly higher than what Labor Minister Bustos Lagos had proposed in February.[70] Just a few days later, Vergara announced an almost identical decision for Schwager. Given the dominance of the Lota and Schwager companies in the region, Horowitz foresaw that "the awards affecting the remaining coal companies [would] follow closely the conditions set by the decisions already rendered."[71]

---

68. In Venezuela, the 1944 dissolution of Communist unions by President Isaías Medina Angarita led to the formation of a national labor confederation under the control of Venezuela's social democratic party, Acción Democrática. See Ellner, *Los partidos políticos*; Alexander, *Rómulo Betancourt*, 180–84, and *Communist Party*, 11.

69. Labor Attaché Report, 3/15–4/15, 1944, 4, USNA, RG 59.

70. Ibid., 5.

71. Ibid.

Although the resignation of government arbiter Aliaga represented a triumph of sorts for the workers, the final contracts were far from the total victory pursued by Deputy Núñez. Indeed, to some observers, they indicated that the National Unity line did entail what Communist leader Luis Corvalán Lépez would later describe as "a certain weakening of the independent fight of the proletariat."[72] Because, however, the contracts were the best deal they could achieve and still maintain a no-strike policy, the workers accepted them. The newspaper of the National Miners' Federation (FNM), *El Chiflón*, described the compromise as a success for all parties, made possible only by the "patriotic attitude of the coal mining workers."[73]

Horowitz disagreed, stressing that capitalist pressure had heavily influenced the outcome of the dispute. One of the pivotal backstage actors behind the tribunal's decision, in fact, was Hernán Videla Lira, who was not only a Liberal Party senator, but also president of the National Mining Society (SONAMI) and brother of the CCIL's general manager. Whereas Aliaga claimed that "political labor leaders" had tried to sway the arbitration outcome, Horowitz gave greater credence to the countercharge of undue lobbying by "political industry leaders."

In support of this countercharge, just a few days after the Lota settlement, the press reported "that the Government was considering a proposal [from the companies] to increase coal prices" to compensate for any loss in profits that might result from the wage raises.[74] Soon after, the companies did hike the price of coal by 30 pesos per ton, which Horowitz estimated would increase their revenues "by approximately the same amount as the increased cost resulting from the improved conditions granted to the workers by the arbitration award."[75] The minister of economics and commerce had publicly stated that the government would not approve any coal price increase "unless the results of an exhaustive study indicated that the increase was justified." Although no such study was undertaken, the government now refused to take the necessary steps to block the companies' move, steps that included declaring coal "a commodity of prime necessity" and setting a maximum price for it. Having agreed to wage raises, the administration took no stand against the coal price increase, once again showing itself unwilling to push forward structural changes in the distribution of industry profits.

72. Corvalán Lépez, *De lo vivido*, 46.
73. *El Chiflón*, May 1944, 30. This article offers a detailed account of the 1943–44 arbitration process.
74. Labor Attaché Report, 3/15–4/15, 1944, 5, USNA, RG 59.
75. Labor Attaché Report, 4/15–5/15, 1944, 5, USNA, RG 59.

The miners' unions, supported by the Confederation of Chilean Workers and the Chilean Communist Party, strongly denounced the increase in the price of coal. This position was consistent with their campaign of opposition to increases in the cost of living, which they blamed on the speculative and monopolistic practices of unpatriotic capitalists. The unions argued that "on the basis of current profit levels in the industry, the companies could absorb the increased labor costs." This point was well substantiated by reputable government officials, including the labor minister himself, who had provided an analysis back in January showing that the 18 percent wage raise he proposed "could be absorbed without a price increase."[76] Even Aliaga had stated that a 20 percent raise was within the limits of the company's profits.[77]

Reminiscent of the 1941 Berguño Report, government arbiter Aliaga's resignation letter had charged that organized labor in the coal mining zone, under Communist control, was instigating disputes for political ends. Explicitly contradicting this charge, Horowitz called on the Chilean government to control inflation so that workers would not have to push the companies so hard for a living wage.[78] In mid-May, Horowitz repeated his conviction that the miners were being compelled into a more aggressive stance, including strike activity, by the struggle simply to feed their families. He concurred with "the many labor officials [who] recognize the dangers involved for the economy in a race between wages and prices," and were "convinced that unless the Government takes strong measures against [the] continued rise in the cost of living," workers will have "no alternative but to press for sufficient wage increases to prevent further deterioration of [their] already low standard of living."[79]

The deepening divisions in the tripartite labor relations system raise at least three key points. First, although government officials and labor actors continued to maneuver within a discourse of cooperation and harmony, their tenuous alliance for the democratization of public processes and the implementation of social reforms would effectively unravel before the end of World War II. This challenges the thesis advanced by many

76. Ibid.

77. Labor Attaché Report, 3/15–4/15, 1944, 3, USNA, RG 59.

78. Cost of living increases in the war years were not unique to Chile. As Leslie Bethell observed, "wartime inflation spurred an unprecedented [political] mobilization" throughout Latin America. Quoted in Rock, *Latin America*, 3.

79. Labor Attaché Report, 4/15–5/15, 1944, 1, USNA, RG 59. Andrew Barnard also noted that inflationary pressures contributed to an undercurrent of industrial unrest during the war years, with a peak of 101 illegal strikes in 1943, involving 46,832 workers. Barnard, "Chile," 69.

scholars that it was the advent of the Cold War that caused the centrist Chilean government to turn against organized labor and the Marxist Left. Even Andrew Barnard, one of the most knowledgeable scholars on this period, is thus mistaken when he says that "antagonisms receded" with the PCCh's move toward Browderism in August 1944, and that it was not until "late 1945 [that] hostilities again broke out as the PCCh began to distance itself from the Browderist heresy and move toward more aggressive policies."[80] It is certainly true that battle lines between government and labor hardened after the war, but, as this chapter shows, the allegedly cooperative period of 1944–45 was rife with conflict.

Second, although the Communists continued to assert the interests of their working-class followers, capitalists fought back, seeking to exploit rightist tendencies within the government. They were quite successful during the Ríos Morales administration, which provoked disillusionment and distrust among the nation's workers and exacerbated tensions between labor and the government. This challenges the widely held thesis that the Democratic Alliance broke apart primarily because of labor's move to an aggressive stance after the war, as articulated by Barnard above.

And third, throughout these years of coalition politics, the workers and residents of the coal communities developed a strong sense of their identity within the nation and a new appreciation of their rights, together with an organizational base from which to press for them, using representational politics and the modern industrial relations system. The miners' struggle for livable conditions was at the same time a contest over the just distribution of industry profits and, in this sense, was intrinsically political, Horowitz's disclaimers notwithstanding. Also political was the loyalty the miners' unions showed to the Confederation of Chilean Workers, to its affiliated federations, and to the Chilean Communist Party. The miners benefited both symbolically and materially by being represented at the highest levels of national decision making; they supported the PCCh's positions in national and international affairs at least in part because the Communists supported them in their battles with the companies.

During the period of so-called collaborationist politics, the workers of the coal mining region tried to improve their circumstances by appealing to government officials and institutions within the terms of the national development model put forth in the 1924 social laws and the 1931 Labor

80. Barnard, "Chile," 72.

Code and then promoted in various ways by the original Popular Front coalition, by Ríos Morales's Democratic Alliance, by the Communists' National Unity line, and by U.S. Vice President Henry Wallace. The society envisioned in this model would be characterized by harmonious labor relations, socioeconomic justice, industrial development, and pluralistic political democracy. The coal miners placed themselves at the forefront of this vision, claiming their rights as citizen workers who patriotically mined for the nation.

The forces behind the centrist governments of the era, however, were deeply divided, and this threatened to derail the project of state-led capitalist development. Within the Ríos Morales administration, certain factions worked continually to undermine possibilities for more radical change and closer cooperation with Communists. The overtly anti-Communist Berguño Report, for example, had condemned shop floor union delegates as agents for international insurrection. Local and regional labor inspectors had charged Communist union leaders with misuse of funds, largely for sending union dues to the National Miners' Federation and the Confederation of Chilean Workers. The carabineros had gunned down workers at a routine union assembly in Lota. And government arbiter Aliaga Cobo had taken the coal companies' side in tripartite negotiations, at least in the view of infuriated workers and Communist leaders.

Yet, in each of these instances where the government had seemingly acted against the interests of labor, the coal miners could also point to official recognition of the rightness of their position. Thus, alongside its anti-Communist charges, the government's Berguño Report offered critiques of company practices that could be used to the workers' advantage in future labor disputes. The shootings in October 1942 resulted in the government's Rettig-Pazols Report, which upheld the right of workers to freely assemble and condemned the Lota company's excessive control of community property. More important, the report also censured Lota Welfare Officer Octavio Astorquiza for his prejudiced, arbitrary, and inflexible behavior toward workers and even called for his dismissal. And, in the case of the March 1944 contract disputes, when government arbiter Aliaga Cobo adopted a position the workers deemed to be pro-capitalist, he felt forced to resign, and his successor offered the workers a slightly better deal. These "victories," however limited, gave credibility to the discourse of Communist political and labor leaders. The path of compromise and alliance building was working to strengthen the coal miners' sense of their importance to the nation and their ability to act effectively in the framework of wartime democratic politics.

Strikes in the Coal Mining Zone: Against Argentina's Juan Perón and Chile's Rightward Shift

While Chilean workers engaged in democratic party politics and alliance building, across the Andes, Argentine popular sectors turned to the emergent figure of Colonel Juan Domingo Perón, a member of the Group of United Officers (Grupo de Oficios Unidos; GOU) that took power by military coup in June 1943. After using his position as labor minister to gain a large following among Argentine workers, in later years, Perón would repress and marginalize Communist, Socialist, and anarchist workers' organizations. Though the Argentine military regime maintained an official position of World War II neutrality, first declared in 1939, many of the GOU officers, including Perón, had ideological and discursive affinities, as well as more formal connections, with both Argentine nationalist groups and European Fascists. Supporters of the Allies condemned the Argentine rulers as Fascist dictators since they refused to break ties with the Axis powers.[81]

As early as February 1944, both the Chilean Communist Party and the Confederation of Chilean Workers had vehemently denounced the Argentine government, and especially its highest labor authority, Juan Perón. Using the same terms with which they had denounced Franco in Spain, Chilean Marxists tried to convince the Ríos Morales administration to take a strong stand against both regimes by exaggerating Fascist threats to national security.[82] In a statement issued in July 1944, for example, the PCCh warned of "the increasing danger that a coup d'état might be undertaken against the [Chilean] Government by Fascist elements in the country."[83] On the same day, the CTCh declared that "there is in progress a vast conspiracy against the democratic regime which may culminate in a coup d'état similar to that which has terrorized the Argentine people."[84] In light of this perceived threat, the CTCh called on "the working class and all democratic elements" to fulfill their "patriotic duty . . . to maintain the strictest vigilance . . . and to fortify their unity and to be mobilized to impede the criminal intentions of the Fifth Column which, together

81. The highpoint of U.S. government opposition to the Argentine regime was its publication of a "blue book" in February 1946, under the misleading title, "Consultation Among the American Republics with Respect to the Argentine Situation." For two excellent sources on this subject, see Vannucci, "Influence"; and Green, "Cold War."

82. Labor Attaché Report, 2/15–3/15, 1944, USNA, RG 59.

83. Labor Attaché Report, 7/16–8/15, 1944, 4, USNA, RG 59.

84. For a full translation of the July 1944 warning by the CTCh National Directorate, see ibid.

with the agents of the G.O.U., work[s] toward plunging the country into civil war."[85]

Responding to this call were the most active and organized sectors of Communist workers in Chile—those in the coal and nitrate mining regions. On several occasions in the latter half of 1944, the longshoremen of the nitrate ports refused to load Spanish ships, and at the very end of the year, the dock workers of the coal mining town of Lota staged the first work stoppage against an Argentine vessel.[86] Soon after, the Confederation of Latin American Workers (Confederación de Trabajadores de América Latina; CTAL), under the leadership of Mexican leftist Vicente Lombardo Toledano, adopted a resolution "calling for [strike] action throughout the continent as a demonstration of solidarity with the Argentine people."[87] Chile was one of the few places in the Americas where the CTAL resolution prompted an energetic response. To express "collective repudiation of the pro-Fascist regime of force which oppresses the sister nation," a ten-minute nationwide work stoppage was scheduled for January 25, 1945.[88] The Communists were not the only political group promoting this bold move; the steering committee for the protest included three representatives of the CTCh (a Communist, a Socialist, and a member of the National Falange) and four members of a new multiparty organization, the Chilean Commission of Solidarity with the Argentine People.[89] The most prominent founder of the solidarity commission was Senator Gabriel González Videla, who headed the left wing of the Radical Party and would soon find himself heading the nation.[90]

Calling on "all our citizens, . . . workers, farm labor[ers], employees, progressive employers, and producers," the strike committee declared, "Fighting for the institutional normality of the Argentine Republic and expressing in an unmistakable manner our [support for] its noble people

85. Ibid.

86. Labor Attaché Report, 10/15–11/15, 1944, 9, USNA, RG 59. I do not know when the first work stoppage in the nitrate ports occurred, but one occurred between June 14 and July 15, 1944, according to the Labor Attaché Report from this period.

87. Labor Attaché Report, 12/15, 1944–1/15, 1945, 1, USNA, RG 59.

88. "Public Statement of Organizers of January 25 [Work] Stoppage, issued January 23," translated from El Siglo, January 24, 1945, as Labor Attaché Report, 1/15–2/15, 1945, Appendix I (henceforth "Public Statement of Work Stoppage Organizers"), USNA, RG 59.

89. The CTCh representatives were Communist Juan Vargas Puebla, Socialist Juan Briones Villavicencio, and National Falange member Alfredo Lorca.

90. Other members of the Solidarity Commission included María Marchant, leader of the woman's organization MEMCh, and César Godoy Urrutia, a Communist senator, formerly of the Workers' Socialist Party (PST). The fourth member was Osvaldo Valencia, about whom I have no information.

now oppressed by the government of the GOU, we not only fulfill our inescapable historic obligations, but we contribute to the extirpation from [the] America[s] of the Nazi-Fascist remnants that hope to survive in order to create new difficulties for the democracies, once weapons succeed in destroying them in Europe, where they have their origin."[91] The declaration also moved to head off criticism that such political action was a violation of national sovereignty and the right of self-determination. Linking the Argentine regime to the horrors of European Fascism, the committee proclaimed, "It has been said by the pacifists and the fifth column elements that the pronouncement against the government of Perón-Farrell constitutes an interference with the internal political problems of another country. From the [perspective] of the present events through which humanity is living, this thesis is not only false, but forms part of the ideological arsenal of totalitarianism. The sovereignty of nations has ceased to be an absolute, irrestrictable concept: it is now complemented by the interdependence of peoples."[92]

The campaign in Chile against the Argentine regime had broad political and social support, and "with a good deal of general publicity," a large portion of the country's industry did cease operations for ten minutes on January 25. Still, the national effort "fell short of achieving its objective of closing down all of industry. Practically no public services were affected and many other industries were affected only partially."[93] In Horowitz's estimation, this was due to "[in]sufficient planning and organization on the local level," and to the government's strong opposition to the work stoppage, which was particularly effective in dissuading public service workers from participating.[94]

Beyond the CTAL's largely unheeded call for continental strikes, opposition to the Argentine regime was also raised in the highest circles of international diplomacy. At the Yalta Conference in February 1945, Stalin secured a promise from Roosevelt "that he would not support the admission of Argentina to the United Nations." Roosevelt's secretary of state, Cordell Hull, publicly declared Argentina to be "the refuge and headquarters in this hemisphere of the Fascist movement."[95] In this context, the efforts by Chilean Communist workers to repudiate the Argentine regime

91. Public Statement of Work Stoppage Organizers.
92. Ibid.
93. Labor Attaché Report, 1/15–2/15, 1945, 1, USNA, RG 59. It is likely that most workers in the coal mining communities adhered to the work stoppage, but I do not have any sources confirming this.
94. Ibid., 3.
95. Cordell Hull, as quoted in Horowitz, "Cold War Continues," 53.

were fully compatible with the PCCh's support of the Allies and the United Nations. In March 1945, Lota longshoremen refused to load coal onto another Argentine ship docked in their harbor.[96]

In the same month, tensions between the Chilean government and labor were greatly exacerbated by the results of the March 1945 congressional elections, in which "the Leftist Parties suffered their most severe set-back since 1938."[97] The right-wing opposition parties gained control of the Senate, and almost won the Chamber of Deputies, leaving the Democratic Alliance parties with "only a slight and unstable majority."[98] Horowitz attributed this shift to an "increased disillusionment" among those who had previously voted for the Left, especially members of the working class:

> The optimism and hope which had characterized most wage earner groups, for example, after the election of the late Pedro Aguirre Cerda as President in 1938, and which had continued to a lesser extent through the congressional elections of 1941 and presidential election of 1942, seem to have disappeared completely. Many wage earners are convinced that the Leftist Parties have, in fact, accomplished little for them. This disillusionment caused many to refrain from voting, vote freely for the Right, or sell their votes to Rightist Parties. In the long run, this factor is perhaps the most important one for the political situation in Chile.[99]

96. Labor Attaché Report, 3/15–4/15, 1945, 10–11, USNA, RG 59. In April, the sailors of the region went on strike, but available information indicates that this was over the Lota and Schwager companies' rejection of the sailors' contract petitions and was not explicitly linked to international politics. Telegrams no. 437 and no. 457, from Ambassador Bowers to Secretary of State, April 6 and April 10, 1945; Labor Attaché Report, 3/15–4/15, 1945, 9, USNA, RG 59.

97. Enclosure no. 1, in Labor Attaché Report, 2/15–3/15, 1945, 1, USNA, RG 59.

98. Ibid. Paul Drake summarizes the national election results: "The 1945 congressional elections registered losses from 1941 for the original Popular Front parties, especially the Socialists, and roughly 6 percent gains each for the Conservatives and Liberals. . . . Although they did not equal their 1941 percentage, the Radicals exceeded their 1937 tally (18.6%) with 20.0% in 1945; so did the Communists with 4.1% in 1937 and 10.2% in 1945. . . . Neither Socialist party alone was as electorally strong as the Communists by 1945. The regular PS [Socialist Party] (7.2 percent) barely outpolled the PSA [Authentic Socialist Party] (5.6 percent). For the Socialists, there was little evidence that participation or nonparticipation in the Ríos government was the key to electoral prominence." Drake, *Socialism and Populism,* 275. The Authentic Socialist Party (PSA) had been founded in July 1944 by longtime Socialist leader Marmaduke Grove in opposition to the Socialist Party's decision "to adopt a stricter Marxist line" and to withdraw from the Ríos Morales government. Faúndez, *Marxism and Democracy,* 80. When the PSA disbanded in mid-1946, some of its members joined the Communist Party, others returned to the main Socialist Party, and a few joined the Radical Party.

99. Labor Attaché Report, 2/15–3/15, 1945, 3, USNA, RG 59.

Even as Chilean Communist workers were denouncing Argentine ruler Juan Perón as a dictator, the March election results led Horowitz to worry whether Chileans might not also move in a similar direction. Horowitz speculated that "the disillusionment with the Leftist Parties may mean loss of faith in democracy. This situation might eventually become a fertile group [lead to] support for a non-democratic government of 'action' of the Argentine type."[100]

Horowitz also foresaw that the March 1945 election results would have "important ramifications upon the labor movement and upon government policy affecting wage earners in general." Even though "the Leftist Parties received a majority of the popular votes cast," the election results "clearly demonstrated the gradual loss of popular support for these Parties which had been developing during the last year."[101] Such a loss of voting support could provoke a tectonic shift in Chile's volatile political alliances. Thus, as Horowitz anticipated, "the labor movement may undoubtedly expect more active opposition from employer groups and less support in the Ministry of Labor, which has already decided that it will 'follow the election returns.'"[102]

Indeed, in a private conversation, the deputy labor minister told Horowitz that "the Ministry will follow a more conservative policy in labor disputes, will use its decree powers more cautiously in settling disputes, and will place more emphasis upon such considerations as keeping production costs down than upon adjusting wages in accordance with cost of living changes."[103] The frankness of this admission strengthened Horowitz's conviction that the mounting tension in labor relations was *not* primarily caused by Communist agitation:

> The employer and government attitudes, which seem to be developing as a reflection of the election returns, [make] it probable that labor disputes will be more difficult to settle than in the past. This

---

100. Ibid.

101. Horowitz's assessment of the March 1945 elections as an unmitigated loss for the leftist parties is disputed by Orlando Millas, who called the elections "a great victory for the Communist Party," which won five seats in the Senate (out of forty-five) and fifteen seats in the Chamber of Deputies (out of one hundred forty-seven). This gave the PCCh more than 10 percent representation in Congress, which was remarkable, Millas thought, given the high degree of electoral corruption and fraud by the right-wing parties. Millas, *En tiempos*, 369.

102. Labor Attaché Report, 2/15–3/15, 1945, 1 , USNA, RG 59.

103. Ibid., 4–5. Since the government's emergency decree powers were often used against the interests of labor, it is not clear to me why using them "more cautiously" would be part of a "more conservative policy."

would appear to be less the result of attempts by "Communists and the C.T.Ch." to foment unrest, as a large sector of the press has characteristically claimed, than the fact that labor unions will apparently attempt to continue their policy of presenting demands and expecting concessions in face of stronger opposition from employers and less sympathetic government intervention.[104]

Recognizing that "the number of labor disputes has continued to increase during the last month," Horowitz turned to the specific cases of copper and nitrate disputes to refute the "accusations that the disputes are a planned campaign of labor disturbances." Rather, he argued, they represented "the customary pattern of collective bargaining," and developed when a number of contracts "happen[ed] to have expired at about the same time." Although insisting that the workers' motivations were entirely "customary," Horowitz again stressed that these disputes took place in a greatly transformed context, in which "the uncertain postwar position of the mining industry has prompted the companies involved to insist that no increases in labor costs are feasible at this time. The position of the government, both because of the election results, as well as its concern with continued foreign markets for copper and nitrate, will apparently support the employer position in general."[105] Thus, at the same time that he saw the mining industry's "uncertain postwar position" pushing the companies to take a harder line in negotiations with their workers, Horowitz also observed the government moving away from its support of labor.[106]

The rightward shift of the Chilean government was paralleled in the United States, where Henry A. Wallace lost the 1944 vice presidential nomination to a far less progressive politician, Harry S Truman. When Roosevelt died on April 12, 1945, and Truman became president, Wallace was appointed secretary of commerce. Less than two weeks later, Truman opened the San Francisco Conference, held from April 25 to June 26, to formally establish the United Nations as an organization for the postwar era. Recalling the promise Roosevelt had made to Stalin regarding Argentina, the Soviet delegation requested that, at the very least, "the question of inviting Argentina to the conference be postponed for a few days for further study." Truman's secretary of state, Edward Stettinius, strongly

104. Labor Attaché Report, 2/15–3/15, 1945, 4–5 , USNA, RG 59.
105. Ibid., 1.
106. Ibid.

opposed the Soviet request, and "it was voted down 28–7, then 31–4, and afterwards Argentina was admitted."[107]

World War II came to a close with the unconditional surrender of Germany on May 8, the Potsdam Conference in July, the nuclear bombing of Hiroshima and Nagasaki on August 6 and 8, and the unconditional surrender of Japan aboard the USS *Missouri* on September 2, 1945. The formal end of the war ushered in a new era, whose contours and direction remained to be seen. Chapter 7 explores how contestation over different visions of the postwar world played out in Chilean labor politics, particularly in the coal mining region.

---

107. Horowitz, "Cold War Continues," 54. See also Niess, *Hemisphere*, 137. Argentina had made concessions to the Allies, and at the last minute, declared war against the Axis. In exchange, the United States promised to support Argentina's entry into the United Nations. On the PCCh's objections to Chile's support of the U.S. position, see Neruda's speeches on September 12 and 13, 1945, reprinted in his *Discursos parlamentarios*, 51–56.

7

GENERAL STRIKES AND STATES OF SIEGE: POLARIZATION IN THE POSTWAR TRANSITION

As World War II drew to an end, the results of the March 1945 congressional elections in Chile exacerbated disputes among the Center and Left parties of the Democratic Alliance that had won the presidency for Radical Juan Antonio Ríos Morales. Votes for Radicals, Communists, and Socialists alike had dropped well below their 1941 totals, especially those for the Socialists, provoking reassessments of strategy and mutual recrimination among all the parties. Although no one was ready to announce the demise of the Popular Front model, efforts at collaboration were clearly giving way to ever more frequent and intense conflict, both within and among the main Center and Left forces.

The Radical Party had been deeply divided since June 1943, when a group of its left-wing members, known as the "Young Turks," issued a manifesto sharply criticizing President Ríos Morales. They opposed him on issues such as his appointment of Liberals to cabinet posts, his failure to control prices and speculation, and his delay in severing Chile's diplomatic ties with the Axis countries.[1] Leading this increasingly powerful leftist bloc were Alfredo Rosende Verdugo and Gabriel González Videla, whom many people looked to "as a caudillo."[2] At its January 1944 convention, the Radical Party created a new governing body called the "National Executive Committee" (Comité Ejecutivo Nacional; CEN), which the

---

1. Barnard, "Chilean Communist Party," 281.
2. Reyes Alvarez, "El presidente," 90, and "Los presidentes radicales," 61–63.

Young Turks quickly came to control. For the next eight months, relations between the party and the Ríos Morales administration deteriorated until finally, in September 1944, the president's own party declared itself in opposition to him.[3]

Left-wing Radicals were concerned about the president's rightist tendencies, especially given the ample room for autonomous executive action granted him by the 1925 Constitution and subsequent legislation. From 1944 to 1946, many of the Radical Party's actions aimed at reimposing congressional restraints on the president. At the same time, voices within the party expressed alarm at the growing strength and militancy of the Communist-led labor movement, which began to flex its muscles at the close of the war. To middle-class Radicals, the increased power of the Communists seemed to presage an imminent "plebeian irruption."[4] The Left-leaning Radicals who now controlled the party apparatus thus navigated between their desire to support a progressive agenda of workers' rights and material improvements, on the one hand, and opposition to Communist leadership of the labor movement, on the other.

The Socialist Party was also deeply divided, largely over the issue of support for the Ríos Morales administration. In June 1943, at the party's Eleventh Ordinary Congress, the Socialists' own group of rising leftists, also referred to as "Young Turks," triumphed over the supporters of party founder Marmaduke Grove. Their standard-bearer, thirty-five-year-old medical doctor Salvador Allende Gossens, was elected secretary-general.[5] Under Allende's leadership, the Socialists withdrew their ministers from Ríos Morales's cabinet, a move supported by about 80 percent of the party's members, but strongly opposed by Grove and his followers. By July 1944, the division was irreparable, and Grove's newly formed Authentic Socialist Party (Partido Socialista Auténtico; PSA) held its own convention, separate from that of the regular Socialist Party (PS), which elected Bernardo Ibáñez Aguila as its secretary-general. The Authentic Socialist Party was, in the words of Paul Drake, "mildly reformist and scarcely Marxist." Seeking to unite all reform parties, it "forged closer alliances with the Radicals, the Communists, and the government than did the

3. See the April 1944 exchange of letters between President Ríos Morales and Radical Party chief Alfredo Rosende Verdugo in Ríos Morales and Rosende, *Dos cartas políticas*. See also Palma Zúñiga, *Historia del partido*, 230–31.

4. Moulian, "Líneas estratégicas," 11. Moulian's concept of "plebeian irruption" is discussed in the final paragraphs of the introduction.

5. The real force behind the internal coup against Marmaduke Grove's more conservative forces was Raúl Ampuero Díaz; Salvador Allende was "a compromise choice for the takeover." Drake, *Socialism and Populism*, 272.

parent party"; in return, its members were awarded cabinet posts and other national and regional government offices throughout the remainder of Ríos Morales's presidency.[6]

The majority Socialist Party shared the left-wing Radicals' concerns both with the president's rightist tendencies and, especially, with the growing strength of the Communists. In the wake of the March 1945 congressional elections, with the Young Turks and Bernardo Ibáñez now in control, the Socialists undertook a "formal process of readjustment." First and foremost, they distanced themselves from the Communists' National Unity line, claiming that it compromised the workers' interests and that it was largely responsible for leftist losses in the recent elections. After their national convention in July, the Socialists tried first to convince the Communists to change their strategy and then to get them excluded from the Democratic Alliance altogether. In August, when it was clear that both efforts had failed, the Socialist Party "declar[ed] its independence of both the government and the coalition."[7]

For their part, the Chilean Communists were also reformulating policies for the postwar era, particularly after French Communist Jacques Duclos famously denounced Earl Browder's moderate line in June 1945.[8] As did Communist Parties around the world, the Chilean Communist Party moved "to distance itself from the Browderist heresy," and throughout the latter half of the year, "the PCCh elaborated a program of reforms designed to speed Chile through its 'bourgeois democratic revolution,' and adopted a tougher policy on labor disputes."[9] During this "process of readjustment," however, the PCCh "continued to express its commitment to National Unity," maintaining the rhetoric of broad, progressive democratic alliances. Observing this, Labor Attaché Daniel Horowitz saw the Chilean Communist Party's postwar transformation as "rather more gradual" and their policies on labor matters still "more conservative" than the positions adopted by the Socialists.[10] Although the Communists supported workers' "pressure upon the government to obtain concessions," they "attempted to stop short of any action which might threaten the stability of the government."[11]

6. Ibid., 274.
7. Barnard, "Chile," 74.
8. Duclos, "On the Dissolution."
9. Barnard, "Chile," 72, 74.
10. Ibid., 74; Labor Attaché Report, 3/15–4/15, 1945, 2, USNA, RG 59.
11. Labor Attaché Report, 10/1–11/25, 1945, 2, USNA, RG 59.

As both the Communist and Socialist Parties moved to regain their strength, momentum, and bargaining positions after the war, their competition for working-class support intensified.[12] In Horowitz's view, the Communist Party's "policy of National [Unity] and of collaboration" was "somewhat less popular among wage earner groups than the policy of aggressive social reform advocated by the Socialists." But, he noted, the PCCh had other assets that enabled it to maintain its following: "The Communist Party is well disciplined, hard-working and offers effective leadership, whereas the Socialist Party is characterized by factionalism, dissension within its own ranks, and by general lack of consistently effective everyday leadership."[13] The problems besetting the Socialists resulted in their loss of control of the Confederation of Chilean Workers (CTCh), whose leadership they now ceded to the Communists.

How could the Communists strengthen their defense of workers' rights and still support the ideal of National Unity against Fascism? Asking workers to continue to refrain from striking—one of the workers' most powerful weapons—would fuel their growing disillusionment with the leftist parties. And yet advocating strikes would be seen by centrist forces as a violation of National Unity and, indeed, as revolutionary provocation. One solution to this dilemma came in the form of patriotic strikes to eliminate the remnants of Fascism still in power around the globe, strikes that were also linked to the coal workers' economic and social grievances.

Strikes in the Coal Mining Zone: For "Democracy" in Argentina and Workers' Rights at Home

Chilean Communists continued their battle against Fascism even after World War II came to an end. Strikes of opposition to the "Fascist" government in Argentina, held sporadically in 1944 and the first half of 1945,

12. In the competition between Socialists and Communists in labor politics, the March 1945 congressional elections gave the PCCh a clear upper hand. Communist Undersecretary of the CTCh Salvador Ocampo won his Senate race from the Ñuble-Concepción-Arauco region by a landslide, and two other Communists on the CTCh's National Directorate won seats in the Chamber of Deputies. *None* of the Socialists on the CTCh, on the other hand, was elected to Congress. Even Secretary-General Bernardo Ibáñez, an incumbent national deputy, lost his race for the Senate. In addition to Ocampo, the other senator elected from the Ñuble-Concepción-Arauco region was Liberal Party leader Gustavo Rivera Baeza, who was then head of the Lebu Coal Mining Company Board of Directors and would soon become president of his party. Labor Attaché Report, 2/15–3/15, 1945, 5, USNA, RG 59; and Pizarro Soto, *Lebu*, 352.

13. Labor Attaché Report, 2/15–3/15, 1945, 5, USNA, RG 59.

now became regular occurrences. Almost always begun by the longshoremen and sailors of the coal mining ports, these strikes quickly spread to the majority of workers throughout the region. Each time, the government would send in Chilean naval personnel as strikebreakers to load the Argentine ships with coal. When they had filled the holds, usually within a day or two, the ships would leave port, and the longshoremen, miners, machinists, and other workers of the region would return to their jobs. Similar strikes were also staged at ports up north, where Communist-affiliated dockworkers refused to load nitrate onto Spanish ships in protest against the Franco regime.

On September 26, 1945, the Argentine ship *Río Diamante* pulled into the port of Lota, and for the third time that year, the longshoremen refused to load it with coal. A Navy destroyer was already docked at the port, seemingly by chance, and when its crew began to fill the holds of the Argentine vessel, all workers in the Lota company walked off the job in protest. The following day, coal miners throughout the provinces of Concepción and Arauco joined the strike, including the large workforce at Schwager.[14] U.S. Labor Attaché Daniel Horowitz noted that "the position of the coal miners was the same as that of the longshoremen—that so long as the Perón government remained in power in Argentina, no coal should be loaded on Argentine ships in Chile."[15] As soon as the Navy men finished loading the ship, it left port on September 28, and the strike came to an end.

Horowitz recognized that "the C.T.Ch. had developed the policy of refusing to load Argentine ships principally as a result of Communist pressure."[16] Nonetheless, he downplayed any subversive political motives, highlighting instead the workers' substantive bread-and-butter grievances: "The month of September has been characterized by a series of general industry strikes which have caused considerable criticism and alarm among some sectors of the population. Actually, they do not appear to represent any immediate threat to political stability, but do represent a reflection of underlying dissatisfaction and discontent."[17] Horowitz

14. Labor Attaché Report, September 1945, 5–6. On the participation of the Schwager workers in the September 1945 strike, see Telegram no. 1236, from Bowers to Secretary of State, September 27, 1945, both in USNA, RG 59.

15. Labor Attaché Report, September 1945, 6; and Telegram no. 1242, from Bowers to Secretary of State, September 29, 1945, both in USNA, RG 59. Reference was already being made to "the Perón government," even though he was but one member of the governing junta, then serving as vice president.

16. Labor Attaché Report, 10/1–11/25, 1945, 4, USNA, RG 59.

17. Labor Attaché Report, September 1945, 1, USNA, RG 59. It is not clear whether Horowitz is referring here to the strikes in the coal mining region.

clearly perceived the frustration that had built up among Chilean workers during the war years, when they had refrained from striking in order to maintain production levels, and thus had not fought for more far-reaching improvements in their working and living conditions. The Chilean government, however, continued to disregard the workers' grievances, insisting instead that the strikes in the coal mining zone were simply "illegal action[s] . . . contrary to [the] national interest." Administration officials were particularly irate since the Argentine ships were bringing crucial deliveries of wheat to Chile in exchange for coal, under a bilateral agreement reached the previous July.[18]

On September 26, the same day the *Río Diamante* pulled into the Lota harbor, President Ríos Morales began to prepare for an official visit to the United States by naming fellow right-wing Radical Alfredo Duhalde Vásquez as interior minister. According to the Chilean Constitution, this meant that, in the president's absence, Duhalde would become vice president and acting head of state.[19] It was thus Duhalde who personally reassured "Argentine steamship agents that [their] vessels would be loaded in compliance with [the] Chilean Government's agreements." Communist-led workers, however, "remained unmoved by [the] Government's insistence," declaring that they would continue their protest actions until the Argentine people were free of fascistic tyranny.[20]

President Ríos Morales had been invited to visit Washington, D.C., during U.S. Vice President Wallace's trip to Chile in March 1943. As Ríos headed north on October 9, all parties hoped the visit would improve U.S.–Chilean relations. After five days of formal meetings and honorary functions in the capital, the president spent another two weeks visiting New York, Philadelphia, Chicago, San Francisco, and Los Angeles. From his Waldorf-Astoria suite in New York on October 16, President Ríos spoke to the press about the military government of Argentina, describing it as "a very sick man who each day grows weaker and weaker" and advocating

18. Airgram no. 540, from U.S. Embassy officer [Hugh] Millard to Secretary of State, October 15, 1945, USNA, RG 59.

19. The 1925 Chilean Constitution did not call for an elected vice president; rather, it provided that in the event of the president's absence, incapacitation, or death, the interior minister would become vice president and acting head of state. Duhalde did so from September 26 to December 3, 1945, and from January 17, 1946, until Ríos Morales's death on June 27, 1946. Duhalde then became acting president, a post he would hold from June 27 to August 3 and from August 13 to October 17, 1946, when he stepped down altogether, and his interior minister, Juan Antonio Iribarren, became acting president.

20. Airgram no. 540, October 15, 1945; see also Telegram no. 1339, October 20, 1945, both from Millard to Secretary of State, USNA, RG 59.

a policy of noninterference so that "he can die in peace."[21] Back in his homeland, however, the workers of the coal mining region disagreed with this passive strategy and continued to boycott Argentine ships docking in their ports.

The working class of Argentina, in whose name the Chilean longshoremen and miners engaged in repeated work stoppages, were also taking to the streets at this time, for quite different reasons. In late 1945, the Argentine governing junta arrested their fellow officer Juan Perón in an effort to halt his growing strength and autonomy. Masses of Perón supporters, referred to as the "descamisados" (literally "shirtless ones"), converged on the Plaza de Mayo in Buenos Aires on October 17–18 to demand their leader's release. This was a defining moment in the emerging populist relation between Perón and the Argentine working class.[22] The Communist-led workers of Chile shared the fervor, but not the political allegiance, of the millions of Argentines who hailed Perón. On October 18, the same day crowds were cheering Perón's appearance on the balcony of the presidential palace in Buenos Aires, the *Río Teuco* arrived at the port of Coronel, and the longshoremen there "continu[ed] their policy of refusing to load coal on any Argentine ships."[23] The next morning, when the crew of a Navy destroyer began filling the holds, the Schwager miners quickly joined the protest strike.

On October 21, when the *Río Teuco*'s holds were full, the ship left port, and following the adopted pattern, the workers returned to their jobs. This time, however, the Schwager company refused to reinstate thirty of the longshoremen, presumably those deemed most politically active and troublesome. In response to the firings, all Schwager dock workers and miners immediately resumed the strike, and that same afternoon, the Lota miners joined them. Unable to reach a negotiated settlement with leftist party and union leaders, the government, now under acting head of state Alfredo Duhalde Vásquez, invoked the internal security laws, under which at least twenty-five strike leaders were immediately arrested. The companies were also now "free to employ new personnel." In response to what they perceived as hostile moves by the government, all mine workers and many others throughout the region declared a sympathy strike.

21. *New York Times*, October 17, 1945, 26. Ríos Morales made similar remarks at a press conference in Washington, D.C., on October 12. *New York Times*, October 13, 1945, 7.
22. The social, political, and cultural dynamics of the mass gathering in La Plata are explored in James, "October 17th."
23. Labor Attaché Report, 10/1–11/25, 1945, 3, USNA, RG 59.

Finally, on October 23, the Schwager company agreed to reinstate the thirty longshoremen, and the striking workers returned to their jobs.[24]

Internal state security laws had been used to put down strikes in the past, but the fact that this was occurring now suggests that even the minimally operative consensus behind the Popular Front project was breaking down. Many leftist and even centrist politicians began to worry about the implications for Chilean democracy of resorting to hard-line measures against labor unrest. The strikes in the coal mining zone were part of a broader wave of national turmoil, which powerful voices in the government perceived as a threat to national security and stability, thus justifying the government's strong response. In the assessment of U.S. Embassy official Hugh Millard, the strikes were driven by "Communist elements conducting [an] active anti-Government campaign."[25] In addition to disturbances in the coal and nitrate mining regions, the same period saw the "most serious strike in several years" at Chuquicamata, the center of the country's vital copper industry, where workers "refused to obey a government order to return to work."[26] According to a U.S. consular agent, the strike began "over a minor technical point," but was then "used as a crucial test between the Communistic dominated National Labor Organization [the CTCh] and the local government." He also noted that the "government appears powerless to carry out its decree" of emergency zone status for the province of Antofagasta.[27]

The Communist and labor leaders fomenting strikes against the Argentine and Spanish regimes intended for them to spread from the longshoremen to the miners, and then to workers throughout the coal mining zone and the nation. Indeed, on October 23, just as the strike in the zone came to an end, U.S. Embassy official Millard warned that Chilean labor leaders were now threatening to declare a national general strike.[28] The Communists believed that the momentum for such actions would be sustained by a large and fervent hemispheric campaign of protest against

24. Ibid. The Lota longshoremen had also refused to load an Argentine ship just a few days before. Airgram no. 540, from Millard to Secretary of State, October 15, 1945, USNA, RG 59.
25. Restricted Telegram no. 1349, from Millard to Secretary of State, October 23, 1945, USNA, RG 59.
26. Labor Attaché Report, 10/1–11/25, 1945, 1, USNA, RG 59.
27. Telegram no. 45, from Ehlers (Antofagasta) to Secretary of State, October 29, 1945, USNA, RG 59. U.S. Labor Attaché Horowitz claimed that when the Chuquicamata strike failed it was largely because the Communist Party had less support in the copper mine than the Socialists and Democratics did. Labor Attaché Report, 10/1–11/25, 1945, 2, 4–5, USNA, RG 59.
28. Restricted telegram no. 1349, from Millard to Secretary of State, October 23, 1945, USNA, RG 59.

the remnants of Fascism in the postwar world. By as late as November 1945, however, Chile seemed to be the only country in which a strike movement in opposition to the Argentine and Spanish governments was under way. Seeking international solidarity, the Confederation of Chilean Workers wrote letters to labor groups in various countries, including both the American Federation of Labor (AF of L) and the Congress of Industrial Organizations (CIO) in the United States, asking if they were going to join the crusade. Daniel Horowitz speculated that the answers from both organizations would be no.[29]

Despite a weak response from other labor sectors in the Americas, Communist-led workers of the Chilean coal mining region continued to heed the CTCh's call for anti-Fascist protest strikes. When the Argentine ship *Río Diamante* reappeared off Chilean shores, this time docking in Coronel on November 11, the longshoremen again refused to load it with coal. As in previous cases, the Navy's move to load the ship was taken as "a signal for the complete shutdown of all coal activity in the entire coal region of Concepción-Arauco." Also joining the strike were machinists, railroad workers, and even the municipal employees of Lota, as well as textile workers in Concepción, who stopped work for several hours to show their opposition to the Argentine government. Altogether, in Horowitz's estimate, "more than 25,000 workers in the area were involved in these stoppages."[30]

Though ostensibly provoked by an international issue, the escalating strikes in the coal mining region were "not solely a gesture of antipathy toward the Argentine regime," as U.S. Ambassador Claude Bowers informed his superiors in Washington.[31] During periods of heightened tension, as at the end of 1945, different disputes and even different motives for the same dispute were tightly intertwined. It was often impossible to distinguish between economic and political strikes. Thus the November 1945 boycott of the Argentine ship *Río Diamante* was also connected to an ongoing dispute about overtime pay; the workers insisted that the company comply with Law no. 7289, a piece of wartime legislation passed in October 1942, which allowed coal mines to operate on Sundays and holidays as long as the miners were paid double time.[32] With the end of the

29. Labor Attaché Report, 10/1–11/25, 1945, 4–5, USNA, RG 59. Horowitz does not explain why he thinks the response would be negative. Both U.S. labor organizations strongly opposed the Farrell-Perón government. See, for example, CIO, "Argentine Regime."

30. Labor Attaché Report, 10/1–11/25, 1945, 3–4, USNA, RG 59.

31. Telegram no. 1425, from Bowers to Secretary of State, November 13, 1945, USNA, RG 59.

32. Ibid. Bowers also mentions that workers of the state-owned railroads were about to strike over wages.

war, the Coal Mining and Industrial Company of Lota (CCIL) unilaterally returned to time-and-a-half pay, even though the law had not been repealed. Although in response to the workers' strike declaration the CCIL declared a lockout for November 12, when the Argentine ship left Coronel on the night of November 14 and the Lota miners ended their strike, the CCIL relented and allowed the workers to return. The dispute over Law no. 7289 remained unresolved.[33]

Thus, even though workers in the coal region engaged in ever larger protest strikes against the Argentine government, they were also motivated by what Horowitz had referred to as their "underlying dissatisfaction and discontent" with their lot at home.[34] In addition to particular grievances, such as company noncompliance with overtime pay laws, the miners were also embroiled in their annual contract negotiations throughout the latter half of 1945, at the same time that the anti-Perón strikes were gaining momentum. Chilean coal miners had long mobilized around a diversity of concerns—from bread-and-butter issues to international politics, but the complex intertwining of their demands seemed to intensify in the immediate postwar months.

Although spokesmen for the Communist-led workers continued to utilize the language of patriotic nationalism, they now added a renewed emphasis on international class solidarity. During the October 1945 work stoppage, for example, when the Schwager company had laid off thirty longshoremen, the Regional Miners' Council of Concepción and Arauco (Consejo Regional Minero de Concepción y Arauco; CRMCA) lauded the "noble attitude of patriotism and solidarity shown by the coal mining workers who refuse to load the ships of the Argentine GOU." In the same article, the CRMCA also lamented the workers' plight in their contract battles, where they sought "improvement in their living and working conditions," but were met with a "campaign of falsehoods and defamation" by company agents.

The regional miners' council argued that, even though Chilean society widely recognized the legitimacy of the workers' demands, neither the companies nor the government wanted a ready "solution" to the labor dispute since prolonging it allowed them to increase their control over

33. Labor Attaché Report, 10/1–11/25, 1945, 3–4; and Telegram no. 1436, from Bowers to Secretary of State, November 15, 1945, USNA, RG 59. The telegram also notes that, on November 15, public school teachers throughout the country began a 24-hour strike for wage increases.

34. Labor Attaché Report, September 1945, 1, USNA, RG 59.

the miners. Careful not to directly name the president or other government officials, the CRMCA leaders nonetheless issued a strong accusation: "The intention . . . is to create the necessary environment for the Companies to refuse wage increases on the pretext of an intransigent or anti-patriotic attitude on the part of the workers, and even to establish a reign of terror and state of siege in the [coal mining] zone, mobilizing the [naval] Squadron and increasing the number of Carabineros personnel and Investigations' agents."[35]

The Lirquén coal miners had submitted their contract petitions back on August 9; the miners and metalworkers of Lota, Schwager, and several smaller companies presented theirs in early October.[36] The demands were similar in all cases, including "a general [wage] increase of 8 pesos daily, adjustments in piece rates to equal this increase, [an] increase in weekly attendance bonuses, [an] increase in family allowance to 40 pesos (20 at present), establishment of 2-peso shift bonus for third shift, and payment of one month's wages for each year of service as severance wages."[37] According to the FNM newspaper El Chiflón, the company representative on the conciliation board for the Lirquén conflict "'recognized' that the wage earned by its workers is insignificant, and that with it, it is impossible to meet the high cost [of] subsistence goods." Nonetheless, he went on, the company "was not prepared to grant any kind of improvement, at least not unless the Government would provide it with 'a subsidy' to finance the greater expense that the wage increase would impose on it." In demanding a wage subsidy, the coal mining capitalists essentially called on the state to take responsibility for the well-being of workers whose production was vital to national industrial progress. In doing so, they were still trying to negotiate to their advantage *within* the broad outlines of the Popular Front national development model. El Chiflón, for its part, bluntly accused the companies of "mocking the workers yet again."[38]

Like the companies, the workers also called on the government to act on their behalf—and to do so beyond the normal limits of mediation. On November 5, after negotiations broke down, approximately 1,200 Lirquén

35. *La Patria* (Concepción), October 18, 1945, as quoted in Molina Urra, *Condición económico-social*, 110.

36. *El Sur*, February 16, 1946, 7; and Labor Attaché Report, 10/1–11/25, 1945, 11–12, USNA, RG 59. I do not know why the Lirquén miners' contract was on a different schedule.

37. Labor Attaché Report, 10/1–11/25, 1945, 11–12, USNA, RG 59. The lists of demands (*pliegos de petición*) from the Lota and Schwager unions were appended to this report. See also *El Chiflón*, November 1945, 9–10, 20.

38. *El Chiflón*, November 1945, 9–10, 20.

workers went on strike, "hop[ing] for an energetic government intervention so that their petitions would be resolved as quickly as possible."[39]
The government did propose a temporary settlement, under which the
Lirquén strikers would return to work pending the outcome of the Lota
and Schwager disputes. The Lirquén company rejected the proposal, however, and the strike continued.[40]

Meanwhile, negotiations in Lota and Schwager were nearing stalemate.
The editors of El Chiflón warned that company intransigence would likely
lead to a regional strike: "This already occurred in Lirquén, and it is most
probable that in Schwager, Lota, Curanilahue, and Colico Sur, the same
thing will occur as soon as the legal measures in the Special Conciliation
Board have been exhausted."[41] Toward the end of November, the Lota and
Schwager unions voted to authorize their leaders "to call a strike whenever [they] deemed advisable." A strike scheduled for November 30 was
postponed, however, when it appeared that a negotiated settlement might
still be reached. And, a few days later, the Lirquén strike ended when the
parties agreed to submit their dispute to a tripartite arbitration tribunal
specifically mandated "to determine whether or not the company could
afford [a wage] increase greater than 3 pesos per day."[42] To represent them,
the workers again chose fiery Communist Deputy Reinaldo Núñez, who
had provoked the resignation of the government arbiter in the coal disputes of the previous year. On December 11, at the urging of Labor Minister Mariano Bustos Lagos, the parties in the Lota and Schwager disputes
also agreed to arbitration.[43]

When labor leaders responded to the government's appeals to call off
their strikes, they expected a degree of reciprocity. On December 22, the
Lota miners' union sent a circular letter to the labor minister, the director
general of labor (DGT), the Concepción intendant, and other regional and
local authorities to "respectfully inform [them] of the multiple and systematic abuses of which the workers have been the victims . . . of humiliation, slander, and extortion of their wages by the Superior Bosses

39. Ibid.; and Labor Attaché Report, 10/1–11/25, 1945, 11–12, USNA, RG 59.
40. Labor Attaché Report, 10/1–11/25, 1945, 11–12, USNA, RG 59.
41. El Chiflón, November 1945, 9–10, 20.
42. Labor Attaché Report, 11/25/45–1/15/4, 1945, 7–8, USNA, RG 59. For a slightly different account, see Stambuck Gallardo, Movimientos sociales, 56.
43. Lota and Schwager formed their own tripartite arbitration tribunals, but with the
same presiding arbiter, Oscar Gajardo Villarroel, vice president of the Chilean Economic
Development Agency (CORFO). Gajardo issued the arbitration decisions in February, but the
companies did not readily comply. At the end of the month, the Regional Miners' Council of
Concepción and Arauco (CRMCA) wrote to Vice President Duhalde to "demand the Supreme
Government obligate the coal companies to apply the award of the Arbitration Tribunal."
Labor Attaché Report, 2/15–3/15, 1946, Appendix IV, 1–2, Despatch no. 13686, USNA, RG 59.

[managers and supervisors] and especially by the Subaltern Bosses [foremen] of the Company." Continuing to use the language of patriotic cooperation in the interests of national development, the letter repeatedly emphasized "the good intentions of the workers to not create difficulties for the Government or for the National Economy, and to increase the production of Coal." The miners had shown their goodwill, the letter explained, by agreeing to arbitration and by forgoing "a legal strike that had been approved by 98% of the workers in the [coal mining] zone." The implication was that, if the miners were again compelled to go on strike, this would have "immeasurable consequences . . . for the stability of our Democratic regime." The letter then described myriad abuses in different sectors of the CCIL, noting, for example, that coal face supervisors had been ordered "to get rid of all the [union] Delegates before the 1st of January."[44]

Highlighting the miners' good-faith efforts to increase coal production alongside the thinly veiled threat of disrupting it, the letter passed over the extent to which the workers had mobilized around national and international political concerns. Yet, on December 27, less than a week after they sent this circular letter, the miners and longshoremen of Lota again demonstrated their opposition to the regime of Juan Perón by halting work when the Argentine ship *Río Neuquén* docked at their port. Following the established pattern, "the strike spread on the next day to all coal mining operations in the Concepción-Arauco area." The ship then went on to Coronel, where its holds were filled by a Navy crew, and when it left port on December 31, the workers returned to their jobs.[45]

Strikes in the Coal Mining Zone: The Politics of Postwar Maneuvering

The complex politics at play in the labor upheaval of the second half of 1945 were brought to the fore by an unusually candid exchange between the National Executive Committee (CEN) of the Radical Party and the Lota CTCh. When the government announced plans to extend the state of siege if the strikes did not cease, both the PCCh and the CTCh condemned the use of military force to quell social unrest. Although Radical Party leaders

44. Oficio no. 80, December 22, 1945, from Lota Industrial Union to Labor Minister et al., FIC, vol. 2320, ANCh.
45. Labor Attaché Report, 11/25/45–1/15/46, 10, USNA, RG 59. A slightly different account was given in *El Sur*, January 2, 1946, 6.

also expressed concern about President Ríos Morales's authoritarian inclinations, after meeting in Santiago at the end of October, they issued a statement insisting that the "Communist Party should modify its activities in these strike[s]."[46] This position enraged union and political leaders in Lota affiliated with the CTCh, who sent a telegram directly to the National Executive Committee (CEN) of the Radical Party in Santiago: "Workers in this zone [are] on their feet in defense of rights achieved, to the point of a general strike if necessary. We demand that [the] government prohibit Fascist ships from docking at port[s] in [the] region, considering it treason to the National interest."[47]

The intertwining issues of the coal mining zone strikes—economic and political, local and international—posed a difficult challenge to the Radical Party, then under the presidency of left-wing leader Alfredo Rosende Verdugo. On November 14, at the conclusion of the regional strike motivated both by the docking of the Argentine ship *Río Diamante* and by the CCIL's noncompliance with overtime pay laws, the Radicals' National Executive Committee issued a lengthy response to the telegram it had received the previous month from the Lota CTCh. Laying out the Radical Party's general position regarding different types of strikes, the letter rejected an absolute distinction between legal and illegal strikes, claiming that such a simplistic view was "not consistent with the social reality in which we are living." The Radical Party would *always* support legal strikes, the executive committee declared, "because it sees in them the best guarantee that the workers [will] progress toward obtaining economic benefits, and that they [will] consolidate their legal institutions." With respect to illegal strikes, the Radicals distinguished between "strikes of a specifically economic nature and essentially just, and strikes of a political nature, or simply of solidarity." Although the Radical Party did not sanction illegal economic strikes, "at the same time," the letter explained, it felt responsible to "contribut[e] decisively toward resolving them." As for illegal political or solidarity strikes, the Radical Party "simply rejects them because of the damage they do to the social interest."[48]

46. Radical Party CEN declaration of October 1945, as quoted in Telegram no. 1350, from Millard to Secretary of State, October 24, 1945, USNA, RG 59.

47. Telegram from Lota CTCh to Radical Party CEN, Santiago, October 24, 1945, included in the "Translation of a letter from Radical Party to Local Lota C.T.Ch. on Chuquicamata and Coal Strikes," November 14, 1945; the letter, originally published in *La Hora* (Santiago), November 15, 1945, was translated and reprinted in Labor Attaché Report, 10/1–11/25, 1945, Appendix I (henceforth "Letter from Radical Party to Lota C.T.Ch."), USNA, RG 59.

48. Letter from Radical Party to Lota C.T.Ch. Less than a week later, regional leaders of the Radical, Democratic, Socialist, and Authentic Socialist Parties met in Antofagasta and

The National Executive Committee letter then turned to the specific case of labor unrest in the coal mining zone "motivated by the refusal of the workers to load Argentine ships" and by "solidarity with others who are engaged in [labor] disputes." Concerned more with national development than with anti-Fascism now that the war was over, the CEN explained that the Radical Party condemned the work stoppages "because this type of strike harms the economic interest of the country, without legitimate or plausible justification."[49] The executive committee reproached the longshoremen and miners for sabotaging trade agreements with Argentina deemed vital to Chile's national interest. What the progressive Radicals then in control of the CEN did not acknowledge, however, was that, in addition to the international politics of protest against Perón, the striking workers were also motivated by bread-and-butter issues, including overtime pay and unjust dismissals.

Yet, even as it condemned the strikes by Communist-led labor sectors, the executive committee also took the Ríos Morales government to task for its excessive use of emergency powers to deal with these strikes:

> The everyday application of the Internal State Security Law—a law of exception—to labor disputes is not proper. In effect, this law [no. 6026] prescribes in its second Article that "those who promote, stimulate, or maintain strikes in violation of the [applicable] legal provisions . . . and [intended] to undermine public order commit a crime against public order." . . . The law of Internal State Security has been applied to phenomena which do not tend to harm the stability of the fundamental institutions of the Republic.[50]

This equivocal language allowed the Radicals to present themselves as defenders both of workers' rights and of democratic principles, while leaving open the possibility that future labor actions might be seen to undermine public order, thereby requiring repressive measures.

The strikes in the coal mining zone also brought to the fore differences in the labor strategies adopted by the Chile's Marxist parties in the early postwar months. "The antagonisms between the Socialists and the Communists have been sharpened in recent weeks," U.S. Labor Attaché Horowitz observed in his October–November 1945 report, "as they have

---

issued a similar declaration condemning the workers' refusal to load Argentine and Spanish ships. Labor Attaché Report, 10/1–11/25, 1945, 5, USNA, RG 59.

49. Letter from Radical Party to Lota C.T.Ch., 6.

50. Ibid., 7.

attempted to apply their divergent policies to specific situations affecting the labor movement."[51] Regarding the strike at the Chuquicamata copper mine, for example, "the Socialists took a 'no-compromise' position, while the Communists urged acceptance of the government decree," ordering the miners to return to work. On the other hand, the Communists continued to support the longshoremen and miners in their refusal to load coal and nitrate onto Argentine and Spanish ships, a policy the Socialists strongly opposed. Thus, in Horowitz's view, the Communists were more willing than the Socialists to compromise in "disputes concerning economic issues," but they continued "promoting their recommended international policy through strike action where circumstances made this desirable."[52]

What Horowitz seemed to underestimate, however, was the strength of voices in the Chilean Communist Party calling for more aggressive action on behalf of the party's working-class base. Labor unrest and antagonism between the Communists and the governing parties had clearly been growing throughout 1944–45. In December 1945, at its Thirteenth Congress, the PCCh formally adopted a new strategic line known as the "battle of the masses."[53] Though it still did not abandon its expressed commitment to National Unity, the party now stressed the need for more rapid and profound transformation of the social and political order; to this end, the Communists "adopted a tougher policy on labor disputes" and became outspoken critics of the Ríos Morales administration.[54] At the same time, their differences with the Socialists over the strikes of late 1945 set the stage for the total collapse of the fragile alliance between Chile's two powerful Marxist parties in the coming months.

51. Labor Attaché Report, 10/1–11/25, 1945, 1, USNA, RG 59.
52. Ibid., 2.
53. The term "battle of the masses [*lucha de masas*]" is used by María Soledad Gómez in her "Factores nacionales," 87. On the PCCh's Thirteenth Congress, see also Lafertte Gaviño, "El Decimotercer Congreso"; Millas, *En tiempos*, 403–4; and Garcés, *Soberanos e intervenidos*, 95–100.
54. Barnard, "Chile," 74. A December 1945 memo from U.S. FBI Director J. Edgar Hoover challenges the idea of growing antagonism between the Communists and the Ríos Morales government. Hoover refers to behind-the-scenes negotiations for the possible entry of Communists into the cabinet. Among other conditions, the Communists insisted that Ríos Morales "adopt a strong Leftist program," and "that diplomatic relations immediately be severed with Argentina and Spain." According to Hoover, the president seriously considered this option, but was leaning toward "a new cabinet composed mainly of Radical Party members, without Communist representation." Hoover added that the administration's "break with Rightist elements appears complete and the Leftist groups have promised Ríos full cooperation." Personal, Confidential Memorandum from J. Edgar Hoover to Frederick B. Lyon, Chief of the State Department's Foreign Activity Correlation Division, December 29, 1945 (henceforth "Hoover Memo, December 29, 1945"), USNA, RG 59.

From Strikes in the Coal Mining Zone to the
Plaza Bulnes Massacre in Santiago

At the beginning of 1946, the operative accords of the preceding years began to unravel at alarming speed. Although most studies of this period focus on the nitrate workers' strikes in the second half of January, the story actually began in the coal mines at the beginning of the month. On January 3, nearly one hundred fifty second-shift miners at the small Colico Sur mine in Curanilahue began an illegal strike by taking two foremen hostage and refusing to leave the mine.[55] According to Horowitz, the company provoked the conflict when it fired six miners, including several union leaders, who "were held responsible for an illegal strike at the company some time ago."[56] An article in *El Sur*, however, claimed that the strike was prompted by the company's refusal to fire twelve workers who would not make payments to the union's Resistance Fund.[57]

Whichever was the truer version, the company responded by laying off all of its four hundred thirty-six workers.[58] The nearby Colico Norte and Plegarias miners quickly declared solidarity strikes and remained inside the mine galleries at the end of their shifts on January 7.[59] On the same day, the Executive issued Supreme Decree no. 42 declaring the provinces of Concepción and Arauco emergency zones under the command of Navy Rear Admiral Immanuel Holger Torres.[60] With fewer than eight hundred workers on strike, the threat these strikes posed to the coal mining industry, to social relations, or to national security did not appear sufficient to

55. Labor Attaché Report, 11/25/45–1/15/46, 8–9, USNA, RG 59; *El Sur*, January 5, 1946, 3, and January 8, 1946, 7; Oficio no. 251, January 8, 1946, from DGT to Labor Minister, FDGT, 1946 Oficios, vol. 1, ARNAD.

56. Labor Attaché Report, 11/25/45–1/15/46, 8–9, USNA, RG 59.

57. *El Sur*, January 8, 1946, 7.

58. The number of workers laid off by the Colico Sur company varies in different sources. See *El Sur*, January 8, 1946, 7, and January 9, 1946, 1; and Telegram no. 32, from Bowers to Secretary of State, January 9, 1946, USNA, RG 59.

59. According to the Curanilahue labor inspector, three hundred first-shift workers at Plegarias remained inside the mine, while one hundred left voluntarily. At Colico Norte, eighty-two first-shift miners also remained inside. Unnumbered telegram, as transcribed in Oficio no. 298, January 8, 1946, from DGT to Labor Minister, FDGT, 1946 Oficios, vol. 1, ARNAD.

60. Immanuel Holger Torres would serve as interior minister under González Videla from 1947 to 1950, during which time an *acusación constitucional*, or "constitutional accusation," was brought against him for his role in repressing the October 1947 coal miners' strike (see chapter 8). Because the acusación constitucional in Chile differs significantly from its nearest U.S. equivalents, "bill of impeachment" and "impeachment proceedings," I use the Spanish term. For more on the acusación constitucional against Holger Torres, which was overwhelmingly rejected by the Chamber of Deputies on November 4, 1947, see chapter 9.

explain the government's peremptory response. The administration may have chosen them, however, an opportunity to communicate its postwar labor policy since, as Andrew Barnard observed, the illegal strike in the Colico Sur coal mine took place in the midst of "sharpening hostilities between the Communists and the Socialists," and "at the precise time that the government decided to do something about the rising tide of industrial unrest."[61]

On the night of January 7, as military forces headed to the region under the emergency zone decree, the Colico Sur miners released their two hostages and left the mine, where they had remained for more than a hundred hours.[62] Even though the company had cancelled the contracts of all its workers and refused to rehire them, El Sur reported that the dispute was resolved and the coal mining zone was tranquil.[63] This assessment proved premature. The following day, the dispute took an "unexpected turn" when the Lota and Schwager miners and longshoremen, together with workers from the CCIL's ceramics factory and other company enterprises, resumed the strike in sympathy with their Colico Sur comrades. From the original handful of Colico Sur miners, the number of workers now on strike increased dramatically, to between seventeen and twenty-five thousand.[64]

U.S. Labor Attaché Horowitz found it quite notable that "a dispute in a relatively unimportant coal mine resulted in a sympathetic shutdown of all activity in the region."[65] Trying to understand this development, he looked to the Communists, "whose greatest strength within the labor movement exists in this region," noting that the PCCh "at the time was agitating for representation in the Cabinet, and it was felt that a general strike in the important coal region might further [their] possibilities."[66] The Lota and Schwager unions did not publicly mention Communist maneuvering for ministerial posts, but simply proclaimed that the "sympathy stoppage would be continued indefinitely unless all workers at Colico Sur [were] reinstated." The unions also insisted that both the general

61. Barnard, "Chile," 75.
62. El Sur, January 8, 1946, 7. If, as El Sur says, the strikers were inside the mine from 3 P.M. on January 3, when the second shift started, to 10 P.M. on January 7, they would have been there for 103 hours, not 62 hours, as El Sur also says.
63. Ibid.
64. These different estimates were given in El Sur, January 9, 1946, 1, and by Ambassador Bowers in Telegram no. 32, from Bowers to Secretary of State, January 9, 1946, USNA, RG 59.
65. Labor Attaché Report, 11/25/45–1/15/46, 1, USNA, RG 59.
66. Ibid., 1, 9.

manager and the Welfare Department chief of the Colico Sur company be "either dismissed or transferred" since the two were seen as fundamentally antagonistic to the workers.[67] As the 1942 Rettig-Pazols Report had warned they might, Welfare Department officers throughout the coal region continued to provoke the workers' indignation.

The government reacted swiftly and categorically to the escalating labor unrest in the region. On January 9, the day after the Lota and Schwager unions joined the strike, President Ríos Morales called a special cabinet meeting where he "announced [the] policy that in illegal strikes legal recognition of [the] participating unions will be withdrawn and union officials discharged from employment."[68] Given the complex procedures in the Chilean Labor Code required for a strike to be declared legal, the vast majority of workers' grievances could only be addressed through illegal strikes, which far outnumbered legal ones throughout most of the twentieth century.[69] In declaring that any union engaged in an illegal strike would lose its legal status (personalidad jurídica), the president was thus adopting an extreme anti-labor position, which, if carried out, would mean the elimination of all unions trying to defend and promote workers' interests. Workers around the country waited on edge to see what the government would actually do.

Even though the labor minister continued to meet with company and labor representatives, following the tripartite model of the preceding decade, the shift toward a more repressive anti-labor stance became clear. On January 9, the government sent a naval warship from Valparaíso to Lota; a few days later, Ambassador Bowers wired that "troops arrived yesterday in coal region and while several arrests have been made no disorder has been reported."[70] In conjunction with the deployment of troops, the Executive issued an ultimatum: all strikers not returning to work by 8 P.M. on January 10 would be subject to arrest under internal state security laws. Contrary to the government's intention, however, the show of force in the region provoked rather than quelled local resistance, at least in the

67. El Sur, January 9, 1946, 1.

68. Telegram no. 39, from Bowers to Secretary of State, January 10, 1946, USNA, RG 59. Ríos Morales's declaration on illegal strikes was included in Labor Attaché Report, 11/25/45–1/15/46, as Appendix VI, USNA, RG 59. As discussed later in the chapter, this policy would be applied by Vice President Duhalde to strikes at the Mapocho and Humberstone nitrate mines later in the month, prompting a rally in Santiago that would be met with state repression. Andrew Barnard is among the few scholars recognizing the role of the coal miners' strike in the adoption of this historic policy. Barnard, "Chile," 75.

69. On Chilean strike laws, see Camu Veloso, Estudio crítica.

70. Telegram no. 48, from Bowers to Secretary of State, January 11, 1946, USNA, RG 59; and El Sur, January 9, 1946, 1.

first few days. On January 11, Bowers reported that the coal strike had "spread to other industries in [the] area yesterday and [the] expected result is [a] general shutdown throughout [the] two provinces [of Concepción and Arauco] by today."[71]

The general strike that Bowers predicted was only narrowly averted. When the national Democratic Alliance of Radicals and Communists sent a three-person commission to Lota to help negotiate a solution, the government extended the return-to-work deadline by one day. By 4 P.M. on January 11, an agreement had been reached, and the third shift returned to work.[72] This settlement did not last, however: contrary to what the workers' representatives understood, the company said it had never agreed to rehire the six Colico Sur miners whose firing originally prompted the strike. Negotiations began again that night and continued until finally the company did agree to rehire the miners, and production resumed throughout the region with the first shift on January 12.[73]

The heavy militarization of the region was clearly significant in bringing the strike to an end, as conveyed in a confidential memorandum from the U.S. naval attaché in Santiago to his superiors in Washington: "A grave strike was broken in the Concepción area by the Minister of Defense, who brought out an Army regiment, two Air Force planes, a Destroyer and a Cruiser. The situation is temporarily quiet."[74] The military's involvement was widely hailed as a positive step, even by leftist elements within the Democratic Alliance. Thus the three-person commission sent to Lota, which included a Lota-born Communist militant and a Democratic Party leader from the Concepción area, credited the "upright, calm, and gentlemanly attitude" of Major Salvador Tapia Muñoz, the military officer in charge of greater Curanilahue, where the Colico Sur mines were located, for helping to resolve the strike.[75] Noting that Major Tapia had

71. Telegram no. 48, from Bowers to Secretary of State, January 11, 1946, USNA, RG 59.

72. El Sur, January 10, 1946, 1, and January 11, 1946, 1, 3.

73. El Sur, January 12, 1946, 1, 7, and January 13, 1946, 13; Telegrams nos. 54 and 56, from Bowers to Secretary of State, January 12 and 14, 1946, USNA, RG 59.

74. Unnumbered confidential memorandum from Navy Department to State Department, January 16, 1946, USNA, RG 59.

75. El Sur, January 13, 1946, 17. Commission member Lorenzo Gallardo Gallardo, a longtime Communist Party militant from Lota, was president of the Lota miners' union in 1940–41 when he was elected to the Lota City Council. Gallardo also served for several years as secretary-general of the CRMCA, the regional branch of the National Miners' Federation (FNM), before moving to Santiago. Commission member Dionisio Garrido Segura, a Democratic Party leader from Tomé, the town next to the Lirquén coal mines, just north of Concepción, represented the coal mining zone in Congress. While working with the Talcahuano maritime union, Garrido Segura joined forces with Juan Pradenas Muñoz in the Democratic Party.

done everything possible to facilitate its work, the commission lauded "his high level of understanding and interest in reaching a satisfactory resolution of the strike" and declared that "his even-tempered and magnanimous attitude" should "serve as an example."[76]

The day the strike ended, the Radicals of Concepción issued a statement condemning "strikes outside the law" in the coal mining zone, and particularly the current strike "affecting around 30,000 workers."[77] They neither distinguished between political and economic strikes nor acknowledged the legitimacy of the workers' grievances, as the National Executive Committee of the party had done. Although many of the original anti-Front Radicals in the coal mining region had eventually come to accept electoral pacts with Communists in both the Popular Front and the subsequent Democratic Alliance, they still remained well to the Right of the dominant forces in the national party. In this sense, Radicals of the coal region provided significant support for President Ríos Morales, who was also at odds with the CEN.

The Radicals of Concepción might also have ignored distinctions between economic and political strikes since, being closer to the conflict, they understood that solidarity with the Colico Sur miners was intertwined with other issues. The workers of the CCIL-owned railroad from Concepción to Curanilahue, for example, joined the strike in solidarity with the Colico Sur miners, but even after the other strikers returned to work, they stayed on strike, insisting that a fire stoker who had been laid off six months earlier be rehired.[78] When the railroad workers tried to convince the miners and metalworkers to rejoin the strike with them, they were told that their cause was different and were offered "only moral support." Not until January 15, three days after the miners' strike was resolved, did the railroad workers negotiate a settlement with the CCIL and return to work.[79]

76. El Sur, January 13, 1946, 17. See also El Sur, January 12, 1946, 1, and January 13, 1946, 13.

77. El Sur, January 12, 1946, 9. The president of the Concepción Radicals at the time was Humberto Enríquez Frödden, who soon headed González Videla's presidential campaign in the Concepción region and then served as his first education minister. For more on the Enríquez Frödden families, see chapter 10, note 13.

78. El Sur, January 11, 1946, 3.

79. El Sur, January 13, 1946, 14, and January 15, 1946, 7. Also in mid-January 1946, Duhalde authorized a fare increase for the CCIL's railroad, which provoked outrage since it was the principal means of transport for bringing consumer goods into the region. Campaigns quickly mounted to have the government expropriate the railroad and convert it into a public utility. See El Sur, January 26, 1946, 1; El Siglo, August 6, 1946, 4, and August 8, 1946, 6.

Economic demands also underlay the January coal miners' strike, though neither the press nor government officials paid heed to this fact. The Lota, Schwager, Plegarias, and Colico Sur miners' unions, as well as the metalworkers of Curanilahue and Schwager and the port workers of Schwager, were all in the midst of collective contract proceedings, which had passed to arbitration tribunals back in December. When the strike ended, the tribunals resumed their work, and the government arbiter spent several days visiting the mines. Settlement decisions were to be announced in the latter half of January.[80]

Following the strike in the coal mining zone, which ended between January 11 and 15, national attention shifted almost immediately to the nitrate mines of Humberstone and Mapocho in the northern province of Tarapacá, where an illegal strike began on January 17. As in the coal mining region, Communists dominated the nitrate miners' unions, both as leaders and as members. One of the immediate causes of this strike was an increase in the price of basic goods in the company store, in direct violation of a previous agreement.[81] The rapid rise in the cost of living was severely affecting workers nationwide; in towns where companies exercised de facto monopolies over the distribution of goods, the situation was worse.

On the very day the strike began, President Ríos Morales temporarily stepped down due to rapidly failing health. Interior Minister Alfredo Duhalde Vásquez, one of the most conservative members of the Radical Party, assumed the office of vice president and acting head of state.[82] Thus, on January 22, with an estimated eight thousand nitrate miners on strike, it was Duhalde who issued an emergency zone decree for the region and sent Army troops and Navy destroyers to the port of Iquique. The following day, in keeping with the policy announced during the coal miners' strike earlier in the month, Duhalde revoked the legal standing of these nitrate unions.[83] Expressions of solidarity flooded in from workers

80. El Sur, January 13, 1946, 11, January 16, 1946, 1, and January 18, 1946, 6, 7. CORFO Vice President Oscar Gajardo headed all the arbitration tribunals, except Colico Sur's. See also Oficio no. 1, January 2, 1946, and Oficio no. 187, January 5, 1946, both from DGT to the Interior Minister, FDGT, 1946 Oficios, vol. 1, ARNAD.

81. Pizarro, La huelga obrera, 125.

82. Anales de la República, 1:454. See also El Sur, January 18, 1946, 1. Even in late December, reliable reports indicated "that Ríos was quite ill and could not be expected to continue in office more than four months." Hoover Memo, December 29, 1945. Though the government denied rumors of the gravity of the president's condition, this proved to be the final phase of his illness; Ríos Morales died in June 1946 without ever again resuming office. See El Sur, January 10, 1946, 4, and January 11, 1946, 4.

83. El Sur, January 22, 1946, 3; letter from Bernardo Ibáñez CTCh Faction to "Compañero Presidente y Compañeros," [ca. 1947], 3, photocopied from personal files of Robert J. Alexan-

around the country, particularly from Communist workers such as the coal miners.

Workers and their representatives saw Duhalde's move against the nitrate unions as an attack on crucial rights won by labor in the preceding decades. On January 26, the National Directorate of the Confederation of Chilean Workers held an emergency meeting to decide how to respond.[84] In a historic move, the leadership voted unanimously in favor of a 24-hour national general strike to be held on January 30—the first such strike ever called by the CTCh.[85] To promote the strike, public rallies were "held simultaneously throughout Chile" on January 28, with the largest in Santiago, where an estimated seven to ten thousand people gathered in the Plaza Bulnes in front of the presidential palace.[86] While national labor and political leaders took to the stage to denounce the government's attack on unions, approximately two hundred fifty national police officers arrived, including a hundred on horseback, arrived on the scene. In a chilling reenactment of the events in Lota on October 7, 1942, the police "encircled [the] crowd," as "the speakers protested." In the midst of what Ambassador Bowers described as "an argument . . . between policemen and spectators," a gun went off, at which point the police opened fire on the crowd and continued firing for nearly five straight minutes, leaving six people dead and close to one hundred wounded, including a Communist national deputy.[87]

In his account of what would come to be called the "Plaza Bulnes massacre," Bowers reported that "when a Communist deputy and others protested [the arrival of the carabineros, the] deputy was beaten by police

der, Rutgers University; Restricted Telegram no. 89, from Bowers to Secretary of State, January 23, 1946, in USNA, RG 59.

84. At this time, the CTCh still had a single National Directorate, headed by Socialist Bernardo Ibáñez, with Communist Bernardo Araya as undersecretary. Yet, since its founding in 1936, the Communists in the CTCh had overtaken the Socialists in numbers of both union affiliates and National Directorate delegates. Thus, as Andrew Barnard observes, the Socialists "could not expect to control the office of secretary-general for very much longer." Barnard, "Chile," 73. See also Labor Attaché Report, 9/15–10/15, 1944, USNA, RG 59; Drake, Socialism and Populism, 279–80; Angell, Politics, 106–14; and Barría Serón, Trayectoria, 1, 5–6.

85. Pizarro, La huelga obrera, 128.

86. Urgent Telegram no. 107, from Bowers to Secretary of State, January 28, 1946, USNA, RG 59.

87. Report from J. Edgar Hoover, FBI Director, to State Department, January 30, 1946 (henceforth "Report from Hoover, January 30, 1946"); Urgent Telegram no. 107, January 28, 1946, and Restricted Telegram no. 110, January 29, 1946, both from Bowers to Secretary of State, all in USNA, RG 59; Pizarro, La huelga obrera, 127. Different sources give different casualty figures. Comparing figures given by El Mercurio and El Siglo, Crisóstomo Pizarro concluded that six people were killed and more than eighty wounded. For more details on the victims, see Millas, En tiempos, 462. Pablo Neruda also named the six dead in one of his numerous poems in their honor. Neruda, Canto general, 189–90.

and, as [the] crowd became more restless, [the] police started shooting." In the official police report, by contrast, it was the crowd that had provoked the violence, throwing stones and attacking the police with sticks. Indeed, the report contended, it was only after "shots from the crowd . . . gravely wounded a police lieutenant" that, "without an order being given to fire, the police in self-defense shot into the air and at the feet of the crowd." The report failed to explain how six people could be killed and nearly one hundred wounded by bullets fired into the air and at the feet of those assembled.[88] At least fourteen policemen were wounded, which many people took as evidence of violence from the crowd, though some accounts indicate that, with bullets flying in all directions, the police actually shot one another.[89]

While the police were clearing the plaza, Vice President Duhalde replaced the civilian interior minister with Navy Commander in Chief Vice Admiral Vicente Merino Bielich. Merino immediately issued Decree no. 620, placing the entire nation under a state of siege for sixty days due to the "extremist agitation prevailing in the country."[90] Under this decree, Army battalions went on alert, and even the municipality of Santiago came under the jurisdiction of a military commander. Not only leftists, but also many centrists, perceived the police shootings and the government's response, especially the declaration of a state of siege, as a turn against both labor and Chilean democracy. "The Communists, Socialists, 'Authentic' Socialists, and Falange Nacional Parties issued official protests during the night," Bowers reported, "condemning [the] government as responsible for [the] Bulnes incident and for the use of armed force in labor disputes."[91]

88. Different versions of the Plaza Bulnes shootings in the Chilean press are discussed in Restricted Telegram no. 110, from Bowers to Secretary of State, January 29, 1946, USNA, RG 59. All quotes in this paragraph are from this source. See also El Sur, January 29, 1946, 1.

89. The January 1946 police shootings in Santiago had many similarities with those in Lota in October 1942, at which time Duhalde Vásquez had been defense minister. Yet because these two incidents occurred at altogether different historical moments, only the January 1946 slayings assumed a prominent place in Chilean memory and history, becoming widely known as "the Plaza Bulnes massacre." Far from being memorialized, the Lota killings do not appear in any Chilean history of which I am aware.

90. This quote is from a statement by Vice Admiral Merino to the press, reprinted in El Sur, January 29, 1946, 1. See also El Sur, January 29, 1946, 3, and Restricted Telegram no. 110, from Bowers to Secretary State, January 29, 1946, USNA, RG 59. Other sources, such as the annual presidential address, indicate that the state of siege decree was for six months. Vice President Duhalde Vásquez, Message to Congress, Chamber of Deputies Session, May 21, 1946, BCNCh. See Duhalde Vásquez, Mensaje (1946), 7.

91. Restricted Telegram no. 110, from Bowers to Secretary of State, January 29, 1946, USNA, RG 59.

Just before the Plaza Bulnes shootings, the Radical Party had met to select its candidate for the 1946 presidential election, and a sharp contest had erupted between Duhalde and Gabriel González Videla, leader of the party's left wing. In repudiation of Duhalde's hard line, the party had nominated González Videla. As its candidate, he now called for the immediate resignation of Duhalde and all the Radicals in his cabinet.[92] Though neither Duhalde nor the Radical ministers heeded González Videla's call, two other cabinet members did step down—Minister of Public Works Eduardo Frei Montalva of the National Falange and Justice Minister Enrique Arriagada Saldías of the Authentic Socialist Party.[93] As explained by U.S. Federal Bureau of Investigation (FBI) Director J. Edgar Hoover, the resignation of these ministers showed "their solidarity with the workers in opposition to the government's actions."[94] When Vice President Duhalde reconstituted his cabinet, he replaced these Left-leaning civilian politicians with military figures: Vice Admiral Vicente Merino Bielich became interior minister, and Army General Manuel Tovarías Arroyo took over as minister of public works.[95]

The appointment of heads of the armed forces to cabinet posts, particularly that of interior minister, was an exception to the rule of government established in 1938. All administrations in the Popular Front era had presidents and interior ministers from the Radical Party, regardless of the composition of the rest of the cabinet. The only exceptions between 1938 and 1952 were in times of national crisis, when top military officers were given control of the Ministry of the Interior or other ministries, such as Defense, "in order to relieve the pressure that was threatening to explode."[96] As Brian Loveman and Elizabeth Lira explain, "The Armed

92. *El Sur*, January 30, 1946, 1.

93. The Authentic Socialist Party (PSA) was founded by Marmaduke Grove in July 1944. See chapter 6, note 98. When the PSA disbanded in 1946, Enrique Arriagada Saldías joined the Radical Party.

94. Report from J. Edgar Hoover, FBI Director to State Department, January 31, 1946 (henceforth "Report from Hoover, January 31, 1946"), USNA, RG 59. See also Pizarro, *La huelga obrera*, 128.

95. *El Sur*, January 29, 1946, 1. See also Barría Serón, *Trayectoria*, 3–4. Both Vice Admiral Merino and General Tovarías remained in the "Socialist-military cabinet" until September 1946, as discussed later in the chapter.

96. Loveman and Lira, *Las ardientes cenizas*, 122; see also Pizarro, *La huelga obrera*, 108. Though Aguirre Cerda did not appoint any military figures to cabinet posts, Ríos Morales named an Army general as defense minister and a Navy admiral as interior minister as early as June 1943. The post of interior minister went to a civilian again in October 1944. President González Videla also appointed military men to cabinet posts, as further discussed in chapter 9.

Forces and the National Police were considered, in moments of acute tension, as the only 'guarantee' of 'social peace.'"[97]

National Disarray in the Wake of the Killings

In the face of "the strong-arm attitude assumed by Vice President Alfredo Duhalde," CTCh leaders of all political persuasions called for a general strike to be held on January 30, the same day as the funeral for the Plaza Bulnes victims.[98] Taking the lead, coal miners, railroad workers, and Braden company copper miners halted work on January 29, joining the Tarapacá nitrate miners who had not returned to their jobs since the initial walkout that prompted the dissolution of their unions and subsequent national protests.[99] The government refused at this time to offer any conciliatory gestures that might have averted a general strike. Indeed, by 7 P.M. on the 29th, Ambassador Bowers reported that "several union leaders both Communist and Socialist are known to have been arrested in Santiago," and arrest warrants had been issued for other top CTCh figures, including its secretary-general, Socialist Bernardo Ibáñez.[100] At 6 A.M. on January 30, the official strike began and was joined by almost all labor groups in the country, with the exception of rural workers, who were inadequately organized and not affiliated with the Confederation of Chilean Workers.[101] In Santiago and other cities, even retail establishments closed their doors.[102]

On the morning of the national general strike, between thirty and forty thousand people in Santiago, primarily "from CTCh unions [and the] Communist and Socialist Parties," marched in a funeral procession for the Plaza Bulnes victims, from CTCh headquarters to the cemetery. The police maintained a low profile, and no violent incidents were reported.

97. Loveman and Lira, *Las ardientes cenizas*, 122.

98. Report from Hoover, January 31, 1946. See also *El Sur*, January 29, 1946, 4.

99. Restricted Telegram no. 110, January 29, 1946, and Telegram no. 114, January 30, 1946, both from Bowers to Secretary of State, USNA, RG 59; Pizarro, *La huelga obrera*, 128; *El Sur*, January 31, 1946, 5. The decision of certain labor groups to begin the strike on January 29 was not the official policy of the CTCh. As FBI Director Hoover reported, immediately after the shootings in Plaza Bulnes, "the crowd regathered . . . and more speeches were made after which a spontaneous parade was formed. It was decided that the general strike [should] begin on January 29 instead of January 30, as originally planned." Report from Hoover, January 30, 1946.

100. Telegram no. 112, from Bowers to Secretary of State, January 29, 1946, USNA, RG 59.

101. Pizarro, *La huelga obrera*, 128.

102. Restricted Telegram no. 114, from Bowers to Secretary of State, January 30, 1946, USNA, RG 59.

According to Ambassador Bowers, the speakers at the cemetery were "relatively reserved" in their criticism of "the Bulnes affair," emphasizing the need both for discipline and responsibility from workers and for cooperation between Socialists and Communists to defend democratic civilian government, which was seen to be under threat.[103] As U.S. FBI Director Hoover noted, "The fear has been expressed in Chilean political circles that Alfredo Duhalde, together with General Manuel Tovarias and Vice Admiral Vicente Merino, are planning a military government."[104] In the face of this possibility, leftist leaders tried to bury their differences and present a united front.

The speakers at the cemetery told the crowd that they had requested a meeting with Vice President Duhalde and that, depending on his responses to their demands, the general strike "would either be terminated [the following] morning or continued indefinitely."[105] Later that night, when CTCh leaders met with Duhalde, they presented a twelve-point memorandum. Its principal points called for an end to the state of siege; the return of all constitutional guarantees; the establishment of a leftist civilian government; the punishment of those responsible for the Plaza Bulnes violence; the indemnification of the victims' families; reestablishment of the legal standing of the Humberstone and Mapocho nitrate miners' unions; a reversal of the government's recent policy regarding illegal strikes; the repeal of emergency zone decrees; and the immediate withdrawal of troops from areas engaged in labor disputes, including the coal mining zone. The memo also insisted that Chile "terminate relations with the governments of Franco, in Spain, and [Perón-]Farrell, in Argentina, [and] cease all shipments of nitrate and coal to them."[106] This was a remarkable demand given the high state of domestic social and political tension. Returning to national matters, the memo further insisted that the government rescind the 1939 Ministry of Labor circular that instructed its personnel not to oversee any union activities in the countryside, thereby making it impossible for rural workers to organize in compliance with the Labor Code. And, finally, it called on the government "to eliminate evictions from homes, price increases, and speculation."[107]

103. Restricted Telegram no. 117, from Bowers to Secretary of State, January 30, 1946, USNA, RG 59.

104. Report from Hoover, January 31, 1946.

105. Restricted Telegram no. 117, from Bowers to Secretary of State, January 30, 1946, USNA, RG 59.

106. Text of the CTCh January 30, 1946, memorandum, as reprinted in *El Siglo*, January 31, 1946, 4.

107. Restricted Telegram no. 117, from Bowers to Secretary of State, January 30, 1946, USNA, RG 59.

Several of the CTCh's demands would have been impossible for Duhalde to meet, at least in the short term. The vice president tried to deescalate the situation by promising first to lift the state of siege if the strikes were ended and production returned to normal and then to work on meeting the memo's other demands as quickly as possible. Duhalde's promise allowed the CTCh leaders to publicly claim victory for their striking supporters while privately returning to negotiations with the government from a position of greater strength. They therefore called an end to the strike after twenty-four hours; on January 31, when workers throughout the country began returning to their jobs, Duhalde lifted the state of siege.[108] The only workers remaining on strike were the northern nitrate miners, who refused to return to their jobs until the government reestablished the legal standing of their unions.[109]

Over the next several days, negotiations and maneuvers among political leaders in Santiago proceeded at a frenetic pace, as the Socialists, under Bernardo Ibáñez, considered whether to accept Duhalde's invitation to join the government or to maintain solidarity with the Communists and insist on Duhalde's compliance with the CTCh's demands. At a meeting of the CTCh's National Directorate, Communist and Socialist leaders agreed to call for a renewal of the general strike, to begin on February 2 and to become total by February 4.[110] By February 2, however, the Socialists had decided to accept positions in Duhalde's new cabinet, and they now condemned the strike, claiming that the government was showing good-faith efforts to meet the CTCh's demands. The next day, Socialists were sworn in to five important ministerial posts, joining the previously appointed military officers, to form what became known as the "Socialist-military cabinet," deplored by both Communists and left-wing Radicals.[111] That night, in a radio address, Bernardo Ibáñez called on

108. Urgent Telegram no. 120, from Bowers to Secretary of State, January 31, 1946, USNA, RG 59; and *El Sur*, February 1, 1946, 1. In his annual address to Congress in May 1946, Duhalde explained that he had lifted the state of siege by Decree no. 626, of January 31, 1946, "considering that other measures adopted would be sufficient to maintain order and tranquility in the country." Duhalde Vásquez, *Mensaje* (1946), 7.

109. Urgent Telegram no. 120, from Bowers to Secretary of State, January 31, 1946, USNA, RG 59.

110. Pizarro, *La huelga obrera*, 133. The call for a staggered strike may have been related to the workweek since February 2 was a Saturday, and not all sectors of the national workforce would be scheduled to work until Monday. See also *El Sur*, February 2, 1946, 1; and Barnard, "Chile," 76.

111. *El Sur*, February 3, 1946, 5. According to the *Anales de la República*, 1:455, Minister of Lands and Colonization Fidel Estay Cortés, of the Democratic Party, was not replaced at this time. Also, the new justice minister was a Radical, not a Socialist. Duhalde described the negotiations leading to the formation of this "Socialist-military cabinet" in his annual address to Congress. Duhalde Vásquez, *Mensaje* (1946), xxx–xxxi.

workers to ignore the strike order, claiming that it was a Communist move to sabotage the democratic government.[112]

Communists saw the Socialists' alliance with Duhalde and their opposition to the second general strike as betrayals, which ushered in what historian Andrew Barnard has described as "a bitter, bloody, and protracted civil war in the union movement that lasted for much of 1946."[113] On the night of February 4, Communist CTCh leader Bernardo Araya Zuleta publicly accused Bernardo Ibáñez of "irresponsibility and demagogy, [for] first supporting [the] general strike and then opposing it when [the] Socialist Party entered [the] government."[114] Araya further denounced Ibáñez for "helping [to] establish military dictatorship in Chile."[115] By February 5, the CTCh formally split into a Communist faction led by Araya and a Socialist faction led by Ibáñez. Despite the larger size of the Communist CTCh, the government, not surprisingly, granted legal recognition only to the Socialist faction.[116]

In this polarized context, local unions decided whether to support the second general strike based on "political sympathies and pressures."[117] Estimates of the total number of striking workers vary widely. Bernardo Ibáñez claimed that only sixty thousand workers participated, whereas Ambassador Bowers gave an estimate of eighty to one hundred thousand, noting that about 60 percent of them were in the coal, copper, and nitrate industries.[118] Indeed, the workers of the coal mining zone were among the first in the country to join the strike. Cosmito miners walked off the job on February 2, and were joined by almost all unions in the region over the next two days.[119] By February 5, Ambassador Bowers warned, "If [this]

112. Restricted Telegram no. 139, from Bowers to Secretary of State, February 4, 1946, USNA, RG 59.

113. Barnard, "Chile," 76; see also Barnard, "Chilean Communists," 358–49.

114. Telegram no. 133, from Bowers to Secretary of State, February 2, 1946, USNA, RG 59. Bowers confirmed the "possibility that Socialists will not support strike although final attitude will be conditioned by whether they reach satisfactory agreement in meantime enabling them to enter government."

115. Restricted Telegram no. 143, from Bowers to Secretary of State, February 5, 1946, USNA, RG 59.

116. Urgent Telegram no. 142, February 5, 1946, and Telegram no. 149, February 6, 1946, both from Bowers to Secretary of State, USNA, RG 59. Bernardo Ibáñez provided a detailed discussion of this period in Memoria de la Confederación, 16–30.

117. Barnard, "Chile," 72; and Restricted Telegram no. 139, from Bowers to Secretary of State, February 4, 1946, USNA, RG 59.

118. More precisely, Bernardo Ibáñez stated that 60,000 workers joined "the revolutionary strike of the Communists" on February 4, but that "over the next four days, fewer and fewer [workers participated]." Ibáñez, Memoria de la Confederación, 24.

119. Oficio no. 491, February 12, 1946, FIC, vol. 2328, ANCh; and El Sur, February 3, 1946, 10.

strike lasts several more days, [a] shortage of coal may affect railroad and public utility operations."[120]

Socialists in the coal mining communities, though a clear minority, tried to defy the strike by "mobilizing their affiliates to go to work."[121] According to Bernardo Ibáñez, the total stoppage of work in the coal mining zone was achieved only by the Communists' "applying their old policy of terror." Ibáñez claimed that a Communist "band of terrorists" had murdered a Socialist worker at a cement factory north of Santiago and that Communists had attacked seven Socialist workers in Lota with knives when they tried to return to their jobs.[122] In retaliation, as Andrew Barnard notes, Socialists used their new power in government ministries "to harass the PCCh," securing the arrest of Communist activists throughout the country.[123]

Government moves to break the general strike included the militarization of the coal mining zone and the arrest of over fifty leaders and workers, who were charged with violating internal state security laws.[124] Although Communist national deputies traveled to the region to meet with the emergency zone chief, Rear Admiral Immanuel Holger Torres, they were unable to secure the release of the detainees.[125] To diminish the bargaining power of the striking workers, the government also moved to procure emergency supplies of imported coal. As Andrew Barnard explains, Duhalde took "the classic first step of all Radical presidents when expecting or planning a confrontation with the Communists—he asked the U.S. State Department to arrange for the shipment of coal to Chile,"

120. Letter from Bernardo Ibáñez CTCh Faction to "Compañero Presidente y Compañeros," [ca. 1947], 7, photocopied from personal files of Robert J. Alexander, Rutgers University; and Restricted Telegram no. 143, from Bowers to Secretary of State, February 5, 1946, USNA, RG 59.

121. El Sur, February 4, 1946, 7, 4. The article referred specifically to "the opposition of the Socialists" in Lirquén and Cosmito.

122. Ibáñez, Memoria de la Confederación, 24.

123. Barnard, "Chilean Communists," 359.

124. El Sur, February 5, 1946, 5, February 8, 1946, 7, and February 13, 1946, 9. One of the lawyers defending those arrested was Raúl Puga Monsalves, a Democratic Party leader who was born in Arauco and lived most of life in Concepción, maintaining close ties with the coal mining communities. Puga Monsalves served in Aguirre Cerda's government both as justice minister and as agriculture minister.

125. El Sur, February 10, 1946, 11. Around this time, Vice Admiral Alfredo Hoffman Hansen replaced Holger Torres as chief of the Concepción-Arauco emergency zone by Duhalde's Supreme Decree no. 220, of February 7. See Decrees no. 16, February 10, 1946, no. 17, February 11, 1946, no. 18, February 14, 1946, and no. 20, February 25, 1946, all issued by Alfredo Hoffman Hansen, and all in FIC, vol. 2332 (Oficios Recibidos de Otros Funcionarios), ANCh. See also El Sur, February 11, 1946, 7, February 13, 1946, 9, and February 22, 1946, 11.

a request that U.S. officials granted quickly and willingly.[126] On February 6, Ambassador Bowers reported that support for the general strike was decreasing in some industries around the country, but not in the coal, copper, and nitrate mining regions, which were still almost totally shut down.[127] By the next day, at least one shipment of U.S. coal was en route to Chile.

On February 7, after long days and nights of difficult talks between CTCh leaders and the interior minister, the government finally issued a response to the twelve-point memo of January 30. In a show of contempt, it sent its response only to Socialist Bernardo Ibáñez, refusing to recognize the majority faction of the CTCh, headed by Communist Bernardo Araya. Despite this affront, the Communist CTCh decided to end the strike, publicly declaring that the government had satisfactorily complied with many of the confederation's demands.[128] In fact, however, the government's reply to the CTCh memo was mostly negative. It stated that the "Socialist-military cabinet" would not be changed, that the government was "obligated to use [the] military to maintain order and to apply emergency law[s] where necessary," and that "breaking relations with Spain and Argentina would be unwarranted internal interference with those countries." On almost all other points as well, the government found reason to refuse the CTCh demands. Thus, as Ambassador Bowers noted, the Communists' decision to call off the strike was motivated, not by the government's assent to their demands, but rather "by [the] increasing difficulty in keeping workers on strike," especially after the government announced that a "coal shortage would be avoided by imported coal."[129]

Even though production in most industries in the country had returned to normal levels by February 9, the coal miners refused to call off their strike. Ambassador Bowers reported with some alarm that coal mining was the "most important industry still shut down, with workers demanding [the] release and reinstatement [of] approximately 50 coal strike leaders arrested during [the] past week."[130] That day, company representatives met with departing Emergency Zone Chief Holger Torres to discuss

126. Barnard, "Chile," 77–78. See also El Sur, February 8, 1946, 4.

127. Restricted Telegram no. 149, from Bowers to Secretary of State, February 6, 1946, USNA, RG 59.

128. Urgent Restricted Telegram no. 158, from Bowers to Secretary of State, February 8, 1946, USNA, RG 59. See also El Sur, February 8, 1946, 1.

129. Urgent Restricted Telegram no. 158, from Bowers to Secretary of State, February 8, 1946, USNA, RG 59.

130. Restricted Telegram no. 164, from Bowers to Secretary of State, February 9, 1946, USNA, RG 59. See also El Sur, February 8, 1946, 7, and El Sur, February 9, 1946, 7.

the terms they were willing to offer to end the strike.[131] A few days later, in a statement delivered from the deck of a Navy warship docked in the Lota harbor, the newly appointed emergency zone chief, Alfredo Hoffman Hansen, called on the strikers to return immediately to their jobs.[132] Unmoved, the miners "repeated their intention to continue the strike indefinitely, as long as they do not receive contrary orders from the top leadership of the CTCh," referring to the Communist faction.[133] As late as February 12, *El Sur* reported that "the coal mining zone—which consists of Lota, Coronel, Schwager, Curanilahue, Lirquén, and Cosmito—remains totally on strike," but it added that the region was completely calm except for a few small street clashes and the arrests of people allegedly preventing others from returning to work.[134] After leading government officials traveled to the region to secure guarantees against company reprisals, on February 13, the coal miners returned to work.[135]

The coal miners had continued their regional strike after the national strike ended on February 9, in part to influence the outcome of their contract disputes, which had been in arbitration proceedings since December. Just days after the miners returned to work on February 13, the arbitration tribunals issued settlement decisions for all the labor disputes in the region.[136] These settlements were to go into effect on February 20, but by February 28, the coal mining companies had still not begun to comply. The unions responded with a memorandum to the government, outlining three central demands: first, the government must require company compliance with the arbitration decisions; second, the Ministry of Labor must rescind a recent order freezing union funds; and, third, action must be taken against companies that illegally retaliated against participants in the general strike.[137] When the government did not respond to their memo, the Lota and Schwager unions held strike votes on March 3,

131. *El Sur*, February 10, 1946, 11.

132. *El Sur*, February 12, 1946, 1.

133. Ibid., 5.

134. Ibid. According to the company's Board of Directors, the Pipilco coal miners were the only coal miners in the region who did not strike a single day in January or February 1946. Acts of Board of Directors, Thirty-ninth Session, February 15, 1946, 105; and Fortieth Session, March 8, 1946, 8, Compañía Carbonífera Pilpilco, Coal company records, consulted at ENACAR, Lota Alto.

135. Restricted Telegram no. 185, from Bowers to Secretary of State, February 14, 1946, USNA, RG 59; *El Sur*, February 13, 1946, 4; and February 14, 1946, 7.

136. The Lirquén settlement decision was announced first. Decisions for the other companies followed a few days later. *El Sur*, February 16, 1946, 7, and February 22, 1946, 7.

137. Telegram no. 257, from Bowers to Secretary of State, March 4, 1946, USNA, RG 59. Cosmito was the only coal mining company charged with discriminating against strike participants.

and on the morning of March 6, the workers of the largest coal mining companies in Chile walked off the job, for the fourth time in two months.

Rear Admiral Immanuel Holger Torres again assumed command of the Concepción-Arauco emergency zone. Justifying this renewed military intervention, Interior Minister Vicente Merino declared that the "Communist Party is determined to produce a revolutionary strike destined to upset our institutions and that [the] Government would take all constitutional and legal measures to guarantee [the freedom to] work."[138] The strike ended on March 8, at least in part because the government threatened to apply the "Labor Code provisions relating to illegal strikes." This was taken to mean that the legal standing of the miners' unions would be revoked, as had happened to the Humberstone and Mapocho nitrate unions.[139]

Nearly two and a half years had passed since the Socialist Party, taking a more aggressive stand for workers' rights and social reform, had withdrawn its ministers from Ríos Morales's cabinet and some six months since Young Turk Bernardo Ibáñez proclaimed his party's total independence from the government. Now, still under Ibáñez's leadership, the Socialists rejoined the government, allying themselves not only with the right wing of the Radical Party, but also with all those supporting the government's use of the military to keep labor in check. In a 1946 CTCh annual report, Ibáñez referred to the national turmoil in February, claiming that "the Government of Sr. Duhalde acted in those moments with exemplary prudence. The recently formed Cabinet demonstrated not only competence and judgment but also a great sense of responsibility."[140] The decision of the Ibáñez Socialists to join the Duhalde regime signaled their willingness to renounce the more radical aspects of their agenda. As U.S. Labor Attaché Horowitz explained, "While the government has continued with a Socialist-Military Cabinet, it has become more evident during recent weeks that the Socialists will be permitted to accomplish very little with respect to the development of government policies for social reform or action in remedying immediate problems."[141]

138. Restricted Telegram no. 274, from Bowers to Secretary of State, March 8, 1946. USNA, RG 59.

139. Restricted Telegram no. 270, from Bowers to Secretary of State, March 7, 1946, USNA, RG 59. Between March 3 and 5, the Lota longshoremen were also on strike, refusing to load the Chilean cruiser *Chacabuco*, but this does not seem to have been principally related to the miners' labor disputes. The longshoremen were fighting for a "100% increase in [the] ordinary loading rate because of special loading conditions." Telegram no. 257, March 4, 1946, Telegram no. 260, March 5, 1946, and Restricted Telegram no. 265, March 6, 1946, all from Bowers to Secretary of State, USNA, RG 59.

140. Ibáñez, *Memoria de la Confederación*, 24.

141. Labor Attaché Report, 2/15–3/15/46, 1, USNA, RG 59.

What the Socialists gained from this move, at least in the short term, was a new position from which to compete with their erstwhile Popular Front allies, the Communists, for working-class support. With their entry into the cabinet, Horowitz noted, the Socialists were "permitted free rein with respect to their anti-Communist policy in the labor unions."[142] Though the reentry of the Socialists into the government would prove fleeting, the intense internal dissent it generated would contribute to "one of the most lasting splits in the party, [that] between the Socialist Party of Chile and the Popular Socialist Party."[143]

The growing anti-Communist sentiment among governing Radicals and Socialists in Chile was also fueled by developments on the international scene. Tensions among the Allied powers had surfaced as early as May 1945, when U.S. President Harry Truman abruptly cut off all aid to the Soviet Union. In July and August of that year, at the final wartime meeting in Potsdam, conflict over the political fate of Eastern Europe surged to the fore. Then, in his famous Fulton, Missouri, speech of March 1946, British Prime Minister Winston Churchill proclaimed that "an Iron Curtain" had "descended across the [European] continent." The international divisions that would come to constitute the Cold War were thus rapidly forming, when, in June 1946, Chilean President Ríos Morales died in office, the second consecutive Radical president to do so.

For another Radical Party candidate to win the presidency, a strong Center-Left coalition was needed. But how could such an alliance be assembled when "civil war [raged] in the union movement" and anti-Communism was gaining momentum?[144] This was the burning question in many minds as the presidential campaign got under way in the Chilean winter of 1946, not only in the backrooms of Santiago party headquarters, but also in union halls and mines, on soccer fields and in taverns throughout the coal mining region and around the country. The results of this presidential election would usher in one of the most eventful periods in Chilean history, when workers' hopes would be raised and then brutally dashed, as we shall see in the next three chapters.

142. Ibid.
143. Angell, Politics, 99–100. The Popular Socialist Party (Partido Socialista Popular; PSP) split off from the Socialist Party (SP) over the 1948 Law for the Permanent Defense of Democracy (LDPD), as further discussed in chapter 10.
144. Barnard, "Chile," 76, and "Chilean Communists," 358–49.

PART III

RUPTURE AND BETRAYAL

"THE PEOPLE CALL YOU GABRIEL":
COMMUNIST-BACKED GONZÁLEZ VIDELA REACHES
THE PRESIDENTIAL PALACE

As the world polarized into pro- and anti-Soviet camps after World War II, left-wing Radical Gabriel González Videla won his party's nomination for president in late January 1946. The man he defeated in late January 1946, acting head of state Vice President Alfredo Duhalde Vásquez, represented the Radical Party's anti-Communist right wing.[1] González Videla, on the other hand, had been one of the most ardent proponents of the original Center-Left coalition in the mid-1930s, and the Communists considered him a strong ally. They had even tried to convince him to break party discipline to run against Ríos Morales back in 1942. Pulling out all stops for González Videla's election, the Chilean Communist Party (PCCh) placed one of its most illustrious and persuasive national leaders, poet Senator Pablo Neruda, at the head of his campaign. For a major rally in Santiago, Neruda wrote a poem entitled "El pueblo lo llama Gabriel" (The People Call You Gabriel), which was quickly taken up as a campaign slogan. Describing González Videla as "a loyal brother," the poem conveyed a sense of intimacy and affection between Chile's working-class people

1. For the 1946 convention proceedings, see Partido Radical, *Declaración de principios.* See also Barnard, "Chile," 78–79. Even after the convention, discontented right-wing Radicals tried to put forward the candidacy of Arturo Olavarría Bravo, but they were defeated in an internal party plebiscite on April 28. See González Videla, *Memorias,* 1:461–62.

and the new Center-Left standard-bearer. González Videla, the Communists proclaimed, would finally push through the reforms promised in the Popular Front decade.[2]

During the presidential campaign of June 1938, Pedro Aguirre Cerda had struggled to rouse small crowds in Lota and other working-class towns throughout the country, much to the disappointment of his campaign manager, Gabriel González Videla. Now, in August 1946, candidate González Videla arrived in Lota Bajo to a tumultuous "holiday" welcome by nearly thirty thousand men, women, and children.[3] Musical bands marched down the streets, "the Communist youth paraded in spectacular uniforms," and cheering supporters waved flags and banners.[4] People from different communities, religions, occupations, and political persuasions had come together with "the mine workers, who went straight from their work sites wearing their work clothes and tools, which made a deep impression on the candidate."[5]

As González Videla made his way to the stage in the main plaza of Lota Bajo to stand alongside local and national Communist leaders, the crowd shouted, "Long live the Communist Party!" Thousands of fists pumped the air in gestures of triumph as this Radical Party leader received a hearty fraternal hug from Carlos Contreras Labarca, secretary-general of the PCCh.[6] Contreras Labarca spoke first, denouncing the acting head of state, Duhalde Vásquez, as an "'oligarchic *latifundista*' who was trying his best to bring the workers' movement to disaster." Contreras Labarca also condemned the Socialist-military cabinet in place since February, and particularly the "ferocious offensive against the unions conducted by the 'Socialist' ministers," with serious "repercussions for the workers' gains."[7]

2. After González Videla turned against the Communists in 1947–48, Neruda tried to downplay his support for him as a candidate. He claimed that he wrote the poem "El pueblo lo llama Gabriel" only at the insistence of his PCCh colleagues and that he had refused to recite or publish it. The poem appeared in the press and later in González Videla, *Memorias*, 1:759. See "Interview with Neruda," *El Siglo*, August 3, 1963, reprinted in Neruda, *Obras completas*, 4:1260–61; see also Olivares, *Pablo Neruda*, 478–82.

3. *El Siglo*, August 13, 1946, 2, and August 12, 1946, 3. *El Siglo*'s estimate of 38,000 people is likely exaggerated, even if many came from surrounding areas, since Lota's total population in 1946 was around 36,000. For photos of the rallies in Lota and Curanilahue, see *El Siglo*, August 13, 1946, 1.

4. *El Siglo*, August 11, 1946, 1.

5. *El Siglo*, August 12, 1946, 3.

6. When the PCCh had tried to convince González Videla to run for president against Ríos Morales in 1942, Contreras Labarca had repeatedly referred to him as "my dear and esteemed friend," as, for example, in a speech he gave in Lota. Unnumbered Providencia Confidencial, April 19, 1942, FMI, vol. 10787, ARNAD.

7. *El Siglo*, August 12, 1946, 3.

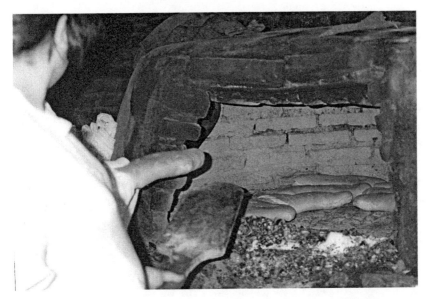

Fig. 8 Miner's bread in a collective oven in Lota Alto, 1997. Photo by Jody Pavilack.

It was from rallies such as this one that González Videla came to be "regarded as 'the Communist candidate.'"[8]

The meeting between González Videla and his supporters in Lota was deeply emotional. Manuel Cifuentes, who attended the rally as a boy of fifteen, later recalled, "With tears in his eyes, [González Videla] cried out—that, under his government, there would no longer be so much suffering—old women, women made old from all they had lived through, they gave him flowers, and a loaf of miner's bread for him to eat—he served himself, and then he said that this loaf was 'very small' and that he was 'going to eat a large loaf.'"[9] With these words, and by eating miner's bread baked in communal ovens (fig. 8), Radical candidate González Videla proclaimed his commitment to improving the daily lives of the coal miners, the most solid and visible bloc of working-class Communist supporters in the country.

González Videla ran against Conservative Eduardo Cruz Coke, Liberal Fernando Alessandri Rodríguez (son of Arturo Alessandri Palma), and Socialist Bernardo Ibáñez Aguila. After more than a decade of urging leftward shifts in national policy, González Videla now promised to fulfill

8. Bethell and Roxborough, *Latin America*, 11.
9. Interview with Pastor Manuel Cifuentes.

many aspirations of Chile's popular sectors. Thus, while maintaining his predecessors' focus on industrial development, he promised to nationalize certain public utilities, to enact moderate agrarian reform, and even to rescind the 1939 ministerial order under which the Aguirre Cerda government had "suspended" the formation of rural unions by ordering labor officials not to participate.[10] He also promised to secure full suffrage rights for women. "It was, in sum, a program designed to advance political democracy and improve conditions for working people," Andrew Barnard explains. "It was also a program intended to finally realize those expectations for change and improvement that had been promoted by the crusade against world fascism but that had not been fulfilled since the end of the war."[11]

The timing of González Videla's ascent, however, complicated his agenda. Now, a year after the end of World War II, the capitalist West, led by the United States, and international Communism, led by the Soviet Union, were drawing new battle lines. In the mounting conflict that would become the Cold War, any national reform program with Communist involvement was likely to come under U.S. suspicion, which could lead to a range of responses, from warnings to credit freezes, to direct intervention. From the outset of his campaign, González Videla thus walked a tightrope: how to clearly commit to making the reforms he, and so many others before him, had promised his working-class supporters, without antagonizing the United States and its allies over policies that could be labeled "communistic."

When the elections were held on September 4, 1946, González Videla received more votes than any other candidate, but his 40 percent plurality was not an absolute mandate.[12] In the coal communities, by contrast, he won a landslide victory, nearly doubling his national average. In Curanilahue, he received 67 percent of the vote, in Coronel more than 75 percent, and in Lota almost 80 percent. His worst showing in the coal mining region was about 50 percent in Lebu and Los Alamos.[13] These figures contrasted sharply with the regional vote given to Popular Front candidate Pedro Aguirre Cerda back in 1938, which was barely at the national average in Lota and Coronel and well below it in Curanilahue and Lebu. A

10. Loveman, Struggle, 123.

11. Barnard, "Chile," 79.

12. Not only did Center-Left standard-bearer González Videla fail to win an absolute majority of votes cast, but the proportion of those voting had dropped significantly, "from 88% of the registered voters in 1938 . . . to 76% in 1946." Drake, Socialism and Populism, 281.

13. Dirección del Registro Electoral, presidential election results, 1946, SERCh.

notable shift to the Left had clearly occurred among the region's voters in the intervening years.

González Videla's Socialist opponent, Bernardo Ibáñez, who had allied his party with Duhalde Vásquez's Right-leaning government and moved aggressively against the Communists when the Confederation of Chilean Workers split in two, received only 2.5 percent of the national vote. The coal communities rejected Ibáñez even more strongly, giving him only thirty-three votes in Lota (0.9 percent), seventeen in Coronel (0.6 percent), two in Lebu, and none in Los Alamos. The only coal town in which Ibáñez fared better than his national average was Curanilahue, where he received forty-one votes (3.1 percent).[14]

Communists Enter the Government on the Eve of the Cold War

That an open ally of the Communists and labor came out ahead in an election six months after Churchill's famous Iron Curtain speech was an extraordinary feat, especially given the strength of anti-Communist and anti-labor forces within Chile. Yet, according to the Constitution, because he had received only a plurality of the vote, González Videla's election as president would have to be confirmed by a joint session of Congress—for the first time in Chilean history. Conservatives quickly moved to block his confirmation by calling on the military to, at the very least, rattle their sabers. That they could not find any officers willing to intervene in the political conflict testified to the preponderance of Constitutionalists in the armed forces at the time.[15]

As the vote in Chile's multiparty Congress neared, González Videla had not only to secure the votes of the Socialists, but also to convince the right-wing Liberal Party to back his bid for office, while retaining the support of the Communists and Radicals. All sides drove hard bargains, and, in the words of historians Simon Collier and William Sater, González Videla "promised all things to all men."[16] The Liberals were especially concerned about González Videla's promise to the Left to rescind the 1939 ministerial order that prevented the formation of rural unions. In return for the Liberals' support, their former archenemy not only offered them cabinet posts, but also agreed to support new restrictive legislation on

14. Ibid.
15. Lafertte, *Vida de un comunista*, 334–35; Barnard, "Chile," 80.
16. Collier and Sater, *History of Chile*, 247.

rural organizing.[17] Finally, on October 24, González Videla won sufficient votes in the Chilean Congress to ascend to the presidency. Showing that his reputation as a skilled politician was well deserved, he received 138 votes to Eduardo Cruz Coke's 46.[18]

The first cabinet organized by the president-elect was a highly unusual political mix, with six Radicals, three Liberals, and three Communists.[19] According to some sources, González Videla also invited the Conservatives to join, but they declined.[20] With the exception of Cuba, where Fulgencio Batista had named two Communists as ministers without portfolio in 1942, this was the first time in the Americas that Communists occupied cabinet posts.[21] González Videla's decision to govern with Communists after the collapse of the U.S.–Soviet alliance was quite bold, especially since the United States was stepping up its pressure on governments around the world to adopt anti-Communist positions.

One of the Communists González Videla personally invited to join his cabinet was the party's secretary-general, Carlos Contreras Labarca, who had accompanied the Radical candidate on his campaign tour, standing

17. In November 1946, González Videla did indeed rescind the 1939 ministerial order, and a "massive wave" of unionization swept the countryside. Drawing on promised support from the president, however, Liberals secured "legal repression of the [rural workers'] right to organize," which [they] had theoretically enjoyed since promulgation of the 1931 Labor Code," with the passage of Law no. 8811 in July 1947. Loveman, *Struggle*, 124; see also Loveman, *Chile*, 215.

18. Reyes Alvarez, "El presidente," 86. Reyes describes González Videla as having a "wheeler-dealer mentality characteristic of parliamentarianism" and favorably compares his negotiating skills with those of the legendary Arturo Alessandri Palma. In a more cynical comparison, Patricio Manns places both González Videla and Alessandri "in the category of chameleon politicians," noting that they were "consummate demagogues" who relied on working-class votes to get elected and, once in power, unleashed state violence against urban and rural workers. Manns, *Chile*, 160–61.

The election of Salvador Allende in 1970 closely resembles that of González Videla in several ways. Having won by an even smaller plurality (36.2 percent), Allende also had to have his claim to the presidency confirmed by Congress. To secure the support he needed, Allende also had to compromise with his political opponents. And, like González Videla's, Allende's enemies, which included the U.S. government in addition to the Chilean right wing, also tried and failed to find military officers willing to prevent him from becoming president.

19. Liberals headed the Ministries of Defense, Justice, and Health, while the Communists—Miguel Concha Quezada, Víctor Contreras Tapia, and Carlos Contreras Labarca—headed the Ministries of Agriculture, Lands and Colonization, and Public Works.

20. See, for example, letter from Bowers to Braden, November 18, 1946, 1–2, USNA, RG 59.

21. On Batista's appointment of two Communists to his cabinet, see Thomas, chap. 62, "Batista the Democratic President," in *Cuba*, 724–36, which draws heavily from Thomas's interview with one of the Communist ministers, Dr. Carlos Rafael Rodríguez. See also Robert J. Alexander's interview with the other Communist minister, Juan Marinello, Havana, August 13, 1947, RJAIC.

side by side with him in front of tens of thousands of coal miners and their neighbors. Contreras Labarca had led the Chilean Communist Party (PCCh) throughout the war years, as the party pursued increasingly collaborationist policies, eventually falling in line with the policies of U.S. Communist leader Earl Browder. At the end of the war, with the PCCh trying to distance itself from what was now known as the "Browderist deviation," Contreras Labarca came under heavy internal criticism. Unlike the Socialists and Radicals, however, the Communists were determined to avoid public discord, let alone schism. Contreras Labarca's appointment as minister of public works was a welcome solution since he then stepped down as party chief.[22] In naming Ricardo Fonseca Aguayo as his successor, the PCCh Central Committee signaled its intent to push forward a program of change: the new secretary-general was seen to be "a more combative leader more closely associated with the worker majority of the party."[23]

When González Videla and his politically mixed cabinet took office on November 3, anti-Communist sentiment was on the rise among U.S. policy makers. Ambassador Claude Bowers proved to be a strong supporter of González Videla; in frequent reports to his bosses in Washington, he minimized and justified the role of Communists in the Chilean government, trying to buy time for the new president. The newly appointed assistant secretary of state for Latin American affairs, Spruille Braden, was the son of an engineer who had founded the Braden Copper Company and other major mining operations in Chile. Braden had served as ambassador to several Latin American republics, most recently Argentina, where he became embroiled in the 1946 presidential campaign, allying himself with both Argentina's extreme Right and the Communists against Juan Perón. Just before the February election there, the U.S. State Department released a blue book, authored by Braden, which attacked Perón as a Nazi supporter. Perón responded with the anti-imperialist slogan "Perón or Braden?" At the polls, Argentines reacted angrily to Braden's interference in their domestic affairs, voting Perón into office by a

22. Contreras Labarca's downfall within the PCCh's leadership occurred between June and December 1945. At the party's Thirteenth Congress in December, the former secretary-general was asked to make a public mea culpa, which he eventually did. For a full analysis of the conflict over the Browderist line, see Barnard, "Chilean Communist Party," 321–26.

23. Drake, Socialism and Populism, 280n30. In his memoirs, González Videla contrasts the two Communist Party leaders, claiming that Contreras Labarca was frank and easy to work with, whereas Fonseca was "furtive, obstinate, and rash." He recalls that "from the beginning" he knew the change in Communist leadership "was going to bring [him] difficulties." González Videla, Memorias, 1:525. Though Contreras Labarca fell out of favor with the party, Fonseca came to occupy a prominent place its history. See PCCh, Ricardo Fonseca.

large margin. Communists were disgraced by their ill-fated alliance with the U.S. ambassador and right-wing forces, and they began to change their stance toward Perón.

Thus, when Ambassador Bowers wrote to Spruille Braden in November 1946, just weeks after González Videla took office, he warned against overt intervention in Chilean domestic politics, recalling that such policies had backfired disastrously in Argentina. Convinced as he was that the new president would disassociate himself from the Communists at the earliest opportune moment, Bowers advised Braden to wait and see. Communist support had been crucial to González Videla's gaining the presidency, Bowers explained, and the new head of state had therefore felt obligated to offer them positions in his cabinet. He could not "force them out immediately after taking office since that would make too easy the charge that they had been tricked." Bowers added that, although it was "shortsighted of the Conservatives" to refuse to join the cabinet, González Videla's inclusion of three Liberals among his ministers would help him achieve a "moderate but progressive" government.[24] Thus, despite the anti-Communist agenda of U.S. foreign policy, Bowers thought "it would be unwise to 'force' the president at [this] juncture . . . to break with the Communists—which would create a difficult situation at the outset of his administration."[25]

Notwithstanding Bowers's belief that González Videla intended a "moderate" regime, two months into his term, the president made a significant gesture to the Left. He replaced his Radical labor minister with Juan Pradenas Muñoz, leader of the Democratic Party's left wing, who was highly esteemed by workers around the country, especially in his home region of Concepción, where the coal mines were located. Soon after, in early February 1947, González Videla met with Carlos Fonseca and other national Communist leaders, who "informed the President that the Communist Party had dedicated itself to cooperate with the Government." In this spirit, they offered a plan of industrial production based on tripartite committees and included a pledge "to make use of the strike solely as an exceptional last measure of defense."[26] At a press conference following the meeting, Fonseca reiterated the party's "no strike pledge" aimed at supporting the new government, but he insisted that "this did

24. Letter from Bowers to Braden, November 18, 1946, USNA, RG 59.
25. Memo of Bowers and Braden telephone conversation, from Ellis O. Briggs, November 12, 1946, USNA, RG 59.
26. Despatch no. 14894, from W.E.D., U.S. Embassy, Santiago, February 6, 1947, 1, USNA, RG 59.

not mean that the Communist Party would leave the workers to their own devices or would fail to support their just demands." Rather, the Communist leaders agreed with the president that "a cordial understanding between capital and labor" could be achieved through legal arbitration procedures.[27]

The Socialist press railed against what it dubbed a "sensational Communist shift." They denounced their Marxist rivals as "traitors to the working classes" who would "break strikes to remain in power."[28] The Communists, however, were playing a subtler hand. Even as the national leadership adopted a conciliatory posture, the party encouraged its working-class supporters to press the new government to fulfill its promises. Although the coal miners certainly had misgivings about González Videla's concessions to the Right, they still considered him a longtime ally. He had been their candidate, and his ascent to the presidency, they believed, gave them access to national power. Expecting González Videla to be responsive to their needs, the coal miners wrote to him directly to keep him apprised of local developments and to convey their positions on national and international issues.

The miners also made clear that their support was not unconditional: it would not be given at the expense of their own interests. Regardless of pledges made by their national leaders, Communist workers of the coal mining zone insisted on their right to strike and declared their willingness to do so if necessary. On the afternoon of February 7, just three days after Fonseca offered González Videla a "no strike pledge," the miners' union of Lota wrote to the president informing him of agreements they had reached in an assembly that morning. The union declared that if three metalworkers who had been unjustly fired were not rehired by 7 A.M. on February 12, all workers in the Lota company would go on strike.[29] The union's letter challenged the idea that "a cordial understanding between capital and labor" existed in the coal mining zone. The Lota workers denounced the company for not paying them their share of profits as mandated by law and insisted that the González Videla government make the company comply. The union also conveyed its "most energetic protest" against the Industrial Hygiene Commission of the General Health Office, which, on a recent inspection of Lota, had ignored the workers and only visited areas shown to them by company officials.[30]

27. Ibid., 2.
28. Ibid., 2, 3, quoting from *La Opinión* (Santiago), February 4, 1947.
29. Letter from Lota Miners' Union to President González Videla, February 7, 1947, Oficio no. 12, February 7, 1947, FIC, vol. 2355, ANCh.
30. Ibid.

The Lota miners then turned to national and international politics. They strongly condemned the "Feudal Oligarchy" for blocking the union-ization of rural workers, referring to the deal the Liberals had forced on González Videla in return for their confirmation of his presidency. They also denounced efforts by "reactionary forces" to postpone the upcoming municipal elections, which would work to the advantage of the right-wing opposition parties. The union repeated its demand that the presi-dent terminate Chile's diplomatic and commercial relations with Franco's Fascist government. It also insisted that the government stop using Chil-ean naval forces to break workers' strikes, especially those staged in oppo-sition to Spain's "bloody and despotic government, seedbed for a new World War."[31]

Notably absent from the letter, however, was the workers' long-stand-ing insistence that the Chilean government also break ties with the "Fas-cist" regime in Argentina. In the wake of Juan Perón's decisive electoral victory in February 1946, Argentine Communists rued their misjudgment in allying with right-wing forces and U.S. Ambassador Braden. When they moderated their opposition to the Peronist regime, Chilean Communists and their working-class supporters in the coal mining zone followed suit.

For his part, as he had in his campaign, so also in his first months in office, González Videla tried to be all things to all people. In certain private conversations, notably with Ambassador Bowers, he let it be known that he would soon break with the Communists. Bowers thus wrote to Braden, then assistant secretary of state, to assure him that "these Communists will not linger long in the Government." A hand-written note next to this sentence, most likely written by Braden, sug-gests that Washington policy makers were not so easily convinced: "Then why not off-load now?"[32] Bowers nonetheless made every effort to keep the Chilean government in the good graces of his bosses. Gonzá-lez Videla was "ashamed of having Communists in [his administration]," Bowers explained to Braden, and the president had made it absolutely clear to them that "the point of view of his Government will be that of a capitalist State." Bowers ended his confidential letter with a direct appeal: "Convinced as I am of his sincerity, I am hopeful that we can help him out of his present predicament."[33]

González Videla's open alliance with the Communists provoked strong opposition not only among U.S. policy makers and Chile's traditional

31. Ibid.
32. Letter from Bowers to Braden, November 18, 1946, USNA, RG 59.
33. Ibid.

right wing, but also among the more conservative forces in the president's own Radical Party. A leading opponent was Radical Arturo Olavarría Bravo, interior minister in the Aguirre Cerda government, who immediately formed the Chilean Anti-Communist Action League (AChA). Organized along paramilitary lines, the AChA consisted of seven regiments around the country that held public demonstrations and engaged in covert actions against Communists.[34] Notable political actors from across the spectrum joined the AChA, including General Jorge Berguño Meneses, author of the overtly anti-Communist 1941 report about the coal mining zone, who was later implicated in a coup conspiracy against Ríos Morales.

Notwithstanding any private conversations he may have had, González Videla publicly continued to denounce Chile's right-wing forces. In a speech given at the presidential palace four months after taking office, González Videla condemned the anti-Communist movement, which, he said, aimed chiefly at "the persecution, the liquidation of the working class." Directing his words both to his "enemies" and to his landowning and industrialist "friends," the president reminded them of his commitment to respect unions and social rights, declaring that "no force either human or divine will ever be able to separate me from the people [or] make me turn my back on them."[35]

Sliding Toward Showdown

On April 6, 1947, a month after González Videla uttered these words, men and women around the country turned out in high numbers to vote in municipal elections. The results showed just how successful the Chilean Communist Party had become since its embrace of electoral politics as the route to state power: with 16.5 percent of the vote the Communists tripled their showing in the 1944 municipal elections. Moreover, they won twice the votes of their Socialist rivals.[36] As in previous elections, their greatest support came from Chile's mining regions, where

34. On the history of the AChA, see Olavarría Bravo, Chile, 2:41–53.

35. Speech by González Videla given at La Moneda, 120 days after taking office, reprinted in part in Neruda, Discursos parlamentarios, 177–78; and, with slightly different wording, in Durán Bernales, El Partido Radical, 426.

36. Drake, Socialism and Populism, 287. See also Baeza Flores, Radiografía política, 282; Etchepare Jensen, "El advenimiento," 89; Bethell and Roxborough, Latin America, 11.

they won majorities of 55 and 63 percent, respectively, in the copper and nitrate mining towns and 71 percent in the coal mining towns.[37]

The 1947 municipal elections revealed the complexities of Chile's multiparty system, with its constantly shifting alliances. As Chilean historian Jaime Etchepare Jensen notes, political parties combined in these elections in the most varied ways, "without paying attention to doctrinaire or programmatic congruencies or discrepancies, or to their situation as a governing or opposition party." In most municipalities, for example, the Liberals, who were in the government, ran together with Conservatives, who were in the opposition, while the Radical Party, in the government, allied with the Socialists, in opposition. Even unlikely combinations of Communists, Socialists, and Liberals occurred in some places. The position of both the National Falange and the Democratic Party also varied greatly across the nation, being pro- or anti-Communist in different locales, "depending on where the sun shone most strongly."[38]

In the coal mining town of Curanilahue, the Socialists, Radicals, and Democrats ran together on a three-candidate list, "with the exclusive goal of regaining the city government that the [Communist Party] has had in its hands during the last two terms." This opposition bloc based its campaign on "a sentiment of protest and frustration shown by merchants and the community over the irregularities committed by the city council in its role as the Local Commissariat of Subsistence and Prices."[39] Two of these candidates won, becoming a minority on a city council with three Communists. The only other parties, besides the PCCh, to gain in these elections were those opposed to González Videla—the Agrarian Labor, the Conservative, and the Socialist Parties. The Radical and Liberal Parties, on the other hand, each with ministers in González Videla's cabinet, suffered major losses. This "made them think about the advisability of breaking an alliance with the Communists that was becoming very costly for them."[40]

The Communists' entrance into the government and their strong showing in the April municipal elections precipitated a domestic political crisis. The United States added to the urgency of the situation by using its control of international credit and financial assistance—of which Chile was in "increasingly desperate need"—to pressure González Videla

37. Drake, *Socialism and Populism*, 287.
38. Etchepare Jensen, "El advenimiento," 89; *Ercilla* (Santiago), April 1, 1947, 5.
39. *La Época*, March 22, 1947, 1.
40. Alba, *Historia del Frente*, 185.

to break with the Communists.[41] From the moment he took office in November 1946, the U.S. government maintained what Julio Faúndez described as "an informal embargo on credits to Chile," blocking loans from the World Bank and the Export-Import Bank of the United States.[42]

Finally, on April 17, under intense internal and external pressure, President González Videla removed the three Communist ministers from his cabinet.[43] Despite some claims that a "wave of revolutionary strikes flared up in the mining and industrial centers,"[44] the only strike in the entire country appears to have been at the small Lirquén coal mine near Concepción. Nearly five hundred Lirquén workers of the first and second shifts walked off the job and were later joined by the third shift in what the national newspaper *El Mercurio* described as "a demonstration of disagreement . . . with the President's solution to the Cabinet crisis and with the distancing of the Government from the Communist Party."[45]

When González Videla removed the Communist ministers from his government, he was trying to appease right-wing forces in Chile and the United States, but he still hoped to prevent a total break with his Marxist friends. The fact that the PCCh did not call on its cadres to initiate a general strike or take to the streets indicated that they also desired a negotiated solution. Yet the president was still "anticipating a showdown," and he began to prepare for "Communist shutdowns of the coal mines."[46] In May and June, González Videla made a series of requests for "an emergency shipment of coal" from the United States. Ambassador Bowers strongly recommended that the United States accede to "Chile's request for a coal stockpile in its struggle to combat Communism," particularly in light of an impending general strike scheduled for late June 1947.[47]

González Videla's efforts to obtain both coal and a World Bank loan at this time were mediated by Earl T. Stannard, president of the Kennecott

41. Barnard, "Chile," 85.

42. Faúndez, *Marxism and Democracy*, 73–75. See also Collier and Sater, *History of Chile*, 248, who attribute the credit squeeze to U.S. Assistant Secretary of State Spruille Braden.

43. By several accounts, González Videla promised the Communists they would soon resume their places in his cabinet, which is why they agreed to step down. See Lafertte, *Vida de un comunista*, 345; Barnard, "Chile," 82; Faundez, *Marxism and Democracy*, 73–75; and Collier and Sater, *History of Chile*, 247–48.

44. Hernán Santa Cruz Barcelo, the Chilean representative to the United Nations, as quoted in Clissold, *Soviet Relations*, 204–5. My attention was directed to this quote by Angell, *Politics*, 114n85.

45. *El Mercurio*, April 18, 1947, 30.

46. Loveman, *Chile*, 220.

47. Claude G. Bowers, as quoted in ibid.

Corporation, which owned the Braden Copper Company, originally founded by the father of Assistant Secretary of State Spruille Braden. Stannard told González Videla that these requests could be met only after the administration had proven its anti-Communism, but, as Thomas Klubock notes, Braden arranged in secret to "immediately ship two cargoes of coal to the Chilean government to help fight off a coal shortage caused by the miners' strike."[48] Though the month of June came and went without a major coal strike, González Videla continued to prepare for a confrontation with the Communists, which he felt was imminent.[49] According to a secret State Department memorandum, "On his recent trip down there Stannard was told by President González that they were now 'buddies' and that he, González, was disgusted with the Communists and desired Stannard's help in fighting them. By September a general strike would occur, the President said, at which time he will insist on a showdown."[50]

As the field was being prepared for battle, González Videla made a precipitous move: on August 2, 1947, he appointed two top military officers—Army General Guillermo Barrios Tirado as defense minister and Navy Rear Admiral Immanuel Holger Torres as interior minister—to an "Administrative Cabinet" that included Liberals, Democrats, and Radicals, but no Communists.[51] In the opinion of General Leonidas Bravo Ríos,

48. Klubock, *Contested Communities*, 265. Although Klubock says the request for coal was in response to a depletion of stocks during a June strike, both Loveman and Bowers assert that coal was requested *in anticipation of* a June strike, which never occurred. A U.S. State Department document places these events in July, when "President González asked Stannard to help him obtain 50,000 tons of coal (20,000 tons of which was to be a working minimum). Stannard said that the Braden Copper Company would be glad to help González acquire this if González would fight the Communists. Two cargoes of this coal have already left, amounting in all to $468,000. The coal is consigned to an Admiral of the Chilean Navy with the Braden Copper Company not appearing as the shipper. The President and Stannard agreed that nothing of this should be made public, but the President, according to Mr. Stannard, has told numerous people about it to the embarrassment of the Company." Secret Memorandum of Conversation, with participants Mr. Armour, Assistant Secretary of State, Mr. Stannard, President of the Kennecott Copper Corporation, and Mr. Wells and Mr. Brundage, both of NWC, July 23, 1947 (henceforth "Secret Memorandum of Conversation, July 23, 1947"), USNA, RG 59.

49. A strike did occur at Schwager from May 23 to 30 and was resumed from June 4 to 9. There was also a "dispute" at Lota, settled on June 6, which does not seem to have been a strike. Another unspecified labor disturbance took place "in the Concepción area" from June 11 to 14.

50. Secret Memorandum of Conversation, July 23, 1947.

51. The Administrative Cabinet replaced the cabinet created in April 1947, which was composed entirely of Radicals, with the exception of Democratic Juan Pradenas Muñoz, who served as labor minister from mid-January 1947 through April 2, 1948. The only other holdover from the preceding cabinet was the Radical minister of public works. With the replace-

a legal adviser for the armed forces, this marked the "beginning of the battle" between González Videla and the Chilean Communist Party.[52] The president's move was particularly offensive to residents of the coal mining zone since the new interior minister, Holger Torres, was already well known and much despised from his days as head of the Concepción-Arauco emergency zone in early 1946.[53]

Fighting for "a Large Loaf": The August 1947 Bread Price Strike

Rises in the cost of living and speculation in basic commodities had long been major rallying points for community mobilization. Created under Decree Law no. 520 in August 1932, the General Commissariat of Subsistence and Prices was given the "authority to set prices for a wide range of goods considered of 'basic necessity.'" The commissariat also had the power "to take charge of distribution of basic commodities, to expropriate or intervene in the administration of firms that refused to cooperate with government economic policies, to requisition production under specified conditions, and otherwise to regulate the operation of private firms."[54] As Brian Loveman sees it, however, the main significance of this government agency was that it "created an expectation among the population that incumbent regimes would control the rate of inflation."[55]

Failure to control inflation and price gouging was indeed one of the chief criticisms levied against both Ríos Morales and Duhalde Vásquez by various leftist groups when they moved into opposition. Despite his campaign pledge that the miners would eat large loaves under his presidency, González Videla now decreed price hikes for flour and bread. Under existing laws, bread producers could sell a certain number of "special loaves" above the price of 4.40 pesos per kilo set by the commissariat after they had sold all their regular loaves. Many unscrupulous bakers, however, seemed to be always "just out" of regular loaves, forcing consumers to buy the more costly "special" loaves. To end this form of price

---

ment of Pradenas Muñoz by Ruperto Puga Fischer, the Administrative Cabinet remained in place from August 1947 until July 1948, when the Conservatives joined the government.

52. Bravo Ríos, *Lo que supo*, 186.

53. On the emergency measures taken in the coal mining zone in early 1946, see chapter 7.

54. Loveman, *Chile*, 203.

55. Ibid.

gouging, González Videla ordered that all flour and bread be sold at the fixed price of 6.40 pesos per kilo.[56]

Communist and labor activists assailed the president's decision, which affected the cost of the most essential good consumed in working-class households across the nation. The price increase would further impoverish workers, they warned, and could precipitate a social upheaval. Lota's Communist mayor, Santos Medel, for example, protested directly to the agriculture minister, whom he had met on several occasions, and to other key government officials. Having risen to local prominence from his beleaguered minority status back in 1938, Mayor Medel now boldly declared, "It is absolutely impossible for the workers and employees of this town to accept such an extreme measure [the price increase for flour and bread] because their wages and salaries are, disgracefully, the lowest in the country." Medel warned that "if the Supreme Government does not maintain the previous prices, there could be a total cessation of work in this locality."[57]

In the mounting conflict between González Videla and Communist labor sectors, August 19, 1947, was an eventful day, with a number of developments occurring in close succession. In the morning hours, "the coal miners at Lota, Coronel, Curanilahue, and Lirquén voted [an] 'indefinite' strike ostensibly to protest recent increase in price of bread."[58] The illegal strike began when, in the words of the Arauco labor inspector, the first-shift workers at Colico Sur and the CCIL's Curanilahue mines "inopportunely paralyzed operations."[59] The strike quickly spread beyond these miners to most of the workers at Lota, Schwager, Lirquén, and Lebu and, by the afternoon, to workers at the small coal mines of Antihuala, Pilpilco, and La Castellana.[60]

With their argument that the price increase threatened the well-being of all, the Communists galvanized a wide range of social and political support for this strike. Not only did miners throughout the region cease work, but so did local bakers and flour mill workers, joined by construction, brewery, gas company, textile, ceramics, railroad, maritime, and

56. Restricted Despatch no. 15579, from Bowers to Secretary of State, August 22, 1947, 1, USNA, RG 59. See also *El Siglo*, August 1, 1946, 8; and PCCh, *Ricardo Fonseca*, 150.

57. Letter from Mayor Santos Medel to Agriculture Minister, Oficio no. 199, August 18, 1947, FIC, vol. 2356, ANCh.

58. Restricted Telegram no. 667, from Bowers to Secretary of State, August 19, 1947, USNA, RG 59. See also Chamber of Deputies Session, October 28, 1947, 419, BCNCh.

59. Telegram no. 196, August 19, 1947, as transcribed in Oficio no. 7733, August 20, 1947, from DGT to Labor Minister, FDGT, 1947 Oficios, vol. 26, ARNAD.

60. Telegram no. 202, August 20, 1947, as transcribed in Oficio no. 7757, August 21, 1947, from DGT to Labor Minister, FDGT, 1947 Oficios, vol. 26, ARNAD.

port workers.[61] Yet, even though the breadth of the strike reflected the widely perceived legitimacy of the strikers' demands, the labor inspector of Lebu continued to claim that the workers were being politically manipulated to join the movement "without just cause."[62]

President González Videla also discounted the broad popular support for the strike. In a radio address on August 19, he declared that "the Communists had seized [on the] apparent increase in [the] price of bread to work against [the] Chilean Government and people and in favor of wheat speculators and black marketers who were trying [to] exploit people."[63] Decades later, González Videla still denounced the strike as a maneuver by the Communists, "owners and lords of the coal mining zone [who] dominated twenty thousand miners with the terror of the Cheka." He claimed that, "as a pretext, they invoked a purely political, and moreover false reason: the increase in the price of bread."[64] González Videla failed to explain how striking over the price of a basic necessity like bread could be purely political. Nonetheless, citing the coal strike as evidence of the Communists' revolutionary agenda, on the same day, August 19, the president "announced that all appointive offices held by Communists are declared vacant."[65] With a stroke of the pen, he threw out of work tens of thousands of civil servants at all levels of government. The PCCh lost its representatives throughout the state apparatus, including those in key labor posts.

Also on August 19, González Videla declared the provinces of Concepción and Arauco an emergency zone under the command of Navy Admiral Alfredo Hoffman Hansen, who had served in this capacity in February 1946.[66] This move was carried out under Internal State Security Law no. 7200, a piece of wartime legislation that authorized "draconian legal measures" with "repressive consequences."[67] In the case of the illegal August

61. For details on unions participating in the August 1947 strike, see Telegrams nos. 199 and 202, from Lebu IPT, as transcribed in Oficio no. 7757, August 21, 1947, and nos. 448 and 451, from Concepción IPT, August 20, 1947, as transcribed in Oficio no. 7759, August 21, 1947, from DGT to Labor Minister, both in FDGT, 1947 Oficios, vol. 26, ARNAD.

62. Telegram no. 199, August 20, 1947, from Lebu IPT, as transcribed in Oficio no. 7757, August 21 1947, from DGT to Labor Minister, FDGT, 1947 Oficios, vol. 26, ARNAD.

63. González Videla, as quoted in Telegram no. 673, from Bowers to Secretary of State, August 19, 1947, USNA, RG 59.

64. González Videla, *Memorias*, 1:629.

65. Telegram no. 673, from Bowers to Secretary of State, August 19, 1947. See also Telegram no. 679, August 20, 1947; and Restricted Despatch no. 15579, August 22, 1947, 2, both from Bowers to Secretary of State, all in USNA, RG 59.

66. Restricted Telegram no. 667, from Bowers to Secretary of State, August 19, 1947, USNA, RG 59. The relevant supreme decrees establishing the Concepción-Arauco emergency zone were nos. 1827 and 1828 of 1947.

67. Loveman and Lira, *Las ardientes cenizas*, 28. Memo no. 68, August 19, 1947, FIC, vol.

strike in the coal mining zone, General Bravo Ríos recalled that "the Government responded with a show of force by the Army and the Navy, which seemed disproportionate at first, but sufficed to get the strikers to return to work. At the same time, it requested extraordinary powers from the Congress, which were immediately granted, placing all the necessary weapons in the hands of the Executive."[68] "Necessary weapons" was not simply an abstract figure of speech. "The 'regimes of exception,'" as Loveman and Lira explain, "gave the Armed Forces almost limitless authority within the affected areas, as if the territory were in a state of war."[69] It was thus under the heavy hand of the military that the strike came to end on August 21. The region remained militarized, however; under the "special powers" granted him by Congress, the president's emergency zone decrees were for a period of six months, with the possibility of renewal in February 1948.[70]

The rise in the price of bread was not the only issue in the illegal August strike. As Ambassador Bowers observed, the strike coincided with the beginning of legal contract proceedings.[71] Between August 7 and 10, at least eight different unions in the region, including miners, metalworkers, and port workers, had submitted their annual contract petitions to their respective companies. All the petitions called for substantial increases in the basic wage, from 30 pesos to 55–70 pesos per day.[72] They also contained demands related to working conditions, health and safety, and operational control at the coal face and on the shop floor, most notably, the perennial call for "recognition by the Company of the section delegates chosen by their fellow workers."[73] The companies rejected the petitions, and the labor disputes began to move through the various

---

2356, ANCh. As discussed in chapter 4, Law no 7200 of 1942 gave the Executive "special powers" in times of crisis, including the authority to declare emergency zones.

68. Bravo Ríos, *Lo que supo*, 186.

69. Loveman and Lira, *Las ardientes cenizas*, 124–25.

70. Law no. 8837 of 1947 granted the Executive extraordinary political and economic powers for six months. It passed in the Chamber of Deputies (82 to 29) on August 21, and in the Senate (22 to 5) on August 22, and was published in *Diario Oficial* on the same day. See Telegram no. 679, August 20, 1947; and Restricted Despatch no. 15579, August 22, 1947, both from Bowers to Secretary of State, USNA, RG 59; González Videla, *Memorias*, 1:629; Chamber of Deputies Session, October 28, 1947, 418, BCNCh; and James D. Bell, U.S. Embassy Second Secretary, "Coal Strike—October 1947," report no. 404, co-signed by Ambassador Bowers; addressed to Secretary of State, December 22, 1947 (henceforth "Bell Report"), 47, USNA, RG 59.

71. Restricted Telegram no. 667, from Bowers to Secretary of State, August 19, 1947, USNA, RG 59.

72. Bell Report, 10.

73. *El Siglo*, September 5, 1947, 7.

stages of government-mediated negotiations. When the August strike broke out, the workers' petitions were under review by a tripartite conciliation board.

Other points of dispute were also at play in the regional upheaval. Less than a week before the strike began, the Schwager miners had been protesting the company's noncompliance with an agreement signed on May 30, particularly regarding "the provision of special clothing and protective devices to the workers."[74] And, in the Colico Norte labor disputes, the company that had operated the mines until March 31 refused to pay any back wages, claiming bankruptcy. The company that took over the mines on April 1 waited until the regional strike began on August 19, and then it, too, declared bankruptcy and shut down all operations, driving the workers and their families into desperate straits.[75]

Workers throughout the region offered monetary and moral support to the Colico Norte miners; as their own contract disputes dragged on, they also began to prepare for a possible strike, despite the heavy military presence in their towns. Thus, in the first week of September, the Lirquén miners "agreed to increase the Resistance Fund and to supply homes with provisions to confront any eventuality that may derive from the bosses' mean-spirited and miserly attitude."[76] In a notable act of regional solidarity, Pilpilco workers, who had joined the August strike even though their contract was not up for renewal, voted to contribute 100 pesos per union member to aid their fellow miners "in order to break the monopolies of the coal barons of Lota and Schwager."[77] While these regional strike preparations were under way, on September 9, police arrested nearly one hundred union and political leaders throughout the coal mining zone and charged them with violating internal state security laws during the illegal August strike.[78]

On September 12, the company and government representatives on the Special Coal Mining Conciliation Board recommended that the Lota and Schwager miners and metalworkers be granted a general wage increase of

74. Oficio no 7499, August 14, 1947, from DGT to Labor Minister, FDGT, 1947 Oficios, vol. 25, ARNAD.

75. On the shutdown of the Colico Norte mines and the desperate situation of the miners and their families, see Oficio no. 8617, September 11, 1947, from DGT to Lebu IPT, FDGT, 1947 Oficios, vol. 29, and Oficio no. 8920, September [22?], 1947, from DGT to Labor Minister, FDGT, 1947 Oficios, vol. 30, ARNAD. See also El Siglo, September 3, 1947, 4, September 8, 1947, 5, September 9, 1947, 7, September 11, 1947, 7, September 12, 1947, 7, September 17, 1947, 7, September 22, 1947, 5, October, 8, 1947, 6, and October 9, 1947, 4.

76. El Siglo, September 8, 1947, 6.

77. El Siglo, September 16, 1947, 1.

78. El Siglo, September 9, 1947, 7.

15 percent for work inside the mine, 10 percent for jobs on the surface, and a 15 percent rise in the family allowance, which Chilean law required companies to pay to their workers. The CCIL's Curanilahue miners received the same offer, while, in Lirquén, the recommendation was for a flat 10 percent raise for all workers.[79] When the unions refused these offers, the board proposed that the case go to voluntary arbitration, but neither side agreed.[80] Emergency Zone Chief Hoffman Hansen then tried to pressure the workers by announcing "that the Government was disposed to declare any strike illegal and to issue a decree for the resumption of work on the basis of wage raises recommended by the majority of the conciliation board."[81]

Such intimidation was reinforced throughout the month of September by continued arrests and trials of local actors who had been involved in the August strike. Leaders of almost all unions in the region and local delegates to both the Confederation of Chilean Workers and the National Miners' Council were targeted, as were municipal officials who had supported the striking workers, including the Communist mayors of Lota and Coronel.[82] By the end of the month, nearly one hundred union and political activists, from twenty-eight different entities, had been charged with violating internal state security laws. Although most of the cases were soon dismissed, almost all leaders directly connected to the coal industry continued to face criminal proceedings in the Concepción Appeals Court.

Also during September, the police repeatedly intervened in union meetings. When they did so at a September 14 Schwager gathering, the outraged metalworkers sent a telegram directly to President González Videla condemning such tactics.[83] Meanwhile, the Concepción provincial labor inspector reported that "the collective dispute affecting the coal workers is proceeding in accordance with the [pertinent] legal and statutory provisions."[84] The Ministry of Economics and Commerce appointed a commission to report on the relationship between the cost of living in the coal mining zone and company profits as reported in tax declarations.

79. Oficio no. 3028, September 16, 1947, from Concepción IPT to DGT, as transcribed in Oficio Urgente no. 8988, September 22, 1947, from DGT to Labor Minister, FDGT, 1947 Oficios, vol. 30, ARNAD.
80. Ibid.
81. Bell Report, 10. See also El Siglo, September 13, 1947, 1.
82. El Siglo, September 9, 1947, 7.
83. El Siglo, September 16, 1947, 1.
84. Oficio no. 2937, September 11, 1947, as transcribed in Oficio no. 8946, September 22, 1947, from DGT to Labor Minister, FDGT, 1947 Oficios, vol. 30, ARNAD.

Reflecting the new role of the military in settling labor disputes, the commission was headed by Emergency Zone Chief Hoffman Hansen.[85]

Repression had risen to a new level in the coal communities, where it was directed first against Communist labor and political leaders and activists. What those who ordered this repression failed to see, however, was that behind the leaders stood tens of thousands of workers who, together with their families and neighbors, had come to give their loyalty to Communists in both trade union and electoral arenas. Even as international Communism rapidly retreated from alliances with Western powers and bourgeois economic and political sectors, in Chile, Communist-led workers had supported the Radical Party candidate, Gabriel González Videla, who had close ties with the Communists and who entered the presidential palace promising that "no force human or divine" would separate him from the Chilean people.

Despite growing evidence that the president was shifting his political allegiances, the Communists clung to hope that their support of González Videla would pay off. They nervously watched events in neighboring Brazil, where President Eurico Gaspar Dutra declared the Communist Party an agent of foreign powers and began to mobilize the force of the state against it. Communist leaders also watched closely as annual contract negotiations took place in the coal mining region. By September 15, all negotiation and mediation possibilities mandated by law had been exhausted, and the conciliation board authorized the workers to hold strike votes.[86] Overseen by Ministry of Labor officials, voting took place in all eight unions between September 23 and 26. No irregularities or disturbances were reported, and in all cases, the results were almost unanimously in favor of declaring a strike, which was scheduled to begin on October 4.[87] The unfolding of this historic strike and its aftermath are the subjects of chapter 9.

85. *El Sur*, September 24, 1947, 8.
86. *El Siglo*, September 16, 1947, 1.
87. On the strike votes, see *El Sur*, September 24, 1947, 8.

THE GREAT BETRAYAL:
GONZÁLEZ VIDELA AND THE COAL MINERS'
STRIKE OF OCTOBER 1947

Eighteen thousand Chilean coal workers began a legally authorized strike on October 4, 1947. The federal government reacted swiftly, unleashing within hours the most extensive repression the miners had ever witnessed. In what Defense Minister Guillermo Barrios Tirado described as a "surprise occupation," Army regiments, Navy warships, and Air Force squadrons attacked the coal mining communities. Acting in concert with local units of the national police, military personnel took control of all institutions and activities.[1] They raided union offices, political party headquarters, social and sports clubs, libraries, municipal halls, and workers' homes. They even took over the mines. As tanks and trucks hauling cannons lumbered down the streets and Air Force planes roared overhead, soldiers on foot and horseback charged through company row houses, overturning furniture and running sabers through mattresses in their relentless search for striking workers. Although some people managed to hide out in the surrounding hills, by the end of February 1948, five months after the start of the strike, at least seven thousand people had been forcibly removed from their homes and deported from the region, either to designated places of internal exile or to military prison

1. Guillermo Barrios Tirado, Chamber of Deputies Session, October 29, 1947, 513, BCNCh.

camps.[2] More than six hundred of these men and women, known as "re-legados," were held at an internment camp in the northern port of Pisagua, commanded for a time by a young Army captain named Augusto Pinochet.[3]

Although the government had used force to break strikes before, this full military assault on an entire working-class region was one of the most extreme occasions.[4] What made it even worse for the residents of the coal mining region was that the man responsible for these acts, Gabriel González Videla, was the very man who had asked for their votes "with tears in his eyes," promising "that under his government there would no longer be so much suffering," the man for whom his campaign manager, Pablo Neruda, had written the poem "The People Call You Gabriel."[5]

Among the Communist leaders who had stood beside González Videla at the Lota campaign rally just over a year earlier was the city's beloved mayor, Santos Medel, who now found himself smuggled out of town in the back of a pickup truck, forced to spend the next several years in hiding.[6] Senator Pablo Neruda spoke out against what he saw as the traitorous persecution of Medel: "He who brought the people's vote to Sr.

2. El Siglo, October, 5, 1947, 1, and October 9, 1947, 1; Acusación Constitucional Against Holger Torres, Chamber of Deputies Session, October 28, 1947, 419, BCNCh. Testimonies of how people tried to hide or flee under cover include that of Omar Sanhueza Segunda, as quoted in Alcalde, Reportaje al carbón, 82–83, and interviews with Pastor Manuel Cifuentes, Emelina Araneda, and Fresia Vidal Ojarse (September 15, 1997).

3. Pablo Neruda, Senate Session, January 13, 1948, reprinted in Neruda, Discursos parlamentarios, 270–84. From the floor of the Senate, Neruda read out the names of 628 men and women interned at the Pisagua military camp. Many more people arrived at the camp over the next months. Pisagua was also used as a detention camp at other points in Chilean history, first under the brutal regime of Carlos Ibáñez del Campo (1927–31) and then at the height of World War II, when foreigners and suspected Fascists were interned there. During the military dictatorship of Augusto Pinochet Ugarte (1973–89), thousands of Chileans were imprisoned and tortured at this northern desert port, and many were executed there. For an innovative look at Pisagua across time, see Frazier, Salt in the Sand, chap. 5.

4. As Steve Stern observes about the repression of the 1970s and 1980s, "The experience of a state turning violently against a portion of its own citizenry is always dramatic. In a society of Chile's size, [it] translate[s] into pervasiveness." Stern, "Introduction to the Trilogy," in Remembering, xxi.

5. Interview with Pastor Manuel Cifuentes.

6. Memories of Santos Medel's flight from Lota vary in interesting ways. Fresia Vidal recalls that he hid in the back of a pickup truck, buried under sacks of potatoes, headed to Nahuelbuta. Medel's nephew, Evaristo Azócar, said that he hid inside a wine cask and was taken by truck to Los Andes, where he dyed his hair and boarded a train for Temuco. Interviews with Fresia Vidal Ojarse (September 15, 1997) and Evaristo Azócar Medel. In later years, from 1961 to 1965, Santos Medel served as national deputy for Lebu, Cañete, and Arauco. He also served on the PCCh Central Committee, until his death on May 1, 1967, at age sixty-two.

González Videla . . . is being hunted by the police, even underground. The day before yesterday, to learn his whereabouts, a little brother of his, twelve years old, was savagely beaten."[7] Just three months later, Neruda himself, who had tirelessly toured the country as González Videla's campaign manager, would be stripped of his congressional immunity for defamation of his former ally, and he, too, would be forced to flee underground to escape arrest.[8]

A Legal Strike Is Declared "Revolutionary"

The events leading up to the dramatic break between González Videla and his Communist supporters in the coal mining region were, to all appearances, quite routine. Throughout the coal miners' contract proceedings, their full compliance with the Chilean Labor Code was never questioned. Government labor officials affirmed that "the collective dispute concerning the coal workers is proceeding in accordance with the [pertinent] legal and statutory provisions."[9] Between September 12 and 14, unions around the region had held assemblies in which they rejected the option of voluntary arbitration, and, in keeping with Article 540 of the Labor Code, they voted to have their representatives seek legal authorization to hold strike votes.

Intimidation in this situation took several forms. The police stepped up the arrest of union leaders and activists, who were charged with violating internal security laws during the illegal strike in August. Coal face and shop floor supervisors stepped up their punitive actions against workers, even refusing to let them look at their own accident reports.[10] And the police also stepped up their surveillance of union and political meetings, as at the Coronel theater on September 14, when a group of officers entered unannounced "to observe" the affairs of the Schwager metalworkers' union. Though no one was arrested, the outraged union members felt that their hard-won rights as workers and as citizens were

7. Pablo Neruda, Senate Session, October 14, 1947, reprinted in Neruda, *Discursos parlamentarios*, 182.

8. Neruda's congressional immunity was revoked because of his January 6, 1948, speech in the Senate, called "I Accuse" for its resemblance to Émile Zola's famous open letter in the Dreyfus Affair. See Neruda, *Passions*, 284–307. For Neruda's account of his escape across the Andes, see his *Memoirs*, 173–92; see also chapter 10.

9. Oficio no. 2937, September 11, 1947, transcribed in Oficio no. 8946, September 22, 1947, from DGT to Labor Minister, FDGT, 1947 Oficios, vol. 30, ARNAD.

10. *El Siglo*, October 4, 1947, 1.

being trampled under foot. In their telegram to President González Videla, they protested such police intervention as a violation both of the Labor Code and of union statutes, which legally prohibited "outside persons" from participating in union meetings. The Schwager leaders reminded González Videla of the promises he had made to the workers during his campaign, especially his guarantee that "union freedom [would] be protected." They ended with their "respectful request" that the president intercede to favorably resolve the workers' contract disputes.[11]

The next day, September 15, the conciliation board authorized the unions to hold strike votes, though the board continued to meet, still hoping for a negotiated solution.[12] At the same time, the government appointed a special commission "to investigate the relationship between miners' wages and the cost of living; the economic capacity of the companies to pay higher wages; and the wisdom of increasing the price of coal if necessary to increase wages."[13] Headed by Emergency Zone Chief Vice Admiral Hoffman Hansen, the commission included representatives from the Ministry of Economics and Commerce and the Internal Revenue Service (Servicio de Impuestos Internos), who arrived in Concepción on September 19.[14] Using recommendations from this special commission, the conciliation board held its last session on September 22, when final offers and counteroffers were presented and rejected; the companies insisted that they could not afford the 15-peso daily wage raise demanded by the unions.[15]

With the breakdown of these last-ditch negotiations, strike votes took place as planned in eight different unions of miners, metalworkers, and port workers throughout the region between September 23 and 26. Voting was overseen by appropriate Ministry of Labor officials, and, at least in the cases of Lota and Schwager, by the much-despised Welfare Officers Octavio Astorquiza and Juan Mococaín, the companies' most visible symbols of power. Despite all efforts to intimidate them, workers everywhere turned out in high numbers and voted overwhelmingly in favor of the strike. According to the National Miners' Federation (FNM), the eight unions had a total of 16,680 members, of which 15,189, or 91 percent, voted. Of all the ballots cast, only sixteen were against the strike, while seventy were discounted as blank, annulled, or illegible.[16]

11. El Siglo, September 16, 1947, 1.
12. Ibid.
13. Bell Report, 10.
14. El Sur, September 21, 1947, 10.
15. Bell Report, 11.
16. El Siglo, September 27, 1947, 1; Bell Report, 11; Telegrams nos. 524 and 525, September 26, 1947, from Concepción IPT, transcribed in Oficio no. 9165, September 27, 1947, from

In no way, then, could this be considered a spontaneous, unauthorized strike. In the week between the vote and October 4, when the strike was to begin, all parties to the labor disputes were in constant contact. On September 27, union leaders from the region accepted an invitation to travel to Santiago to meet with Ministry of Labor officials, and, they hoped, with the president himself.[17] As they began these direct negotiations with the government, the workers' representatives considered Labor Minister Juan Pradenas Muñoz their closest ally. Pradenas Muñoz would "take it upon himself to resolve the problem," the Communist newspaper *El Siglo* declared, since "he had lived with the workers of the zone in his childhood and was himself a worker." He thus understood "the anguish with which the working class has always struggled against the arrogance and the antisocial and inhuman treatment of the miners by the companies."[18]

In addition to trusting Pradenas Muñoz, union leaders also held out the hope that their former ally González Videla would, in the end, take up the workers' cause, especially after they had made the long trip to the capital to see him. They were therefore "especially bitter [when] they were not received by the President and could not succeed in getting him to intervene in the negotiations."[19] Although González Videla shunned the union leaders, his wife, First Lady Rosa Markmann, met with a delegation of women from the coal mining zone on their way home from the Second National Women's Congress in Valparaíso. Led by Communist Councilwoman Eusebia Torres Cerna from Coronel, the women appealed to the First Lady to help secure fair resolution of the regional labor disputes. The impending strike, they insisted, was about pressing bread-and-butter issues, especially the high price of basic goods.[20]

As late as October 1, Labor Minister Pradenas Muñoz was still meeting with top officials of the Lota, Schwager, and Lirquén companies.[21] On October 3, he held a final meeting with Bernardo Araya, secretary-general of the Communist faction of the CTCh, together with FNM delegates and

DGT to Labor Minister, FDGT, 1947 Oficios, vol. 31, ARNAD; Report on Schwager Union Assembly of January 26, 1941, prepared by Chief of Community Security Juan Mococaín H., Schwager Welfare Department, January 27, 1941, FIC, vol. 2228, ANCh.

17. Oficio no. 9273, September 29, 1947, FDGT, 1947 Oficios, vol. 31, ARNAD; and Bell Report, 11.

18. *El Siglo*, September 29, 1947, 1.

19. Bell Report, 11.

20. *Mujeres Chilenas*, October 1947, 2.

21. Oficio no. 9361, October 1, 1947, from DGT to Labor Minister, FDGT, 1947 Oficios, vol. 32, ARNAD.

labor leaders from the region. He explained to them that the president and his ministers were working "in search of a resolution of the coal industry labor disputes to be implemented once the strike had begun."[22] This led *El Siglo* to conclude that, having failed to prevent the strike (with some question as to whether this was their true intent), government officials were now planning use all legal means to break the strike once it began, as they had done in a recent strike of Valparaíso dock and boat workers.[23] According to Barrios Tirado, Emergency Zone Chief Hoffman Hansen issued a "secret directive" on October 3 ordering the military, as soon as the strike was declared, to take over the mines and arrest all Communist agitators, including not only workers and labor leaders but also city officials and visiting national deputies and senators. If politicians of other parties were found in the region, they were to be immediately removed. The secret directive also indicated that the government would order the strikers to return to work, thus confirming *El Siglo's* speculation in this regard.[24]

The workers and their leaders seem to have been moving in two directions in the days prior to October 4. Even as their leaders continued negotiating in Santiago to prevent the strike, the workers also began to prepare for it, stockpiling as many basic provisions as they could. Later reports of enormous stores are almost certainly exaggerated, however, since an average family in the coal mining zone could scarcely meet its daily needs, let alone accumulate a sizable surplus. The unions' resistance funds were also quite low after sustaining workers through the August strike.

On Friday, October 3, unions throughout the region held roughly concurrent assemblies to clarify when and how they would begin the strike the following day. It was decided that the Schwager miners would stop work at 2 P.M., followed by the Schwager metalworkers and the Plegarias and Curanilahue workers at 3 P.M., and the Lota miners and port workers at 4 P.M.[25] At these same meetings, just one day before the strike was set

22. *El Siglo*, October 4, 1947, 1.

23. Ibid.

24. Barrios Tirado discusses "the subversion in the coal zone" in his unpublished memoirs. González Videla included an abridged and edited version of that discussion as part 13 (pp. 655–87) of his own memoirs. On the "secret directive," see Barrios Tirado, in González Videla, *Memorias*, 1:655.

25. Telegram no. 535, from Concepción IPT, and Telegrams nos. 124 and 233, from Arauco IPT, all to DGT and all transcribed in Oficio Urgente no. 9472, October 4, 1947, from DGT to Labor Minister, FDGT, 1947 Oficios, vol. 32, ARNAD. I do not know why this document did not mention the Lota metalworkers or the Lirquén unions. The staggered start times may have been due to different shift schedules.

to begin, the unions elected their strike committees. The delay in taking such an important organizational step may have been due to the union leaders' prolonged absence from the region, or it may have been a strategic move to prevent preemptive arrests and persecution of strike committee members. With the strike committees finally in place, on October 4, at the start of the respective second shifts in Lota, Schwager, and Lirquén, an estimated sixteen thousand workers declared themselves on strike.[26] The miners walked out of the pits and off the grounds slowly, milling around, talking loudly to cut through the tension. The armed forces were already firmly in place throughout the region: indeed, in his first telegram to Washington announcing the start of the strike, Ambassador Bowers reported, "Army control zone tranquil."[27]

Despite the massive influx of military personnel and equipment, neither the workers nor their leaders foresaw the degree of repression about to befall them. They were not, after all, living under dictator Carlos Ibáñez, but rather in a democratic republic led by a Left-leaning president they themselves had helped put into office. Moreover, the coal mines had been declared an emergency zone and occupied by the military several times in the preceding years, without resort to draconian measures. Indeed, during the January 1946 occupation, some Communist politicians had praised the "upright, calm, and gentlemanly attitude" of the military officers, whose presence helped resolve the labor-management disputes.[28] Finally, even though the coal mining region had been under formal military rule continuously since August, only about twenty people still faced criminal charges for their involvement in that *illegal* strike. Now, less than two months later, the workers were carrying out a labor action in full conformity with the letter of the law. Regional leaders and activists were given no warning that the rules of the game were about to change.

Thus, rather than going into hiding when the strike began, leaders and activists headed to the mine entrances to set up pickets. There they were arrested en masse. On the first day of the strike, the military seized at least forty people, and arrests continued in the coming weeks.[29] The first

---

26. Oficio no. 9556, October 6, 1947, from DGT to Labor Minister, FDGT, 1947 Oficios, vol. 32, ARNAD. Regarding the number of striking workers, Bowers estimated 18,000, whereas the Bell Report says 16,000. The latter figure appears most frequently in other sources. Telegram no. 772, from Bowers to Secretary of State, October 4, 1947, USNA, RG 59; and Bell Report, 15.

27. Telegram no. 772, from Bowers to Secretary of State, October 4, 1947, USNA, RG 59.

28. *El Sur*, January 13, 1946. For fuller discussion of the role of military officers in labor-management disputes, see chapter 7.

29. Bell Report, 12.

wave of detainees included many of the region's top labor leaders, mayors, council members, governors, CTCh officials, and Communist Party militants. According to *El Sur*, for example, at dawn on October 6, police arrested thirty people at the Lota and Schwager mine heads, where they were allegedly armed with clubs and knives, trying to keep strikebreakers from entering. The group at Schwager was led by three prominent Communists—Isaías Fuentes Reyes, former governor of the department of Coronel; Fidel Mellado, current mayor of the city of Coronel; and Humberto Pineda Pacheco, the municipal secretary.[30] In a confidential telegram, Ambassador Bowers confirmed that the military had "arrested and [exiled] to [the] far south 30 armed Communist pickets who were terrorizing workers at Lota and Schwager mine heads."[31] In describing the same arrests, however, *El Siglo* reported that the mines were so heavily guarded no one could get near them and that former governor Isaías Fuentes had been picked up leaving the Coronel movie theater, where union and political meetings were frequently held.[32]

Measures against detainees varied and could include court-martial, confinement on a Navy ship, exile from the region under military or police supervision, or internment in an Army prison camp. The term "relegación" (exile or banishment) referred to both of the latter two measures, and internal exiles as well as prison camp detainees were called "relegados." According to *El Siglo*, at least seven of the thirty people arrested on October 6 were held on the Navy destroyer *Videla*, anchored in the Lota harbor. Others were taken to military camps on Quiriquina Island, in Concepción Bay, or Santa María Island, off the coast of Lota and Coronel in the Gulf of Arauco.[33] From these temporary jails on Navy ships and offshore islands, some people were forcibly relocated to designated places outside the coal mining zone, where they were required to report to local officials at regular intervals. Others were transported under military guard to the makeshift internment center at the port of Pisagua, in Chile's desolate northern desert.[34] Coal zone residents exiled to Pisagua would

30. *El Sur*, October 7, 1947, 1.

31. Confidential Telegram no. 779, from Bowers to Secretary of State, October 7, 1947, USNA, RG 59. Contrary to Bowers's report, at least three of the leaders of these pickets— Fuentes Reyes, Mellado, and Pineda Pacheco—were not deported to the south, but rather were interned at Pisagua.

32. *El Siglo*, October 7, 1947, 1.

33. Ibid.

34. Evidence indicates that people designated as "relegados" were being interned at Pisagua even before the coal miners' strike, but I have been unable to determine their identities, numbers, or origins. Several communications from the Tarapacá police chief to the Tarapacá intendant, dated between September 24 and October 3, 1947, discuss the medical problems of the internees (Documents nos. 1151, 1166, 1177, and 1198). Lessie Jo Frazier pro-

soon be joined by hundreds of other political prisoners from around the country. As noted above, by mid-January 1948, over six hundred people were being held at Pisagua, and by the end of February, over seven thousand had been exiled from the coal mining region. Communist Senator Pablo Neruda and others decried that many of these people were not even informed of the charges against them.[35]

In order to justify turning against his former allies and repressing workers whom he had lauded as democratic patriots over the preceding years, President González Videla had to transform their legal strike into a revolutionary action directed from Moscow, which threatened national security. In effect, he came to the same solution advocated back in 1941 by the staunchly anti-Communist Brigadier General Jorge Berguño Meneses. The Berguño Report had recommended a two-pronged strategy: addressing some of the miners' legitimate grievances while forcefully moving to undermine, if not eliminate, Communist control in the region. To this end, in the early days of the strike, González Videla repeatedly emphasized the favorable terms the miners were offered to return to work and their continued refusal to do so. "This confirms the revolutionary and political nature of the conflict," he said in an October 10 press statement, "which follows a coldly premeditated plan in accordance with foreign directives."[36]

To support the charge that international Communist intrigue lay behind domestic unrest, González Videla focused his attack on two Yugoslav diplomats, one who had resided in Chile for many years and another who was visiting from Argentina. The president claimed to have received intelligence reports linking these diplomats to insurgent strike activity; on October 8, the government expelled them and broke ties with Yugoslavia.[37] Two days later, González Videla declared, "The President of the Republic reaffirms the unwavering objective of eliminating once and for all

vided me transcriptions of these documents, which she consulted in the Archivo Intendencia de Tarapacá (AIT), Iquique.

35. Pablo Neruda, Senate Session, January 13, 1948, reprinted in Neruda, *Discursos parlamentarios*, 270–84.

36. Gabriel González Videla, press statement issued on October 10, 1947, published in *El Sur*, October 11, 1947, and reprinted in González Videla, *Memorias*, 1:642–43. The Bell Report refers to a statement by the president with similar wording, but dates it from October 5. Bell Report, 24.

37. For the full text of the government's October 9 statement about the expulsion of the Yugoslav diplomats, see the *New York Times*, October 10, 1947, 1, 4. See also Barrios Tirado, in González Videla, *Memorias*, 1:676–79; Bowers, *Chile*, 166–69; *Time*, October 20, 1947, 37. The Chilean government broke ties with the Soviet Union and Czechoslovakia on October 21 and 22, respectively.

Communist Party control over the working masses." He called on the nation to make the necessary sacrifices to achieve this end.[38]

Why the Strike Did Not End

In moving against the Communists, González Videla adopted something quite like Berguño's two-pronged strategy, probably on the advice of the military officers in his "Administrative Cabinet." First, to undermine the strikers' sense of power and confidence and to deprive them of their leadership, he deployed a full array of military force without warning. Then, based on Article 547 of the Labor Code, which dealt with "crimes against the freedom to work," he directed Labor Minister Juan Pradenas Muñoz to issue Decrees nos. 977 and 978 requiring workers to return to their jobs at once under temporary contracts drawn up by the government. Finding it politically expedient to offer the most favorable terms possible, the González Videla administration issued return-to-work decrees that provided for a 40 percent increase in the basic wages of workers inside the mines and a 30 percent increase for those on the surface.[39] These terms were widely lauded, both at the time and in later accounts. Even Jorge Barría Serón, a Socialist historian highly critical of González Videla, noted that the decrees offered material improvements "superior to what the workers would have been able to negotiate."[40]

González Videla and his supporters cited the coal miners' refusal to work, despite the magnanimity of the government's terms, as clear evidence that the strike was politically motivated. This was an important strategy to persuade those who were convinced of the legitimacy of the workers' socioeconomic grievances. As Ambassador Bowers recalled in his memoirs, "These miners, inadequately paid and improperly housed, had legitimate reasons for complaint, and at the beginning, they had the sympathy of many conservative citizens." But, after the administration announced "concessions that exceeded what was asked [for] by the miners" and the Communists still "demanded that the strike should proceed,"

38. Gabriel González Videla, October 10, 1947, press statement, published in *El Sur,* October 11, 1947, and reprinted in González Videla, *Memorias,* 1:642–43.

39. Acusación Constitucional Against Holger Torres, Chamber of Deputies Session, October 28, 1947, 418, BCNCh. Decree no. 977 was published in *El Siglo* on October 5, 1947, 13, and translated in the Bell Report as Appendix III. As far as I could determine, Decree no. 978 duplicated Decree no. 977 but applied specifically to workers at the Lirquén company.

40. Barría Serón, *Trayectoria,* 11.

the "purely revolutionary program of the Communists could no longer be doubted."[41]

On October 6, the Socialist Party publicly declared its support of the return-to-work decrees, whose terms, it said, "satisfied the demands of the workers to a greater degree than the gains achieved in the various strikes staged by the Communist Party in the previous fifteen years. In such circumstances, the continuation of the strike lacked economic justification and only represented a political maneuver. Such an attitude put democratic stability in danger."[42] The Army's official history of this period also claimed that the continuing coal strike was "driven by the Communists, who incited the workers to disobey the return-to-work decree[s]"—"despite the efforts of the Executive."[43]

In these accounts, the strikers appear as beguiled victims of Communist manipulation, duplicity, and terror. The initiatives taken by the González Videla administration and the armed forces—the "bastion of democracy" and "the only 'guarantee' of 'social peace'"—were therefore not repressive, but emancipatory, intended to free the miners from Communist domination.[44] This view, however, overlooked the element of consent—how, in the preceding decade, feelings of gratitude, attachment, and loyalty to Communist labor leaders and the Chilean Communist Party had been woven into the cultural, social, and political fabric of the region and into the hearts and minds of its residents. The importance of this aspect of regional working-class culture in the trajectory of the strike was alluded to in the December 1947 Bell Report on the strike, authored by U.S. embassy official James Bell and signed by Ambassador Bowers. "Despite the arrest of a large number of strike leaders and strict military control designed to protect those wishing to return to work," the report noted, "the response of the average miner was very disappointing. Although supposedly freed from the alleged influence of Communist leaders practically none of the 16,000 on strike returned to work. Reports that this was due to 'agitation and continuous meetings' seem to be incorrect as military control prohibited meetings and the more militant agitators had been arrested."[45]

41. Bowers, Chile, 167, 166.
42. Jobet, Historia del Partido, 194–95.
43. Estado Mayor General del Ejército de Chile, Historia, 50.
44. Sala de Touron, "Guerra fría," 21; and Loveman and Lira, Las ardientes cenizas, 122.
45. Bell Report, 15. James Bell did not stay long in Latin America, but his work in Chile seems to have been viewed favorably; in the 1950s and 1960s, he served as ambassador to Indonesia and Malaysia and director of Southwest Pacific affairs (1960–63).

Why, then, did the strikers refuse to return to work? Part of the answer lies in questionable claims made about the decrees that ordered them to do so. Ambassador Bowers, for example, claimed that "González Videla summoned the mine owners and secured concessions that exceeded what was asked by the miners, and this was announced the day before the strike was to begin."[46] Other reliable sources refute this claim, however. As noted above, on October 3, Labor Minister Pradenas Muñoz told the workers' representatives that a decree granting such concessions was likely, but he did not divulge its content.[47] The October 3 secret directive described by Defense Minister Barrios Tirado also referred to an imminent return-to-work decree, but indicated that it would not be issued until after the start of the strike.[48] The government and military certainly had plans for how to break the strike once it began, combining severe repressive measures with a wage increase that could be readily propagandized as evidence of good will. But all sources concur that the decrees themselves were issued only after the strike had begun. If the administration had wanted to avoid the strike and the total militarization of the zone, it could have made the terms of the decrees known well before then.

As soon as the decrees were publicly released, the increasingly censored press and the speeches of certain members of Congress raised a number of controversial questions.[49] Many national political and labor leaders defended the strikers' refusal to comply with the return-to-work order. The supposedly favorable terms, they explained, were issued unilaterally by the government and did not constitute an agreement between workers and their employers.[50] The companies had not formally endorsed the decrees and were not legally bound by them once they regained control of mining operations. Pursuing this question, the centrist newspaper El Sur contacted an official of the Lota company, who declared that "in the face of the rumor propagated by agitators that the Company would not comply with the wage increases established in the Supreme Government decree[s] once operations return to normal, I can assure you that

46. Bowers, Chile, 166–67.
47. El Siglo, October 4, 1947, 1.
48. Barrios Tirado, in González Videla, Memorias, 1:655.
49. See, for example, El Siglo, October 5, 1947, 1. On October 5, the government issued Decree no. 5610, which ordered censorship of the Communist newspaper El Siglo and other suspect media. For a translation of the decree, see Bell Report, Appendix V
50. On October 8, for example, the Confederation of Chilean Workers submitted a memo of "patriotic propositions" to Labor Minister Pradenas Muñoz, their perceived ally in the administration, calling on the government to clarify and refine the terms of the return-to-work decrees and to guarantee full compliance by the companies. El Siglo, October 9, 1947, 1.

this rumor is completely inaccurate and that the Company I represent has accepted and will uphold the decreed raises."[51]

Yet this statement by an unidentified company official was published at the prompting of a regional newspaper five days after the decrees were issued, leading some observers to wonder whether the government had really tried its best to resolve the labor disputes peacefully. If the companies had agreed to the contract terms before the decrees were issued, why was this fact not made widely known, especially to the workers? The conclusion reached by Communists and other more surprising supporters of the strike was that the government may have withheld such information in order to perpetuate conditions that could justify repression. Even Marmaduke Grove, leader of the moderate Authentic Socialist Party (PSA), made this argument on the floor of the Senate on October 14, ten days after the start of the strike:

And I ask my Honorable colleagues: Does anyone believe that a solution would not have been reached if the problem had been dealt with in an atmosphere of cordiality, if the workers had not been surrounded by troops and machine guns and if the Government had demonstrated to them, as has been said here, that this decree favored their interests and that the companies accepted what the Executive was proposing? Because this latter point has been spoken about very softly, so softly that we didn't even know about it; I've just learned about it here in this room, that the compan[ies] had accepted, by way of a letter, the proposition of the Government.

When Communist senators Neruda and Contreras Labarca agreed that no one had been told about any deals with the companies, Grove concluded that the government had not really been interested in the workers' accepting the terms of its return-to-work decrees.[52]

A further question raised about the supposedly magnanimous government decrees was the way attendance bonuses would be calculated after the strikers returned to work. Defending the government, Interior Minister Holger Torres said that it was incorrect that the decreed changes would be detrimental to the workers. But, at the same time, he also noted that on October 21, two new decrees were issued superseding the terms

51. El Sur, October 9, 1947, 7.
52. Marmaduke Grove, "Conflicto Obrero en la Zona del Carbón," Senate Session, October 14, 1947, reprinted in Neruda, Discursos parlamentarios, 188.

disseminated on October 4.[53] In other words, the government recognized the legitimate basis for the workers' objections to the attendance bonus clauses in the original decrees, yet for more than two weeks failed to rectify the problem. In the intervening period, miners' deliberations about whether to return to work were based on the original clauses. The decrees also contained other "gaps and contradictions," according to strike supporters, including the fact that they applied only to certain segments of the workforce. As congressional critics explained, "they do not consider economic improvements for diverse [other] groups of workers, such as the drillers and haulers, who work by quantity-based contracts, and the metalworkers, maritime workers, and others, who are remunerated according to special agreements they have with the Companies."[54]

Another reason given for why the strikers did not return to their jobs had to do with the democratic rights of citizen workers. Under the military occupation of the region, the workers were prevented from holding meetings to discuss and vote on the government's terms, a practice entrenched in the political culture of the region by this time. As later charged by Communist Senator César Godoy Urrutia, police and military forces were constantly "preventing workers from meeting in assemblies, closing union offices, seizing documents and other property of the unions, refusing to recognize the Strike Committees, detaining their members, and so on." At 7 P.M. on October 4, for example, shortly after the decrees were announced, a group of about forty Lota port workers gathered at their union headquarters to discuss how to proceed. Almost immediately, as recounted by Godoy, "two police officials arrived, accompanied by twelve policemen and six Investigation agents, and they intimidated the workers into leaving the place at once, and they also asked the whereabouts of the union president."[55]

Military officers in the emergency zone not only interrupted the workers' meetings, but also tried to hold workers' assemblies under the officers' own control. According to El Siglo, the workers told them they would

53. Holger Torres's Defense Against the Acusación Constitucional, Chamber of Deputies Session, November 4, 1947, 563, BCNCh. For a translation of one of the October 21, 1947, decrees (no. 1014), see Bell Report, Appendix IV.

54. Acusación Constitucional Against Holger Torres, Chamber of Deputies Session, October 28, 1947, 418, BCNCh.

55. César Godoy Urrutia, Chamber of Deputies Session, November 4, 1947, 579, BCNCh. Interior Minister Holger Torres flatly "reject[ed] the charge that he had prohibited the celebration of any union assembly, or failed to recognize the existence of any strike committee, nor had he arranged closings or requisitions." Report of the Special Commission on the Acusación Constitucional Against Holger Torres, Chamber of Deputies Session, November 4, 1947, 561, BCNCh.

meet only "when the censorship of their organizations [had] been lifted and they [could] debate in full freedom in the presence of their own leaders."[56] González Videla and his advisers had underestimated the ties of reciprocity and trust that had developed between the workers of the coal mining region and their mostly Communist leaders. The administration presumed that once they removed the leadership cadres from the scene the workers would readily accept material offerings in the form of favorable work contracts. This did not occur. As explained in the Bell Report, "The military had made serious attempts to inform the miners of benefits provided by the Government decree[s] but failed to convince them of the desirability of immediately resuming work. Probably the best explanation of this recalcitrant attitude is that given by a reporter for *Ercilla* who found that leaders of coal unions had gained the respect of miners to such an extent that the average worker at the coal fields was suspicious of any settlement not endorsed by union leaders."[57]

This "recalcitrant attitude" shown by "the average worker" altered the terms of battle in ways that González Videla had perhaps not fully anticipated. Because the coal miners and their fellow strikers still rejected his terms, even after their leaders had been arrested, the president was forced to acknowledge, at least implicitly, the legitimacy of his former Communist allies in the eyes of the workers. On the third day of the strike, when the return-to-work decrees went unheeded, González Videla sent Ambassador Bowers an "urgent request" to meet. In a confidential telegram wired after the meeting on October 6, Bowers reported that the president "was at war with Communism" and believed that this now required battling not just readily identifiable Communist leaders and agitators, but the coal miners themselves since indoctrination had put them beyond possible redemption. To this end, the president planned to recall to active duty 16,000 striking miners who were also Army reservists. Moreover, he planned to "move out coal miners (60 percent of whom he judged had reached [a] point of fanaticism due [to] Communist agitation) and replace them with entirely new elements (since he and [the] Army felt miners would not work even if [called back to active duty]); he said this was the only course."[58] Bowers stressed that Chile was an important test case to show that Communist strength could "be routed and discredited." He ended his report by proclaiming, "I consider it of utmost importance that

56. *El Siglo*, October 7, 1947, 1.

57. Bell Report, 15.

58. Confidential Telegram no. 776, from Bowers to Secretary of State, October 6, 1947, USNA, RG 59. See also Bowers, *Chile*, 166–69.

we give full immediate assistance to the President, who has today thrown down the gauntlet to our common enemy."[59]

Also on October 6, the same day González Videla told Bowers about the plan, Defense Minister Barrios Tirado issued Decree no. 2191 recalling to active duty all Army reservists in the coal mining zone, which, according to Chilean law, automatically included all men who had completed their year of obligatory military service.[60] Recalling the miners to military service put them under the jurisdiction of military law and made their refusal to work grounds for court-martial. Then, putting into effect a policy that "those who didn't work, didn't eat," the military removed provisions from workers' homes and tightly rationed further sales. When it became known that residents were subsisting on the fruits of the sea, "fishing was subsequently prohibited."[61] In response to such measures, a delegation calling itself the "United Women of Lota" met with Vice Admiral Hoffman Hansen to request permission to stage a "march of empty pots." The emergency zone chief refused the request, and carabineros were sent in to disperse the hundreds of women gathered outside military headquarters.[62] The armed forces further consolidated their control of the coal mining zone by cordoning off entry and exit points and implementing a "safe conduct" system; beginning on October 11, no male over age fifteen could transit into or out of the region without a pass. Passes could be obtained only in person at designated military offices.[63] Despite these measures, by as late as October 16, fewer than three thousand miners— fewer than one in six—had returned to work, most of them at the point of a machine gun or bayonet.

Even coal company administrators grew frustrated at what seemed to them excessive measures involving undue intervention in their affairs by the military authorities. Back in 1942, after publication of the Rettig-Pazols Report, the Lota company had simply ignored intrusive government recommendations, such as to dismiss its Welfare Department chief. But now, with all mining operations and personnel decisions firmly in the

---

59. Confidential Telegram no. 776, from Bowers to Secretary of State, October 6, 1947, USNA, RG 59.

60. For a translation of Decree no. 2191, see Bell Report, Appendix VIII. See also Confidential Telegram no. 783, from Bowers to Secretary of State, October 9, 1947, USNA, RG 59; and Bravo Ríos, Lo que supo, 188–89.

61. Bell Report, 17.

62. El Siglo, October 9, 1947, 1.

63. Garrison Order no. 5, October 10, 1947, FIC, vol. 2356, ANCh. Andrew Barnard provides a good summary of the extreme measures used to break the strike in his "Chile," 83–85.

hands of military officers by executive decree, the companies could not just carry on with their own agenda while paying lip service to the government. At the beginning of the strike, company administrators believed that military intervention would be short-lived and would serve to remove the most active leaders and agitators. To this end, they agreed to respect the wage raises offered in the government decrees, which were indeed much higher than what they had offered during the negotiations. At the same time, the companies turned their personnel records over to military officers and compiled lists of persons they considered troublemakers. As the number of workers arrested and removed continued to rise, however, company officials felt helpless to stop what they saw as the near elimination of their workforce.

González Videla's plan to arrest some 60 percent of the miners and to replace them with entirely unskilled rural migrants met with increasing opposition from the companies. On October 14 and 15, when Defense Minister Barrios Tirado traveled to the coal mining zone to meet with military officials, the Marine commander of Coronel denounced the Schwager company for "not collaborating . . . not subordinating itself to the authorities installed in the zone." After hearing similar reports around the region, the general made an urgent call to President González Videla to inform him that the situation there was not yet completely under control. Barrios Tirado noted two principal reasons for the delay: "First, the companies resisted cooperating with the removal of two to three thousand men from the zone, to have them replaced with others brought in from the South. Second, there was evidence of a climate of hatred, of passive resistance, among the working masses, who were bowed but not beaten."[64]

The lengths taken by the government to break the strike and tear apart the social, political, and cultural fabric of the coal communities were in many ways a measure of the resistance shown by the miners and their families and neighbors. Yet, at the same time, the repressive measures themselves prompted resistance. More than any particular aspect of the return-to-work decrees, the most powerful reason for the strikers' "recalcitrant attitude" and the "climate of hatred [and] of passive resistance" was their outrage at being treated as less than citizen workers. After a decade of showing patriotic support for democratic procedures and centrist bourgeois politicians—including President González Videla himself—the miners were now being hunted down as criminals, and they

64. Barrios Tirado, in González Videla, *Memorias*, 1:662, 664. See also Bravo Ríos, *Lo que supo*, 189.

refused to submit calmly to such humiliation. Again, as Senator Marmaduke Grove asked his colleagues, "Does anyone believe that a solution would not have been reached if the problem had been dealt with in an atmosphere of cordiality, if the workers had not been surrounded by troops and machine guns?"[65] Even during the persecution of the 1920s, the workers had not felt such an acute sense of betrayal—that the nation for which they had been mining and the state in which they had reposed their deepest hopes had turned brutally against them.

Strikebreakers and Mass Deportations

While arrests and internal deportations were under way, the military began to carry out the plan announced by González Videla to replace the striking workers with "entirely new elements."[66] On the morning of October 15, trains began to pull into the Lota and Coronel stations filled with strikebreakers from rural areas in the South. All told, some fifteen hundred of these strikebreakers would be brought to the mines, a move cited by General Bravo Ríos as "one of the factors that most contributed to the triumph" over the strikers.[67] Recruiting labor for the mines through trickery was widely referred to as an "enganche," meaning a "snare" or "hook." According to most testimony, military agents lured these country folk with false promises about living and working conditions. Many did not even know that the miners were on strike and or that the coal mining zone was militarized. One such unwitting strikebreaker was Davíd Padilla Rodríguez, who was working on a rural estate near Temuco when, drawn by the prospect of better wages, he boarded a train bound for the coal mines. As recounted by his daughter Raquel, who grew up listening to his stories,

> Somewhere midway between Temuco and Concepción, they had already gone a fair stretch, he said, when . . . all the trains filled up with military guys [milicos] with machine guns, and they began to cover the trains with flags, those trains, freight trains, continued on . . . , plastered with flags. Then, my father said, they began to get worried. . . . They tried to get off, but the military guys pointed guns at them and said no, they couldn't get off. They said they were

65. Marmaduke Grove, "Conflicto Obrero en la Zona del Carbón," Senate Session, October 14, 1947, as reprinted in Neruda, *Discursos parlamentarios*, 188.
66. Confidential Telegram no. 776, from Bowers to Secretary of State, October 6, 1947, USNA, RG 59.
67. Bravo Ríos, *Lo que supo*, 189.

bound for a destination and they had to arrive there. So then my father became afraid, terror seeped in, . . . they really didn't know what they had gotten themselves into.[68]

Covering the trains that transported the strikebreakers with Chilean flags was only the beginning of the military's manipulation of patriotic symbols to break the strike. When the trains pulled into the coal mining towns, the rural recruits "were received with fanfare including a [military] band and appropriate speeches," arranged by the local emergency zone authorities.[69] Yet, after this festive welcome, the recruits were led under military guard to makeshift quarters in local schoolhouses and gymnasiums, and each day, they were sent into the mines at the point of guns and bayonets, even though they had no training for this kind of work. As Raquel Padilla described her father's arrival in Schwager,

> They tossed all the people there to sleep on the floor, imagine that, . . . and the next day they already had to go down in the mine. . . . My father said they cried, all the people were crying, because they didn't know what to do. . . . They didn't know what they had gotten themselves into because [the military agents] had brought them there by deception, they had offered them houses, good wages, that they would live well, all those things, but then they went four months without any communication with their families, because they wrote, but no letter ever left Schwager, and no letter ever came in.[70]

Just before the arrival of these rural workers, turned into strikebreakers by military force, unusually high tides had stranded large schools of hake (*merluza*) on the beach of Lota Bajo, and the hungry "men, women and children of Lota hurried to gather [them] up."[71] When many of the new arrivals began to fall victim to injuries and illness in the unfamiliar and difficult circumstances, people remarked that they were so out of their element, they would soon die off just as the stranded hake had done. This group thus became known in collective memory as the "merluzas con banda," roughly translated as "hake with a band" or "stranded fish with fanfare," referring back to the military band and flags with which

68. Interview with Raquel del Carmen Padilla Vergara.
69. Bell Report, 18.
70. Interview with Raquel del Carmen Padilla Vergara.
71. *El Siglo*, October 13, 1947, 1.

they were first greeted at the train station.[72] Although many people resented the new migrants for breaking the strike, they also understood the deception that had lured them to the region and the mistreatment and coercion to which the migrants had been subjected. Nevertheless, the few who survived their crash apprenticeship in the mines and stayed in the region were marked as "merluzas" for their rest of their lives, and the stigma was even passed on to their children.[73]

One young observer of the desperate lot of the rural recruits was Juan Alarcón, a sixteen-year-old errand boy, or "junior," in the Schwager management offices, who continued to work throughout the strike. As an errand boy, he reported directly to the military officers who took over the running of the mines, and he witnessed firsthand the treatment of strikebreakers from the South, many of whom were indigenous Mapuches:

> Many people died here . . . because [the military] led them into the mine without [their having any] knowledge of mining, . . . to work in the mine because they wanted to break the strike. And I remember Mapuche fathers, Mapuche mothers, who arrived to claim their dead sons, and they had to use a translator because they didn't speak any Spanish. . . . When the bosses noticed [the Mapuche workers], they would say, "How's it going for you, Juan Caiman Mariqueo?" . . . "Hey, this one's an Argentine," they would say, and all the employees would laugh, yeah, "This one is Argentine," "This one's Bolivian," "This one's Austrian," "This one's European," because they were all pure Mapuche names, eh? So they would laugh,

72. Almost every person I interviewed in Lota told some version of this story. Beyond the literal translation of *merluza* as "hake," the term also refers to inebriation, as in "coger una merluza" or "estar con la merluza," which mean to get or be drunk. Because the more established working-class movement in the region had long sought to distinguish itself from a culture of degradation and debauchery, the identification of the rural migrants as "merluzas" may also be part of the effort to highlight the respectability of the "true miners." The stranding of fish occurred only in Lota, and the expression "merluzas con banda" was not incorporated into popular memory in Coronel, only 8 kilometers (about 5 miles) away, where the strikebreakers are referred to as "huasos con banda," or "countryfolk with fanfare."

73. When Luis Fuentealba Medina (d. 2009), Communist council member from Lota and former national deputy (1969–73), told me the story of the "merluzas con banda," he referred to them in the third person and noted that within ten to fifteen years, the majority had died or left the region. Interview with Luis Fuentealba Medina. Other people told me that Fuentealba himself was one of the rural workers who arrived in Lota in October 1947. As Daniel James's work has shown, fissures and silences in testimony often point toward places of shame in identity formation. See James, *Doña María's Story*, esp. 239–43.

and then . . . they had them sleeping in the market, they had them sleeping in a school, all crammed together like that, because they didn't have any other place.[74]

By mid-October, then, coal extraction was under way with an eclectic group of strikebreakers. Local workers like Juan Alarcón, who stayed on the job for various reasons, were joined by rural folk lured to the coal mining zone with promises of good wages, housing, and even small plots of land.[75] Other strikebreakers arrived with explicitly political motives, such as the Socialist detachments sent by Bernardo Ibáñez. In addition to the regular military troops sent to work in the mines, the Army called up thousands of reservists in the region under threat of court-martial, as described above. Many of the workers who refused to report voluntarily were eventually dragged out of their hiding places and sent into the mines at bayonet point. All of these different groups worked together under military guard. At the end of their shifts, local workers went to the same homes they had been living in for years, while the "merluzas con banda" slept under tight watch in makeshift quarters around town and the Army reservists were confined in police barracks.

Military and government officials in charge of resolving the conflict in the coal mining zone believed that using strikebreakers to renew production would convince the regular workforce—most of whom were in hiding in the towns themselves or in nearby hills—that the strike had failed. By as late as October 16, however, only about three thousand miners had returned to work. At this point, the repression entered a new phase; the military now moved against "the miners who, although not leaders, were recalcitrant." These people were to be banished from the zone together with their families, according to criteria summarized in the Bell Report as follows:

> Determinations as to which miners were to be permitted to continue their employment in the mines were made by a Commission on the Qualifications of Workers composed of officers of the Armed Forces. Four categories of miners to be removed from the area were established as follows:
>   1. Ringleaders who "direct agitation and sow panic."
>   2. Miners who carry out the orders of ringleaders . . . to be moved to any point in Chile of their choice.

74. Interview with Juan Alarcón.
75. El Siglo, October 10, 1947, 2.

3. Those who failed to comply with the order to return to work by 3 P.M. on October 15 were to be tried by military courts and, if guilty, were subject to three to five years' imprisonment.

4. Those who requested a legal vacation at the time of the strike and thus did not work were to be investigated.[76]

Bell then gave estimates of the number of people arrested and deported in each of these categories through mid-December, when he prepared his report. He noted, for example, that 150 to 200 people were deemed "ringleaders" in category one and were interned at a military camp on Quiriquina Island. Returning from a visit to the region, Defense Minister Barrios Tirado confirmed these detentions, saying that 149 workers had been sent to Quiriquina.[77] As the Bell Report continued, "Approximately 1,500 to 1,800 were found to fall into the other three categories and were removed (with their families) from the coal mining zone. They were first taken to the station of Chepe near Concepción and sent from there to any point in Chile they requested. Due to the size of the movement and the lack of preparations, there seems to have been some hardship imposed on those evacuated."[78]

For the relegados, the people who experienced these arrests and deportations, James Bell's reference to "some hardship" was a gross understatement. As with the "merluzas con banda," the story of the detainees at the Chepe train station came to occupy a critical place in the region's collective memory. Descriptions of what occurred there were central in congressional debates at the time, and would be included in the testimony of many residents in years to come. Beginning the third week of October, between five hundred and several thousand detainees from the coal mining towns were taken to the Chepe train station on the outskirts of the city of Concepción.[79] From there, they were to be exiled, sent to a place of their choosing outside the region, where they would reside under police surveillance. The military screenings and the actual departures were delayed, however, in many cases up to four days. During the delay, the detainees—including hundreds of women and children—were kept inside

76. Bell Report, 18.

77. *El Siglo*, October 19, 1947, 5.

78. Bell Report, 19.

79. Although Communist sources report that several thousand were detained at the Chepe station, pro-government estimates are much lower. After his November visit to the zone with the president, for example, Radical Senator Pedro Opitz Velásquez testified that only 480 people had been "accidentally" detained there. Senate Session, November 4, 1947, 431, BCNCh.

the freight and cattle cars that would transport them to their destinations; they were provided little food and water, denied medical attention, and in general, held in a situation widely described as immoral, unsanitary, and inhumane.

The image of men, women, and children packed into freight and cattle cars raised the issue of the violation of the rights and dignity guaranteed to all Chilean citizens perhaps with greater poignancy than any other during the strike. It stood in sharp contrast to the government's pronouncements about the necessity, legality, and humaneness of the measures taken to rout the Communists. And this particular scene—railroad cars packed with human beings en route to detention centers—took on a heightened significance in the immediate wake of World War II, when stories of Nazi atrocities flooded the international press. Playing on the public's sense of horror at news from Europe, Communists referred to Quiriquina Island and Pisagua as "concentration camps." Their acclaimed spokesman Pablo Neruda went even further: "While the UN is debating the crime of genocide—and the Chilean delegate will surely make a few emotional speeches on the subject—Señor González Videla is responsible for that very crime, perpetrated against his own countrymen."[80]

Talk of genocide was groundless hyperbole; indeed, there is no evidence that anyone died as a direct result of military actions in 1947–48.[81] Nonetheless, this was certainly "a massive repression,"[82] though the exact number of people arrested and deported from the region may never be known. As noted above, the Bell Report claims that in addition to the 150 to 200 people charged as "ringleaders" and sent to internment camps, another 1,500 to 1,800 people "were removed (with their families) from the coal [mining] zone." This estimate seems to be fairly accurate, based on extrapolations from two official lists of persons to be deported. The first list, dated October 25, 1947, was sent from the Lota military delegate

80. Pablo Neruda, "Carta íntima para millones de hombres," *El Nacional* (Caracas), November 27, 1947; translated as "Intimate Letter to Millions of People" and reprinted in Neruda, *Passions*, 274.
81. In his November 1947 "Intimate Letter," Neruda claimed that "children and adults died as a result of" their detention on railroad cars. He also noted that "corpses of miners appeared in the hills, and no one could investigate since no one was allowed to enter the zone." Neruda, *Passions*, 274. A few people did die at the Pisagua internment camp in 1948, but whether from natural causes or from the hardships of camp life is not clear (see chapter 10).
82. Interview with Omar Sanhueza Segunda, September 10, 1997.

to the intendant of Concepción.[83] The opening paragraph states that the people on this list were to be sent to Concepción, together with their families, and from there, given passage to destinations of their choosing (they may well have been among those held for days at the Chepe station). The list specifies the number of family members traveling, their preferred destinations, and the presence or absence of the head of household. Of the forty-three named persons, all are male except for two married women: Sra. de Heraldo Aravena and Sra. de Pedro Fuentes.[84] An average of three to four family members traveled with each named person, giving a total of approximately 150 people to be deported from the zone. Some of the destinations were nearby—Concepción, Arauco, Chillán, Los Angeles; others were farther south—Valdivia, Curicó, Cauquenes, Osorno; while seven families headed to Santiago. None of the relegados was listed as heading north, where the copper and nitrate mines were sites of potential employment, probably because military officials prohibited travel to other areas of labor unrest. Indeed, just two days before this list was issued, Defense Minister Barrios Tirado responded to illegal strikes in the Chuquicamata and El Teniente copper mines and in several nitrate mines by declaring the provinces of Tarapacá, Antofagasta, Atacama, and O'Higgins emergency zones.[85]

One of the people named on the October 25 list was Roberto Gómez Sandoval, a Communist secretary of the Lota miners' union, who had won his post in the highly contentious 1942 elections.[86] He was now to be sent to Chillán with nine family members. Also named was José Segundo Martínez Suazo, who had been working on the CCIL docks in December 1945 when he was arrested, along with five other workers, for allegedly attacking a company agent (most likely a spy or infiltrator).[87] A third man

83. Oficio no. 120, October 25, 1947, from Lota Emergency Zone Military Delegate to Concepción Intendant, FIC, vol. 2356, ANCh.

84. There is also a María Duarte Rojas, who could be a woman but was more likely a man since she would be the only woman on the November 30 list.

85. Barrios Tirado, in González Videla, *Memorias*, 1:691.

86. The 1942 union elections had been scheduled for May 24, but on that date, a dispute broke out between the workers and the local labor inspector over how they would be run. After tense negotiations, the elections were finally held in June. See Díaz Iturrieta, "Historia"; and Damián Uribe Cárdenas, Chamber of Deputies Session, June 2, 1942, 325–26, BCNCh. I do not know what Roberto Gómez Sandoval was doing between 1942 and 1947. All five union leaders elected in June 1942 were Communists, but Gómez Sandoval is the only one named on this early list of relegados.

87. Oficio no. 80, circular letter from Industrial Union of Lota Miners, December 22, 1945, FIC, vol. 2320, ANCh. Interestingly, Martínez Suazo's name was not removed from the electoral registers under the 1948 Law for the Permanent Defense of Democracy (LDPD), which indicates that he did not fit any of the broad criteria for being labeled a "Communist."

on the October list was Luis Moraga Moraga, who was to be sent to Trai-guén with seven family members, "tomorrow," according to a handwritten notation next to his name. Luis Moraga had been named treasurer of the strike committee in the October 3 union assembly.[88]

The second list of people to be internally deported was issued by Emergency Zone Chief Hoffman Hansen with Decree no. 14, on November 30, 1947. "In the interest of maintaining public order and guaranteeing the freedom to work," the decree states, "it is not convenient" for certain persons described as "dangerous" due to "their background or their actions in recent events" to remain in the coal mining zone. "From this day forward," Hoffman Hansen ordered, "the persons indicated below may not transit through nor remain in the Province of Arauco, nor in the Department of Coronel, of the Province of Concepción."[89] The list is divided into people from Lota (499), Coronel (320), Curanilahue (76), and Lebu (13), giving a total of 908 named individuals, all of whom seem to be men. Next to the typed name of each man is the number and issuing location of his identification card, but there is no indication of where he was to be sent, nor with how many family members, as was the case on the previous list. Every person on the October 25 list also appears on the November 30 list, except for the two married women, whose husbands do appear on the November 30 list.

These two lists were clearly incomplete, for several reasons. Many more women were arrested and deported from the coal mining zone in their own right, not just accompanying their condemned spouses, and these women must have been named on separate lists.[90] The most famous woman arrested in Lota was Blanca Elvira Sánchez Sagredo, a schoolteacher and Communist Party militant, who was sent to the Pisagua internment camp. Also arrested during the October strike was Eusebia Torres Cerna, a Communist councilwoman from Coronel who had been charged with violating internal state security laws during the illegal August strike. In September, Torres led the regional delegation to the Second National Women's Congress that met with First Lady Rosa Markmann on their return through Santiago.

88. El Siglo, October 4, 1947, 1. What is quite puzzling is that no other members of the Lota Strike Committee were named on the first (October 25) list of relegados, nor were any of the region's top labor and political leaders.

89. Decree no. 14, November 30, 1947, issued by Concepción-Arauco Emergency Zone Chief Alfredo Hoffman Hansen, FIC, vol. 2356, ANCh.

90. An October 31 document from the Llanquihue intendant, for example, named three women forcibly deported there from the coal mining zone, but I have no further information about them. Oficio no. 137, October 31, 1947, from Llanquihue Intendant to Maritime Services Chief, FIC, vol. 2356 (Oficios Recibidos de Otros Funcionarios), ANCh.

During the October strike, the Communist Party put out two issues of *Mujeres Chilenas*, a newspaper designed to garner public sympathy by relaying images of women and children suffering under government repression. The publication denounced the arrests and deportations of women such as Blanca Sánchez and Eusebia Torres, and told the story of national Communist leader Julieta Campusano, who entered premature labor and delivered her first child in police custody.[91] The paper also heralded the formation of a national Committee of Solidarity with the Women and Children of the Coal Mining Zone.

Without the separate lists that were likely produced, it is impossible to know the total number of women deported from the coal mining region or other parts of the country. Moreover, the lists discussed above do not include people exiled from smaller mining towns in the department of Concepción, such as Lirquén and Cosmito.[92] Adding all the cases of exiled persons who were *not* named on the November 30 list to the nine hundred who *were* named brings the total very close to James Bell's estimate of 1,500 to 1,800 people. What the Bell Report does not make clear, however, is that each of these people traveled with an average of four family members, which raises the total to between 6,000 and 7,000 people removed from the zone.

Smaller lists of detainees to be exiled continued to appear after the submission of the Bell Report in late December, all produced by military authorities and all worded just like Decree no. 14. Decree no. 15, issued by Hoffman Hansen on January 2, 1948, lists twenty-four men, twenty-three from Lota and one from Coronel.[93] Though the document itself does not indicate why these people were being exiled, cross-referencing the names with other evidence helps us understand whom the military was targeting. Froilán Sánchez Sánchez, for example, was a Communist city council member in Coronel from 1944 to 1947.[94] And Carmen Alarcón Romero had headed the Communist Party's electoral committee in Lota for González Videla's presidential campaign.[95] Decree no. 17, of February 23, 1948, also

91. Among the many sources relating Julieta Campusano's story, see, for example, Neruda, "Intimate Letter," in *Passions*, 275.

92. Since the department of Coronel was the only part of the province of Concepción included in the November 30 decree, other decrees must have been issued during the course of the strike to expand the area prohibited to the relegados; otherwise, it would have been impossible for people from Lirquén to have been deported, as other evidence clearly indicates they were.

93. Decree no. 15, January 2, 1948, issued by Concepción-Arauco Emergency Zone Chief Alfredo Hoffman Hansen, Talcahuano, FIC, vol. 2364, ANCh.

94. Dirección del Registro Electoral, municipal election results, 1944, SERCh.

95. *El Siglo*, August 5, 1946, 2.

issued by Hoffman Hansen, names six people from Chiguayante, Coronel, and Lirquén, including Juan Lorenzo Córdova Beltrán, a Communist leader of the Lota miners' union back in 1942, when he was arrested during the October 7 clash with police.[96]

Extrapolating from all available sources gives a total of at least seven thousand people exiled from the coal mining zone in the five months from October 1947 through February 1948. Just under half these people were from Lota, with a population of about forty thousand, which means that one in every twelve city residents was forcibly removed and banished from the region.[97] Other estimates given at the time were even higher: Communist Deputy César Godoy, for example, stated that ten thousand coal mining zone residents had been deported.[98] Around the country, other areas had also been declared emergency zones, and some observers estimated that nationwide fifteen thousand people or more were arrested, banished from their homes, and blacklisted from employment.[99]

In the coal mining towns, whenever a worker who resided in company housing was arrested, the family was given a maximum of eight days to vacate the house, which would then be turned over to strikebreakers.[100] Usually with no other sources of income, the evicted women and children would be forced to migrate to growing city slums or to live with relatives in the countryside; at times, they would follow their husbands and fathers to places of internment or exile—including the "concentration camp" at Pisagua. The disruptions of community life in the coal mining

96. Decree no. 17, February 23, 1948, issued by Concepción-Arauco Emergency Zone Chief Hoffman Hansen, Talcahuano, FIC, vol. 2364, ANCh. There was likely a Decree no. 16, which I did not come across. Córdova Beltrán is mentioned as a leader of the Lota miners' union in all of the following sources: El Sur, July 3, 1941, 13; La Época, July 11, 1942, 5; Díaz Iturrieta, "Historia"; El Sur, October 8, 1942, 7; El Siglo, October 8, 1942, 1; El Sur, October 10, 1942, 12. The other two men from Chiguayante, Carlos H. Rodriguez Leal and Manuel Riffo Stuardo, may have been previously deported from the zone, as a result of the January-February 1946 strike, but the source referring to this deportation does not provide full names. Resoluciones del Consejo Provincial de la CTCh de Concepción, June 26, 1946, FIC, vol. 2333, ANCh. Both of the men from Coronel are on the LDPD list.

97. In the 1940 Census, the comuna of Lota had 34,445 residents, and in the 1952 Census, 45,411 residents. For the smaller city of Lota, the Bell Report gives a 1947 population estimate of 23,000. Bell Report, 4.

98. César Godoy Urrutia, Acusación Constitucional Against Holger, Chamber of Deputies Session, November 4, 1947, 577, BCNCh. Because the lists I extrapolated from are incomplete, Godoy Urrutia's estimate of ten thousand may well be closer to the actual number.

99. See the 1951 pamphlet El Estado policial o la Ley de Defensa de la Democracia by the Comité Nacional de Solidaridad y Defensa de las Libertades Públicas (National Committee for Solidarity and the Defense of Civil Liberties).

100. Barrios Tirado, in González Videla, Memorias, 1:662.

zone were thus immense, as railroad cars packed with detainees and ex- iled families headed out of the region en masse and incoming trains brought campesinos to work in the mines under military guard.

Last Stand in the Coal Mines and Confrontation in the Halls of Congress

With manhunts, arrests, and mass deportations under way, the strikers who remained in the region began to drift back to work, joining up in the coal pits with the "merluzas con banda" and other strikebreakers, such as the Socialists sent by Bernardo Ibáñez. Observing these diverse groups working under tight military control, James Bell wrote, "By October 20, it appeared that the measures outlined above had succeeded in ending the strike. Production was approaching normal at Lota, and the Schwager mine was working."[101] Defense Minister Barrios Tirado con- firmed that "in Coronel "on [October] 16th, more than 2,500 men showed up for the 2 P.M. shift, and on the 20th, work continued and achieved near normal production."[102] Having in large part been forced back to work, the miners now engaged in a final protest. On October 21, about 2,000 miners at Schwager and 600 at Lirquén took over the mines: they refused to leave at the end of their shifts and used dynamite explosions to repel the mili- tary troops sent to dislodge them. By acting out so violently and demand- ing that all political prisoners be released and all military forces leave the region, the workers made it clear that taking over the mines was not about their contract petitions, but about the trampling of their demo- cratic rights.

Accounts of how this final protest ended vary widely. According to the official Army history, twenty-four-year-old Lieutenant Eleodoro Neu- mann went down into the Schwager coal pit with about fifty soldiers to forcibly remove the miners.[103] Meeting with strong resistance, which

101. Bell Report, 20.

102. Guillermo Barrios Tirado, Chamber of Deputies Session, October 29, 1947, 514, BCNCh.

103. The official Army account of the October 21 Schwager mine occupation quotes from several interviews with Lieutenant Neumann, and González Videla's *Memoirs* include a lengthy excerpt from the lieutenant's report to the president. Both sources also mention that González Videla decorated Lieutenant Neumann and his soldiers at a formal ceremony in the city of Chillán on November 16, 1947. Estado Mayor General del Ejército de Chile, *Historia*, 51–54; González Videla, *Memorias*, 669–75. Other accounts citing Army Lieutenant Neumann as the hero of the day include Bravo Ríos, *Lo que supo*, 189–92; Bell Report, 20; and *El Sur*, October 22, 1947, 1. Barríos Tirado, speaking to Congress, also described the episode, but did not name the "valiant officer" who led fifty soldiers into the Schwager mine. Guil-

included explosions of dynamite, the troops retreated to the surface, where they pumped tear gas into the ventilation system. When the miners emerged, dizzy and choking, military officers screened them and arrested more than two hundred "leaders of the movement." As the Bell Report states, "They were charged with being a Communist terrorist group referred to by Government officials as the 'Cheka.' Handbills urging a sit-down strike were found on some miners."[104] Armando González Uribe was one of the men arrested as part of this alleged "Cheka." His daughter, Julia González Figueroa, describes what took place:

> The miners crossed their arms and threw themselves into a sit-down strike inside the mine. . . . After [the soldiers] started to throw down [tear gas], the miners had to leave, to get out of the pits, and at the exit, they were there arresting them, those they were most familiar with, those who were most combative, who participated in the assemblies, who spoke out, all those they took away to the Navy ships. . . . They held them about three or four days without eating, without water, without anything, without beds, sleeping on the floor.[105]

On board the Navy destroyer *Araucano*, one of the men responsible for interrogating the arrested Schwager miners was Admiral Fernando Campos Harriet. What is most notable in his own account of this experience is that, unlike those who were not there, such as González Videla and Ambassador Bowers, Campos Harriet made no mention of the Communist Party, or any other political motives for the strike. To the contrary,

---

lermo Barríos Tirado, Chamber of Deputies Session, October 29, 1947, 514, BCNCh. Other credible accounts, however, say that it was Navy Captain Oscar Manzano Villablanca who led a contingent of Navy troops into the Schwager mine. See, for example, Pedro Opitz Velásquez, Senate Session, November 4, 1947, 431, BNCh. According to retired Navy officer Manuel Chamorro Moreno, González Videla awarded Captain Manzano a Medal of Honor on November 6, 1947, for his brave leadership during the mine occupation. Also awarded Medals of Honor were several men who accompanied Captain Manzano, including First Lieutenant Mariano Campos Menchaca, who, in 1952, would be named by the CCIL Board of Directors to replace Octavio Astorquiza as head of the company's Welfare Department. See Manuel Chamorro Moreno, "Histórico reconocimiento presidencial" (November 22, 2004) and "Vicealmirante Hugo Castro Jiménez" (July 24, 2009), in Fundación Mar de Chile, http://www.mardechile.cl/ (accessed July 2010). Although no accounts discuss the Lirquén mine occupation in such detail, James Bell reported that "no attempt was made to evict [the miners there]" and that they "voluntarily came to the surface after about 48 hours without food." Bell Report, 20.

104. Bell Report, 20.

105. Interview with Julia González Figueroa.

he explicitly stated that the upheaval in the coal mining zone was due to the workers' "demand . . . for an improvement of their economic situation." After recounting the sequence of events, Campos Harriet described his reaction to the physical appearance of the miners he interrogated:

> From all that, there's something I can't forget since it offended my sensibilities as a native of Concepción. When I asked the age of the detainees, most, to my astonishment, confessed to being 20, 22, or 24. They gave the appearance of being much older. Their pallor [and] bad teeth were striking. Since then, I have thought that if there were any privileged class in Chile, it should be the coal mine workers, who do not even enjoy that unique natural treasure—the only one that Socrates required—just a little bit of sunlight.[106]

The comments of Admiral Campos Harriet reveal what Chilean sociologist Jorge Marambio describes as a "double discourse," in which the coal miners were seen as at once heroic, to be honored by the nation, and undisciplined, thus "subject to permanent repression."[107] Even sympathetic views varied widely, with some emphasizing the miners' strength, productivity, and boldness, and others, their victimization and martyrdom. On the one hand, the coal miners were heroes of the working-class struggle, of national production and bourgeois development, of democratization, and of many political campaigns. And, on the other hand, they were victims of Communist demagoguery, of ignorance, poverty, and debauchery, and of capitalist exploitation and government repression.

Many stories told of the October 1947 strike bring to life what Marambio described as "this classic identity" of the coal miners as it developed within the national imagination—productive heroes, beleaguered victims, *and* dangerous Reds. It is in this vein that we can best understand the numerous accounts that characterize the October strike as entirely political, orchestrated by the Communist Party, while also acknowledging the coal miners' grievances as legitimate. The recollections of General Leonidas Bravo Ríos, a military judge involved in these events, convey just such a double discourse: "The 4th of October, the Communist Party initiated the great offensive with which it tried to bring down the government through a strike in Lota and Coronel." Yet, having thus explained the strike, on the same page, Bravo Ríos goes on to say that "the living

106. Campos Harriet, *Historia de Concepción*, 272.
107. Marambio, *Identidad cultural*, 78–79.

conditions of the Lota workers were shameful, which drew sympathy toward them from everyone who knew the state of things. General Jorge Berguño, in [his] thorough and useful [1941] report issued at the request of a previous government, had deliberated thoroughly on this subject, but instead of addressing [his] conclusions . . . a political discussion developed around it, and nothing was done. Now those affected were trying to demand what should have been given to them out of good will."[108]

For their part, the Communists were outraged at the repression unleashed in the coal mining zone, and they engaged in one last protest against the tide of events. On October 28, a week after the Schwager mine occupation, which brought the strike to an end, ten Communist national deputies introduced an *acusación constitucional* (constitutional accusation) against Interior Minister Holger Torres.[109] The deputies also condemned the actions of Defense Minister Barrios Tirado but they did not formally initiate proceedings against him. "Our accusation," they wrote, "is directed against the Minister of the Interior, Sr. Holger, exclusively in his character as a direct representative of the Executive charged with overseeing the maintenance of public order, although we recognize that the principal responsibility lies with the Minister of National Defense because of the way that the so-called emergency zones are being applied."[110] In two long subsequent sessions, the deputies grappled with different accounts of events in the coal mining region the previous month. In the process, they found themselves engaged in a fierce debate about "the history of humanity, the fundamental values of human beings, and the meaning of

108. Bravo Ríos, *Lo que supo*, 187. In his capacity as legal adviser for the armed forces (*auditor de guerra*), General Bravo Ríos not only advised on the interpretation and application of laws, but also at times served as judge.

109. Acusación Constitucional Against Holger Torres, Chamber of Deputies Session, October 28, 1947, 418–22, BCNCh. An acusación constitucional in Chile was "a constitutional procedure similar to, but not exactly equivalent to, impeachment in the U.S. constitutional system." Loveman and Lira, "Truth," 52. Among other differences, an acusación constitucional could be introduced up to six months after an official left office, and it could lead to criminal prosecution. On the history of the acusación constitucional procedure in Chile, dating back to the Spanish *residencias* and nineteenth-century Chilean constitutions, see Loveman and Lira, *Las acusaciones*, esp. 7–10. Loveman and Lira provide a detailed discussion of many significant acusaciones constitucionales in Chilean history, including one in 1939 brought against former president Arturo Alessandri Palma, for violating the Constitution during his handling of the September 5, 1938, Nazi youth occupation of the Workers' Insurance Fund building (see chapter 3). Because "bill of impeachment" is not an exact equivalent to the Chilean acusación constitucional, I follow the lead of Loveman and Lira and use the Spanish term.

110. Acusación Constitucional Against Holger Torres, Chamber of Deputies Session, October 28, 1947, 418, BCNCh.

patriotism."[111] Finally, on November 5, 1947, the Chamber of Deputies rejected the acusación constitucional by a vote of 91 to 16, with 8 abstentions.[112]

While Holger Torres was defending the government's actions in the halls of Congress, González Videla and First Lady Rosa Markmann headed south to Temuco on October 30 to attend an agriculture and livestock exposition. Accompanying the presidential couple were Defense Minister Barrios Tirado and his wife, as well as several national deputies and senators. Speaking to crowds largely of rural landowners, González Videla railed against international Communist plots in Chile and stressed that the threat to the nation justified recent drastic measures. Whose approval or absolution was he seeking for his actions? Certainly, the president had heard from emergency zone officials that walls and railroad cars throughout the coal mining zone were covered with the epithet "Gabriela González de Truman," despite the high risk activists ran painting graffiti under military occupation. Rationally, the president may well have expected such hostility, but the news that he was now portrayed as the wife of a yanqui imperialist could not have been easy to accept,[113] especially when he recalled his campaign experiences in Lota and Schwager, where tens of thousands of people had cheered him and given him flowers and loaves of miner's bread.

During the trip south, González Videla told Defense Minister Barrios Tirado of his decision to visit the coal mining zone "to make contact with the miners and the people" and to show he was not afraid to go to "a place he knew was hostile to him." Barrios Tirado thought the president's plan was imprudent and tried to talk him out of it. Security for his life could not be guaranteed, the defense minister said, if the president set foot "where there existed such deep wounds [and] such intense hatred directed against him personally."[114] González Videla would not be dissuaded; he scheduled a visit to Lota and Coronel for November 3. The president's arrival took almost everyone by surprise because only top

111. Loveman and Lira, *Las ardientes cenizas*, 123. The debates themselves are in Chamber of Deputies Sessions, November 4, 1947, 558–82, and November 5, 1947, 589–625, BCNCh.

112. For the final vote on the acusación constitucional against Holger Torres, see Chamber of Deputies Session, November 5, 1947, 625, BCNCh. The sixteen votes in favor were cast by thirteen Communists and three National Falange deputies.

113. Bell Report, 15n2. The "de Truman" in "Gabriela González de Truman" refers to the customary form of the husband's name taken by a Chilean woman when she marries. In her recent study of the nitrate mining region, Lessie Jo Frazier documents that the slogan "Videla de Truman" was also painted on walls in Iquique. Frazier, *Salt in the Sand*, 234n27.

114. Barrios Tirado, in González Videla, *Memorias*, 1:665.

emergency zone officials had been forewarned. Surrounded by security forces, González Videla delivered four different speeches, each to several thousand people. No violent attacks or major incidents occurred, although, as Barrios Tirado observed, the president was besieged by desperate, weeping women "whose family members had been deported and imprisoned [and] who refused to leave the zone, convinced that their husbands would soon return."[115] In his first speech, delivered in Lota from the back of a jeep, the president said he regretted that he had been forced to take extreme measures, but that when the security of the Republic was threatened by foreign intrigues, he would never hesitate to defend it. "The Chilean worker," he told them, "is deceived and is serving a foreign power; therefore, the Communists who serve those interests will be dealt with as traitors to the nation [la patria]."[116] He exhorted the workers to free themselves from their bondage to professional agitators and to work hard at their jobs in full confidence that, as paraphrased by Astorquiza and Galleguillos, "the Government would see to their increasing advances in the field of social gains."[117]

After lunching with military personnel in Lota, González Videla went to the Pique Grande mine shaft, where he spoke to about 3,000 workers who had just finished the second shift. From there, he went on to the Schwager mine head in Coronel, where he also spoke to workers during their shift change. Radical Senator Pedro Opitz Velásquez, who was among the president's entourage, remarked that even though the Schwager miners lived and worked in better conditions than their Lota counterparts, most remained "impassive," and some were openly hostile. "At no time," Opitz reported, "did anyone applaud the president's words, even though he explained to them the reason for the measures that had been taken and the benefits they had gained with his return-to-work decree[s]."[118] Later in the afternoon, González Videla gave another address, described by the defense minister as "the most vehement [el más violento] of his speeches against Communism." During his visit to Coronel, González Videla also met personally with Lieutenant Neumann, who had gone down into the Schwager mine during the workers' last-ditch takeover on October 21. The president thanked Neumann for his heroic service to the

115. Ibid.,1:666. Astorquiza describes González Videla's speech on an improvised stage in front of the Matías Cousiño School in Astorquiza and Galleguillos V., Cien años, 139. See also Senate Session, November 4, 1947, 430–38, BCNCh; and Bell Report, 25, 49.
116. Gabriel González Videla, as quoted by Barrios Tirado, in González Videla, Memorias, 1:667–68.
117. Astorquiza and Galleguillos V., Cien años, 139.
118. Pedro Opitz Velásquez, Senate Session, November 4, 1947, 431, BCNCh.

nation. In Barrios Tirado's estimation, the president's visit to Lota and Coronel was a complete success because he "demonstrated to the people his strength [*su virilidad*] and his personal concern for resolving the problems of the working class."[119]

One month later, on December 5, 1947, González Videla traveled to Concepción, just 30 kilometers (some 20 miles) north of Coronel, on the edge of the Bío-Bío River, which served as the military control point for passage into and out of the coal mining region. From the balcony of the provincial government building (Intendencia), the president once again beseeched the "deceived" and "manipulated" workers to recognize that they had become pawns of international Communism. He stressed that his administration "had never authorized" repressive actions "against the deceived and exploited masses," but only against the "responsible militants of the Communist Party." Yet he quickly added that "some mistakes [may] have been made, given the extraordinarily threatening circumstances in which the measures are being carried out." Any such mistakes, he insisted, would be immediately rectified.[120]

To absolve his administration of responsibility for using state violence to control domestic social forces, the president shifted the blame to the burgeoning international conflict that would soon become known as the "Cold War." Only in this way could the repression of the coal mining communities be presented as a crucial measure of state security. "Because I love Democracy and Freedom," he said, "because my fundamental duty is to preserve and maintain for Chile this regime of freedom, I will not hesitate for an instant to oppose force with force, to destroy at its very outset any new attempt at aggression that originates beyond our borders. The President of the Republic has the absolute certainty, as this massive demonstration proves, that the whole country supports his action in defense of the Republic, of social peace, and of the working class itself."[121]

In delivering such a speech, González Videla may still have hoped to save face with his former working-class and leftist supporters by convincing them that his actions stemmed from the highest principles, shared by all. More likely, however, the president intended his words for middle- and even upper-class Chileans, including many of his fellow Radicals,

119. Barrios Tirado, in González Videla, *Memorias*, 1:666.

120. Gabriel González Videla, "To the People of Concepción: Defense Against the Actions of the Communist Party," speech delivered from the balcony of the Concepción provincial government building (Intendencia), December 5, 1947, Document no. 5, FGGV, vol. 99, 153–96, ANCh.

121. Ibid.

who had come to believe in the midcentury project of democratization and who were now dismayed at their leader's antidemocratic turn. Gonzá-lez Videla was moved to defend himself as a man of integrity and to claim that "the whole country" supported his actions. In language similar to what Chilean dictator Augusto Pinochet would use after the coup of September 11, 1973, González Videla declared, "It is not, then, the President of Chile who has betrayed the Chilean people [but the Communists]. What he has done is to energetically prevent International Communism from spreading general chaos to secure the triumph of its hidden agenda of unconditional support for Soviet political, military, and economic interests."[122] As González Videla's actions came under increasing attack, rather than moderate his anti-leftist, anti-labor measures, he intensified them. Chapter 10 provides a glimpse at the human suffering and political consequences of Gonzalez's Videla's assault on a significant segment of the Chilean people.

122. Ibid.

DEMOCRACY UNDER SIEGE:
GONZÁLEZ VIDELA'S "DAMNED LAW," INTERNMENT CAMPS,
AND MASS DEPORTATIONS

In the decade leading up to the 1946 presidential campaign, Gabriel González Videla earned a reputation as one of the most progressive leaders of
the Radical Party. He had staunchly defended the Communists' participation in Chilean political and social life and had consistently promoted
Center-Left alliances. Yet less than a year after winning the presidency
with crucial Communist backing, González Videla turned sharply against
striking coal miners and their Communist leaders. When diverse actors—
from the National Falange, the Socialist Party, and even his own Radical
Party—voiced mounting alarm at what they perceived as the president's
antidemocratic measures, rather than moderate his position, González
Videla intensified his assault. Perhaps it was because his actions in late
1947 contrasted so sharply with his long-held principles that he felt he
had to assert his new stance with full force. In mid-1948, he secured passage of one of the most draconian anti-Communist laws in the Americas:
the Law for the Permanent Defense of Democracy (LDPD). People across
the political spectrum, including many who had supported the repression
of the coal miners' strike, strongly condemned this legislation. In the
wake of González Videla's abrupt turn to the Right in the late 1940s, both
he and his party fell into such extreme "political ostracism" that neither
would ever fully recover.[1]

1. González Videla himself used the phrase "political ostracism" to describe his life
from 1953 to 1973, in a section of his memoirs entitled "Abandoning My Political Ostracism."

The choices made by González Videla in the early postwar years stood in sharp contrast to those of another longtime progressive politician, former U.S. Vice President Henry A. Wallace, who played a significantly different role in the emerging Cold War context. In the years after his March 1943 visit to Chile and other Latin American republics, Wallace repeatedly warned of the dangers of hard-line anti-Communism for world peace and social justice. His message was highly controversial, especially in light of President Truman's increasingly belligerent stance toward the Soviet Union. In 1946, while González Videla stood side by side with Communists in his campaign for the presidency, then–Secretary of Commerce Wallace was publicly denouncing Truman's anti-Soviet line. In early September, as voters went to the polls in Chile, Wallace spoke at a meeting of labor organizations in Mexico, where he again insisted on a progressive definition of democracy: "We do believe in the common man. We do believe in the people. . . . We believe that in democracy, properly understood, sovereignty comes directly from the people, and therefore a good government is one which will serve the interests of the people."[2]

A week later, back in the United States, Wallace delivered what has been described as "one of the most explosive speeches in American political history"—his "Way to Peace" address on September 12 at Madison Square Garden, which amounted to a full-scale indictment of Truman's foreign policy.[3] Ironically, on the same day, Ambassador Bowers sent a telegram to President Truman conveying González Videla's "earnest wish" that Henry Wallace be selected to represent the United States at his inauguration. The president-elect argued that Wallace's presence would undercut Communist propaganda against the United States since "the Chilean masses would never believe that Wallace was either an imperialist or a reactionary." Bowers endorsed the idea, emphasizing Wallace's extreme "popularity" among the "same working classes [that] had elected González Videla."[4] U.S. Ambassador to Argentina George Messersmith,

---

This is part of a larger section, "Twenty Years Later: Historical Vindication of My Presidential Term," which he sees to have occurred with the military overthrow of Salvador Allende's Marxist government. González Videla, *Memorias*, 2:1239–63. González Videla's controversial actions and what some might describe as his "disgrace," were key factors in the Radical Party's decline. Also significant were the exhaustion of import substitution industrialization (ISI) strategies and the party's image as a network of corrupt politicians connected to powerful economic sectors. Indeed, Carlos Ibáñez would win the 1952 elections as a populist, above partisan politics, waving a broom to sweep out Radical corruption.

2. Henry A. Wallace, as quoted in Schapsmeier and Schapsmeier, *Prophet in Politics*, 149.

3. Walton, *Henry Wallace*, 100.

4. Hrenchir, "Claude G. Bowers," 257.

and many others, strongly disagreed, arguing that an official visit by Wallace to Chile would signal "that the United States gave a blessing to the extreme left that supported González Videla." The matter was soon eclipsed, however, by fallout from the "Way to Peace" speech: on September 20, an outraged President Truman asked Wallace to resign from his cabinet. Truman then sent his chief of staff and chairman of the Joint Chiefs of Staff, Admiral William Leahy, who "arrived in Chile along with the American fleet," to attend the inauguration.[5]

As close as they had been ideologically and strategically in the fall of 1946, just one year later, the positions of Wallace and González Videla diverged dramatically. González Videla threw in his lot with U.S. hardliners, and the epithet "Gabriela González de Truman" appeared on walls throughout the coal and nitrate mining towns, then under military control. Wallace, on the other hand, made the difficult decision to break with the Democrats and run for president on the Progressive Party ticket. In his 1948 campaign, he called for an end to the House Committee on Un-American Activities, which was investigating alleged Communist infiltration of labor unions and government agencies.

Had Henry Wallace won the presidency, the Cold War as we know it would likely never have been waged, and González Videla's moves against Chilean Communists and workers would have been internationally condemned. Though, in the end, Wallace garnered only 2.4 percent of the vote, his story highlights an alternative path open to González Videla. Even as many international voices were calling for escalation of the U.S.-Soviet conflict, Wallace and his followers remained committed to the ideal of global peace based on socioeconomic justice. González Videla's actions in 1947–48 were not historically inevitable. By brutally reversing the progress toward greater social and political inclusion, they brought Chilean democracy to a crisis, not for the first time, but in a way that would mark the rest of the twentieth century.

The Law for the Permanent Defense of Democracy: "An Atomic Bomb Dropped [on] Our Republican Principles, Habits, and Customs"

In April 1948, six months after the fierce repression of the coal miners' strike, President González Videla and Interior Minister Immanuel Holger Torres submitted a bill to the Chamber of Deputies called the "Law for

5. Ibid., 257–58, 259, 260.

the Permanent Defense of Democracy" (Ley de Defensa Permanente de la Democracia; LDPD).[6] The proposed legislation targeted the president's former allies—those whose votes had carried him into office and whom he now described as "the Stalinist Communist Party, which, in name of Soviet imperialism and with the absence of even the most basic patriotism, seeks to subordinate the country to the interests of a foreign power."[7] The president and other proponents of the LDPD argued that existing internal state security laws were insufficient to combat the intrigues of international Communism on Chilean soil. They cited the threat of "civil wars and Communist uprisings, as had occurred in Paraguay, Costa Rica, and Colombia, which was the danger [the government] thought it saw in the October 1947 coal miners' strike, since the world was facing constant war by the 'invisible armies of traitors to democracy.'"[8]

The LDPD bill proposed a series of drastic measures designed to destroy the Chilean Communist Party and to prevent the recurrence of anything remotely like what Chilean scholar Tomás Moulian described as a "plebeian irruption."[9] After nearly a month of heated debate, on May 12, the Chamber of Deputies approved the bill by a vote of 93 to 20, with 1 abstention.[10] Those opposed were the Communists, the National Falange, the majority of the Socialists, who would soon form the Popular Socialist Party (PSP), and a few renegade Radicals. Those voting in favor were the Conservatives, the Liberals, the majority of the Radicals, some Socialists, and (however tentatively) members of the Agrarian Labor Party. The Popular Front era, it seemed, was coming to a definitive and inglorious end

6. Good sources on the Law for the Permanent Defense of Democracy (LDPD) include Huentemilla Carrasco, "Antecedentes de la Ley"; Trabucco Godoy, *Tesis sobre la Ley*; Miranda Casanova, *Los delitos en la Ley*; Mera Figueroa, González, and Vargas Vivanco, "Función judicial"; Bopp Blu, "La Ley," Caffarena de Jiles, *El recurso*, and Daire Tolmo, "Derogación de la Ley."

7. Gabriel González Videla, Message to Congress, Chamber of Deputies Session, April 21, 1948. See González Videla, *Mensaje* (1948), 5.

8. Huentemilla Carrasco, "Antecedentes de la Ley," 122, quoting from Chamber of Deputies Session, April 21, 1948, 6, BCNCh. Paraguay was racked by civil war from March to August 1947 as a coalition including Liberals and Communists sought to keep hard-line military forces from assuming power. The Costa Rican civil war, caused by a dispute over presidential elections in March–April 1948, was the bloodiest episode in the country's history, even though it lasted only forty-four days. In Colombia, the murder of populist presidential candidate Jorge Eliécer Gaitán on April 9, 1948, set off mass rioting and police repression, known as the "Bogotazo," which led to a decade of violence ("La Violencia"), in which hundreds of thousands of Colombians were killed.

9. The concept of "plebeian irruption," which comes from Moulian, "Líneas estratégicas," 11, is discussed in the final paragraphs of the introduction.

10. Chamber of Deputies Session, May 12, 1948, 215, BCNCh. See also Loveman and Lira, *Las ardientes cenizas*, 125–32; and Trabucco Godoy, *Tesis sobre la Ley*, 195–97.

at the hands of one of its earliest and most ardent proponents, Gabriel González Videla, who had played a key role in bringing together the original coalition back in April 1938.[11]

As the bill moved to the Senate, debates about the LDPD raged far beyond the halls of Congress. In late June, at the height of Senate deliberations, the "Most Serene Great Leader" of the Chilean Masons, Orestes Frödden Lorenzen, wrote directly to President González Videla, a fellow Mason, condemning his actions as undemocratic.[12] Frödden Lorenzen was an engineer who had served in the Navy and worked in nitrate mining, for Westinghouse Electric, and in the state-owned railroad. He came from a powerful Concepción family of Radical Party supporters.[13] In his letter, he summarized the principles of Freemasonry with regard to politics,

11. On the Popular Front Convention of 1938 and González Videla's role in it, see chapter 3.

12. The Chilean Masonic Lodge published the June 1948 exchange of letters between Frödden Lorenzen and González Videla as a pamphlet later in the year. In an epilogue, they included letters about the Chilean situation from Masons in Mexico, Cuba, Colombia, and Panama, all of which glossed over the substantive conflict and heralded the democratic virtue of such a healthy exchange of views, "overflowing with pure patriotism." In essence, the Masons promoted reconciliation, claiming that now, five months after the initial communication between Frödden Lorenzen and González Videla, "a certain calm and tranquility has been achieved in the spirit of our fellow citizens, which is promising for the restoration of the order threatened by those who would trample the lofty ideals of patriotism and democracy for their petty, shameful interests." Frödden Lorenzen and González Videla, "Defensa de la democracia," 2–3.

13. Orestes Frödden Lorenzen was born in Concepción in 1892. After studying engineering at the Naval Academy, he worked as an electrical and mechanical engineer for the nation's largest brewery and then for the state-owned railroad. His family had previously lived in the coal mining region. His older brother, Carlos, was born in Coronel and attended school in Lebu for a number of years. Carlos later joined the Marines and eventually became a top-ranked admiral. After serving both as interior minister and as defense minister under Carlos Ibáñez in the early 1930s, Carlos T. Frödden Lorenzen retired from the Marines in 1941. In the same year, he became an advisor to the CORFO, and was then appointed vice president of the agency after 1952. *Diccionario biográfico* (1949), 448–49; *Diccionario biográfico* (1967), 540.

Orestes and Carlos Frödden Lorenzen were first cousins of another prestigious trio of siblings in the Concepción area—Humberto, Inés, and Edgardo Enríquez Frödden, who were also Masons and distinguished members of the Radical Party. Humberto was born in Concepción in 1907. After heading González Videla's presidential campaign in the region and then serving as his first education minister, Humberto was elected national deputy from the region from 1949 to 1961 and senator from 1961 to 1969. He was president of the Radical Party in 1965. Inés (de Saez) was the intendant of Concepción in 1950, and then, in 1951, she became the first woman in the country elected to the Chamber of Deputies from the Concepción region. Their brother, Edgardo, a prestigious medical doctor and rector at the University of Concepción, was the father of Miguel and Edgardo Enríquez, two of the founders of the Revolutionary Left Movement (MIR), who were killed by the military after the coup of 1973. See the three-volume autobiographical work by Enríquez Frödden, *En el nombre*.

emphasizing its fundamental belief in democratic rights, he then explained to González Videla how the proposed LDPD contravened these principles, especially its Transitory Article 2, which eliminated members of the Chilean Communist Party from electoral registers, thereby "depriv-[ing] them of the right of citizenship."[14] Frödden Lorenzen argued that "the elimination of a group of our fellow countrymen from the exercise of their natural rights and from the citizenship conferred on them by their free birth, in a free land, under the protection of a libertarian regime of government, that is to say, under the jurisdiction of a Democracy, contravenes the fundamental principles of Freemasonry: freedom of thought, political tolerance, universalist humanitarianism, ethical liberalism, philosophical relativism."[15]

González Videla was clearly concerned about losing the moral, social, and political backing of the Grand Mason.[16] He sent a reply just a week later trying to convince Frödden Lorenzen that the extent of Communist intrigue and insurgence justified his actions as a necessary *defense* of Chilean democracy. He pointed out that Communist agitators had resorted to "the most dreadful of all strikes" when they forcibly occupied the Schwager and Lirquén mines, even though these were last-ditch protests staged after the region had been under military control for nearly three weeks. González Videla defended the "rapid and energetic measures" he had taken in the face of this "grave danger," but he also stressed "the care with which the repression of the strike was organized," so that it had not been necessary "to employ violence against anyone."[17] He was seeking exoneration, it seems, by tacitly comparing his mode of repression with much more violent episodes in Chilean history, such as the 1907 Santa María de Iquique massacre, when President Pedro Elías Montt (1906–10), who also drew on working-class support for his election, ordered security forces to fire on striking nitrate miners.[18]

González Videla faced sharp criticism from other leading members of the Radical Party as well, including Raúl Rettig Guissen, who, back in October 1942, had been commissioned by President Ríos Morales to investigate the killing of miners by police at a public rally in Lota.[19] Together

14. Frödden Lorenzen and González Videla, "Defensa de la democracia," 16.

15. Ibid., 17.

16. Not only were González Videla and Frödden Lorenzen Freemasons, but so, too, were many crucial political actors across the globe in these years, including Franklin D. Roosevelt, Winston Churchill, Harry S Truman, and Henry A. Wallace, as well as Chileans Raúl Rettig, Salvador Allende, and many others.

17. Frödden Lorenzen and González Videla, "Defensa de la democracia," 38, 39.

18. See Devés, *Los que van a morir*; and Frazier, *Salt in the Sand*, chap. 4.

19. In 1948, thirty-nine-year-old Raúl Rettig Guissen had been a member of the Radical Party for seventeen years, including a period as president of the Concepción Assembly. Born

with several of his colleagues, Rettig met with González Videla a number of times to warn him "about the dangers inherent in dictating this law in such an extreme form."[20] Their efforts were unsuccessful, however, and once it became clear that the Executive was determined to push the law through, "party discipline was imposed," defied by only two Radical senators, who abstained from voting. "Fortunately," Rettig recalled in a later interview, "I did not have to vote for the law . . . since I was not yet a Senator."[21]

Openly opposing the bill was Raúl Rettig's good friend, Communist Senator Pablo Neruda, joined by other Communist and National Falange politicians, as well as several Socialists, including Marmaduke Grove and Salvador Allende, who had tentatively supported the repression of the coal miners' strike six months before. In a lengthy speech on the Senate floor just days before the vote, Allende—also a Freemason—stressed that the Socialist Party had been "the most tenacious and constant adversary of the Communists." Thus it was not out of some kind of Marxist camaraderie that Socialists denounced the proposed law, but rather, Allende explained, because the LDPD "violates the fundamental bases that sustain the democratic organization of the country." Drawing on potent imagery from the recent World War, Allende continued, "I maintain, Sr. President [of the Senate], that the initiative of the Executive is an atomic bomb dropped in the midst of our republican principles, habits, and customs." The Socialists, he added, were keenly aware that they could easily be the next target of such a law.[22]

One of the most surprising opponents of the bill was former Vice President Alfredo Duhalde Vásquez, who had moved decisively against Communist-led workers in January 1946, at the time of the Plaza Bulnes massacre and the ensuing general strike. Going into the 1946 elections, when the majority of the Radical Party opted for the leftist candidacy of

---

in Temuco, as was Pablo Neruda, the two men became fast friends, despite their political differences. Rettig, a lawyer by profession, worked in government throughout the Popular Front decade. He served as deputy interior minister in 1938–39, as an official in the Ministry of Foreign Relations in 1940, and as director of information and culture in 1942. He won a seat in the Chilean Senate in 1949 and became the president of the Radical Party in 1950. During the Salvador Allende's government (1970–73), Rettig was Chile's ambassador to Brazil, and, in the aftermath of the Pinochet dictatorship, he chaired the Truth and Reconciliation Commission.

20. Rettig Guissen, *Historia de un "bandido,"* 42.

21. Ibid., 42.

22. Salvador Allende Gossens, Senate Session, June 18, 1948, 722–23, BCNCh. This Senate speech is also available at the Archivos Salvador Allende, http://www.salvador-allende.cl/Documentos/1939-49/leymaldita.html/ (accessed July 2010).

Gabriel González Videla, Duhalde led a Right-leaning breakaway group, known as the "Democratic Radical Party," which now continued its strong opposition to González Videla, even though this meant opposing a law aimed at destroying the Chilean Communist Party.[23]

With such diverse criticism of the proposed LDPD, members of Congress worked to modify some of its more draconian aspects, limiting the acts punishable under the new law and defining "its concepts with greater legal precision."[24] On June 22, the Senate finally approved the bill, by a vote of 31 in favor, 8 opposed, and 2 abstentions.[25] With the passage of Law no. 8987, on September 3, 1948, not only was the Communist Party outlawed, but also some forty thousand people nationwide lost the right to vote, to participate in formal politics, and to belong to labor unions, thus being deprived of their basic rights both as citizens and as workers.[26] Nearly 15 percent of the disenfranchised hailed from the coal mining zone, a remarkable figure given that the region accounted for less than 3 percent of the nation's total population.[27] The zone was home to activist men and women who had supported the Communist Party and had contributed significantly both to the Popular Front project of the preceding decade and to González Videla's presidential election just two years before. This was a strategic locus in the country where transformative politics—public action aimed at fundamentally changing society—had taken firm root, and where a plebeian irruption seemed most imminent.

23. For views of the LDPD held by Democratic Radicals, see Ruiz Solar, Duhalde V., and Durán, *Análisis del mensaje*. The Democratic Radical Party, which dissolved in 1949, when its members rejoined the parent party, reemerged in 1970, in opposition to the Radicals' support of presidential candidate Salvador Allende.

24. Bowen Herrera, *Nuestro derecho*, 6.

25. The votes in the Senate in favor of the LDPD were cast by the Liberals, all but one of the Conservatives, most of the Radicals, all but one of the Democratic Radicals, the Agrarian Laborites, and one Socialist. Voting against the law were Communist Senators Contreras Labarca, Lafertte Gaviño, and Guevara Vargas, Socialist Senators Allende Gossens, Grove Vallejos, and Martínez Martínez, Conservative Senator Cruz-Coke Lassabe (leader of the Social Christian faction), and Democratic Radical Senator Duhalde Vásquez. Abstaining were Radical Senators Ortega Masson and Jirón Latapiat. See Trabucco Godoy, *Tesis sobre la Ley*; Gómez, *Factores nacionales*, 118; Loveman and Lira, *Las ardientes cenizas*, 127.

26. *Diario Oficial* published the LDPD on September 3, but the definitive text was in Supreme Decree no. 5839, of September 30. See Neruda, *Discursos parlamentarios*, 292. The number of people disenfranchised strictly by the LDPD was approximately 26,650, but the names of another 16,408 were removed in a clerical purging of the registers. These figures are further discussed below.

27. The 1952 Census gives the national population as 5,932,995. The combined population for the comunas of Coronel, Lota, Curanilahue, Lebu, Los Alamos, and Penco was 136,454, or 2.3 percent of the national population. Adding up the population of the departments of Coronel, Arauco, and Lebu, and the city of Penco gives a total of 161,245, or 2.7 percent of the national population.

The new legislation consolidated the Chilean government's anti-Communist position and its alignment with the United States in the burgeoning Cold War. As its name suggested, the law was intended to "permanently" eliminate all forms of disruptive agitation from Chilean national life. Referred to by opponents and leftist scholars as the "Damned Law" ("Ley Maldita"), the LDPD ushered in a shocking and often overlooked time of crisis in the history of twentieth-century Chilean democracy. After a decade of fighting for, and to some extent achieving, more inclusionary ideals and practices at the local and national levels, Chilean workers now faced a sudden and brutal contraction of the polity.

For the occasion of President González Videla's annual address to Congress on May 21, 1949, Ramón Zañartu, director of the National Electoral Registry, submitted a report describing how the LDPD was to be implemented.[28] The first step was to revoke the legal standing of both the Chilean Communist Party (PCCh) and the National Progressive Party (Partido Progresista Nacional), which was the alternate designation used by the Communists in elections before 1946. Zañartu had been given ten days from the date of the law to effect this revocation, but he issued the decree the very next day, September 4. As Zañartu's report explained, "the Communist Party was thus eliminated as a Political Party for all legal effects, and . . . would not be able to present candidates for any elected position, thereby preventing Communism from spreading its infamous propaganda in the [Congress] and from sheltering under constitutional protections."[29] This also meant that Communists who had been freely elected to local and regional positions in the coal mining region and throughout the country, including city council members and union officers, were forced to step down. Zañartu also declared vacant the Communists' twenty seats in Congress—five in the Senate and fifteen in the Chamber of Deputies—though he did not call for a special election, and their now empty seats were not filled until March 1949. By this act, then, the Executive nullified the expressed will of the electorate, a move that even many anti-Communist centrists perceived as a dangerous violation of democratic practices.

---

28. The report from the National Electoral Registry (Dirección del Registro Electoral) was included in the Interior Ministry Report appended to the published version of Gabriel González Videla, Message to Congress, May 21, 1949. See González Videla, *Mensaje* (1949), 36–40. This report was closely based on a series of memoranda written by Ramón Zañartu E. a few months earlier, "Partidos Politicos ante la Elección Ordinaria de Congreso Nacional en 6 de marzo de 1949," and attached oficios, SERCh.

29. National Electoral Registry Report, in González Videla, *Mensaje* (1949), 36.

Then, in a measure unprecedented anywhere in the Western hemisphere, the law gave the director of the Electoral Registry one hundred days to cancel the national and municipal voter registration of all current "members" of the Chilean Communist Party, as broadly defined by the following criteria in Article 3:

(a) persons who hold or have held elected positions in representation of the Chilean Communist Party or the National Progressive Party: Senators, Deputies, Municipal Councilmen;

(b) persons who have been candidates of said parties for elected positions, or have been representatives of those candidates, or have been electors promoting the declarations of those candidacies;

(c) persons who belong to or have belonged to leadership bodies of said parties: Central, Departmental, or Local Directorates constituted for the purposes of the Law of Elections before the National Electoral Registry;

(d) persons who belong to or have belonged to national, regional, or local leadership bodies of said parties or to cells of said parties (secret leadership bodies and Party militants); and,

(e) persons who have occupied positions as Ministers of State, Intendants, Governors, Subdelegates, and District Inspectors in representation of the Chilean Communist Party.

In other words, one did not have to be a card-carrying member of the PCCh to be deprived of citizenship rights. In fact, according to item (b) above, any person who had promoted the declarations of a Communist candidate in any election could be placed on this national blacklist. This criterion could be readily applied to almost all Socialists and Radicals who had participated in the Center-Left alliances of the preceding decade, and even to González Videla himself, who had frequently campaigned on behalf of his Communist compatriots. Having been given the right to vote in municipal elections in 1935, women were also subject to disenfranchisement according to the LDPD.

The names of people removed from the electoral registers according to these criteria were to be published in both regional newspapers and the *Diario Oficial*, starting in December 1948. This was the same month the United Nations approved the Universal Declaration of the Rights of Man, Article 3 of which proclaimed the right to life, liberty, and security of person.[30] Those whose names were published had ten days to file a complaint with the Electoral Court (Tribunal Calificador de Elecciones). The lists first submitted to the Electoral Registry from all provinces in the country named 40,687 persons; adding the 3,768 public servants denounced by the Ministry of the Interior raises the total to 44,455 persons initially classified as Communist-affiliated. Of those named, 16,101 were listed with incomplete or questionable information, such that they could not be clearly identified in the electoral registers or their political affiliation could not be sufficiently proved. Thus, on December 13, 1948, when the 100-day procedure came to a close, 26,498 men and 1,856 women—a total of 28,354 people—were formally removed from the electoral registers under the terms of Law no. 8987. As of thirty days before the congressional elections in March 1949, 1,704 of these expunged electors had been reinstated through appeals to the Electoral Court, leaving 26,650.[31]

At the same time, however, an additional 16,408 people were disenfranchised through a clerical purge of the registers, which eliminated voters whose information was deemed incomplete or inaccurate—for an overall total of 43,058 disenfranchised electors. Many of the 16,408 clerically purged voters were likely the same as the 16,101 who were initially classified as Communists but could not be proved as such. Critics of the "Damned Law" thus spoke of "the 40,000 citizens who have been eliminated from the electoral registers," as did Salvador Allende in a 1952 Senate debate about a possible amnesty law. His use of this figure went unchallenged even by right-wing opponents.[32] Table 2 shows the number of persons from the coal mining towns and surrounding areas removed from the electoral registers in accordance with the LDPD; it does not reflect those subject to the clerical purge.

The 404 women from these three coal mining departments constituted 22 percent of the national total of 1,856 women whose hard-won right to vote, even if only at the local level, was now taken away. In the case of the men, the 3,626 from the coal mining region represented almost 15 percent

30. For a discussion of the LDPD in relation to international human rights accords, see Trabucco Godoy, *Tesis sobre la Ley*, 194.

31. The estimate of 26,650 is only slightly higher than that given by other sources, such as Andrew Barnard, who says that "some 23,000 Communists were eventually struck off the electoral roll," and Cole Blasier, who states that "some 25,000 Communists, a huge number for a small country like Chile, had been disenfranchised." Barnard, "Chile," 89; Blasier, "Chile," 373.

32. See Allende's dialogue with Fernando Aldunate, Senate Session, June 3, 1952, 124–37, BCNCh.

Table 2 Number of coal mining zone residents on LDPD blacklists, January 1949

Location	Estimated population[a]	Men on blacklists[b]	Registered male voters[c]	%[d]	Women on blacklists[b]	Total people blacklisted	% of total by location
Department of Coronel	86,403	3,087	9,149	34	313	3,400	84
Coronel	34,217	1,232	3,930	31	239	1,471	37
Lota	42,670	1,829	4,643	39	74	1,903	47
Santa Juana	9,516	26	576	5	—	26	1
Department of Lebu	18,056	264	1,828	14	47	311	8
Lebu	9,462	223	1,175	19	44	267	7
Los Alamos	8,595	41	653	6	3	44	1
Department of Arauco	28,032	275	3,250	8	44	319	8
Arauco	15,144	36	1,282	3	7	43	1
Carampangue	(1,370)	35	—	—	0	35	1
Curanilahue	12,888	187	1,644	11	31	218	5
Llico	(665)	17	324	5	6	23	0.5
Totals	132,490	3,626	14,227	26	404	4,030	100

[a]Calculated from 1940 and 1952 census data.

[b]Calculated from Dirección del Registro Electoral, "Ciudadanos Eliminados del Registro de Electores en Conformidad a la Ley no. 8987 de Defensa de la Democracia," Nómina anexa a oficio no. 3067 (December 15, 1948), *Oro Negro*, January 15, 1949, 3–46; *Oro Negro*, January 23, 1949, 3–8; *El Minorista* (Lebu), January 10, 1949, 1–3; and January 14, 1949, 1–2; *El Minorista*, January 25, 1949, 1; *El Regional* (Curanilahue), January 8, 1949, 1–2, 4, and January 15, 1949, 1–3; *El Regional*, January 29, 1949, 3.

All the men's lists for these comunas include a category called "permanente," the significance of which I have not been able to ascertain. Thus, for example, 171 of the 1,829 men listed from Lota are designated "Lota permanente." The women's lists do not have this designation.

Several of the comunas in this table (Santa Juana, Arauco, Carampangue, and Llico) did not have coal mines, and a few places with coal mines (Cosmito, Lirquén) are not included. Also, a few people appeared on the lists published in the *Diario Oficial* list but not in the departmental newspapers. Because my tallies are drawn from the latter, they may understate the number of people from the coal region deprived of citizenship rights under the terms of the LDPD.

[c]Calculated from Dirección del Registro Electoral, presidential election results, 1946. SERCh. Women were not eligible to vote in the 1946 presidential election, and therefore would not have been included in these numbers of registered voters. I have not been able to find accurate figures for the number of registered women voters in each location at the time LDPD went into effect.

[d]Percentage of registered male voters on LDPD blacklists.

of the national total of more than 26,000 disenfranchised male electors. Both were notably high percentages. The greater number of men on these lists reflected the overall state of gender relations in Chile, where women were less likely to belong to political parties or unions and where they could only vote in municipal elections.[33] Yet, even though both the Chilean Communist Party and the coal industry were strongly dominated by men, women in the coal mining region tended to be more publicly active and militant than their counterparts around the country.

Not only did the LDPD deprive people of the right to vote; it also severely infringed on their rights to belong to trade unions, to participate in strikes, and to reap benefits from Chile's progressive social system. Beyond making the Chilean Communist Party illegal and disenfranchising its supporters, the LDPD introduced sweeping modifications of electoral laws, labor and social security codes, and the country's internal state security legislation, which was centered on Law no. 6026, of February 12, 1937, described by a North American legal scholar as "the first comprehensive and full-fledged Public Order Act of its kind in Latin America, a veritable anti-revolutionary code."[34] All of the LDPD's amendments to Law no. 6026 aimed at expanding its reach and strengthening its punitive consequences. Many acts previously deemed common crimes or misdemeanors, for example, were now categorized as state crimes, with much higher penalties.[35] Situating the LDPD in Chile's long history of controlled democracy, Brian Loveman and Elizabeth Lira explain that "in many senses, it was a law combining the most restrictive elements of the laws limiting or suspending constitutional rights and guarantees from the time of [Interior Minister Diego] Portales [in the 1830s]. It was like bringing up to date, for the Cold War, the Portalian and Montt-Varista inquisitorial traditions, as well as the repressive measures implemented between 1925 to 1948."[36]

In terms of Chilean labor law, the original LDPD bill severely curtailed "the right of union association, the right to strike, the right of class representation, the right to the administration of union patrimony, and the right of employed union leaders to job security."[37] But, in doing so, it generated a number of legal muddles and political quagmires. According to the 1931 Labor Code, "The right of union association is recognized for

33. See Rosemblatt, *Gendered Compromises*, esp. 241–51.
34. Loewenstein, "Legislation," 368–69.
35. Bowen Herrera, *Nuestro derecho*, 5.
36. Loveman and Lira, *Las ardientes cenizas*, 126.
37. Bowen Herrera, *Nuestro derecho*, 5–6. See also Camu Veloso, *Estudio crítica*, 34–37.

persons of both sexes, more than eighteen years old, who work in the same enterprise, work site, or who exercise the same job or profession, or similar or connected jobs or professions, whether they be of intellectual or manual character."[38] Article 7, Paragraph 1 of the LDPD bill as submitted to Congress by the González Videla administration called for the addition of the following clause: "No persons may belong to any union, however, who execute acts prohibited by the Internal State Security Law [no. 6026] and its modifications, or who have been excluded from the Electoral or Municipal Registers." By this wording, not only would the twenty-seven thousand people on the published lists be prohibited from belonging to unions, but so would anyone who participated in any illegal strike. This was a sharp blow to the power of organized workers since the Labor Code made it difficult for strikes to be classified as legal. After much debate, Congress rejected the wording "persons who execute acts" and replaced it with "persons declared prisoners or condemned for crimes sanctioned by Law no. 6026 and its modifications."

During these congressional debates, González Videla realized that his original bill was seen as an attack on the right to unionize, which was widely considered "one of the most valued gains in the field of labor rights."[39] The law was criticized for cutting deeply not only into democratic political rights, but also into hard-won social rights, central to the state's claims of legitimacy since the 1920s, and particularly under the governments of the Popular Front era. Seeking to head off further protests and denunciations in this regard, González Videla used his executive power to effect an additional change to Article 7. He wanted to make it clear that the prohibition of union membership to persons deemed Communist or subversive was not intended to deprive them of the benefits provided by unions. González Videla thus secured the addition of a clause specifying benefits to which *all* workers would be entitled. In its final form, then, Article 7 of Law no. 8987 included two paragraphs that substantially altered the Chilean Labor Code, such that it now read,

> The right of union association is recognized for persons of both sexes, more than eighteen years old, who work in the same enterprise, work site, or who exercise the same job or profession, or similar or connected jobs or professions, whether they be of intellectual or manual character.

38. Article 362, Title I, Book III, in Rojas Valenzuela and Ruiz de Gamboa A., *Código del Trabajo*, 101.

39. Bowen Herrera, *Nuestro derecho*, 10.

No persons may belong to any union, however, who have been declared prisoners or condemned for crimes sanctioned by Law no. 6026 and its modifications, nor those who have been excluded from the Electoral or Municipal Registers.

Notwithstanding the stipulation in the above clause, the persons affected by it will have the right to participate in the [company] profits established in Article 405, and, if they pay the dues they are obligated to pay, [they will have the right to participate] in the cultural, educational, cooperative, solidarity, and protective benefits that the union provides, in conformity with its statutes and regulations.[40]

These Labor Code changes, Chilean law professor Alfredo Bowen Herrera explains, created "a sui generis type of union member who, stripped of the designation 'member,' . . . nonetheless enjoyed a series of social benefits." This was indeed peculiar since those excluded from membership were still required "to pay their obligatory dues" to a union to which they could no longer belong. In Bowen Herrera's opinion, a right of association could still be said to exist, although "it is quite a distinct thing that, by force of law, these members lack voice and vote in social assemblies, which seems to be the principal effect of said modification."[41]

The labor courts and conciliation boards in 1949–50 then faced the question of whether these "alienated" persons (extraños) could be present for the election of union leaders even though they could not vote. They were also unclear about whether the rights and obligations subscribed to by the union in collective contracts were legally applicable to this group of sui generis workers. In Bowen Herrera's judgment, there was no doubt that all collective agreements applied to these workers since such agreements constituted one of the principal "benefits of solidarity" referred to above. Offering a solution to the legal muddle generated by the law, even a seemingly anti-Communist scholar such as Bowen Herrera, came to the conclusion that

it is not necessary to exclude those workers from such rights in order to achieve the social tranquility intended by Law no. 8987, an objective that would be obtained, in the judgment of the legislator, by depriving these persons of the right to voice [their views] and

40. Ibid., 12.
41. Ibid., 12, 13.

vote in the union assemblies, and by making them ineligible to be elected to the union directorate. The contrary interpretation, on the other hand, would carry things far beyond what is necessary and what is just, giving the legal prohibition under discussion a penal and punitive reach that the legislator did not have in mind for this part of the law.[42]

The LDPD also raised a number of other problems for Chilean labor relations. In his annual address to Congress in May 1949, for example, President González Videla defended the law against the charge that it prevented workers from exercising their constitutional right to strike. He claimed that, although twenty-seven legal strikes had occurred in 1947, "when the Communist Party maintained all of its Empire," in 1948, the year the law was passed, there were still twenty legal strikes.[43] González Videla's trajectory and image as a friend of the working class, combined with Chilean society's respect for labor legislation, meant that the president, unlike his counterparts in Brazil and elsewhere in Latin America, could not openly embrace the disciplinary state project on which he had embarked. He continued presenting himself as a progressive politician, even as this became less and less credible. In all his public pronouncements, he stressed that the state's repressive actions aimed exclusively at the Chilean Communist Party, although clear evidence showed that many non-Communists had been arrested, exiled, and disenfranchised. In the Chilean context of the late 1940s, anti-Communist and anti-labor initiatives were not easily distinguishable.

Notwithstanding the president's assertions, the LDPD did have a major impact on strikes, even according to the labor minister's own report, presented as part of the same May 1949 address to Congress. Nationwide, he said, thirty-seven legal strikes occurred in 1947, not twenty-seven as González Videla claimed, and they involved nearly eighteen thousand workers and seventy employees. The twenty legal strikes in 1948, by contrast, involved only seven thousand workers and thirty employees.[44] González Videla's statements were also misleading because he did not mention illegal strikes, which had always far outnumbered legal ones, since the requirements for the latter were difficult to meet.[45] According to the labor minister, more than 51,000 workers and nearly 500 employees

42. Ibid., 14–15.
43. González Videla, *Mensaje* (1949), xv.
44. Ibid., 310.
45. Camu Veloso, *Estudio crítica*, esp. 8, 79–91, 111–15.

participated in 127 illegal strikes in 1947. In 1948, on the contrary, there were only six illegal strikes, involving 1,200 workers and no employees.[46] Thus, from 1947 to 1948, the total number of striking workers fell by nearly 90 percent, from almost seventy thousand to slightly more than eight thousand.[47]

Despite González Videla's insistence that his measures had not curtailed the right to strike, the labor minister dated the decline of strikes, especially illegal ones, from August 22, 1947, with the passage of Law no. 8837, which granted the Executive extraordinary powers against "extremist activities" that threatened the country's productive enterprises. He observed that 114 illegal strikes were held between January and August 1947, whereas only 13 illegal strikes occurred from September to December. This was an average of fourteen illegal strikes per month in the first period, and only three in the second, a decline that clearly continued into 1948, when only six illegal strikes occurred, all of which "were easily resolved."[48] At the regional level, not a single strike—legal or illegal—was staged in any industry or occupation in the provinces of Concepción and Arauco in the year 1948.[49]

Organizing efforts were renewed in the coming years; indeed, many younger residents of the coal mining region, such as Juan Alarcón and Evaristo Azócar Medel, described the repressive aftermath of the October 1947 strike as a time of radicalization. Coming of age under military control, Alarcón recalled, raised his political consciousness. As soon as he turned twenty-one in 1952, he joined the then-clandestine Communist Party, in which he remained active for the next half century.[50] For his part, Evaristo Azócar Medel said that it was precisely on October 4, 1948, the one-year anniversary of the coal miners' strike, that he joined the Popular Socialist Party (PSP), just formed by the breakaway, anti–LDPD faction of the Socialist Party and led by figures such as Raúl Ampuero and Salvador Allende.

Azócar was the nephew of Lota's beloved Communist mayor, Santos Medel, who had been smuggled out of town in the early days of the strike.

46. González Videla, Mensaje (1949), 325. See also Loveman, Chile, 204.

47. See also Silva, Los partidos, 236.

48. González Videla, Mensaje (1949), 310, 325–26.

49. Ibid., 324. This is a table of strikes by province.

50. Interview with Juan Alarcón. By the end of the 1950s, Alarcón worked in the Schwager machine shop; from 1965 to 1973, he was a leader of the Industrial Union of Schwager Metalworkers. After surviving detention and exile during the military dictatorship of Augusto Pinochet (1973–89), Alarcón had returned to Coronel by the mid-1990s, where he was elected to the city council on the PCCh ticket.

318 RUPTURE AND BETRAYAL

Azócar's decision to bypass his uncle's party and join the PSP was related to a tragic family story. In 1943, Azócar had entered the National Mining School in Copiapó with grants from the Communist-dominated CTCh and the Lota municipality, headed by his uncle.[51] In September 1945, when his stepfather killed a locally powerful fellow Communist in a drunken brawl, the Communists cut off Azócar's funding and he was forced to leave the school. Back in Lota, he got a job building ship and railroad parts in the machine shop, and soon became an active member of the metalworkers' union. In October 1947, twenty-two years old and recently married, Azócar continued working through the strike, in part, he said, to spite the Communists, who had blackballed his family. In the ensuing weeks and months, however, as the police and military hauled away his friends and neighbors, Azócar's anger toward the government grew. After a trip to Concepción, where he witnessed people being held inside freight and cattle cars prior to their deportation, he decided to take political action. "I was so enraged about what happened at the Chepe [train station]," Azócar explained, "I had to join a party to move forward with my rebellion, and I chose the Socialist Party . . . to fight hard against the dictatorship of González Videla."[52] The "atomic bomb" denounced by Senator Allende had fallen not only on the Chilean Communist Party, but on the homes, workplaces, and lives of tens of thousands of Chilean men and women.

"As Forsaken as the Birds": Internees, Exiles, and Those Left Behind

While national figures like the Grand Master of the Masonic Lodge were denouncing González Videla's antidemocratic measures, a younger generation of outraged local activists, such as Evaristo Azócar, was becoming radicalized. At the same time, the nearly ten thousand people who had been banished from the coal mining region and other turbulent areas around the country were struggling simply to survive, as they searched for a way to get back home. These "relegados"—miners, civil servants,

51. Interview with Evaristo Azócar Medel; and Lota Municipal Acts, April 28, 1943, vol. 2, 4/43–4/52, 4, BML.

52. Interview with Evaristo Azócar Medel. By 1951, Azócar was a leader of the Professional Union of Lota Metalworkers. Lobo Moraga, *Guía sindical*, 168–69. By 1958, he was a city council member and subsequently mayor of Lota. During the Allende years, when the coal mines were nationalized, Azócar served as the chief welfare officer for the newly established state-owned company, ENACAR. During the Pinochet dictatorship, he lived in exile in Argentina, and when he returned, he opened a restaurant on Playa Blanca.

teachers, dockworkers, men and women of all occupations and ages—experienced multiple forms of hardship, from the psychological stress of betrayal and disillusionment to the material struggle to earn a living and support their families while blacklisted from jobs and harassed by public authorities in often unfamiliar locations. Perhaps most painful of all, many suffered the loneliness and longing of forced separation from their families and friends.

Those left behind—family members as well as neighbors, pastors, and shopkeepers—were also victimized by the repression. Indeed, everyone in the region was affected in one way or another. In response to the socio-political movement based on popular notions of democratization and progressive reform that had been developing in the coal mining communities over the previous decade, the policy of the González Videla government was literally reactionary: it sought not only to repress Communists and labor leaders, but also to dismantle social, political, and cultural institutions, which had come to threaten the existing distribution of national resources and long-standing hierarchies of power.

One of the "extremist agitators" banished from his hometown was Juan de la Cruz Leal Vega, a twenty-five-year-old Schwager coal miner.[53] In September 1948, while living in the city of Concepción, Leal Vega wrote to the intendant requesting protection against future detentions.[54] His story highlights the overlapping experiences of those detained or interned and those sent into internal exile, all of whom were referred to as "relegados." On October 7, 1947, three days into the strike, the armed forces occupying Coronel detained Leal Vega. They first sent him to Quiriquina Island and then to the internment camp at Pisagua. Some time later, he was released from Pisagua, along with sixty-two other people, and taken to Concepción aboard the Navy warship *Araucano*. Adding a strange detail in his letter to the intendant, Leal Vega noted that, upon release, each person was given 250 pesos, as "a gift from the company."

53. Though his letters clearly identify him as a Schwager miner, Leal Vega appears on the November 30, 1947, relegados list with a Lota identity card. Decree no. 14, November 30, 1947, issued by Concepción-Arauco Emergency Zone Chief Alfredo Hoffman Hansen, FIC, vol. 2356, ANCh.

54. Letter from Juan de la Cruz Leal Vega to Concepción Intendant, September [23?], 1948, FIC, vol. 2362, ANCh. More specifically, Leal Vega was requesting *recurso de amparo preventivo*, a right granted in the 1925 Constitution, roughly equivalent to habeas corpus, which could be sought when a person was subject to intimidation or surveillance and feared imminent arrest. During states of emergency, however, Chilean habeas corpus rights were drastically restricted. On the articles in the 1925 Constitution that address due process, see Loewenstein, "Legislation," 372. On modifications of these rights during states of emergency, and especially under the LDPD, see Caffarena de Jiles, *El recurso de amparo*; and Hilbink, *Judges Beyond Politics*, 67–70.

In Concepción, Leal Vega went for a long time without work before finally landing a job as a city plumbing assistant. But just when his fortunes seemed to be looking up, the police arrived at his boarding house, shortly before midnight on April 28, 1948, to arrest him on "suspicion of conspiracy." After five days in jail, he was released and left town immediately. "Since I didn't have anything to do with what they accused me of," he explained to the intendant, "I became indignant and took off for the countryside." A month later, Leal Vega heard a rumor that the military had suspended the requirement for safe conduct passes to enter the coal mining zone, so he made his way back to Coronel. His father was ailing, he said, and one of his brothers had been injured in a mine accident.[55] Since border control had indeed eased, Leal Vega was able to cross the bridge over the Bío-Bío River from Concepción to Coronel. This did not mean, however, that he was no longer a marked man. Indeed, no one who had been deported from the region was legally allowed back until the late 1950s. Soon after his return to Schwager, Leal Vega was again arrested "on suspicion," and he spent several days in detention before being sent back to Concepción.

In his letter to the intendant, Leal Vega declared his great love of the Chilean nation—his "Happy Homeland Paradise" (Patria Feliz de Eden)—matched only by his great love of sports, which, he said, is what led him into the Communist fold in the first place, and into all his troubles. He had been elected president of the Communist Youth, he claimed, "because of the great enthusiasm for sports that I had."[56] Athletic prowess, particularly on the soccer field, could certainly have made a young man popular among his peers in the coal mining towns of the 1940s and could even have gotten him elected to a political office, but it does not in itself explain his decisions to join the Communist Youth and then to serve as its president. Leal Vega's letter reveals a complex mix of raw emotions and tactical rhetoric, as he downplayed his political militancy and ideological convictions, admitted but repented his party affiliation, and expressed anger at the false accusations and unjust persecution to which he was

55. Since the start of the strike, all males over age fourteen had to show a safe conduct (salvo conducto) pass granted by emergency zone officials in order to enter or leave the coal mining zone. Garrison Order no. 5, from Concepción Garrison Commander, October 10, 1947, FIC, vol. 2356, ANCh. See also Report of the Special Commission on the Acusación Constitucional Against Holger Torres," Chamber of Deputies Session, November 4, 1947, 560, BCNCh.

56. Letter from Juan de la Cruz Leal Vega to Concepción Intendant, September [23?], 1948, FIC, vol. 2362, ANCh.

subjected. His tone alternates from apologetic and supplicating to righteously indignant.

Leal Vega was not alone in directing letters to the Concepción intendant, a civic figure who the desperate relegados hoped would help them defend their citizenship rights, even though he could not legally supersede the authority of the emergency zone military officers. Froilán Carrillo Verdugo was another man exiled from the coal mining zone by military decree, who also sent a number of letters to the intendant in January and February 1948.[57] In 1934, Carrillo Verdugo had been among those arrested when the police raided a house in Coronel and found illegal weapons.[58] Though he never worked for the Schwager company, by 1939, this young activist had become a leader in the Coronel CTCh.[59] In his first letter to the intendant, Carrillo Verdugo stressed his long service as a civic employee, in his capacity as secretary of the Coronel Police Court (Juzgado de Policía). He then gave a brief account of his internment on Quiriquina Island and at Pisagua. Unlike Leal Vega, Carrillo seemed to understand clearly the terms of his exile: "After going through all this," he wrote, "I was freed by Supreme Decree, but conditionally, without being allowed to live where I want."[60] He knew he could not legally return to his hometown.

Carrillo Verdugo was also less apologetic about his affiliation with the Communist Party than was the much younger Juan de la Cruz Leal Vega, though both men, in different ways, emphasized their patriotic love of their country. Carrillo boldly told the intendant, "The only thing I know is that I am a Chilean Communist and Patriot because I want the betterment of my country, and I have never denied my political affiliation when I have been asked." Yet, believing that the repression was meant to target the miners, he added, "I have never worked in the Schwager Company, nor have I have thought of doing so; I don't have anything to do with it."[61]

After telling his story, Froilán Carrillo Verdugo appealed to the intendant to allow him to return to his home in Coronel. When his individual

57. Carrillo Verdugo was named on the November 30, 1947, list of relegados.

58. Oficio Confidencial no. 3, January 27, 1948, from Military Chief of Schwager Mines, FIC, vol. 2362, ANCh. This document is on Schwager letterhead, with "Emergency Zone" typed directly beneath the company name.

59. *El Obrero*, July 15, 1939, 6; Report on Schwager Union Assembly of January 26, 1941, prepared by Chief of Community Security Juan Mococaín H., Schwager Welfare Department, January 27, 1941, FIC, vol. 2228, ANCh.

60. Letter from Froilán Carrillo Verdugo to Concepción Intendant, January 9, 1948, FIC, vol. 2362 (Oficios Recibidos de Particulares), ANCh.

61. Ibid.

appeal was unsuccessful, he began to organize other relegados in the area toward some form of collective statement or action. The next letter he sent to the intendant, about a month later, came from the "Committee of the Unemployed from the Coal Mining Zone Residing in Concepción" (Comité de Cesantes de la Zona del Carbón Radicados en Concepción), with Carrillo Verdugo signing as secretary and a man named Alfredo Rojas Molina signing as president. Their main request at this time was simply that the intendant "give [them] a chance to put up some small shacks on the banks of the Bío-Bío River."[62] This desperate petition was made particularly on behalf of Rojas Molina, who had nine young children with him, as well as another man with four children, neither of whom had a place to live. Many relegados had moved with or been joined by their families, making their need for employment and makeshift housing all the more urgent.

Another man who appealed to the Concepción intendant for help was José René Villanueva Leal, a young Schwager miner who had been deported from the coal mining zone sometime in late October or early November 1947. Writing to the intendant in May 1948 from Talcahuano, Villanueva explained that he was trying to get a job at the newly opened steel mill, Huachipato. Unfortunately, he wrote, after "finding me on a list of coal workers, they refused me, believing me to be a Communist." Throughout the letter, Villanueva denied Communist affiliation, describing himself as apolitical. He did admit that he had remained in the Schwager mine during the October 21 takeover, but he claimed this was "against my will, since the true Communists threatened us with death if we didn't obey their orders." Thus echoing the charges levied by the government and other anti-Communist sectors, he lamented, "I am now prohibited from working honorably . . . because of a few who harm many workers who don't have anything to do with them." Villanueva implored the intendant to contact the appropriate authorities to remove his name from "the list that appeared at Huachipato . . . once it is proven that, in fact, I have never belonged to the Communist Party."[63]

Villanueva's letter passed through the hands of various emergency zone officials, one of whom noted that this was likely the same Villanueva

62. Letter from Alfredo Rojas Molina, President, and Froilán Carrillo Verdugo, Secretary, Committee of the Unemployed from the Coal Mining Zone Residing in Concepción to Concepción Intendant, February 10, 1948, FIC, vol. 2364, ANCh.

63. Letter from José René Villanueva Leal to Concepción Intendant, [May 11, 1948], FIC, vol. 2362, ANCh. I estimate the date of the letter to be about May 11, 1948, since the intendant's handwritten note at the bottom, which orders the letter to be sent on to the Talcahuano emergency zone chief, is dated May 12.

Leal listed as a relegado on decree no. 14, of November 30, 1947.[64] The military delegate in Coronel provided further details, confirming that Villanueva had remained in the San Pedro section of the Schwager mine during the October 21 occupation and was fired on October 27, "by Order of the Supreme Government." He had also been fired by Schwager on three previous occasions for missing work and had been suspended twice.[65] Notwithstanding this negative profile, the final paragraph of the military report concluded, "Having studied this citizen's record and having made inquiries with the personnel of Investigations, the Police, the Company, and [his] neighbors, it has not been possible to verify that he belongs to any political party or that he participated in any activity against the Company."[66]

The next reviewer of the case, acting Intendant Inés Enriquez de Saez, handwrote her opinion on the back of the military report. Villanueva should be "removed from the official lists of Communist Party militants," she recommended, "since it has not been possible to prove that he belongs to any party." She sent the letter on to the emergency zone chief, who replied that, whether or not Villanueva's political affiliation could be proved, the very fact that he had been involved in the Schwager mine occupation made it "inadvisable for [him] to be removed from said list," referring to Decree no. 14 of November 30, 1947.[67] Again, labor activism and Communist militancy were largely conflated in the eyes of the military officials sent to control the coal mining zone.[68]

Another relegado whose case came to public light was an unabashed Communist, Humberto Pineda Pacheco, the municipal secretary of Coronel from at least April 1945 to the October 1947 strike.[69] In mid-October, Pineda and other detained municipal officials wrote to then–President of the Senate Arturo Alessandri, protesting that they had not been informed

64. Oficio Confidencial no. 126, from Emergency Zone Chief for Province of Arauco and Departments of Tomé and Talcahuano to Concepción Intendant, May 19, 1948, FIC, vol. 2362, ANCh.

65. The expression used to describe Villanueva Leal was "fallero," which roughly translates as "slacker." Villanueva was fired in December 1942, August 1943, and May 1944. He was also suspended for six days in July 1946, for sleeping inside the mine, and for three days in October 1946, for not using his hard hat.

66. Oficio no. 303, June 9, 1948, from Chief Military Delegate of Coronel to Concepción Emergency Zone Chief, FIC, vol. 2362, ANCh.

67. Note from Concepción Emergency Zone Chief, [June 1948], FIC, vol. 2362, ANCh.

68. Villanueva Leal was not named on the list of those removed from the electoral registers in Coronel according to the terms of the Law for the Permanent Defense of Democracy (LDPD).

69. El Sur, April 21, 1945. Pineda's name appears as "Pinto" and as "Pineda" in different sources, but they clearly refer to the same person.

of the reasons for their arrest.⁷⁰ A year and a half later, Coronel's Socialist newspaper *Oro Negro* interviewed Pineda, who had just returned home after fifteen months of internment in "various places" around the country, including the camps on Quiriquina Island and at Pisagua.⁷¹ Pineda again emphasized that during the entire period of his detention, he was never informed of the charges against him, in violation of the Chilean equivalent of habeas corpus, *recurso de amparo*. As set forth in the 1925 Constitution, recurso de amparo was a basic right of citizenship, fundamental to the republican institutions that Salvador Allende and others saw to be under attack. After his release in February 1949, Pineda returned directly to Coronel, whereas Leal Vega, released from Pisagua and sent to Concepción sometime before April 1948, was still prohibited from entering the coal mining zone.

As did many other eyewitness accounts, Pineda's letter stressed the diversity of people interned at Pisagua in terms of occupation, gender, generation, and political affiliation. The fact that not all men and women exiled to distant places were Communist Party militants was personally experienced by Villanueva and was confirmed by James Bell:

> Although the Government apparently tried to exercise care that only Communists were arrested during the coal strike and the subsequent sympathy strikes in nitrate and copper mines, there is considerable evidence that members of other political parties were also detained and sent to remote areas. A reporter for the magazine *Vea* visited the submarine tender *Araucano* just before it left with 120 people to be taken to Pisagua. He found that [not] all 120 were . . . miners nor were they all Communists. He reported that some were employees and some travelling vendors and small business men. Falangists and Socialists, as well as some who belonged to no political party, were among them.⁷²

One such victim, belonging to no political party, was Enrique Pereira Rojas, a young Lirquén coal miner who had joined the Pentecostal Wesleyan Mission in 1943. Almost a half century later, Chilean theologian Manuel Ossa interviewed Pereira at his home in Penco, where he had been named a Wesleyan pastor in 1982, and subsequently, superintendent of

70. *El Siglo*, October 15, 1947, 1. See Confidential Telegram no. 779, from Bowers to Secretary of State, October 7, 1947, USNA, RG 59.

71. *Oro Negro*, February 19, 1949, 1.

72. Bell Report, 21.

the Wesleyan Mission's northern district. Pereira directly linked his life as a strong union activist to the mission's teachings, claiming that "when he was a worker in Lirquén, he learned in the Bible to defend his rights." In the wake of the sit-down occupation of the Schwager and Lirquén mines on October 21, Pereira's shift boss accused him of "having tried to block or tackle the [military] men when they came to make us leave [the mine]." He declared he was innocent of this charge and could produce witnesses, "but at that time no one listened to anything," and he was arrested. Together with a group of about twenty other people from Lirquén, he was taken by train under military guard to Punta de Parra, and was then sent on a Navy warship to the detention center on Quiriquina Island in Concepción Bay.[73]

At the time of his arrest, this young Wesleyan labor activist had been married for less than a year. In the coal mining town of Lirquén, he left behind an eighteen-year-old wife, Fresia Correo de Pereira, with their one-month-old daughter, Rosita. After surviving three weeks without her husband or his wages, Fresia Correo sat down, with the baby nursing at her breast, to write to Rosa Markmann de González, who had visited Coronel with the president earlier that month. "With tears in my eyes and my heart destroyed," she beseeched the First Lady, "without anyone to turn to, I address myself to you because I know clearly that, after God, you are the only one who can fix my sad situation." Fresia Correo then presented the case of her husband, who "had fallen into the net of incarceration on Quiriquina Island." Although proclaiming her husband's innocence, she added that, if he were guilty, it was "just because of the influence of others." Trying to convince Rosa Markmann to secure her husband's release, Fresia Correo stressed that they were religious and had never belonged to any political party, "nor do we even know what it means."[74] She tried to elicit sympathy by both humbling herself and praising the First Lady—"Sra. Rosita"—as the only person who might be willing and able to save her:

> I find myself as forsaken as the birds, I and my little daughter Rosita of 1 month 22 days, and we wail day and night, awaiting the return of my husband. Sra. Rosita, do it for your own little granddaughter who you adore so much, I have touched on this point because I believe it will be the deepest, and I know that what you desire my

73. Enrique Pereira Rojas, 1989 interview, as quoted in Ossa, *Espiritualidad popular*, 193–94; see also 124n167.

74. Letter from Fresia Correo de Pereira, Lirquén, November 22, 1947, FGGV, vol. 19, 151–52, ANCh.

President will agree to it. . . . It has not yet been a year that we've been married, I am 18 years old and am not yet a woman with experience in these sufferings, which is why I turn to you since I believe you are the only person who will take this anguish from my heart.

In a final gesture of humility, Fresia Correo begged Sra. Markmann's forgiveness for "all the mistakes" in the letter.[75]

The first lady's response is unknown, but Fresia Correo's husband was not released. After a month on Quiriquina Island, the young Wesleyan coal miner was taken by Navy destroyer to the internment camp at Pisagua, where, with six to eight hundred other internees, he lived under constant military surveillance. The small port town had insufficient facilities to meet the housing, food, medical, and other basic needs of so many people, who struggled to survive in cramped and difficult conditions. Thrown together were leaders and activists from different parts of the country, different industries, and different political parties, though certainly Communists were in the majority. Enrique Pereira thus commented that during his year in Pisagua, he "learned a lot about labor laws and union rights from other exiled compañeros."[76] Despite the embittering experiences of having a legal strike brutally crushed and being stripped of their democratic rights, Chilean Communists did not turn to insurrectionary rhetoric or politics, as did their counterparts in Brazil and elsewhere in Latin America at the time. Rather, as Pereira indicated, they held onto the promise of working within legal, democratic institutions and continued to emphasize the fundamental rights of citizen workers within Chile's laws and labor relations system.

In January 1948, about the time that Pereira came to Pisagua, a young Army captain named Augusto Pinochet Ugarte also arrived there, together with two other officers and sixty men, to take over the running of the camp. During the coal miners' October strike, Pinochet had been sent to the nitrate pampas "to arrest Communist agitators and transfer them to Pisagua" in an effort to prevent solidarity strikes.[77] With his promotion to military chief of Pisagua, Pinochet interacted on a daily basis with the alleged "extremists" interned there and with socially conscious centrist

75. Ibid.

76. Ossa, *Espiritualidad popular*, 194, paraphrasing from his 1989 interview with Enrique Pereira.

77. Pinochet Ugarte, *Camino recorrido*, 114. See also Estado Mayor General del Ejército de Chile, *Historia*, 54.

and leftist politicians, including Senator Salvador Allende, who traveled to the camp to investigate the state of affairs firsthand.[78]

Although he had been called on to control what the González Videla regime considered to be the most subversive elements in the country, in his memoirs, Pinochet accorded a remarkable degree of respect, and even friendship, to many of the Communist internees. In his contorted narration of the period, however, he also referred to defiant internees, especially "women of a certain age, [who were] quite violent and excessively vehement."[79] Yet what most caught the young captain's attention was precisely the type of educational work that young Wesleyan Enrique Pereira had praised the Communists for. Pinochet complained to his superiors that, despite all his efforts at surveillance and control, the Communists "were transforming the Pisagua camp into a true Marxist-Leninist university" and preparing cadres of "future agitators in labor activities." After a chance encounter with President González Videla, who seemed favorably impressed with the young captain, in February 1948, Pinochet was transferred to the coal mining region, where he served as military commander of Schwager for over a year.[80]

Shortly after Pinochet's departure from Pisagua, more than three hundred detainees staged the first of three hunger strikes, "to protest the abject conditions of the camp and the complete denial of due process." At the same time, "associations of prisoners' wives and families conducted hunger strikes and demonstrations in their home communities."[81] The first strike, lasting just over a week, was brought to an end at the urging of Communist leaders from Santiago.[82] By December, word circulated that the Pisagua internment camp had produced its first martyr—Ángel Veas Alcayaga, a former national deputy who had been appointed intendant of Tarapacá by González Videla and for whom Augusto Pinochet expressed the utmost respect.[83] A number of other deaths in the camp followed: a nitrate miner's wife died (allegedly of starvation while on a hunger strike), as did the former governor of the department of Coronel, Isaías

78. According to Pinochet, Camino recorrido, 117–18, Allende and the other senators and national deputies with him did not have proper authorization, and he therefore refused them permission to enter the camp to meet with the relegados. No other source confirms this story.

79. Ibid., 115.

80. Ibid., 117, 118–23.

81. Frazier, Salt in the Sand, 166. For more details on the hunger strikes by Pisagua prisoners, see Senate Sessions, November 16, 1948, 310, 316, and December 7, 1948, 561, BCNCh; Lafertte Gaviño, Vida de un comunista, 349–50; Corvalán Lépez, De lo vivido, 26.

82. Frazier, Salt in the Sand, 323n23.

83. Pinochet, Camino recorrido, 116–17.

Fuentes Reyes, and at least three others.[84] In addition to hunger strikes, another form of passive resistance at Pisagua was flight, and the Intendancy of Tarapacá was flooded with reports of escaped detainees.[85] With another hunger strike in January 1949 and criticism mounting around the country, the González Videla administration began to release internees from Pisagua in February, though within six months new waves of relegados were being sent to the camp.

Among those released in February 1949 was Enrique Pereira, but unlike openly Communist Froilán Carrillo, who returned to Coronel the same month, Pereira was denied permission to reenter the coal mining zone, indicating a degree of arbitrariness in decisions about relegados. As with thousands of others in internal exile, Pereira described being "stigmatized"—unable to find work wherever he went. Recalling her father's similar experience, Julia González Figueroa explained that "the government launched a campaign throughout the country to slander the good name of the miners, [to tell people] that the miners were criminals, that the miners were barbarians, so that . . . in other places, people thought the worst of the miners . . . and no matter where they went, the exiled miners couldn't get jobs anywhere."[86]

Eventually, Pereira settled in a fishing town outside Concepción, where he spent four years working at different jobs, including market vendor and stevedore. In the latter job, Pereira again emerged as a labor activist and was soon fired, at which point he joined up with twenty-five other people in desperate situations to apply for fishing licenses. When they were denied this simple livelihood, Pereira said that he prayed to God and received the vocation to organize a union. As Pereira's interviewer, Manuel Ossa, observed, "His testimony is enough to show once more the lived and practiced synthesis between religious faith and social and political

84. Communist Senator Guillermo Guevara Vargas named all four men, claiming that they died due to "torture received at said concentration camp." Senate Session, December 7, 1948, 561, BCNCh. Communist leader Luis Corvalán Lépez, however, recalls that Isaías Fuentes died several years later, having left the Pisagua camp very ill and weak. Corvalán Lépez, De lo vivido, 26. Neruda names these martyrs, including Margarita Naranjo, the nitrate miner's wife, in Canto general, 245–46.

85. See, for example, Oficio no. 1003, July 2, 1948, from Tarapacá Police Chief to Tarapacá Emergency Zone Chief, listing six escapees, one of whom, Marcelino Gajardo Fonseca, was head of the Lota CTCh back in 1942, then head of the Concepción provincial CTCh, and by 1947 was a national CTCh leader. See also Documents no. 46, November 22, 1948, no. 1831, December 14, 1948, no. 1904, December 26, 1948, no. 6, January 13, 1949, and no. 8, March 21, 1949. Lessie Jo Frazier provided me transcriptions of these documents, which she consulted in the Archivo Intendencia de Tarapacá (AIT), Iquique.

86. Interview with Julia González Figueroa.

dedication" in the Wesleyan Mission.[87] Pereira was not the only Wesleyan persecuted under the LDPD, regardless of his political affiliation or lack thereof; "several members had been labeled Communist and were persecuted for the sole fact of having [supported] just union demands."[88]

In the same vein as Fresia Correo's letter, many other women in the coal mining zone appealed to Rosa Markmann to intervene in the personal tragedies wrought by the repression, particularly after the first lady's visit with her husband to Lota and Coronel on November 3, 1947.[89] Luisa Bueno de Figueroa, for example, wrote on November 16, from her home in Coronel, where she was left alone with seven children after her husband's arrest. Bueno boldly recalled a promise Markmann had made to her: "In your recent tour in this zone, you offered me your help to intervene on behalf of my husband, don Teodoro Figueroa, who finds himself detained on Quiriquina Island; according to you, we just had to wait a few more days."[90] Another woman from Lota, who watched as soldiers arrested her husband in their home in front of their children, wrote to the first lady "as a citizen and a Chilean woman . . . full of pain." She pleaded for her husband's release, claiming that he had been unjustly detained (though she failed to mention that he was secretary of the Lota Strike Committee).[91] Such letters were filled with stories of the sufferings of families left behind in the coal towns and other besieged workers' communities.[92]

First Lady Rosa Markmann de González did try to intervene on behalf of at least some of the desperate women who appealed to her. In late November 1947, for example, she wrote to the military commander for Lota and Coronel, Brigadier General Santiago Danús Pena, inquiring

87. Ossa, *Espiritualidad popular*, 195.

88. Ibid., 124.

89. Letters written to First Lady Rosa Markmann were not exclusively or even primarily about these detentions. The Gabriel González Videla Collection (FGGV) consists of 154 volumes, 96 of which exclusively contain letters written to the president's wife. See Veneros Ruiz-Tagle, "El epistolario," "Sufragismo," "Testimonio histórico"; and Escobar Guic, "Documentos."

90. Letter from Luisa Bueno de Figueroa, Coronel (Villa Mora), November 16, 1947, FGGV, vol. 19, 3–4, ANCh. Bueno's husband, Teodoro Figueroa, was elected Schwager union treasurer in May 1947; his name was removed from the Coronel electoral registers under the terms of the LDPD.

91. Letter from Mary de Alvárez, Lota, January 9, 1948, FGGV, vol. 22, 118–20, ANCh.

92. Other examples include letters from María Fereira de Muñoz, Schwager, November 5, 1947, FGGV, vol. 18, 56; Irma Acosta de Sanhueza, Schwager, November 6, 1947, FGGV, vol. 18, 77; (illegible name), Arauco, January 23, 1948, FGGV, vol. 22, 276–78; María Inzunza de Maldonado, Tomé, March 16, 1948, FGGV, vol. 24, 179–80, ANCh.

about several families. He responded that their whereabouts were unknown "since they were forced to leave the coal mining zone but had not been found in the places they declared as their new residences."[93] In at least one documented case, appeal to Rosa Markmann brought about rapid, positive results. Julia Sánchez de Morales wrote to the First Lady on April 14, 1948, from Pisagua, where she and her aging mother-in-law and several young children had accompanied her husband after his arrest from their home in Curanilahue. Sánchez made her case on behalf of her husband using the same charges against the Communists promoted by González Videla: As a municipal employee in a Communist-controlled town, she explained, her husband had been "forced to comply with their orders," or else they would kill him or "dynamite the house in which we lived." After his arrest and internment at Pisagua, her husband renounced his affiliation with the Communists. It was when they began to persecute him that she and her family moved to be near him, as a form of protection.

At Pisagua, Julia Sánchez worked hard to establish good relations with local authorities and influential townspeople. Back in Curanilahue, she said, they were unable to have one of their daughters baptized because of their forced association with the Communists; now, when the bishop of Iquique visited Pisagua, he gladly baptized the child, with the head of the internment camp, Army Captain Augusto Pinochet, serving as her godfather.[94] Rosa Markmann took a special interest in the plight of this family, appealing directly to Interior Minister Immanuel Holger Torres to secure their release. Just two weeks after Julia Sánchez wrote to the first lady, her husband was freed and the family headed back home.[95]

Pablo Neruda Versus González Videla: The Construction of Memories and Meanings

Almost all of the women who wrote letters of supplication to First Lady Rosa Markmann used the most humble, often sycophantic, tones. Even the relegados who wrote to public officials to convey their despair or

---

93. Letter from Brigadier General Santiago Danús Pena to Rosa Markmann, December 31, 1947, FGGV, vol. 21, ANCh. He refers to Markmann's letter dated November 28, 1947.

94. Letter from Julia Sánchez de Morales, Pisagua, April 14, 1948, FGGV, vol. 25, 175–76, ANCh.

95. Note from Interior Minister Holger Torres to Rosa Markmann, April 22, 1948, FGGV, vol. 25, 177; and letter from Deputy Interior Minister to Rosa Markmann, April 28, 1948, FGGV, vol. 25, 178, ANCh.

outrage or to demand their rights refrained from criticizing the president directly. And the leftist press, trying to get past government censors, also only alluded to the president's duplicity and disloyalty to the Communists and the working class, still addressing him with terms of respect. Thus, on October 4, El Siglo ran as its lead article a declaration by Bernardo Araya, secretary-general of the Communist faction of the Confederation of Chilean Workers: "In his presidential campaign, Sr. González Videla declared on repeated occasions in front of the workers that he would respect the inalienable right to strike. I hope that yesterday's candidate and today's President of the Republic will keep these promises."[96] And, even when González Videla instead called on the military to occupy the region, the Communists' usually partisan press refrained from denouncing him as a traitor. Throughout October, as El Siglo reporters struggled to follow what was happening on the ground in the cordoned-off zone, the newspaper mostly reported on basic facts, such as the arrival of military units, the issuance of government decrees, and the arrests of miners.

This restraint was most powerfully cast aside by Communist poet and senator Pablo Neruda on November 27, 1947. In his "Intimate Letter for Millions of People," published in El Nacional of Caracas to circumvent Chilean censors, Neruda characterized the events of the preceding months as "the direct and personal responsibility" of González Videla, a man he called a "traitor to democracy" who had ushered in "a climate of tyranny and corruption."[97] A month later, on January 6, 1948, from the floor of the Chilean Senate, Neruda again lashed out at the president, in what became known as the "I accuse" speech for its resemblance to Emile Zola's famous open letter during the Dreyfus Affair of 1898. González Videla was enraged. He charged Neruda with treasonous defamation of the head of state, revoked his congressional immunity, and ordered his arrest. Though the president quickly made clear that he had no intention of prosecuting the now world-famous poet, he had already given this preeminent public relations man more than enough material with which to run, both literally and figuratively.

After fleeing into exile across the Andes and then into Mexico, Neruda lambasted González Videla at every turn, in every possible forum. In addition to articles and interviews in newspapers and journals, he circulated clandestine pamphlets of both poetry and prose. In 1949, Neruda put out

---

96. Bernardo Araya, statement on strike in coal mining zone, El Siglo, October 4, 1947, 1.
97. Neruda, "Carta íntima para millones de hombres," reprinted in La verdad, 23–32.

a vitriolic pamphlet entitled *González Videla, the Laval of Latin America: Brief Biography of a Traitor.* Invoking the infamous Nazi collaborator of Vichy France, Pierre Laval, the cover of the pamphlet graphically depicted a flesh-eating skull spewing out the blood of its martyred victims (fig. 9). Neruda drew on a repertoire of tropes from the Spanish Civil War and World War II to render in words and images a brute struggle between good and evil. As the opening lines of the pamphlet proclaim, "González Videla will pass into history as 'The Rat,' the rat who gnaws away at the sacred foundations of his own nation."[98] This was the beginning of the Cold War in Chile.

During his exile from Chile in the late 1940s, Pablo Neruda completed his masterwork *Canto general*, which gives central prominence to the traitor González Videla and "the great betrayal." In passage after passage of this epic poem, Neruda bitterly denounces his former ally:

> Wretched clown, miserable
> mixture of monkey and rat, whose tail
> is combed with a gold pomade on Wall Street,
> it won't be long before you fall from your tree
> and become the pile of conspicuous filth
> that pedestrians will bypass on the street corners!
> And so it has been. *Betrayal* was Chile's
>   Government.
> A traitor has bequeathed his name to our history.
> *Judas* flourishing a grinning skull
> sold out my brother and sister,
>   poisoned my
>   country,
> founded Pisagua, demolished our star,
> profaned the colors of a pure flag.
>
> *Gabriel González Videla.* Here I leave your name,
> so that when time has erased
> ignominy, when my country cleans
> its face illuminated by wheat and snow,
> those who later seek here the heritage
> that I leave in these lines like a hot green coal
> will also find the name of the traitor who brought
> the glass of agony that my people refused.[99]

98. Neruda, *González Videla*, 1.
99. Neruda, *Canto general*, 201.

Fig. 9   Cover of a clandestine 1949 pamphlet by Pablo Neruda. Artist unknown.

Neruda's prophecy that González Videla would soon pass into history as "a pile of conspicuous filth" ignored by passersby was almost literally fulfilled. González Videla fell out of favor not only with the Left, but also with his own centrist partisans. Even the citizens of La Serena, where he was born and where he lavished government funds, failed to embrace him as a hometown luminary.[100] Nearly fifty years after his presidency, lifelong Lota resident Fresia Vidal Ojarse traveled more than a thousand miles to La Serena to curse González Videla at his tomb, which she found in a state of total abandon. Shaking with renewed rage, she recalled that day:

> I talk to him, and I tell him, look, you were such an ingrate, such a tyrant and bad leader, and look at you now, all that pride you had, now they don't even come to clean your tomb; it's left filthy. . . . Not even your wife will pay someone to clean up around here. . . . I tell you, you pay for everything [you do] in life. . . . Who is going to believe that a President of the Republic is buried in here? Sure, the building is beautiful, but it is so dirty and uncared for.[101]

Along with many others who lived through those dark times, Fresia Vidal Ojarse recalled highly personal, emotional experiences, which she connected to a broader sense of justice and solidarity. The daily human suffering she had witnessed as a young girl growing up in Lota related directly to the battles being waged over the meaning of democracy in Chilean society at the start of the Cold War, as the political openings and possibilities for social gains of the preceding decade rapidly closed. The connection between personal experiences and collective, historical meanings may be glimpsed in Fresia's narration of her face-to-face encounter with González Videla in November 1947, when he visited the coal mining zone at the height of its repression:

> I argued with the authorities about the injustices they were committing; since I was just a girl, they didn't take reprisals against

100. While still in office, for example, González Videla traveled to La Serena with a visiting Brazilian dignitary, who commented in his memoirs on the remarkably low turnout and enthusiasm shown by the crowds toward their president. At the time of his visit, João Café Filho was a former vice president of Brazil; he would later become president. See his memoirs, *Do sindicato*, 1:265.

101. Interview with Fresia Vidal Ojarse, August 15, 1996.

me . . . to defend some neighbors they had taken to [Quiriquina] Island, I argued and I fought with González Videla himself when he came to Schwager. I grabbed him here [she grabs the collar of her shirt], impulsive me. I remember that he was wearing a gray suit and a white shirt and a red tie, and I grabbed him here and I said to him, "What kind of president are you?" when he had asked for the support of the Communists and now he was protecting himself by doing away with the Communists, for what? To punish everyone, because here not all [the people] were Communists, but, they'd just take anyone, the most innocent, the most quiet, they took them away. . . . It was awful.[102]

The people Fresia Vidal tried to defend were her neighbors—men, women, and children, with names, faces, and personal histories. Her recollections, however, resonate deeply with the more universal portrayal of human agony and resilience in Neruda's poetry. Just as Neruda drew from his intimate knowledge of the coal miners' stories, so, too, did residents like Fresia Vidal imbibe Neruda's words as their own memories developed over time.

While Pablo Neruda was in exile abroad denouncing González Videla's crimes to the world, activists who remained in Chile took to writing of another kind. At great risk to themselves under the military occupation, young people throughout the coal and nitrate mining regions, mostly from the Communist Youth (JJCC), covered the walls of their towns with seditious and incendiary graffiti: "Down with Tyranny," "Down with 8987," "Death to Videla the Traitor," "Out with the Sellouts of the Nation," "Long Live the P.C.," "Freedom for Political Prisoners," and, of course, the hammer and sickle.[103] Undeterred from his chosen path, in April 1950, González Videla embarked on a two-week trip to the United States, where he and First Lady Rosa Markmann met several times with President and Bess Truman (fig. 10).[104] Back in Chile's working-class communities, these visits only served to strengthen the image of "Gabriela González de Truman," an epithet that young coal miners and workers across the country

102. Ibid.
103. Document no. 574, April 19, 1948, from Tarapacá Deputy Police Chief; and Document no. 949, July 1949, from Tarapacá Police Chief, both to Tarapacá Intendant. Lessie Jo Frazier provided me transcriptions of these documents, which she consulted in the Archivo Intendencia de Tarapacá (AIT), Iquique.
104. For excellent photos and detailed description of the Chilean dignitaries' U.S. visit, see Watson, *Visita del Excelentísimo* (1951).

Fig. 10   U.S. President Harry S Truman and First Lady Bess Truman with Chilean
President Gabriel González Videla and First Lady Rosa Markmann, ca. April 12,
1950, Washington, D.C. Photo by Abbie Rowe, U.S. National Park Service; courtesy
of Harry S Truman Library.

would write on walls for years to come.[105] In 1952, González Videla would
end his presidency with a magnanimous gesture, pardoning several people who had been charged with internal state security violations.[106]
Among those pardoned was Pablo Neruda, González Videla's former campaign manager and Chile's greatest poet. Neruda was unmoved.

105. At least in part to counter this image, on his last day in office, November 8, 1952,
González Videla and his wife, Rosa Markmann, dined at the presidential palace, La Moneda,
with their invited guest, visiting dignitary Eleanor Roosevelt. The previous day, the former
first lady had attended a reception at the beautiful country estate of Arturo Cousiño Lyons,
then president of the Coal Mining Company of Lota (CCIL) and grandson of its founder. See
Roosevelt's newspaper columns for November 3, 8, 10, 1952, available at http://www.g-
wu.edu/~erpapers/myday/ (accessed August 2009).

106. Decree no. 4969, of September 17, 1952. For a copy of this decree, as well as other
amnesties and related laws from the Popular Front era, see Loveman and Lira, *Leyes de
reconciliación*, 113–42.

CONCLUSION:
COALITION POLITICS IN THE HISTORY
OF CHILEAN DEMOCRACY

From North to South, where the dead
were ground or burned,
they were buried in darkness
or burned at night in silence,
heaped in mine shafts,
or their bones spit into the sea:
nobody knows where they are now,
they have no grave, their martyred fingers
are dispersed in the country's roots:
their executed hearts:
the Chileans' smile:
the pampa's valiant:
the captains of silence.

Nobody knows where the assassins
buried these bodies,
but they'll rise from the earth
to redeem the fallen blood
in the resurrection of the people.[1]

1. Neruda, "The Massacres," *Canto general*, 187.

This is poet Pablo Neruda denouncing state violence, heralding the ghosts of the dead whose bodies have not been found. Miners and their families, campesinos, Mapuches—Chileans across the country—were arrested in droves, sent to "concentration camps," such as the one in the northern nitrate town of Pisagua. These camps would gain international notoriety as the places where hundreds of Chileans disappeared during the dictatorship of Augusto Pinochet, when the Popular Unity (1970–73) burst, both literally and figuratively, into flames. It is not to these massacres, however, that Neruda here refers. Rather, he wrote these lines about bodies with no graves in the late 1940s, at the very outset of the Cold War, when it was the Center-Left project known as the "Popular Front" that exploded in a frenzy of anti-Communist persecution.

This was also the moment when Chile was at the height of its presumed long history of peaceful democracy before 1973. In the segment of the *Canto general* above, Neruda blends an account of the January 1946 police shootings of six people in Santiago's Plaza Bulnes with the subsequent attack on thousands of Communists and working-class families following the coal miners' strike of October 1947. Far from being buried in secret, however, as Neruda asserts, the bodies of the six people shot dead in front of the presidential palace in 1946 were accompanied to their graves by tens of thousands of angry Chileans. And, of the nearly seven thousand people who were banished from their homes in the coal mining region and forced into internal exile (*relegación*) from 1947 to 1949, there is no evidence to prove that any were killed or disappeared. That said, Neruda's poetic invocation of "martyred fingers," "executed hearts," and "bones spit into the sea" now stands as an eerie prophecy of the murderous brutality that would mark the apogee of the Cold War in Chile in the 1970s.[2]

Many scholars over the years have challenged the notion of Chilean exceptionalism—the idea that prior to September 11, 1973, Chile was historically exempt from the volatility and autocratic violence experienced by most of its continental counterparts. In the words of French journalist

2. On January 5, 2001, a Chilean human rights roundtable commission (la Mesa de Diálogo, 1999–2001) submitted its final report to President Ricardo Lagos. Among the findings that the president made public on January 7 was information, largely obtained from anonymous military sources, about the fate of one hundred and eighty persons who had been arrested and "disappeared" by the regime between 1973 and 1976. Much to the horror of family members and friends, the remains of one hundred and twenty of these victims were reported to have been thrown by helicopter into lakes, rivers, and the ocean, thus tragically fulfilling Neruda's prophetic words in *Canto general* about "bones spit into the sea."

Régis Debray, "Chilean history does not look like the smooth democratic ideal with which it is often confused. It is certainly, but in a rather subterranean way, one of the most violent, perhaps one of the bloodiest [nations] in Latin America, as much for its civil wars of the past century . . . as for the frequency, since the beginning of this century, of great assassination campaigns conducted by the repressive apparatus against *campesinos* and workers, culminating in brutal episodes."[3] Debray and others are certainly right to challenge the myth of smooth, peaceful Chilean democracy up to 1973 by pointing out its violence. The story of the coal miners in the 1930s and 1940s certainly supports this view, with episodes of repression ranging from the little-remembered police slaying of unarmed workers in Lota in October 1942 to the massive military force unleashed by González Videla in response to the October 1947 strike.

In bringing to light new information and a regional perspective, *Mining for the Nation* has tried to show that, as with the coup of September 11, 1973, these mid-twentieth-century episodes of state violence were responses to organization and mobilization from below. The history of the coal miners in the 1930s and 1940s was one of complex strivings for fuller participation in Chilean democracy, not as an end in itself, but as a way to achieve greater socioeconomic justice. In their aspirations and actions, the workers were not the passive victims of manipulation by the Communist Party or by the bourgeois state. For the coal miners, the realization of democratic ideals did not mean peace at any price, simply to avoid class conflict and generate national wealth. Rather, they took advantage of the political openings engendered by the cross-class national development model to push their own interests. The period was thus also marked by highly contentious and often violent daily struggles of workers in mine galleries, corner taverns, and municipal halls. As with Augusto Pinochet's military takeover in 1973, González Videla's turn to the Right in 1947 did not come about because of acquiescence and compromise by political forces representing the working class. Rather, it was a fearful reaction to the workers' success in organizing and mobilizing under a Center-Left coalition government. In October 1947, as in September 1973, the deep structure of feeling for those directly affected was betrayal—betrayal of a democratic opening, of a progressive agenda, and of the workers' own newfound sense of protagonism as citizens of the nation.

Other eras in Chilean history before 1973 more closely approximate Debray's description of "great assassination campaigns"—from the 1907

---

3. Debray, *Conversación con Allende*, 18.

massacre of nitrate miners at Santa María de Iquique to the years of the
Carlos Ibáñez dictatorship. But what makes the 1930s and 1940s most interesting in terms of the exceptionalism debate is that this was a period
when Chile was presumably most democratic. Thus the reactionary tendencies and irruptions of violence under the mid-century model of "progressive, harmonious national development" must be understood in
conjunction with the Chilean workers' increasingly powerful assertion of
their identity, aspirations, and rights, with coal miners at the fore. Drawing on Debray's notion of subterranean contestation, twentieth-century
Chilean history might be imagined not just as one of seething undercurrents of oligarchic and bourgeois violence beneath a placid democratic
surface, but also as a history of miners pushing and prodding from below
to expand their place as citizen workers in the nation above. Many centrist, often quite progressive, politicians believed they could mobilize
working-class aspirations, yet keep them under control. They were mistaken, not only in the 1960s and 1970s, but also in the 1940s.

Operating within the legal industrial relations system and constitutional, electoral democracy, coal industry workers in the 1930s and 1940s
appropriated prevailing discourses about patriotism and national development—"mining for the nation"—in order to advance their interests. At
times, they were even able to turn capitalist aggression and episodes of
state violence to their advantage. When the police shot and killed unarmed workers in Lota in October 1942, for example, the miners' patriotic
decision not to strike gave them symbolic capital. In light of the miners'
sacrifice, union leaders insisted, the state should intervene in their contract disputes and force the companies to settle in their favor. Participating in modes of resolution that were not directly or violently
confrontational also produced benefits when government representatives
Raúl Rettig and Osvaldo Pazols released their report about the shootings
in Lota. Largely sympathetic to the workers' position, they called for the
government to intervene in the running of the Lota company and especially to replace its much-loathed Welfare Department chief. The coal
miners' understanding of themselves as significant actors in the nation
and the world was reinforced on March 30, 1943, when esteemed New Deal
leader U.S. Vice President Henry Wallace stood side by side with the
mayor of Lota and other locally revered Communist leaders, hailing the
miners as valiant "soldiers of democracy." Growing worker empowerment
within the legal, democratic model was also evident during the arbitration of labor disputes in early 1944, when the workers' representative,

Communist Deputy Reinaldo Núñez, publicly charged the government arbiter with colluding with the company and caused him to resign.

The residents of the coal mining zone embraced a new sense of themselves as citizen workers in a democratic republic that was embarking on a path of industrial development, in which coal was a vital commodity. In doing so, they supported the efforts of the Chilean Communist Party (PCCh) to form alliances with progressive national forces, especially after the 1935 Comintern Congress, when the Popular Front strategy, aimed at defeating Fascism and pushing forward a bourgeois-democratic revolution, was formally proclaimed. Under this model, national development in Chile was to be achieved through an alliance of patriotic workers and progressive capitalists, with the impartial and just mediation of an interventionist state. Yet the story of the coal miners in the 1930s and 1940s shows that, although the orthodox Popular Front line called for workers to collaborate with the national bourgeoisie, in practice, working-class cadres and leaders, at least in this particular region, usually did not. Chilean coal miners supported the Popular Front only insofar as it opened up spaces for them to press their collective interests and benefit from favorable representation. Fundamentally, it was their increased sway in decision-making forums that led them to "fully place [their] hopes in the State."[4]

Even eminent scholars studying the national politics of the Popular Front era have overlooked the class conflict taking place on, or under, the ground, beneath Central Committee pronouncements, Radical Party platitudes, and congressional wheeling and dealing.[5] Though the Popular Front model explicitly called for collaboration between workers and national capitalists, the story of the coal mining region in the 1930s and 1940s indicates that the Communist-led workers there did not befriend, sympathize with, or support their bosses. The story of the coal miners also shows that the reforms they fought for in these years had as much to do with shifting the balance of political and social power in the region as with securing immediate gains in wages and welfare. Despite the theoretical placement of national capitalists as allies in the pursuit of freedom, democracy, and industrial growth, in practice, workers were not willing to grant their bosses concessions to their own detriment. The ideal of nationalist cross-class cooperation coexisted with often aggressive attacks both by employers against their workers and by workers and their representatives against national capitalists.

4. Marambio, *Identidad cultural*, 78.
5. See, for example, Drake, "International Crises," 130–31.

This coexistence of the Communists' theoretical line and their actual practice was physically embodied—seen, felt, and heard—in the streets and taverns, on soccer fields, in mine pits, and union halls throughout the region in the form of local leaders, many of whom had themselves "excavated beneath the sea, / spread out in the wet cave, / and extracted the mines' black clump / with sweat and blood."[6] Communist influence on the coal zone residents had little to do with programmatic decrees wired from party headquarters in Santiago or Moscow, as many reductive references to this "Red zone" would have us believe. Rather, the men and women who supported the Communist Party in large numbers in the 1930s and 1940s did so because its ideology and discourse resonated with their own experiences, and because they felt camaraderie with, and trust for, the leaders who acted on their behalf. Activist miners and local and regional labor leaders and politicians strove to adapt the national and international policies and tactics of the Communist Party to the perspectives and needs of their communities. Together with their national counterparts, they also worked to mediate internal tensions and conflicts between the party's different levels and objectives and to negotiate with broader non-Communist circles.

The complex process of identification among Communists, labor activists, and the Popular Front is seen in the biography of local figures, such as coal miner Damián Uribe Cárdenas, who, in the late 1930s, was chosen by his peers as a mine floor union delegate. He was then elected secretary of the powerful Lota miners' union, in which capacity he served until 1941, when he washed the coal dust from his face, put on a tie, and set off for the Chamber of Deputies to battle directly with Conservative and Liberal politicians, many of whom were major shareholders and top directors of the coal mining companies.[7] Deputy Uribe quickly became known for his fiery speeches, which were always based on his intimate knowledge of living and working conditions in the coal mining towns.

Damián Uribe's story highlights changes in the ways class conflict, as manifest in the coal miners' battles, played out under the Popular Front model. It was clear that the attitudes and actions of the coal mining capitalists, so thoroughly represented in the congressional right wing, in no

6. Neruda, *Canto general*, 197.
7. Nearly all of Chile's leading right-wing politicians were members of the nation's industrial, financial, and agrarian elite. In the case of the coal mining industry, see, for example, the biographies of Fernando Aldunate Errázuriz, Pedro Poklepovic Novillo, Hernán Videla Lira, Gregorio Amunátegui Jordán, Guillermo Correa Fuenzalida, Maximiliano Errázuriz Valdés, Joaquín Prieto Concha, Gustavo Rivera Baeza, and Alvaro Santa María.

way corresponded to those of a progressive national bourgeoisie. For the organized working-class communities that Uribe represented, this situation called for the decisive intervention of the state to rectify the fundamental imbalance of power between the "progressive" proletariat and a bourgeoisie that was "reactionary" in thought and practice. The state was to imbue social relations with the justice and equality perceived by Chile's popular sectors as fundamental to the advance of democracy. In other words, the state's role could not be impartial when Chilean political and social relations were still structured around opposing and asymmetrical interests, that is, along the lines of class conflict, all rhetoric of harmony notwithstanding. Workers and coal mining capitalists alike were certainly aware of the dilemma this posed for government actors in the Popular Front years, and both groups constantly pushed for the resolution of the contradiction in terms most favorable to their interests.

In this context, the fragile alliance the Communists forged with the Radicals and their tumultuous relations with the Socialists assumed paramount importance in Chilean history, precisely because a Lota miner, who a few years before was signing union documents in a barely literate hand, now was able to directly represent his compañeros and compañeras of the coal mining region in the sphere of national politics. Our understanding of modern Chilean history and politics needs to go beyond the dichotomies of reform versus revolution and continuously peaceful democracy versus violent dictatorship. Indeed, what the story of the coal miners in the 1930s and 1940s shows most clearly is that democracy, as it was embraced by Marxist parties and their working-class followers in mid-twentieth century Chile, was an intrinsically contentious project. Organization and mobilization from below came to be seen by workers not as a way to overthrow Chilean democracy or halt its capitalist advance, but rather as a way to participate fully. Workers were prepared to fight within existing systems rather than against them, but this did not mean an end to class conflict. Coal miner Damián Uribe Cárdenas was not revolutionary in the sense of violently taking control of the state, but his presence in the Congress, and the bold tenor of his speeches there, speak clearly to the substantive shifts in social and political power that took place between 1935 and 1947.

The hopes and possibilities of this era came to an end in late 1947, when Gabriel González Videla, the third Radical President elected with Communist support, summarily quashed the coal miners' legal strike, declaring it a "revolutionary" move to cripple the Chilean economy. As discussed above, González Videla tried to justify his use of state force to repress Chilean workers in the following terms: "It is not, then, the President of Chile who has betrayed the Chilean people [but the Communists]. What he has done is to energetically prevent International Communism from instilling general chaos in order to secure the triumph of the hidden agenda of unconditional support for Soviet political, military, and economic interests."[8] Such language reads like a template for junta pronouncements after September 11, 1973, when, as was the case twenty-six years earlier, Communists were also targeted for blame, although both repressive regimes cast a much wider net than any particular party, social sector, or region.

On September 11, 1973, when the presidential palace came under attack, Salvador Allende is said to have expressed concern about the welfare of Augusto Pinochet, whom he had named chief of the armed forces less than a month before. Allende feared that coup leaders had detained Pinochet to prevent him from defending the constitutional government. In both moments, then, 1947 and 1973, there emerges the figure of a traitor and the act of betrayal—with its multiple layers of meaning.[9] In neither case was this simply a story of palace intrigues, of a falling out among top government and political leaders. Rather, both historic moments gave rise to a profound feeling of betrayal throughout Chilean society. In 1947, as in 1973, what was fundamentally betrayed were the hopes, struggles, and gains of the Chilean people during two critical, yet quite distinct, periods of democratization. One participant in the battle at the presidential palace on September 11 recalled that when leaders of Allende's personal guard decided to topple the marble statues of former presidents to use as barricades against the onslaught of gunfire, they gave the order that all should be used but one—that of Pedro Aguirre Cerda—the beloved President of the Popular Front, "the century's first popular-democratic experience on the continent."[10]

The Popular Front and the Popular Unity were both Center-Left political alliances that relied on support from progressive capitalists and middle-class sectors and the nation's mass of rural and urban workers. Both

8. Gabriel González Videla, "To the People of Concepción: Defense Against the Actions of the Communist Party," speech delivered from the balcony of the Concepción provincial government building (Intendencia), December 5, 1947, Document no. 5, FGGV, vol. 99, 153–96, ANCh.

9. In Allende's last words to the Chilean people, broadcast over jammed airways as the presidential palace came under attack, he described the overthrow of his government as a betrayal; this part of his farewell speech is engraved on his tomb. See Timossi, *Grandes alamedas*, 227–32.

10. Ibid., 117.

projects aimed at expanding participation and deepening the social dimensions of Chilean democracy without sacrificing economic growth.
And both projects also carried with them the threat of a plebeian irruption, which was categorically forestalled with the exertion of state power,
albeit of a different kind and to a different degree in each case. Notwithstanding these similarities, in a 1971 interview with Régis Debray, President Allende highlighted distinctions between the Popular Unity
coalition of the 1970s and the Popular Front of the 1930s and 1940s, in
which he participated as a Socialist leader, senator, and health minister.
The Popular Front governments, he explained, were led by the Radicals,
representing presumably progressive middle-class sectors, whereas his
Popular Unity government was led by a Socialist "compañero presidente,"
representing the working class.[11] What Allende did not live long enough
to add was that while both he and González Videla had made promises to
the effect that "no force either human or divine" would ever make them
abandon the Chilean people, only Allende kept his word to the end.[12]
Whereas the violent quashing of the popular upsurge in 1973 came from
forces external to the Allende government, in 1947, the turn to the Right
came from within, starting in the presidential palace itself.

After the collapse of the Popular Front and the repression unleashed
by González Videla, Salvador Allende led his supporters in a new leftist
coalition that would become the Popular Action Front (Frente de Acción
Popular; FRAP; 1956–69). Under this alliance between the Socialists and
Communists, with other smaller leftist groups, Allende ran for president
three times (1952, 1958, 1964), before eventually forming the Center-Left
Popular Unity coalition and winning the election of September 4, 1970.
During his organizing efforts of the 1950s and 1960s, Allende said that
one of the most important lessons to take from the Popular Front was
that leftist parties and their working- and middle-class supporters had to
achieve unity before reaching out to centrist or right-wing forces. It
therefore makes sense that he tried to publicly distance his new project
from the Popular Front, juxtaposing the "failed reformism" of the earlier
period with his would-be successful peaceful road to revolution.

In this portrayal of the Popular Front, however, Allende fell into the
same contradiction that Chilean sociologist Tomás Moulian did when he
described the era as both the bourgeois co-optation of the hapless masses

11. Debray, *Conversación con Allende*, 63, 66–67, 114–15, 120.
12. See speech by González Videla given at La Moneda, 120 days after taking office,
reprinted in part in Neruda, *Discursos parlamentarios*, 177–78.

and the threat of plebeian self-assertion. If the Popular Front were indeed neither revolutionary nor even radical in the sense of organizing and mobilizing from below, why did the coal workers of the late 1940s elicit such a reactionary backlash? Their story shows that the centrists' perception of a threat from below derived from the complex politics of the preceding decade, when popular sectors organized in alliance with Marxist parties to assert their rights as citizen workers in a democratic republic.

Allende was not alone among political actors of the 1960s and 1970s who forged their careers and outlooks from their experiences of the 1930s and 1940s. The Christian Democratic president from 1964 to 1970, Eduardo Frei Montalva, had served as minister of public works in the 1940s, until he resigned in opposition to the January 1946 police shootings in Plaza Bulnes. Likewise, Raúl Rettig Guissen, head of the 1990 Truth and Reconciliation Commission, had gained favor with workers when he investigated the October 1942 police shootings in Lota. On the other side of the political spectrum, young Army Captain Augusto Pinochet served in 1947–48 both at the Pisagua internment camp and in the coal mining town of Coronel, which is where, he later claimed, he first became convinced of the dangers of Communism.

In addition to these well-known public figures, hundreds of thousands of working-class men and women across Chile also lived through both the 1940s and the 1970s. One such man was Lota native Omar Sanhueza Segunda, a local Communist leader, who was president of the Lota coal miners' union at the time of the September 11, 1973, coup. He vividly recalled the torture he experienced in clandestine detention centers during the Pinochet regime and cried when he talked about the arrest and disappearance of his son at the hands of the military. Yet he also vividly recalled the incidents of October 1947, when, as an eleven-year-old boy in Lota, he watched his older brother taken away in a railroad car and sent into exile in southern Chile: "They arrived [at the Chepe station] with the people to be exiled in '47 . . . in those cars they used before to transport animals; that's why I always say that, in spite of the painful situation I lived during the seventeen years of the [Pinochet] dictatorship, the people of '47 suffered more than us because '47 was a massive repression, they threw people out en masse, so that many died, sure, many died then, too."[13]

For many residents of the coal mines, the events of the 1940s and the 1970s became closely intertwined. Fresia Vidal Ojarse, for example, recalled a visit by President González Videla to the coal mining region on

13. Interview with Omar Sanhueza Segunda, September 10, 1997.

the occasion of a mine explosion: "And he came here," she said, "but he came with Pinochet because they were good friends." She also compared the two leaders, describing González Videla as "an ungrateful, tyrannical, evil ruler . . . a tremendous pirate, only slightly less evil than Pinochet."[14] Omar Sanhueza put it more bluntly: "Pinochet was just a son-of-a-bitch. González Videla was a traitor."[15]

Even González Videla found the significance of the 1940s to be integrally tied to the events of the 1970s, and vise versa. After twenty years of what he described as "political ostracism," in late 1972, González Videla begin to write his memoirs. He felt compelled to, he stated in the preface, because "International Communism has once again taken over my country and has it on the verge of civil war."[16] When he completed his two-volume memoirs in 1975, González Videla was well aware of the violent acts committed by the military dictatorship. Yet he still included a section he titled "Twenty Years Later: Historical Vindication of My Presidency," in which he explicitly linked 1947 and 1973: "Among the great satisfactions destiny has brought me . . . is to see my vision as a Leader—to put a halt to Communism in our country—justified twenty years later."[17]

The former president claimed that the upheaval and violence of the 1970s might well have been avoided if his moves against the Communists in the late 1940s had not been tempered and undermined. "If the Law for the Defense of Democracy had not been overturned," he wrote, "the country would not have fallen under the influence of the Communist Party and our institutional regime would have survived without the destruction it experiences today, as the only alternative, to wipe out, clean, and neutralize that perfidious ulcer transmitted from foreign lands: International Communism." Just about the time González Videla was writing these words, his former ally Pablo Neruda lay dying, as the military ransacked his various homes. These two men had traveled a long way since the 1946 presidential campaign, when Neruda wrote the poem "The People Call You Gabriel." Now fiercely defending his anti-Communism, González Videla tried to counter the charges spread for decades by Neruda's fiery pen, denouncing everything Neruda, Allende, and the coal miners stood for in both 1947 and 1973: "The truth is that time and the Marxist Government, which left nothing intact, undestroyed, uncorrupted, are now the most

14. Interview with Fresia Vidal Ojarse, August 15, 1996.
15. Interview with Omar Sanhueza Segunda, September 13, 1997.
16. González Videla, *Memorias*, 1:7.
17. Ibid., 2:1241.

eloquent and reliable testaments for reestablishing historical truth. Without my inexorable personal intervention in 1947, Chile might have experienced then the bloodbath brought on [today] by Communism."[18]

After the defeat of Pinochet in a 1988 plebiscite, Chile's first civilian government in more than fifteen years was another multiparty Center-Left coalition, called the "Concertación." The new political alliance was led by the Christian Democrats, who had replaced the Radicals as the dominant force in the Center, together with the Socialist Party, which had undergone dramatic changes since the 1970s. Chilean Communists had also walked a difficult path through the Pinochet years, and now, under the leadership of first Luis Corvalán and then Gladys Marín, the PCCh adopted its most radical position since the 1920s—refusing to support another Center-Left coalition. Christian Democrats headed the Concertación ticket for the first decade of its life, with the presidencies of Patricio Alywin (1990–94) and Eduardo Frei Ruiz-Tagle (1994–2000; son of Eduardo Frei Montalva). The Socialists then rose to the fore with Presidents Ricardo Lagos (2000–2006) and Michelle Bachelet (2006–2010).

If we are to understand the fundamental undercurrents in Chilean society that led to the events of 1947 and 1973—"reestablishing historical truth," as González Videla himself called for—we must reexamine the nature of social contestation during the Popular Front of the 1930s and 1940s. González Videla's sense of ostracism and the Lota miners' sense of betrayal are part of the same story. Both camps believed they were sacrificing for the nation. The actions of the mobilized workers and the often violent reactions against them ought not to be understood as "exceptions" to some kind of genteel Chilean democracy. Rather, it is precisely the intensity of the battles waged in the Popular Front era that helps us achieve a more nuanced understanding of Chilean democratic history. Whereas the myth of Chilean exceptionalism paints a landscape of rolling hills, the real story of twentieth-century Chilean democracy was far more jagged, with all the deep crevices, subterranean fires, and shifting tectonic forces of the Andes, the same forces that long ago produced Chilean coal.

18. Ibid.

BIBLIOGRAPHY

Archival Records and Collections

Archivo Nacional de Chile (ANCh), Santiago.
 Fondo de Gabriel González Videla (FGGV), vols. 1–131, 1920s–1950s.
 Fondo de la Intendencia de Concepción (FIC), Oficios, Solicitudes, Correspondencia, Comunicaciones, 1936–52.
 Fondo de Pedro Aguirre Cerda (FPAC), vols. 25–72, 1920s–1950s.
Archivo Nacional de la Administración Central del Estado (ARNAD; formerly Archivo Siglo XX), Santiago.
 Fondo de la Dirección General del Trabajo (FDGT), Oficios and Providencias, 1936–52.
 Fondo del Ministerio del Interior (FMI), Oficios and Providencias, 1936–52.
 Servicio de Observación, Fondos Varios, vols. 669–70, 1944–45.
Archivos Salvador Allende, http://www.salvador-allende.cl/. Digitized documents from 1930s–1950s and many secondary sources. See esp. "Textos—1933–1949," "Archivos del PS," "Otros Archivos," and "Biblioteca."
Biblioteca del Congreso Nacional de Chile (BCNCh), Santiago. Chamber of Deputies and Senate Sessions, 1935–53. Laws and Legal Codes, 1920s–1950s.
Biblioteca Municipal de Lota (BML), Lota Bajo. Acts of Lota Municipal Sessions, 1936–50.
Biblioteca Nacional de Chile (BNCh), Santiago.
 Dirección General de Estadísticas. Census data, 1920, 1930, 1940, 1952, 1960.
 Political pamphlets and speeches, coal company statutes and work regulations, maps and photographs; newspapers and periodicals, 1920s–1950s.
Centro de Documentación de la Iglesia Metodista Episcopal (CDIME), Santiago.
 Acts of the Annual Conference of the Episcopal Methodist Church of Chile, 1931–47.
Dirección del Trabajo, Santiago. Labor Relations Department. Union registers, documents, letters, 1920s–1950s.
Empresa Nacional del Carbón (ENACAR), Lota Alto.
 Coal company records. CCIL administration letters and documents, financial and shareholders' records, employment, wage, and attendance registers, 1920s–1950s. Acts of board of directors' meetings from Compañía Carbonera Colico Sur, 1941–45, Compañía Carbonífera Pilpilco, 1942–50, and Compañía Carbonífera Victoria de Lebu, 1943–45. Housed in basement of ENACAR Casa de Cultura.
Compañía Carbonífera e Industrial de Lota (CCIL) personnel files, 1930s–1940s. Housed in dynamite bunker on surface of Lota mines.

Henry A. Wallace Papers. Special Collections, University of Iowa Libraries, Iowa City.
Mayor's Office, Coronel. Acts of Coronel Municipal Sessions, 1937–45.
Memoria Chilena: Portal de la Cultura de Chile, http://www.memoriachilena.cl/. Web site of Dirección de Bibliotecas, Archivos, y Museos (DIBAM), Santiago. Digitized published and unpublished primary and secondary sources.
Robert J. Alexander Papers: Interview Collection, 1947–94. (RJAIC). Edited by John D. French and released on microfilm by IDC Publishers, 2002. Robert J. Alexander Papers, Special Collections and University Archives, Rutgers University Libraries.
Servicio Electoral República de Chile (SERCh), Santiago. Dirección del Registro Electoral. Election results, laws, and decrees, 1935–53.
United States National Archives, Record Group 59 (USNA, RG 59), Washington, D.C. Embassy and State Department telegrams and correspondence, Labor Attaché reports, 1935–53.

Newspapers and Other Periodicals

Boletín Minero. National mine owners' association (SONAMI) magazine, 1925–50.
Carbón de Lirquén. Company social club newsletter, Lirquén, 1941–44.
Chile Pentecostal. Pentecostal Methodist church newletter, Santiago, 1943–45.
El Chiflón. National Miners' Federation (FNM) newspaper, Santiago, 1942–53.
La Época. Independent newspaper, Concepción, 1936–48.
Ercilla. Independent magazine, Santiago, 1936–52.
La Esmeralda. Radical newspaper, Coronel, 1885, 1935–44.
Frente Popular. Political coalition newspaper, Concepción, 1937–40, and Santiago, 1936–40.
El Golfo de Arauco. Democratic newspaper, Coronel, 1943–48.
La Hora. Radical newspaper, Santiago, 1936–51.
Ideales. Catholic youth newsletter, Lota, 1935.
La Información: Minas Schwager. Coal mining company newsletter, Coronel, 1937–45.
La Justicia. Communist workers' federation (FOCh) newspaper, Santiago, 1924–27.
El Mercurio. Independent newspaper, Valparaíso and Santiago, 1935–53.
Mujeres Chilenas. Communist newspaper, Santiago, 1947.
Mundo Nuevo. Communist youth newsletter, Santiago, 1938–47.
New York Times. U.S. newspaper, 1935–52.
Nueva Alborada. Methodist youth newsletter, Lota, 1939–40.
El Obrero. Socialist newspaper, Coronel, 1936–42.
La Opinión. Coal mining company (CCIL) newsletter, Lota, 1924–62.
Oro Negro. Independent newspaper, Coronel, 1948–53.
La Patria. Independent newspaper, Concepción, 1935–53.
Principios. Communist magazine, Santiago, 1939–47, 1951–73.
El Regional. Independent newpaper, Curanilahue and Coronel, 1927–51.
Revista del Trabajo. National labor office (DGT) newsletter, 1935–50.
El Siglo. Communist newpaper, Santiago, 1940–53.
El Sur. Independent newspaper, Concepción, 1930–53.
Time. U.S. magazine, 1935–52.
La Trinchera. Socialist newspaper, Coronel, 1942–46.

Interviews (conducted and transcribed by author unless otherwise noted)

Alarcón Medina, Juan. Former Schwager coal miner; Communist municipal council member. Coronel, December 4, 1997.

Araneda, Emelina. Lifelong resident of coal mining region. Chiguayante, September 11, 1997. Transcribed by Verónica Garcés Fuentes.

Azócar Medel, Evaristo. Lifelong resident of Lota and Coronel; former coal miner; Socialist Party militant; nephew of Lota's Communist mayor in 1940s, Santos Medel Basualto. Playa Blanca, June 18–19, 1998.

Azocar Santo, Orlando, and Maria Estelina Salazar Montalva, with their daughter Silvia Azocar Salazar. Former Lota coal miner and his family. Lota Alto, October 16 and November 23, 1997.

Basa Ramírez, Manuel. Lota baker. Lota Bajo, October 22, 1997. Transcribed by Verónica Garcés Fuentes.

Cabeza Insunsa, Juan, and René Reyes Olivar. Octogenarian Lota coal miners. Lota Bajo, August 10, 1996. Transcribed by Verónica Garcés Fuentes.

Carrillo, Víctor Manuel. Retired Lota coal miner; Catholic union activist; local Christian Democrat politician. Lota Alto, October 20, 1997. Transcribed by Verónica Garcés Fuentes.

Centro de Adultos Mayores de Lota Bajo. Collective interview with elderly Lota residents during walking excursion just outside Lota, December 4, 1997.

Cifuentes, Manuel. Interview conducted by Mario Garcés Durán. Santiago, June 1993. Transcription provided to me by Garcés Durán, with permission of Pastor Cifuentes.

Corporación de Desarrollo Social de la Cuenca del Carbón. Collective interview with former Schwager union leaders. Coronel, February 15, 1998.

Corvalán, Gregorio. Lifelong resident of coal mining region; investigator of regional folklore and history; provincial government employee. Multiple interviews in Coronel, 1997–98.

Corvalán Lépez, Luis. Long-time national PCCh leader. Interview co-conducted with Mario Garcés Durán. San Bernardo, Greater Santiago, July 3, 1998. Transcribed by Verónica Garcés Fuentes.

Díaz, José Luis. President of ENACAR Lota employees' union. Lota Alto, October 23 and December 5, 1997.

Fuentealba Medina, Luis. Long-time Lota resident; Communist city council member; former national deputy. Lota Bajo, August 8, 1996.

García, Vicente. Former Schwager coal miner and Socialist union leader; 1956 Middle-Weight Boxing Champion of Chile. Santiago, November 14, 1997.

Garrido Riquelme, Pastor Roberto. Pastor of Wesleyan Mission of Lota. Lota Bajo, September 15 and December 5, 1997.

González, Jerman. Leader of National Miners' Confederation (Confederación Nacional Minera; CNM); former Lota miners' union leader (1968–73). Santiago, August 2, 1996.

González Figueroa, Julia. Lifelong Coronel resident; daugther of Communist organizer. Coronel, May 16, 1998.

Hernández, Hortensia, and Florencia Leal Rodríguez. Lifelong Plegarias residents, coal mining town near Curanilahue. Plegarias, February 10, 1998.

Iturra, Víctor, and Juana Riquelme. Lota coal miner, retired with 1999 closure of National Coal Mining Company (ENACAR), and his wife. Multiple interviews in their Lota Bajo home, often with other family members and neighbors, 1996–97.

Jara Contranzo, Ireneo, and Irma Rivera. Lifelong Lota residents and coal company employees. Ireneo played on Chile's national soccer team in 1952 Olympics. Lota Alto, September 10 and 15, 1997; October 17, 1997.

Jerez, José María. Former CCIL forestry worker; founder of Curanilahue Agrarian Labor Party; former mayor. Curanilahue, February 4, 1998.

Labraña, Moisés. President of National Miners' Confederation (CNM). Santiago, August 2, 1996.

Luco Garrido, Aníbal. Administrator of ENACAR's Lota Maintenance Division. Lota Alto, August 1996.

Muñoz Eyppert, Víctor. Coronel communal labor inspector (ICT). Coronel, December 4, 1997.

Naín Zambrano, José. Mine engineer and shift boss at ENACAR's Trongol Norte mine, near Curanilahue. Interview conducted in his office and during full-day tour of mine interior, February 11, 1998.

Padilla Vergara, Raquel del Carmen. Lifelong Coronel resident; daughter and wife of coal miner. Coronel, May 21, 1998.

Pagueguy, Juan, and Berta Aguayo Bueno. Lifelong Curanilahue residents; former coal miner. Multiple interviews, often with their children and neighbors. Curanilahue, 1998–99.

Peña Contreras, Elva del Rosario. Wife of former carabinero in Coronel and Curanilahue. Coronel, February 1998.

Pradel Benavides, Leocadí. Lifelong Coronel resident (b. 1900); wife of miner exiled from region by González Videla. Interview co-conducted with Dr. Hugo Monsalvez and Mario Garcés Durán. Coronel, May 16, 1998.

Ramírez Flores, Juan Osvaldo. Second-generation Lota native; son of Lota coal company white-collar employee; local historian. Coronel, February 14, 1998.

Rivas, Alicia, Marcelino Solis Ortega, and other members of Lota Pensioners' Club. Collective interview, Lota Bajo, August 11, 1996.

Salazar Montalva, María Estelina, and Silvia Azocar Salazar. Lifelong Lota residents; wife and daughter of coal miner. Lota Alto, October 18, 1997.

Sanhueza Segunda, Omar. Former coal miner; brother of miner exiled from region in 1947; Communist leader of Lota miners' union (1968–70; 1971–73). Lota Alto, September 10 and October 13, 1997.

Silva Torres, Pedro. Lifelong Coronel resident; geographer; author of thesis on regional development; former Socialist leader. Coronel, August 13, 1996.

Tagle, Julio. Former Communist, arrested under González Videla. Interview co-conducted with historian Oscar Ortiz. Santiago, November 14, 1997.

Vidal Ojarse, Fresia. Lifelong Lota resident; political activist. Lota Bajo, August 15, 1996, September 15, 1997, and May 22, 1998.

Books, Articles, Theses, and Select Published Documents

Abbott, Roger S. "The Role of Contemporary Political Parties in Chile." American Political Science Review 45 (June 1951): 450–63.

Aggio, Alberto. Frente Popular, radicalismo, e revolução passiva no Chile. São Paulo: Annablume / FAPESP, 1999.

Agüero Hugel, Luis Sergio. Métodos de colaboración estatal patronal-obrero para solucionar los conflictos colectivos del trabajo. Licenciatura thesis, Universidad de Chile, 1945. Santiago: Imprenta Dirección General de Prisiones, 1945.

Aguilera Muñoz, César. *Antología personal.* Coronel: Impresos García, 1997.

———. *Carbón: Pueblo y poesía.* Coronel: Editorial Adonai, 1993.

Aguirre Cerda, Pedro. *Epistolario de Pedro Aguirre Cerda, 1938–1941.* Edited by Leonidas Aguirre Silva. Santiago: DIBAM / LOM / Centro de Investigaciones Barros Arana, 2001.

———. *Mensaje de S.E. el Presidente de la República (don Pedro Aguirre Cerda) en la apertura de las sesiones ordinarias del Congreso Nacional, 21 de mayo 1939.* Santiago: Imprenta Fiscal de la Penitenciaría, 1939.

———. *El problema industrial.* Santiago: Prensas de la Universidad de Chile, 1933.

Alba, Víctor. *Historia del Frente Popular: Análisis de una táctica política.* Mexico City: Libro Mex, 1959.

Alberdi, Juan Bautista. *The Life and Industrial Labors of William Wheelwright in South America.* Boston: A. Williams, 1877.

Alcalde, Alfonso. *El auriga Tristán Cardenilla y otros cuentos.* Prologue by Jaime Concha. Santiago: Editorial Nascimento, 1971.

———. *Reportaje al carbón.* Santiago: Quimantú, 1973.

Aldebarán, Julio. *Tiempo de Arena.* Santiago: Editorial Universitaria, 1981.

Aldunate Errázuriz, Fernando. *Lejislación carbonífera.* Licenciatura thesis, Universidad de Chile, 1917. Santiago: Sociedad Imprenta-Litografía Barcelona, 1917.

Aldunate Phillips, Arturo. *Un pueblo en busca de su destino: Chile, país industrial.* Santiago: Editorial Nascimento, 1947.

Alegría, Fernando. *Mañana los guerreros.* Santiago: LOM, 1997.

Alessandri Palma, Arturo. *Recuerdos de gobierno.* 3 vols. Santiago: Editorial Nascimento, 1967.

Alexander, Robert J. *Communism in Latin America.* New Brunswick: Rutgers University Press, 1957.

———. *The Communist Party of Venezuela.* Stanford: Hoover Institution Press, 1969.

———. *Labor Relations in Argentina, Brazil, and Chile.* New York: McGraw-Hill, 1962.

———. *Organized Labor in Latin America.* New York: Free Press, 1965.

———. *Rómulo Betancourt and the Transformation of Venezuela.* New Brunswick: Transaction Books, 1981.

———. "Social Security in Chile." *Social Forces* 28 (October 1949): 53–58.

———. *Trotskyism in Latin America.* Stanford: Hoover Institution Press, 1973.

Allende Gossens, Salvador. *La contradicción de Chile: Régimen de izquierda; política económica de derecha.* Santiago: n.p., 1943.

———. *Obras escogidas 1933–1948.* Vol. 1. Compiled by Patricio Quiroga. Santiago: Editorial LAR, 1988.

———. *El P.S. proclama el 25 de octubre como fecha de reconquista; el secretario general, c. Salvador Allende, analizo en su vibrante discurso, el significado histórico del triunfo del pueblo sobre las fuerzas reaccionarias y fascistas. . .* Santiago: Talleres Olmos 3246, 1943.

———. *La realidad médico-social chilena.* 1939. 2nd ed. Santiago: Editorial Cuarto Propio, 1999.

El alma que canta con hermosas tonadas y cuecas chilenas dedicadas al Frente Popular. Santiago: n.p., [ca. early 1940s].

Álvarez Gallardo, Oscar A. *Condiciones de vida y trabajo del obrero de las minas en Chile.* Licenciatura thesis, Universidad de Chile, 1952. Santiago: Editorial Universitaria, 1952.

Ameringer, Charles D. *The Cuban Democratic Experience: The Auténtico Years, 1944–1952.* Gainesville: University of Florida Press, 2000.

Anales de la República: Textos constitucionales de Chile y registro de los ciudadanos que han integrado los poderes ejecutivo y legislativo desde 1810. Compiled by Luis Valencia Alvaria. 2 vols. Santiago: Imprenta Universitaria, 1951.

Angell, Alan. *Politics and the Labour Movement in Chile.* London: Oxford University Press, 1972.

Antezana-Pernet, Corinne [Corinne A. Pernet]. "Chilean Feminists, the International Women's Movement, and Suffrage, 1915–1950." *Pacific Historical Review* 69 (November 2000): 663–88.

———. "El MEMCh en provincia: Movilización femenina y sus obstáculos, 1935–1942." In *Disciplina y desacato: Construcción de identidad en Chile, Siglos XIX y XX,* edited by Loreno Godoy et al., 287–329. Santiago: SUR / CEDEM, 1995.

———. "Mobilizing Women in the Popular Front Era: Feminism, Class and Politics in the 'Movimiento Pro-Emancipación de la Mujer Chilena' (MEMCh), 1935–1950." Ph.D. diss., University of California at Irvine, 1996.

———. "Peace in the World and Democracy at Home: The Chilean Women's Movement in the 1940s." In *Latin America in the 1940s: War and Postwar Transitions,* edited by David Rock, 166–86. Berkeley and Los Angeles: University of California Press, 1994.

Apey Guzmán, Alfredo. *Geografía de la actividad minera.* Geografía de Chile 15. Santiago: Instituto Geográfico Militar, 1987.

Aracena, Francisco Marcial. *Apuntes de viaje: La industria del cobre en las provincias de Atacama y Coquimbo y los grandes y valiosos depósitos carboníferos de Lota y Coronel en la provincia de Concepción.* Valparaíso: Imprenta del Nuevo Mercurio, 1884.

Arias Escobedo, Osvaldo. *La prensa obrera en Chile, 1900–1930.* Chillán: Universidad de Chile, 1970.

Arrate, Jorge, and Eduardo Rojas. *Memoria de la izquierda chilena.* Vol. 1, *1850–1970.* Santiago: Javier Vergara Editor, 2003.

Astorquiza, Octavio. *Lota: Antecedentes históricos, con una monografía de la Compañía Minera e Industrial de Chile.* Concepción: Sociedad Imprenta y Litografía Concepción, 1929.

———. *Lota: Antecedentes históricos, con una monografía de la Compañía Carbonífera e Industrial de Lota, en ocasión de celebrar el noventa aniversario de la explotación de sus minas, 1852–1942.* Valparaíso: Universo, 1942.

Astorquiza, Octavio, and Oscar Galleguillos V. *Cien años del carbón de Lota, 1852–septiembre 1952: Antecedentes históricos, monografía, y estudios sobre el desarrollo industrial, económico, y social de las minas Carboníferas de Lota en su primer siglo de vida.* Compañía Carbonífera e Industrial de Lota, 1952.

Aylwin, Mariana, et al., eds. *Chile en el siglo XX.* 2nd ed. Santiago: Planeta, 1990.

Baeza Flores, Alberto. *Radiografía política de Chile.* Mexico City: B. Costa-Amic Editorial, 1972.

Bari M., David. *El ejército ante las nuevas doctrinas sociales.* Santiago: Talleres del Estado Mayor Jeneral, 1922.

Barnard, Andrew. "Chile." In *Latin America Between the Second World War and the Cold War, 1944–1948,* edited by Leslie Bethell and Ian Roxborough, 66–91. Cambridge: Cambridge University Press, 1992.

———. "The Chilean Communist Party, 1922–1947." Ph.D. diss., University of London, 1977.

———. "Chilean Communists, Radical Presidents, and Chilean Relations with the United States, 1940–1947." *Journal of Latin American Studies* 13 (November 1981): 347–74.

———. "El Partido Comunista de Chile y las políticas del tercer período (1931–1934)." *Nueva Historia* (April–December 1983): 211–50.

Barrera, Manuel. "Perspectiva histórica de la huelga obrera en Chile." *Cuadernos de la realidad nacional* (September 1971): 119–55.

———. *El sindicato industrial como instrumento de la lucha de la clase obrera chilena.* Santiago: Instituto de Economía y Planificación, Universidad de Chile, 1971.

Barría Serón, Jorge. *El movimiento obrero en Chile: Síntesis histórico-social.* Santiago: Ediciones de la Universidad Técnica del Estado, 1971.

———. *El sindicalismo, fuerza social chilena.* Santiago: DERTO, Universidad de Chile, 1978.

———. *Trayectoria y estructura del movimiento sindical chileno, 1946–1962.* Santiago: INSORA, 1963.

Barrio, Paulino del. *Noticia sobre el terreno carbonífero de Coronel i Lota i sobre los trabajos de esplotación en el emprendidos.* Santiago: Imprenta Nacional, 1857.

Barr-Melej, Patrick. *Reforming Chile: Cultural Politics, Nationalism, and the Rise of the Middle Class.* Chapel Hill: University of North Carolina Press, 2001.

———. "Sowing 'Seeds of Goodness' in Depression-Era Chile: Politics, the 'Social Question,' and the Labor Ministry's Cultural Extension Department." *Americas* 59 (April 2003): 537–58.

Bauer, Arnold J. "Industry and the Missing Bourgeoisie: Consumption and Development in Chile, 1850–1950." *Hispanic American Historical Review* 70 (May 1990): 227–53.

Behrens, Julio G. "Estudio sobre el carbón chileno." *Revista de Marina* (Valparaíso) 1 (September 1, 1885): 290–322.

Berger, Henry W. "Union Diplomacy: American Labor's Foreign Policy in Latin America, 1932–1955." Ph.D. diss., University of Wisconsin at Madison, 1966.

Bergquist, Charles W. *Labor in Latin America: Comparative Essays on Chile, Argentina, Venezuela, and Colombia.* Stanford: Stanford University Press, 1986.

Bermúdez Miral, Oscar. *El drama político de Chile.* Santiago: Editorial Tegualda, 1947.

Bethell, Leslie, and Ian Roxborough, eds. *Latin America Between the Second World War and the Cold War, 1944–1948.* Cambridge: Cambridge University Press, 1992.

Bicheno, H. E. "Anti-Parliamentary Themes in Chilean History: 1920–70." *Government and Opposition* 7 (Summer 1972): 351–88.

Bizzarro, Salvatore. *Historical Dictionary of Chile.* 2nd ed. Metuchen, N.J.: Scarecrow Press, 1987.

Blanckenhorn, F. *El carbón de Lota y su aplicación: Manual de consumidor de carbón de Lota.* Santiago: Universo, 1952.

Blasier, S. Cole. "Chile: A Communist Battleground." *Political Science Quarterly* 65 (September 1950): 353–75.

———. "The Cuban and Chilean Communist Parties, Instruments of Soviet Policy (1935–1948)." Ph.D. diss., Columbia University, 1954.

Bollaert, William. "Observations on the Coal Formation in Chile, S. America." *Journal of the Royal Geographical Society of London* 25 (1955): 172–75.

Bongiorno León, Carlos. *1925–1945: Los sindicatos obreros y su relación con las leyes sociales.* Antofagasta: Imprenta Ibérica, 1945.

Bopp Blu, Gustavo. *La Ley de Seguridad Interior del Estado en relación con la libertad de imprenta (con el texto de las modificaciones pertinentes introducidas por la Ley de Defensa Permanente de la Democracia).* Licenciatura thesis, Universidad de Chile, 1948. Santiago: Talleres Gráficos Simiente, 1948.

Borzutsky, Silvia. *Vital Connections: Politics, Social Security, and Inequality in Chile.* Notre Dame: University of Notre Dame Press, 2002.

Bosworth, Stephen David. "The Impact of Coal Strikes on the Formation of the Chilean Government's Policy Toward the Coal Industry, 1920–1931." Master's thesis, University of Texas at Austin, 1996.

———. "A True State of Crisis: Coal Workers, the State, and the Politics of Energy in Chile, 1902–1938." Ph.D. diss., University of Texas at Austin, 1999.

Bowen Herrera, Alfredo. *Nuestro derecho del trabajo y la Ley de Defensa de la Democracia.* Santiago: Editorial San Pancracio, 1950.

Bowers, Claude G. *Chile Through Embassy Windows.* New York: Simon and Schuster, 1958.

Bravo Ríos, Leonidas. *Lo que supo un auditor de guerra.* Santiago: Editorial del Pacífico, 1955.

Bray, Donald W. "Peronism in Chile." *Hispanic American Historical Review* 48 (February 1967): 38–49.

Breslin, Patrick Edward. "The Development of Class Consciousness in the Chilean Working Class." Ph.D. diss., University of California at Los Angeles, 1980.

Browder, Earl. *Teheran: Our Path in War and Peace.* New York: International, 1944.

Bulnes Aldunate, Luis. *La Corporación de Fomento de la Producción.* Licenciatura thesis, Universidad de Chile, 1943. Santiago: Escuela Tipográfica La Gratitud Nacional, 1943.

Butland, Gilbert James. *The Human Geography of Southern Chile.* London: G. Philip, 1957.

Caballero, Manuel. *Latin America and the Comintern, 1919–1943.* Cambridge: Cambridge University Press, 1986.

Cabero, Alberto. *Recuerdos de don Pedro Aguirre Cerda.* Santiago: Imprenta Nascimento, 1948.

Café Filho, João. *Do sindicato ao catete: Memorias politicas e confissões humanas.* Vol. 1. Rio de Janeiro: J. Olympio, 1966.

Caffarena de Jiles, Elena. *El recurso de amparo frente a los regímenes de emergencia.* Santiago: n.p., 1957.

Campos Harriet, Fernando. *Concepción en la primera mitad del siglo XX.* Santiago: Museo Histórico Nacional / Talleres Gráficos Andes, 1985.

———. *Historia de Concepción, 1550–1970.* Santiago: Editorial Universitaria, 1979.

Camu Veloso, Arnoldo. *Estudio crítica de la huelga en Chile.* Santiago: Editorial Jurídica, 1964

Carr, Barry. *Marxism and Communism in Twentieth-Century Mexico.* Lincoln: University of Nebraska Press, 1992.

Casanueva Valencia, Fernando and Manuel Fernández Canque. *El Partido Socialista y la lucha de clases en Chile.* Santiago: Quimantú, 1973.

Castillo Sibilla, Marcelo. "La agonía de la zona del carbón." *Revista Punto Final* (July 29–August 11, 1991): 16–17.

Castro Sauritain, Carlos. *Carbón del Bío-Bío.* Santiago: Alfabeta Impresores, 1988.

Ceballos Contreras, Avelino. *Lota: Historia y tradición.* Santiago: Supergráfica Ltda, circa 1996.

Centenario de Coronel: Revista conmemorativa de primer centenario del puerto de Coronel. Edited by Carlos Martínez Andreo. Coronel: n.p., December 1954.

Centner, Charles William. "Great Britain and Chilean Mining, 1830–1914." *Economic History Review* 12, nos. 1–2 (1942): 76–82.

Cerda Hernández, Daniel. "La guerra fría y la Ley de Defensa Permanente de la Democracia: Influencia de Estados Unidos en la creación de la Ley no. 8987." Licenciatura thesis, Universidad Católica, 2007.

Cerdas Cruz, Rodolfo. *La otra cara del '48: Guerra fría y movimiento obrero en Costa Rica, 1945–1952.* Heredia, Costa Rica: EUNED, 1998.

Céspedes, Mario, and Lelia Garreaud. *Gran diccionario de Chile (biográfico-cultural).* 2nd ed. 2 vols. Santiago: Importadora Alfa, 1988.

Chamudes Reitich, Marcos. *Libro blanco de mi leyenda negra.* 2nd ed. Santiago: Ediciones P.E.C., 1964.

Chelén Rojas, Alejandro. *Trayectoria del socialismo: Apuntes para una historia crítica del socialismo chileno.* Buenos Aires: Editorial Astral, 1967.

Claudín, Fernando. *The Communist Movement: From Comintern to Cominform.* Vol. 2, *The Zenith of Stalinism.* Translated by Francis MacDonagh. New York: Monthly Review Press, 1975.

Clissold, Stephen, ed. *Soviet Relations with Latin America, 1918–68: A Documentary Survey.* London: Oxford University Press, 1970.

Colin Alturarra, Michelle. "Mecanismos de control sobre la mano de obra minera en las explotaciones carboníferas de Lota, 1875–1890: Aproximaciones a un estudio de relaciones entre la Compañía Explotadora de Lota y Coronel y los mineros del carbón." Licenciatura thesis, Universidad Gabriela Mistral, 1999.

Collier, Ruth Berins, and David Collier. *Shaping the Political Arena: Critical Junctures, the Labor Movement, and Regime Dynamics in Latin America.* Notre Dame: University of Notre Dame Press, 2002.

Collier, Simon, and William F. Sater. *A History of Chile, 1808–1994.* Cambridge: Cambridge University Press, 1996.

Comité Nacional de Solidaridad y Defensa de las Libertades Públicas. *El Estado policial o la Ley de Defensa de la Democracia.* Pamphlet. Santiago: Imprenta Imperio, 1951.

Confederación de Trabajadores de Chile (CTCh). *Memoria de la Confederación de Trabajadores de Chile, presentada por su Secretario General Bernardo Ibáñez, 1943–46.* Santiago: El Progreso, 1946.

Congress of Industrial Organizations (CIO), Committee on Latin American Affairs. *The Argentine Regime: Facts and Recommendations to the United Nations Organization.* New York: CIO, Committee on Latin American Affairs, 1946.

Contreras Labarca, Carlos. "La gran experiencia del Frente Popular." *Principios* (July–August 1967): 25–46.

Corkill, David R. "The Chilean Socialist Party and the Popular Front, 1933–41." *Journal of Contemporary History* 11 (July 1976): 261–73.

Corporación de Fomento de la Producción (CORFO). *Cinco años de labor, 1939–1943.* Santiago, 1944.

——. *CORFO: Veinte años de labor, 1939–1959.* Santiago: Editora Zig-Zag, 1962.

Cortés, Lía, and Jordi Fuentes. *Diccionario político de Chile.* Santiago: Editorial ORBE, 1967.

Corvalán B., Gregorio R. "Modo de vida de los mineros del carbón, Golfo de Arauco." In *Mundo minero: Chile, siglos XIX y XX*, edited by Marcela Orellana Muermann and Juan G. Muñoz Correa, 125–50. Santiago, 1992.

———. *El papel de la mujer en la cultura kuyulche (gente del carbón)*. Concepción: n.p., 1989.

Corvalán B., Gregorio R., and Marcos Vargas M. *Condiciones de vida del minero en la superficie*. Working paper no. 17. Concepción: INPRODE, 1989.

Corvalán Lépez, Luis. *Algo de mi vida*. Mexico City: n.p., 1977.

———. *Los comunistas y la democracia*. Santiago: LOM, 2008.

———. *De lo vivido y lo peleado: Memorias*. Santiago: LOM, 1997.

Couyoumdjian, Ricardo. "'La Hora,' 1935–1951: Desarrollo institucional de un diario político." *Historia* (Universidad Católica) 31 (1998): 5–56.

Cruz-Coke, Ricardo. *Geografía electoral de Chile*. Santiago: Editorial del Pacífico, 1952.

———. *Historia electoral de Chile, 1925-1973*. Santiago: Editorial Jurídica, 1984.

Cruz Salas, Luis. "Historia social de Chile, 1931–1945: Los partidos populares, 1931–1941." Licenciatura thesis, Universidad Técnica del Estado, 1969.

Cunill, Pedro. *Visión de Chile*. Santiago: Editorial Universitaria, 1972.

Daire Tolmo, Omar Alonso. "Derogación de la Ley de Defensa de la Democracia: Legalidad al comunismo en Chile, 1958." Licenciatura thesis, Universidad Católica, 1989.

Darwin, Charles. *Geological Observations of the Volcanic Islands and Parts of South America Visited During the Voyage of the HMS "Beagle."* 3rd ed. New York: Appleton, 1896. Originally published in 2 parts, 1844 and 1846.

Debray, Régis. *Conversación con Allende: ¿Logrará Chile implantar el socialismo?* Mexico City: Siglo Veintiuno Editores, 1971. Published in English as *Conversations with Allende*. London: New Left Books, 1971.

Delcourt, Edmundo. *Estudio sobre la cuestión carbonera en Chile*. Santiago: Ministerio de Obras Públicas / Universo, 1924.

DeShazo, Peter. *Urban Workers and Labor Unions in Chile, 1902-1927*. Madison: University of Wisconsin Press, 1983.

Devés, Eduardo. *Los que van a morir te saludan: Historia de una masacre: Escuela Santa María, Iquique, 1907*. 3rd ed. Santiago: LOM, 1997.

Devés, Eduardo, and Carlos Díaz, comps. *El pensamiento socialista en Chile: Antología, 1893-1933*. Santiago: América Latina Libros, 1987.

Díaz, Carlos, Roberto Figueroa, and Carlos Sandoval. *Historia de los trabajadores del carbón, 1844-1900*. Working paper no. 2. Santiago: CEDAL, 1985.

Díaz Iturrieta, José. "Historia de una elección." *El Chiflón*, July 1942, 19, 30, 34, 39.

Diccionario biográfico de Chile, 1948-49. 7th ed. Santiago: Empresa Periodística de Chile, 1949.

Diccionario biográfico de Chile, 1965-67. 13th ed. Santiago: Empresa Periodística de Chile, 1967.

Dimitrov, Georgi. "The Fascist Offensive and the Tasks of the Communist International in the Struggle of the Working Class Against Fascism," main report, and "Unity of the Working Class Against Fascism," concluding speech, Seventh World Congress of the Communist International, August 2 and 13, 1935. http://www.marxists.org/reference/archive/dimitrov/index.htm/ (accessed August 2007).

———. *La unidad de la clase obrera en la lucha contra el fascismo*. Santiago: Sud-América, 1935.

———. *La unidad de la clase obrera en la lucha contra el fascismo: Discurso pronunciado en el VII Congreso de la Internacional Comunista, el día 2 de agosto de 1935.* Madrid: Ediciones Europa-América, 1935.

Dinamarca, Salvador. "On Friendly Relations Between Chile and the United States." *Hispania* 18 (October 1935): 329–32.

Di Tella, Torcuato, et al., eds. *Sindicato y comunidad: Dos tipos de estructura sindical latinoamericana (Lota y Huachipato).* Buenos Aires: Editorial del Instituto, 1967.

Donoso, Ricardo. *Alessandri, agitador y demoledor: 50 años de historia política de Chile.* Mexico City: F.C.E., 1952.

Dorn, Glenn J. "The United States, Argentina, and the Inter-American Order, 1946–1950." Ph.D. diss., Ohio State University, 1997.

Drake, Paul W. "Chile, 1930–1958." In *Chile Since Independence*, edited by Leslie Bethell, 87–128. Cambridge: Cambridge University Press, 1993.

———. "The Chilean Socialist Party and Coalition Politics, 1932–1946." *Hispanic American Historical Review* 53 (November 1973): 619–43.

———. "International Crises and Popular Movements in Latin America: Chile and Peru from the Great Depression to the Cold War." In *Latin America in the 1940s: War and Postwar Transitions*, edited by David Rock, 109–49. Berkeley and Los Angeles: University of California Press, 1994.

———. *Socialism and Populism in Chile, 1932-1952.* Chicago: University of Illinois Press, 1978.

Duclos, Jacques. "On the Dissolution of the Communist Party of the United States." Published in *Cahiers du Communisme*, April 1945. Reprinted in *Marxism-Leninism vs. Revisionism*, edited by William Z. Foster et al., 21–35. New York: New Century, 1946.

Duhalde Vásquez, Alfredo. *Gobiernos de izquierda.* Santiago: Imprenta Amistad, 1951.

———. *Mensaje de S.E. el Vice presidente de la República don Alfredo Duhalde Vásquez en la apertura de las sesiones ordinarias del Congreso Nacional, 21 de mayo de 1946.* Santiago: Imprenta Fiscal de la Penitenciaría, 1946.

Duncan, R. E. "Chilean Coal Mining and British Steamers: The Origins of a South American Industry." *Mariners Mirror* 61 (1975): 271–82.

Durán Bernales, Florencio. *El Partido Radical.* Santiago: Editorial Nascimento, 1958.

———. *La política y los sindicatos.* Santiago: Ediciones Andes, 1963.

Echeverría Bascuñán, Fernando, and Jorge Rojas Hernández. *Añoranzas, sueños, realidades: Dirigentes sindicales hablan de la transición.* Santiago: Ediciones Sur, 1992.

Ellner, Steve. *Los partidos políticos y su disputa por el control del movimiento sindical en Venezuela, 1936–1948.* Caracas: Universidad Católica Andrés Bello, 1980.

———. "The Venezuelan Left in the Era of the Popular Front, 1936–45." *Journal of Latin American Studies* 2 (May 1979): 169–84.

Endlicher, Wilfried. "Lota: Desarrollo histórico-genético y división funcional del centro carbonífero." *Revista de Geografía Norte Grande* 13 (1986): 3–19.

Enríquez Frödden, Edgardo. *En el nombre de una vida.* Mexico City: Universidad Autónoma Metropolitana, 1994.

Ervin, Roger E. "Industry in the Concepción Area of Chile." *American Journal of Economics and Sociology* 14 (April 1955): 271–86.

Escobar Guic, Dina. "Documentos: 'Mujeres que escriben al Estado: Chile, 1946–1952.'" *Dimensión Histórica de Chile*, nos. 13, 14 (1997–98): 275–331.

Escobar Zenteno, Aristodemo. *Compendio de la legislación social y desarrollo del movimiento obrero en Chile.* Santiago: n.p., 1940.

Espech, Román. *El ferrocarril de Concepción a los ríos de Curanilahue.* Santiago: Imprenta Victoria, 1890.

Espinoza Betancourt, Enrique. "Historia, mujeres, huelgas y religiosidad: Aportes a la historia local de Schwager en tres momentos del Siglo XX." Master's thesis, Universidad Católica, Valparaíso, 1995.

Estado Mayor General del Ejército de Chile. *Historia del Ejército de Chile,* vol. 9, *El Ejército después de la Segunda Guerra Mundial, 1940-1952.* Santiago: Estado Mayor General del Ejército de Chile, 1985.

Etchepare Jensen, Jaime Antonio. "El advenimiento de Gabriel González Videla al gobierno y el fracaso de la Unión Nacional, 1946-1948." *Revista de Historia* 2, no. 2 (1992): 73-101.

———. *Surgimiento y evolución de los partidos políticos en Chile, 1857-2003.* Concepción: Universidad Católica de la Santísima Concepción, 2006.

Etchepare Jensen, Jaime Antonio, and Hamish I. Stewart. "Nazism in Chile: A Particular Type of Fascism in South America." *Journal of Contemporary History* 30 (October 1995): 577-605.

Etchepare Jensen, Jaime Antonio, Víctor García Valenzuela, and Mario Valdés Urrutia. *Historia de Curanilahue: La busqueda de un destino.* Concepción: Municipalidad de Curanilahue / Universidad de Concepción, 1986.

Faúndez, Julio. *Marxism and Democracy in Chile: From 1932 to the Fall of Allende.* New Haven: Yale University Press, 1988.

Fenner, Ricardo. "Análisis de los factores que restringen la explotación en las minas de carbón." *Boletín Minero* (October 1939): 1057-64.

———. *Situación actual de la industria carbonera nacional: Conferencia dada ante los miembros del Instituto de Ingenieros de Minas de Chile el 6 de julio de 1936.* Santiago: Imprenta Nascimento, 1936.

Fernández C., Juan F. *Pedro Aguirre Cerda y el Frente Popular Chileno.* Santiago: Ediciones Ercilla, 1938.

Fernández Darraz, Enrique. "Carbón y sociedad, 1910-1920: Antecedentes para un estudio de la huelga larga del 20 en los yacimientos de Lota y Coronel." Licenciatura thesis, Universidad de Concepción, 1991.

Fernández Larraín, Sergio. *Informe sobre el comunismo rendido a la convención general del Partido Conservador Unido el 12 de octubre.* Santiago: n.p., 1954.

———. *El problema del carbón: Control absoluto del PC en la producción de este combustible—Exposición hecha en la Cámara de Diputados en sesión de fecha 29 de julio de 1941.* Santiago: Imprenta El Imparcial, 1941.

Ferrada, Alejandra. "Mujeres de la zona minera del carbón." In *Relatos, testimonios, historias de vida,* working paper no. 1, Programa Interdisciplinario de Estudios de Género, 87-117. Santiago: Facultad de Ciencias Sociales, Universidad de Chile, 1994.

Figueroa, Pedro Pablo. *Historia de la fundación de la industria del carbón de piedra en Chile: Don Jorge Rojas Miranda.* Santiago: Imprenta del Comercio, 1897.

Figueroa Araya, Jaime. *Bosquejo y crítica de nuestro régimen sindical.* Licenciatura thesis, Universidad de Chile, 1945. Santiago: Talleres Gráficos Simiente, 1945.

Figueroa Garavagno, María Consuelo. *Revelación del subsole: Las mujeres en la Sociedad Minera del Carbón, 1900-1930.* Master's thesis, Universidad de Santiago, 1999. Santiago: ICSO / Centro de Investigaciones Diego Barros Arana, 2009.

Figueroa Ortiz, Enrique, and Carlos Sandoval Ambiado. *Carbón: Cien años de historia, 1848-1960*. Santiago: CEDAL, 1987.

Finer, Herman. *The Chilean Development Corporation: A Study in National Planning to Raise Living Standards*. Montreal: International Labour Office, 1947.

Finn, Janet L. *Tracing the Veins: Of Copper, Culture, and Community from Butte to Chuquicamata*. Berkeley and Los Angeles: University of California Press, 1998.

Fox Przeworski, Joanne. "Mines and Smelters: The Role of the Coal Oligopoly in the Decline of the Chilean Copper Industry." *Nova Americana*, no. 1 (1979): 169-213.

Francis, Michael J. *The Limits of Hegemony: United States Relations with Argentina and Chile During World War II*. Notre Dame: University of Notre Dame Press, 1977.

———. "The United States and Chile During the Second World War: The Diplomacy of Misunderstanding." *Journal of Latin American Studies* 9 (May 1977): 91-113.

Frazier, Lessie Jo. *Salt in the Sand: Memory and State Violence in the Postcolonial Nation-State (Chile, 1890-present)*. Durham: Duke University Press, 2007.

Frei Montalva, Eduardo. *La política y el espíritu*. Santiago: Ediciones Ercilla, 1940.

———. *Sentido y forma de una política*. Santiago: Editorial del Pacífico, 1951.

French, John D. *The Brazilian Workers' ABC: Class Conflict and Alliances in Modern Sao Paulo*. Chapel Hill: University of North Carolina Press, 1992.

———. "Workers and the Rise of Adhemarista Populism in São Paulo, Brazil, 1945-47." *Hispanic American Historical Review* 68 (February 1988): 1-43.

French, John D., and Daniel James, eds. *The Gendered Worlds of Latin American Women Workers: From Household and Factory to the Union Hall and Ballot Box*. Durham: Duke University Press, 1997.

French, William E. *A Peaceful and Working People: Manners, Morals, and Class Formation in Northern Mexico*. Albuquerque: University of New Mexico Press, 1996.

———. "*Progreso Forzado*: Workers and the Inculcation of the Capitalist Work Ethic in the Parral Mining District." In *Rituals of Rule, Rituals of Resistance*, edited by William H. Beezley, Cheryl English Martin, and William E. French, 191-212. Wilmington, Del.: SR Books, 1994.

Frödden Lorenzen, Orestes, and Gabriel González Videla. *Defensa de la democracia: Cartas cambiadas entre el Serenísimo Gran Maestro [Orestes Frödden L.] y S.E. el Presidente de la República don Gabriel González Videla*. Santiago: [Logia Masónica de Chile], 1948. Also reproduced as appendix to González Videla's *Memorias*.

Furci, Carmelo. *The Chilean Communist Party and the Road to Socialism*. London: Zed Books, 1984.

Furniss, Edgar S., Jr. "American Wartime Objectives in Latin America." *World Politics* 2 (April 1950): 373-89.

Gaddis, John Lewis. *The United States and the Origins of the Cold War, 1941-1947*. 2nd ed. New York: Columbia University Press, 2000.

Gaete Berríos, Alfredo. *Derecho del trabajo*. Prologue by Arturo Alessandri Rodríguez. Santiago: Zig-Zag, 1943.

———. *El principio de la libertad sindical y la legislación chilena*. Santiago: Imprenta Artes y Letras, 1949.

————. *Tratado elemental de derecho del trabajo: Doctrinas sociales, legislación y política social conforme al programa oficial de la Universidad de Chile*. Santiago: Editorial Jurídica de Chile / Zig-Zag, 1946.

Gallardo, Lorenzo. "Problemas nacionales de Chile: Los comités tripartitos en la zona carbonífera." *Principios*, no. 18 (December 1942): 12–13.

Gandarillas Matta, Javier. *La producción i el consumo del carbón i su influencia en el desarrollo de las naciones*. Santiago: Universo, 1917.

Garcés, Joan E. *Soberanos e intervenidos: Estratégias globales, americanos y españoles*. Mexico City: Siglo Veintiuno Editores, 1996.

Garcés Durán, Mario. *Crisis social y motines populares en el 1900*. 2nd ed. Santiago: LOM, 2003.

————. *FOCh, CTCh, CUT: Los centrales unitarias en la historia del sindicalismo chileno*. Santiago: ECO, 1988.

————. "Movimiento obrero en la década del treinta y el Frente Popular." Licenciatura thesis, Universidad Católica, 1985.

García, Leonidas. "Industria minera: Estado actual de las minas de carbon fósil de Lota i Lotilla en la provincia de Concepcion." *Anales de la Universidad de Chile* 19 (July 1861): 29–38.

Gariazzo, Alicia. "Origenes ideológicos de los movimientos obreros chileno y argentino." *Revista Paraguaya de Sociología* 18 (June–September 1981): 59–96.

Gil, Federico Guillermo. *The Political System of Chile*. Boston: Houghton Mifflin, 1966.

Godoy, Loreno, et al., eds. *Disciplina y desacato: Construcción de identidad en Chile, siglos XIX y XX*. Santiago: SUR / CEDEM, 1995.

Gómez, María Soledad. "Factores nacionales e internacionales de la política interna del Partido Comunista de Chile, 1922–1952." In *El Partido Comunista en Chile: Estudio multidisciplinario*, compiled by Augusto Varas, 65–139. Santiago: CESOC / FLACSO, 1988.

Góngora, Mario. *Ensayo histórico sobre la noción de Estado en Chile en los siglos XIX y XX*. Santiago: Editorial Universitaria, 1981.

González, Marcial. *El carbón mineral i las industrias en Chile*. Santiago: Imprenta Nacional, 1862.

González Araneda, Ricardo. "La huelga larga de 1960 en la zona del carbón, Coronel y Lota." Licenciatura thesis, Universidad de Concepción, 1991.

González Videla, Gabriel. *Informe a la convención: Política internacional y economía, 1943*. Santiago: Imprenta Sud-América, 1944.

————. *Memorias*. 2 vols. Santiago: Editorial Gabriela Mistral, 1975.

————. *Mensaje de S.E. el Presidente de la República don Gabriel González Videla al Congreso Nacional al inaugurar el período ordinario de sesiones, 21 de mayo de 1948*. Santiago: Imprenta Fiscal de la Penitenciaría, 1948.

————. *Mensaje de S.E. el Presidente de la República don Gabriel González Videla al Congreso Nacional al inaugurar el período ordinario de sesiones, 21 de mayo de 1949*. Santiago: Imprenta Fiscal de la Penitenciaría, 1949.

Gotz Betancourt, Shirley Elizabeth, and José Arturo Montecino Parra. "La evolución de los salarios y las condiciones de vida en la zona del carbón, 1930–1940." Licenciatura thesis, Universidad de Concepción, 1993.

Grandin, Greg. *The Last Colonial Massacre: Latin America in the Cold War*. Chicago: University of Chicago Press, 2004.

Grandón, Edison. *El adiós del minero: Crónicas desde Lota*. Santiago: CESOC, 1998.

Green, David. "The Cold War Comes to Latin America." In *Politics and Policies of the Truman Administration*, edited by Barton J. Bernstein, 149–95. Chicago: Quadrangle Books, 1970.

———. *The Containment of Latin America: A History of the Myths and Realities of the Good Neighbor Policy*. Chicago: Quadrangle Books, 1971.

Grez Toso, Sergio. *La "cuestión social" en Chile: Ideas y debates precursores, 1804–1902*. Santiago: DIBAM / Centro de Investigaciones Diego Barros Arana, 1995.

———. *De la "regeneración del pueblo" a la huelga general: Génesis y evolución histórica del movimiento popular en Chile (1810–1890)*. Santiago: DIBAM / Ediciones RIL, 1998.

Grugel, Jean. "Nationalist Movements and Fascist Ideology in Chile." *Bulletin of Latin American Research* 4, no. 2 (1985): 109–22.

Grugel, Jean, and Monica Quijada. "Chile, Spain, and Latin America: The Right of Asylum at the Onset of the Second World War." *Journal of Latin American Studies* 22 (May 1990): 353–75.

Guerrero Jiménez, Bernardo, ed. *Vida, pasión y muerte en Pisagua*. Iquique: CREAR, 1990.

Gunther, John. "Popular Front in Chile." In *Inside Latin America*, 234–70. New York: Harper, 1941.

Guzmán Hernández, Jorge. *Gabriel González Videla: Biografía y análisis crítico de su programa*. Santiago: Universo, 1946.

Halperin, Ernst. *Nationalism and Communism in Chile*. Cambridge, Mass.: MIT Press, 1965.

Hartford, Robert Bartlett. "The Miners of Lota, Chile, and Lower-Class Puerto Ricans: A Cross-Cultural Test of the Theory of Demographic Transition." Master's thesis, University of Georgia, 1968.

Healey, Mark Alan. *The Ruins of the New Argentina: Peronism and the Remaking of San Juan After the 1944 Earthquake*. Durham: Duke University Press, forthcoming.

Heinz, Wolfgang S., and Hugo Fruehling. *Determinants of Gross Human Rights Violations by State and State-Sponsored Actors in Brazil, Chile, and Argentina*. Boston: Martinus Nijhoff, 1999.

Hernández Gurruchaga, Hilario. "El gran Concepción: Desarrollo histórico y estructura urbana; Primera parte. Génesis y evolución: De las fundaciones militares a la conurbación industrial." *Informe geográfico de Chile* 30 (1983): 47–70.

Hernández Salgado, José [Andrés Transal]. *Coronel en el tiempo*. Lota: Impresos Primavera, 1985.

———. *Leyendas y creencias de la zona del carbón*. Coronel: Editorial Adonai, 1993.

Herring, Hubert Clinton. *Chile en la presidencia de don Pedro Aguirre Cerda*. Buenos Aires: Editorial F. de Aguirre, 1971.

Hilbink, Lisa. *Judges Beyond Politics in Democracy and Dictatorship: Lessons from Chile*. New York: Cambridge University Press, 2007.

Hoover, Rev. W. C. *Historia del avivamiento, origen y desarrollo de la Iglesia Evangélica*. Santiago: Corporación Iglesia Evangélica Pentecostal, 1978. Published in English as *History of the Pentecostal Revival in Chile*. Santiago: Imprenta Eben-Ezer, 2000.

Horowitz, David. "The Cold War Continues, 1945–1948." In *Trends and Tragedies in American Foreign Policy*, edited by Michael Parenti, 42–71. Boston: Little, Brown, 1971.

Houseman, Philip Joseph. "Chilean Nationalism, 1920–1952." Ph.D. diss., Stanford University, 1960.

Hrenchir, Mary Josephine. "Claude G. Bowers and American Foreign Relations." Ph.D. diss., University of Nebraska, 1993.

Huentemilla Carrasco, Eladio. "Antecedentes de la Ley de Defensa Permanente de la Democracia." Licenciatura thesis, Universidad Católica, 1992.

Humeres Magnan, Héctor. La huelga. Santiago: Editorial Jurídica de Chile, 1957.

Humphreys, Robert Arthur. Latin America and the Second World War. 2 vols. London: Athlone Press for the Institute of Latin American Studies, University of London, 1981.

Huneeus, Carlos. La guerra fría chilena: Gabriel González Videla y la ley maldita. Santiago: Editorial Debate, 2009.

Huneeus, Carlos, and Luz María Díaz de Valdés. "Neruda, González Videla, y la ley maldita." Revista Siete + 7 (online), 119 (July 16, 2004): [not paginado; 2 pages].

Hutchison, Elizabeth Q. Labors Appropriate to Their Sex: Gender, Labor, and Politics in Urban Chile, 1900–1930. Durham: Duke University Press, 2001.

Illanes, María Angélica. Cuerpo y sangre de la política: La construcción histórica de las visitadores sociales, Chile, 1887–1940. Santiago: LOM, 2005.

——. "Ella en Lota-Coronel: Poder y Domesticación. El primer servicio social industrial de América Latina." Mapocho 49 (2001): 141–48.

——. "En el nombre del pueblo, del Estado y de la ciencia . . .": Historia social de la salud pública, Chile 1880–1973. Santiago: Colectivo de Atención Primaria, 1993.

Infante Barros, Marta. Testigos del treinta y ocho. Santiago: Editorial Andrés Bello, 1972.

Instituto de Economía, Universidad de Chile. Desarrollo económico de Chile, 1940–1956. Santiago: Editorial Universitaria, 1956.

——. La migración interna en Chile en el período 1940–1952. Santiago: Instituto de Economía, Universidad de Chile, 1959.

——. Ocupación y desocupación: Concepción, Talcahuano, Lota, Coronel. Santiago: Instituto de Economía, Universidad de Chile, 1968.

James, Daniel. Doña María's Story: Storytelling, Personal Identity, and Community Narratives. Durham: Duke University Press, 1999.

——. "October 17th and 18th, 1945: Mass Protest, Peronism, and the Argentine Working Class." Journal of Social History 21 (Spring 1988): 441–61.

——. Resistance and Integration: Peronism and the Argentine Working Class, 1946–1976. Cambridge: Cambridge University Press, 1988.

Jara Garrido, Mario. Chillán desaparece, 1939. Documentary film. Santiago: La Academia Centro Cultural, 2005.

Jobet, Julio César. Ensayo crítico del desarrollo económico y social de Chile. Santiago: Editorial Universitaria, 1955.

——. Historia del Partido Socialista de Chile. Santiago: Editorial Documentas, 1987.

——. El Partido Socialista de Chile. 2 vols. Santiago, Ediciones Prensa Latinoamericana, 1971.

——. "El Partido Socialista y el Frente Popular en Chile." Revista Arauco 7 (February 1967): 13–47.

——. "Síntesis interpretativa del desarrollo histórico de Chile durante el siglo XX." 3 parts. Atenea (June, July, August 1947): 347–63, 105–11, 227–46.

Kaempffer Villagran, Guillermo. *Así sucedió, 1850-1925: Sangrientos episodios de la lucha obrera en Chile.* Santiago: Arancibia, 1962.

Klein, Marcus. "The New Voices of Chilean Fascism and the Popular Front, 1938-1942." *Journal of Latin American Studies* 33 (May 2001): 347-75.

Klubock, Thomas Miller. *Contested Communities: Class, Gender, and Politics in Chile's El Teniente Copper Mine, 1904-1951.* Durham: Duke University Press, 1998.

———. "Copper Workers, Organized Labor, and Popular Protest under Military Rule in Chile, 1973-1986." *International Labor and Working-Class History* (Fall 1997): 106-33.

———. "The Politics of Forests and Forestry on Chile's Southern Frontier, 1880s-1940s." *Hispanic American Historical Review* 86 (August 2006): 535-70.

Knight, Alan. "Cardenismo: Juggernaut or Jalopy?" *Journal of Latin American Studies* 26, no. 1 (February 1994): 73-107.

———. "Mexico, 1930-1946." In *The Cambridge History of Latin America*, vol. 7, *Latin America Since 1930: Mexico, Central America, and the Caribbean*, edited by Leslie Bethell, 671-78. Cambridge: Cambridge University Press, 1990.

Labarca Goddard, Eduardo. *El Chile de Luis Corvalán: Una entrevista de 27 horas.* Barcelona: Editorial Fontamara, 1975.

Lafertte Gaviño, Elías. "El Decimotercer Congreso del Partido." *Principios* (January 1946): 3-7.

———. *Hacia la transformación económica y política de Chile por la via de la unión nacional.* Santiago: Ediciones Nueva América, 1945.

———. *Vida de un comunista: Páginas autobiográficas.* Santiago: Empresa Editora Austral, 1957.

Lafertte Gaviño, Elías, and Carlos Contreras Labarca. *Los comunistas, el Frente Popular, y la independencia nacional: Discursos.* Santiago: Antares, 1937.

Lagos Valenzuela, Tulio. *Bosquejo histórico del movimiento obrero en Chile.* Santiago: Imprenta El Esfuerzo, 1941.

Lalive d'Epinay, Christian. *Haven of the Masses: A Study of the Pentecostal Movement in Chile.* London: Lutterworth Press, 1969.

Leonard, Thomas M., and John F. Bratzel. *Latin America During World War II.* Lanham, Md.: Rowman and Littlefield, 2007.

Lillo, Baldomero. *Sub-terra: Cuadros mineros.* 1904. 12th ed. Santiago: Editorial Nascimento, 1986.

Lizama, Carlos. "Remezón." In *Historias para un fin de siglo: Primer concurso de historias locales y sus fuentes*, 34-44. Santiago: ECO, 1994.

Lobo Moraga, Sergio. *Guía sindical de Chile 1951.* Santiago: Talleres Gráficos La Nación, 1951.

Lobos Araya, Marina. "La industria carbonífera y la legislación, propiedad, tenencia y comercio hullero (1840-1888)." Master's thesis, Universidad de Santiago, 1988.

———. "La legislación carbonífera chilena: un ejemplo de casuismo y pragmatismo en el siglo XIX." *Historia Nuestra*, no. 2 (1990): 48-74.

Loewenstein, Karl. "Legislation for the Defense of the State in Chile." *Columbia Law Review* 44 (May 1944): 366-407.

Loveman, Brian. *El campesino chileno le escribe a su excelencia.* Santiago: ICIRA, 1971.

———. *Chile: The Legacy of Hispanic Capitalism.* New York: Oxford University Press, 2001.

———. *The Constitution of Tyranny: Regimes of Exception in Spanish America.* Pittsburgh: University of Pittsburgh Press, 1993.

————. *For la Patria: Politics and the Armed Forces in Latin America*. Wilmington, Del.: Scholarly Resources, 1999.

————. *Struggle in the Countryside: A Documentary Supplement*. Bloomington: International Development Research Center, 1976.

————. *Struggle in the Countryside: Politics and Rural Labor in Chile, 1919-1973*. Bloomington: Indiana University Press, 1976.

Loveman, Brian, and Elizabeth Lira. *Las acusaciones constitucionales en Chile: Una perspectiva histórica*. Santiago: LOM / FLACSO, 2000.

————. *Las ardientes cenizas del olvido: Vía chilena de reconciliación política, 1932-1994*. Santiago: LOM / DIBAM, 2000.

————. *Las suaves cenizas del olvido: Vía chilena de reconciliación política, 1814-1932*. Santiago: LOM / DIBAM, 2000.

————. "Truth, Justice, Reconciliation, and Impunity as Historical Themes: Chile, 1814-2006." *Radical History Review* (Winter 2007): 43-76.

————, eds. *Los actos de la dictadura: Comisión investigadora, 1931*. Santiago: DIBAM / Centro de Investigaciones Diego Barros Arana / Universidad Jesuita Alberto Hurtado, 2006.

————, eds. *Arquitectura política y seguridad interior del Estado, Chile, 1811-1990*. Santiago: DIBAM / Centro de Investigaciones Diego Barros Arana / Universidad Jesuita Alberto Hurtado, 2002.

————, eds. *Historia, política, y ética de la verdad en Chile, 1891-2001: Reflexiones sobre la paz social y la impunidad*. Santiago: LOM, 2001.

————, eds. *Leyes de reconciliación en Chile: Amnestias, indultos, y reparaciones, 1819-1999*. Santiago: DIBAM / Centro de Diego Barros Arana / Universidad Jesuita Alberto Hurtado, 2001.

Loyola Tapia, Manuel, and Jorge Rojas Flores, comps. *Por un rojo amanecer: Hacia una historia de los comunistas chilenos*. Santiago: ICAL, 2000.

Macintyre, Stuart. *Little Moscows: Communism and Working-Class Militancy in Inter-War Britain*. London: Croom Helm, 1980.

MacKay, Juan. *Recuerdos y apuntes, 1820 a 1890*. Concepción: A. L. Murray, 1912.

Maldonado Prieto, Carlos. *AChA y la proscripción del Partido Comunista en Chile, 1946-48*. Working paper no. 60. Santiago: FLACSO, 1989.

————. *La Milicia Republicana: Historia de un ejército civil en Chile 1932-1936*. Santiago: Servicio Universitario Mundial, 1988.

————. "'La Prusia de América del Sur': Acerca de las relaciones militares germano-chilenas, 1927-1945." *Estudios Sociales*, CPU, no. 72 (1992): 75-102.

————. "Right-Wing Paramilitary Groups in Chile, 1900-1950." Partnership for Democratic Governance and Security, 1999. http://www.resdal.org/Archivo/doooooba.htm/ (accessed August 2010).

Manns, Patricio. *Chile: Una dictadura militar permanente, 1811-1999*. Santiago: Editorial Sudamericana, 1999.

Marambio, Jorge. *Identidad cultural en la zona del carbón*. Santiago: LOM, 1996.

Marín, Juan. *Viento negro*. Santiago: Editorial Nascimento, 1944.

Martínez Elissetche, Pacian. "Coronel, auge, y caida." *Boletín de la Academia Chilena de la Historia*, no. 92 (1981): 253-55.

Martinic B., Mateo. "La minería del carbón en Magallanes entre 1868 y 2003." *Historia* (Universidad Católica) 37 (January-June 2004): 129-67.

Martner, Cecilia. *Contribuciones y carencias del discurso educacional de la izquierda chilena, 1938-1952*. Santiago: ECO, 1986.

Martz, John D. "Marxists and Coalitions in Latin America." In *Coalition Strategies of Marxist Parties*, edited by Trond Gilberg, 135–72. Durham: Duke University Press, 1989.

Mazzei de Grazia, Leonardo. "Antiguos y nuevos empresarios en la región de Concepción en el siglo XIX." *Revista de Historia* (Universidad de Concepción) 7 (1997): 177–88.

———. "Los británicos y el carbón en Chile." *Atenea* 475 (1997): 137–67.

———. "Expansión de gestiones empresariales desde la minería del norte a la del carbón, Chile, siglo XIX." *Boletín de Historia y Geografía* 14 (1998): 249–65.

———. "Matías Cousiño antes de Lota: Formación y proyecciones de un empresario minero." *Atenea* 480 (1999): 85–128.

———. "Orígenes del establecimiento británico en la región de Concepción y su inserción en la molinería del trigo y en la minería de carbón." *Historia* (Universidad Católica) 28 (1994): 217–39.

———. *Sociedades comerciales e industriales y economía de Concepción, 1920-1939*. Santiago: Editorial Universitaria, 1991.

———. "Terratenientes de Concepción en el proceso de modernización de la economía regional en el siglo XIX." *Historia* (Universidad Católica) 31 (1998): 179–215.

Mella, Omar. "Curanilahue: Una historia para sobreviver." In *Historias para un fin de siglo: Primer concurso de historias locales y sus fuentes*, 19–33. Santiago: ECO, 1994.

Meneses Ciuffardi, Emilio. *El factor naval en las relaciones entre Chile y los Estados Unidos, 1881-1951*. Santiago: Ediciones Pedagógicas Chilenas, 1989.

Mera Figueroa, Jorge, Felipe González, and Juan Enrique Vargas Vivanco. *Función judicial, seguridad interior del estado, y orden público: El caso de la Ley de Defensa de la Democracia*. Working paper no. 5. Santiago: Programa de Derechos Humanos de la Academia del Humanismo Cristiana (PDHAHC), July 1987.

———. *Los regímenes de excepción en Chile durante el período 1925-1973*. Working paper no. 4. Santiago: PDHAHC, July 1987.

Millas, Orlando. *En tiempos del Frente Popular—Memorias*. Santiago: CESOC, 1993.

Miller, Eugene D. *A Holy Alliance? The Church and the Left in Costa Rica, 1932-1948*. Armonk, N.Y.: M. E. Sharpe, 1996.

———. "Labour and the War-Time Alliance in Costa Rica, 1943-1948." *Journal of Latin American Studies* 25, no. 3 (October 1993): 515–41.

Milos, Pedro. *Frente Popular en Chile: Su configuración, 1935-1938*. Santiago: LOM, 2008.

Miranda Casanova, Hugo. *Los delitos en la Ley de Defensa Permanente de la Democracia*. Licenciatura thesis, Universidad de Chile, 1959. Santiago: Editorial Universitaria, 1959.

Molina Jiménez, Iván. *Anticomunismo reformista: Competencia electoral y cuestión social en Costa Rica, 1931-1948*. San José: Editorial Costa Rica, 2007.

Molina Urra, Silvestre. *Condición económico-social de los mineros en la zona carbonífera*. Licenciatura thesis, Universidad de Chile, 1948. Concepción: Escuela Tipográfica Salesiana, 1948.

Montecinos, Daniel. "Los mineros del carbón." In *Así trabajo yo*, 3:30–65. Nosotros los chilenos 7. Santiago: Quimantú, 1971.

Monteón, Michael. *Chile and the Great Depression: The Politics of Underdevelopment, 1927-1948*. Tucson: University of Arizona Press, 1997.

Moore, Jason Kendall. "Maritime Rivalry, Political Intervention and the Race to Antarctica: U.S.-Chilean Relations, 1939-1949." *Journal of Latin American Studies* 33 (November 2001): 713-38.

Morris, James Oliver. *Elites, Intellectuals, and Consensus: A Study of the Social Question and the Industrial Relations System in Chile.* Ithaca: New York State School of Industrial and Labor Relations, Cornell University, 1966.

Morris, James Oliver, Roberto C. Oyaneder, and INSORA. *Afiliación y finanzas sindicales en Chile, 1932-1959.* Santiago: Facultad de Ciencias Económicas, Universidad de Chile, 1962.

Moulian, Tomás. *Contradicciones del desarrollo político chileno, 1920-1990.* Santiago: LOM / Universidad Arcis, 2009.

———. *Conversación interrumpida con Allende.* Santiago: LOM / Universidad Arcis, 1998.

———. "Desarrollo político chileno entre 1938 y 1973." *APSI* (July–October 1982): 13-20.

———. *Evolución histórica de la izquierda chilena: Influencia del marxismo.* Working paper no. 139. Santiago: FLACSO, 1982.

———. *La forja de ilusiones: El sistema de partidos, 1932-73.* Santiago: Universidad Arcis / FLACSO, 1993.

———. *Fracturas: De Pedro Aguirre Cerda a Salvador Allende, 1938-1973.* Santiago: LOM, 2006.

———. *Los frentes populares y el desarrollo político de la década de los sesenta.* Working paper no. 191. Santiago: FLACSO, 1983.

———. *Líneas estratégicas de la izquierda: "Frentismo," populismo, antireformismo, 1933-1973.* Working paper no. 142. Santiago: FLACSO, 1982.

———. *El régimen del gobierno, 1933-1973: Algunos problemas institucionales.* Working paper no. 406. Santiago: FLACSO, 1989.

Moulian, Tomás, and Germán Bravo. *Debilidad hegemónica de la derecha en el Estado de Compromiso.* Working paper no. 129. Santiago: FLACSO, 1981.

Moulian, Tomás, and Isabel Torres Dujisin. *Discusiones entre honorables: Las candidaturas presidenciales de la derecha, 1938-1946.* Santiago: FLACSO, 1987-88.

Muñoz, Diego. *Carbón: Novela.* Santiago: Editorial Austral, 1953.

———, ed. *Poesía popular chilena.* Santiago: Quimantú, 1972.

Muñoz Gomá, Oscar. "Algunas reflexiones sobre la política de reconversión en la industria del carbón." Santiago: Corporación de Estudios para Latinoamérica (CIEPLAN), 1995.

———. *Chile y su industrialización: Pasado, crisis, y opciones.* Santiago: CIEPLAN, 1986.

———. *El crecimiento industrial de Chile, 1914-1965.* 2nd ed. Santiago: Instituto de Economía, Universidad de Chile, 1971.

Neruda, Pablo. *Canto general.* Translated by Jack Schmitt. Berkeley and Los Angeles: University of California Press, 1991.

———. *Carta a México.* Mexico City: Fondo de Cultura Popular, A.C. / Editorial Popular, 1947.

———. "Carta íntima para millones de hombres." *El Nacional* (Caracas), November 27, 1947.

———. *Discursos parlamentarios de Pablo Neruda, 1945-1948.* Edited by Leonidas Aguirre Silva. Santiago: Editorial Antártica, 1996.

———. *González Videla, el Laval de América Latina: Breve biografía de un traidor.* Mexico City: n.p., 1949.

———. "El marxismo a la luz de los libros: 'Teheran' de Browder." *Principios*, no. 43 (January 1945): 33–34.

———. *Memoirs.* Translated by Hardie St. Martin. New York: Farrar, Straus, and Giroux, 1977. Originally published as *Confieso que he vivido: Memorias.* Barcelona: Seix Barral, 1974.

———. *Obras completas.* Vol. 4, *Nerudiana dispersa I, 1915–1964.* Edited by Hernán Loyola. Barcelona: Galaxia Gutenberg, Círculo de Lectores, 2001.

———. *Passions and Impressions.* Translated by Margaret Sayers Peden. Edited by Matilde Neruda and Miguel Otero Silva. New York: Farrar, Straus, and Giroux, 1983. Originally published as *Para nacer he nacido.* Barcelona: Seix Barral, 1978.

———. *La verdad sobre las rupturas: Carta íntima: Yo acuso.* Buenos Aires: Editorial Anteo, 1948.

———. *La verdad sobre las rupturas: Revelaciones sensacionales: Discurso pronunciado en el Senado de la República, en la sesión del miercoles 10 de diciembre de 1947.* Santiago: Imprenta Moneda, 1947.

Niblo, Stephen R. *Mexico in the 1940s: Modernity, Politics, and Corruption.* Wilmington, Del.: Scholarly Resources, 1999.

Nienhuser R., Germán. *La industria del carbón en su aspecto legal y económico: Proyecto de legislación carbonera.* Licenciatura thesis, Universidad de Chile, 1928. Santiago: El Globo, 1928.

Niess, Frank. *A Hemisphere to Itself: A History of U.S.-Latin American Relations.* London: Zed Books, 1984.

Nocera, Raffaele. *Chile y la guerra, 1933–1943.* Santiago: LOM / Centro de Investigaciones Diego Barros Arana, 2006.

———. "Ruptura con el eje y alineamiento con Estados Unidos: Chile durante la Segunda Guerra Mundial." *Historia* 2 (July–December 2005): 397–444.

Olavarría Bravo, Arturo. *Chile entre dos Alessandri.* 4 vols. Santiago: Editorial Nascimento, 1962. Andrés

Olcott, Jocelyn. *Revolutionary Women in Post-Revolutionary Mexico.* Durham: Duke University Press, 2005.

Olivares B., Edmundo. *Pablo Neruda: Los caminos de América: Tras las huellas del poeta itinerante III, 1940–1950.* Santiago: LOM, 2004.

Ortega Martínez, Luis. "The First Four Decades of the Chilean Coal Mining Industry, 1840–1879." *Journal of Latin American Studies* 14 (May 1982): 1–32.

———. "La frontera carbonífera, 1840–1900." *Mapocho* 31 (1992): 131–48.

———. *La industria del carbón de Chile entre 1840 y 1880.* Santiago: Universdad de Santiago, 1988.

———. "El mundo del carbón en el siglo XIX." In *Mundo minero: Chile, siglos XIX y XX,* edited by Marcela Orellana Muermann and Juan G. Muñoz Correa, 101–50. Santiago: Universidad de Santiago, 1991.

———. "La primera crisis del carbón en Chile: Mercados y tecnología a comienzos del siglo XX." *Contribuciones Científicas y Tecnológicas* (Universidad de Santiago) 25 (August 1995): 105–17.

Ortega Martínez, Luis, Carmen Norambuena Carrasco, Julio Pinto Vallejos, and Guillermo Bravo Acevedo. *Corporación de Fomento de la Producción: 50 años de realizaciones, 1939–1989.* Santiago: n.p., 1989.

Ortiz Alvarez, Elizabeth, and María Eliana Vega Soto. *Identidad y cultura minera.* Concepción: Impresos Rehue, 1994.

Ortiz Letelier, Fernando. *El movimiento obrero en Chile, 1891-1919.* Madrid: Ediciones Michay, 1985. Reprint, Santiago: LOM, 2005.

Ortiz V., Óscar. *Nuevas crónicas anarquistas de la subversión olvidada.* Santiago: Editorial La Simiente, 2008.

Ossa, Manuel. *Lo ajeno y lo propio: Identidad pentecostal y trabajo.* Santiago: Centro Ecuménico Diego de Medellín, 1991.

———. *Espiritualidad popular y acción política: El pastor Víctor Mora y la Misión Wesleyana Nacional: 40 años de historia religiosa y social, 1928-1969.* Santiago: Centro Ecuménico Diego Medellín, 1990.

Pacheco Silva, Arnoldo. "El fenómeno de migración del campo a la ciudad, Concepción, 1850-1880." *Revista de Historia* (Universidad de Concepción) 7 (1997): 189-202.

Palma, Martín. *Un paseo a Lota.* Valparaíso: Imprenta y Librería del Mercurio de S. Tornero, 1864.

Palma, Samuel, and Hugo Villela. *Salir del mundo; Salir de la mina: Identidad minera e identidad evangelica de la zona del carbón.* Santiago: SEPADE, 1997.

Palma Zúñiga, Luis. *Historia del Partido Radical.* Santiago: Editorial Andrés Bello, 1967.

———. *Pedro Aguirre Cerda: Maestro, estadista, gobernante.* Santiago: Editorial Andrés Bello, 1963.

Parada S., Enrique, and Humberto Valdivieso A. *El léxico de las minas del carbón.* Santiago: Universidad de Concepción, Instituto Central de Lenguas, 1974.

Partido Comunista de Chile (PCCh). *Chile Unido en la Coalición Mundial Anti-Nazi: Informes y resoluciones aprobados en la Duodécima Sesión Plenaria del C.C. del P.C de Chile, celebrada en los días 21 al 24 de enero de 1943.* Santiago: D.I.A.P., 1943. Cited as "PCCh Central Committee Resolutions (1943)."

———. *Las grandes luchas revolucionarias del proletariado chileno: Tesis del Buro Sudamericano de la Internacional Comunista.* Santiago: Editorial Marx-Lenin, 1932.

———. *Ricardo Fonseca: Combatiente ejemplar.* Santiago: Talleres Gráficos Lautaro, 1952. Luis Corvalán Lépez is listed as author in later editions.

Partido Radical. *Declaración de principios: Estatutos y voto político aprobado en la Décimosexta Convención Nacional Ordinaria, Valdivia, 24 a 27 de enero de 1946.* Santiago: Imprenta La Salle, 1946.

Partido Socialista (PS). *El libro negro del Partido Comunista (Sección Chilena de la Tercera Internacional de Moscú).* Santiago: Departamento Nacional de Propaganda del Partido Socialista, 1941.

Pedreros, Guillermo. *La huelga grande del carbón, 1920 [Una huelga en el carbón].* Santiago: Cepeda y Rodríguez, 1965. Reprint, Chilpancio: Universidad Autónoma de Guerrero, 1983.

Pereira Gigogne, Hugo. "Lota: Cronología de una historica urbana." *Arquitecturas del Sur* (Concepción), no. 9 (1987): 6-8.

Peri Fagerstrom, René. *Apuntes y transcripciones para una historia de la función policial en Chile.* 4 vols. Santiago: Carabineros de Chile, 1983.

Petras, James. *Politics and Social Forces in Chilean Development.* Berkeley and Los Angeles: University of California Press, 1969.

———. *El radicalismo político de la clase trabajadora chilena.* Buenos Aires: Centro Editor de América Latina, 1969.

Petras, James, and Maurice Zeitlin. "Miners and Agrarian Radicalism." *American Sociological Review* 32 (August 1967): 578-86.

————, eds. *Latin America: Reform or Revolution.* New York: Fawcett, 1968.

Pike, Fredrick B. *Chile and the United States, 1880-1962: The Emergence of Chile's Social Crisis and the Challenge to United States Diplomacy.* Notre Dame: University of Notre Dame Press, 1963.

Pinochet Le-Brun, Tancredo. *Aguirre Cerda: Un hombre pequeño para un país grande.* Santiago: Gálvez, 1938.

Pinochet Ugarte, Augusto. *Camino recorrido: Biografía de un soldado.* Santiago: Imprenta del Instituto Geográfico Militar de Chile, 1990.

————. *El día decisivo.* 4th ed. Santiago: Editorial Andrés Bello, 1980.

Pinto Santa Cruz, Aníbal. *Antecedentes sobre el desarrollo de la economía chilena, 1925-1952.* Santiago: Editorial del Pacífico, 1954.

————. *Chile, un caso de desarrollo frustrado.* Santiago: Editorial Universitaria, 1962.

Pizarro, Crisostomo. *La huelga obrera en Chile, 1890-1970.* Santiago: SUR, 1986.

————. "El rol de los sindicatos en la evolución de la sociedad chilena." *Ensayos* 1, no. 1 (1978): 89–122.

Pizarro Soto, J. Alejandro. *Lebu, de la Leufumapu a su centenario, 1540-1962.* Santiago: Editorial Ñielol, 1991.

Plath, Oreste. *Folclor del carbón en la zona de Lota.* Santiago: Editorial Grijalbo, 1998.

Poblete N., Dario, and Alfredo Guillermo Bravo. *Historia del Partido Radical y del Frente Popular.* Santiago: Imprenta La República Independencia, 1936.

Poblete Troncoso, Moisés. *Derecho del trabajo y la seguridad social en Chile.* Santiago: Editorial Jurídica, 1949.

————. *Evolución del derecho social en América.* Santiago: Editorial Nascimento, 1942.

————. *El movimiento obrero latinoamericano.* Mexico City: Fondo de Cultura Económica, 1946.

————. *La organización sindical en Chile y otros estudios sociales.* Santiago: Imprenta Ramón Arias, 1926.

Pollack, Benny. "The Chilean Socialist Party: Prolegomena to Its Ideology and Organization." *Journal of Latin American Studies* 10 (May 1978): 117-52.

Pollitt, Penelope A. "Religion and Politics in a Coal Mining Community in Southern Chile." Ph.D. diss., Cambridge University, 1981.

Polumbaum, Ted, and Nyna Brael Polumbaum. *Today Is Not Like Yesterday: A Chilean Journey.* Cambridge, Mass.: Light and Shadow, 1992.

Poppino, Rollie E. *International Communism in Latin America: A History of the Movement, 1917-1963.* New York: Free Press of Glencoe, 1964

Pradenas Rojas, María Ester, ed. *Lota "Sudor herido": Trabajadores del carbón en la literatura.* Santiago: Rumbos, 1993.

Ramírez Necochea, Hernán. *Los Estados Unidos y América Latina, 1930-1965.* Santiago: Editora Austral, 1965.

————. *Historia del movimiento obrero en Chile: Antecedentes del siglo XIX.* Santiago: Editorial Siglo XX, 1954.

————. *Origen y formación del Partido Comunista de Chile: Ensayo de historia política y social de Chile.* Santiago: n.p., 1965.

Ravines, Eudocio. *La gran estafa.* 4th ed. Santiago: Editorial del Pacífico, 1957.

————. *El rescate de Chile.* Mexico City: Empresa Editora e Impresora, 1974.

Recabarren, Luis Emilio. *Obras escogidas.* Santiago: Editorial Recabarren, 1965.

————. *El pensamiento de Luis Emilio Recabarren: Recopilación de escritos.* Santiago: Editorial Austral, 1971.

Rettig Guissen, Raúl. *En defensa de la doctrina radical: Discurso pronunciado en el debate político en la 15a. Convención Radical, realizada en la ciudad de Concepción.* Santiago: Continente, 1944.

———. *La historia de un "bandido": Raúl Rettig, entrevista de Margarita Serrano.* Santiago: Editorial Los Andes, 1999.

Reyes Álvarez, Jaime. *Los presidentes radicales y su partido, Chile, 1938-1952.* Working paper no. 120. Santiago: Centro de Estudios Públicos, May 1989.

———. "El presidente y su partido durante la época radical: Chile, 1938-1952." *Estudios Públicos,* no. 35 (1989): 71-101.

Reynolds Neira, Michael. "Movimiento mancomunal y conciencia de clase en la frontera carbonífera, 1903-1907." Licenciatura thesis, Universidad Arcis, 2006.

Ríos Morales, Juan Antonio. *¡Expulsado! Discurso pronunciado en la Asamblea Radical de Concepción por el Senador y Ex-Presidente del Partido Radical Dr. Juan Antonio Ríos.* Concepción: Talleres Gráficos El Sur, 1932.

Ríos Morales, Juan Antonio, Pablo Neruda, and Julio Moncada. *Altitud democrática de Chile [por el] president de la nación, escritores y pueblo: Unidos para la democracia y el progreso.* Lima: Ediciones Hora del hombre, 1943.

Ríos Morales, Juan Antonio, and Alfredo Rosende. *Dos cartas políticas, cambiadas entre el presidente de la República y el presidente del Partido Radical.* Santiago: Dirección General de Informaciones y Cultura, 1944.

Riquelme Segovia, Alfredo. *Visión de Estados Unidos en el Partido Comunista Chileno.* Vol. 1, *La "Era Rooseveltiana," 1933-1945.* Working paper no. 239. Santiago: FLACSO, 1985.

Riquelme Segovia, Alfredo, and Alonso Daire. *Visión y discurso sobre Estados Unidos en el Partido Comunista Chileno, 1945-1973.* Working paper no. 311. Santiago: FLACSO, 1986.

Riveros C., Luis, Emma S. Salas Neumann, and Luis Merino Reyes. *Don Pedro Aguirre Cerda: Estadista y educador.* Santiago: Club de la República, 1996.

Rock, David, ed. *Latin America in the 1940s: War and Postwar Transitions.* Berkeley and Los Angeles: University of California Press, 1994.

Roddick, Jacqueline. "The Failure of Populism in Chile: Labour Movement and Politics Before World War II." *Boletín de Estudios Latinoamericanos y del Caribe* 31 (December 1981): 61-89.

Rojas Flores, Jorge. *La dictadura de Ibáñez y los sindicatos, 1927-1931.* Santiago: Centro de Investigaciones Diego Barros Arana, 1993.

———. "Historia, historiadores y comunistas chilenos." In *Por un rojo amanecer: Hacia una historia de los comunistas chilenos,* compiled by Manuel Loyola Tapia and Jorge Rojas Flores, 1-79. Santiago: ICAL, 2000.

———. *El sindicalismo y el Estado en Chile, 1924-1936.* Santiago: Colección Nuevo Siglo, 1986.

———. "Trabajo infantil en la minería: Apuntes históricos." *Economía y Trabajo en Chile, Informe Anual,* no. 8 (1998): 227-303.

Rojas Valenzuela, Armando, and Alberto Ruiz de Gamboa A. *Código del trabajo y su reglamentación.* 2nd ed. Santiago: Editorial Nascimento, 1935.

Rokha, Pablo de. *Monografía de la Compañía Minera e Industrial de Chile.* Concepción: Imprenta y Litografía Concepción, 1924.

Romualdi, Serafino. *Presidents and Peons: Recollections of a Labor Ambassador in Latin America.* New York: Funk and Wagnalls, 1967.

Rosemblatt, Karin Alejandra. "Charity, Rights, and Entitlement: Gender, Labor, and Welfare in Early Twentieth-Century Chile." *Hispanic American Historical Review* 31 (November 2001): 555–85.

———. *Gendered Compromises: Political Cultures, Socialist Politics, and the State in Chile, 1920–1950.* Chapel Hill: University of North Carolina Press, 2000.

———. "Por un hogar bien constituido: El Estado y su política familiar en los frentes populares." In *Disciplina y desacato: Construcción de identidad en Chile, siglos XIX y XX,* edited by Loreno Godoy et al., 181–222. Santiago: SUR / CEDEM, 1995.

Rotary Club de Lebu. *Contribución al estudio del problema carbonero: Disertaciones leídas en el Rotary Club de Lebu, durante el año 1940–1941.* Concepción: Sociedad Imprenta y Litografía Concepción, 1941.

Ruiz Solar, Marcelo, Alfredo Duhalde V., and Julio Durán. *Análisis del mensaje presidencial: Discurso del Presidente del Partido don Marcel Ruiz Solar—Ley de Defensa de la Democracia.* Santiago: Partido Radical Democrático, 1948.

Sala de Tourón, Lucía. "La guerra fría y el cambio espectacular en aspectos de la política del gobierno presidido por Gabriel González Videla." *Hoy es Historia* (Montevideo) 7 (November–December 1990): 16–22.

Salazar Hermosilla, Sergio. "Los chinchorreros de Playa Blanca, El Chute y Pueblo Hundido." In *Así trabajo yo,* 1:49–66. Nosotros los chilenos 2. Santiago: Quimantú, 1971.

Salazar Vergara, Gabriel. *Labradores, peones, y proletarios: Formación y crisis de la sociedad popular chilena del siglo XIX.* Santiago: SUR, 1985.

———. *Violencia política popular en las "grandes alamedas": Santiago de Chile, 1947–1987.* Santiago: SUR, 1990.

Salazar Vergara, Gabriel, and Julio Pinto Vallejos. *Historia contemporánea de Chile.* 5 vols. Santiago: LOM, 1999–2002.

Salinas, Maximiliano C. *Historia del pueblo de Dios en Chile: La evolución del cristianismo desde la perspectiva de los pobres.* Santiago: Ediciones Rehue, 1987.

Samaniego M., Augusto. "Origen de una larga política: Informe de Carlos Contreras Labarca al Décimo Congreso del Partido Comunista de Chile, 1938." In *Por un rojo amanecer: Hacia una historia de los comunistas chilenos,* compiled by Manuel Loyola Tapia and Jorge Rojas Flores, 213–25. Santiago: ICAL, 2000.

Sánchez Guerrero, Juan. *Hijo de las piedras.* Santiago: Zig-Zag, 1963.

Santa Cruz, Hernán. "Letter from the Permanent Representative of Chile (Santa Cruz) to the Secretary-General of the United Nations (Lie), March 12, 1948." *International Organization* 2 (June 1948): 408–10.

Santis Cerda, Raúl Antonio. *El carbón en la economía chilena.* Licenciatura thesis, Universidad de Chile, 1951. Santiago: Imprenta Dirección General de Prisiones, 1951.

Sarasin, Luciano Claude. "La Corporación de Fomento de la Producción y el problema de los combustibles en Chile." *Anales del Instituto de Ingenieros de Chile* 44 (February 1944): 49–68.

Schapsmeier, Edward L., and Frederick H. Schapsmeier. *Prophet in Politics: Henry A. Wallace and the War Years, 1940–1965.* Ames: Iowa State University Press, 1970.

Schwartzberg, Steven. *Democracy and U.S. Policy in Latin America During the Truman Years.* Gainesville: University Press of Florida, 2003.

Segall, Marcelo. "Biografía social de la ficha salario." *Mapocho* 2 (1964): 97–131.

———. *Desarrollo del capitalismo en Chile: Cinco ensayos dialécticos.* Santiago: Editorial del Pacífico, 1953.

Sherman, John W. "Reassessing Cardenismo: The Mexican Right and the Failure of a Revolutionary Regime, 1934–1940. *Americas* 54, no. 3 (January 1998): 357–78.

Silva, J. Pablo. "The Origins of White-Collar Privilege in Chile: Arturo Alessandri, Law 6020, and the Pursuit of a Corporatist Consensus, 1933–1938." *Labor* 3, no. 1 (2006): 87–112.

———. "White-Collar Revolutionaries: Middle-Class Unions and the Rise of the Chilean Left, 1918–1938." Ph.D. diss., University of Chicago, 2000.

Silva, Miguel. *Los partidos, los sindicatos, y Clotario Blest, La CUT del '53.* Santiago: Mosquito Editores, 2000.

Silva, Patricio. "State, Public Technocracy, and Politics in Chile, 1927–1941." *Bulletin of Latin American Research* 13 (September 1994): 281–97.

Silva Torres, Pedro. "Impacto de la actividad carbonífera en la región de Arauco: Un análisis regional." Licenciatura thesis, Universidad Católica, 1986.

Silvert, Kalman H. "The Chilean Development Corporation." Ph.D. diss., University of Pennsylvania, 1948.

Smith, David. "Tonypandy 1910: Definitions of Community." *Past and Present* (May 1980): 158–84.

Snow, Florrie, ed. *Testimonio de fe y vida de Reginaldo Octavio Beldar.* Santiago: Ediciones Metodistas, 1994.

Stambuck Gallardo, Juana. "Movimientos sociales durante el Frente Popular." Licenciatura thesis, Universidad Técnica del Estado, Instituto Pedagógico, 1970.

Stern, Steve. *Battling for Hearts and Minds: Memory Struggles in Pinochet's Chile, 1973–1988.* Vol. 2 of *The Memory Box of Pinochet's Chile.* 3 vols. Durham: Duke University Press, 2006.

———. *Remembering Pinochet's Chile: On the Eve of London, 1998.* Vol. 1 of *The Memory Box of Pinochet's Chile.* 3 vols. Durham: Duke University Press, 2004.

Stevenson, John Reese. *The Chilean Popular Front.* Philadelphia: University of Pennsylvania Press, 1942. Reprint, Westport, Conn.: Greenwood Press, 1986.

Super, Richard Raymond. "The Chilean Popular Front Presidency of Pedro Aguirre Cerda, 1938–1941." Ph.D. diss., Arizona State University, 1975.

———. "The Seguro Obrero Massacre." In *The Underside of Latin American History,* edited by Daniel M. Masterson and John F. Bratzel, 43–66. East Lansing: Latin American Studies Center, Michigan State University, 1977.

Sutulov, Alexander. *Minería Chilena, 1545–1975.* Santiago: CIMM, 1976.

Sznajder, Mario. "A Case of Non-European Fascism: Chilean National Socialism in the 1930s." *Journal of Contemporary History* 28 (April 1993): 269–96.

———. "El nacional socialismo chileno de los años treinta." *Mapocho* 32 (1992): 169–93.

Taller Nueva Historia (New History Workshop). *Historia del movimiento obrero, 1820–1970.* Working paper no. 2. Santiago: Vicaría de Pastoral Obrera, 1980.

———. *Historia del movimiento obrero, 1820–1984.* 6 vols. Santiago: CETRA, 1983–84.

Tarrow, Sidney. "Transforming Enemies into Allies: Non-Ruling Communist Parties in Multiparty Coalitions." *Journal of Politics* 44 (November 1982): 924–54.

Teitelboim, Volodia. *Antes del olvido II: Un hombre de edad media.* Santiago: Editorial Sudamericana Chilena, 1999.

————. *Hijo del salitre*. 1952. Reprint, Havana: Instituto Cubano del Libro, 1972.

————. "Lota aguerrida y heroica." *Principios* (May 1946): 21–23.

————. *Pisagua: La semilla en la arena*. Santiago: Quimantú, 1972.

Thomas, Hugh. *Cuba, or, The Pursuit of Freedom*. Updated ed. New York: Da Capo Press, 1998.

Timossi, Jorge. *Grandes alamedas: El combate del presidente Allende*. Havana: Editorial de Ciencias Sociales, 1974.

Tinsman, Heidi. *Partners in Conflict: Sexuality and Labor in the Chilean Agrarian Reform, 1950–1973*. Durham: Duke University Press, 2002.

Tironi Barrios, Ana. "La ideología del Partido Radical Chileno en los años treinta, 1931–1938." Licenciatura thesis, Universidad Católica, 1983.

Toenges, Alberto Louis. "Coals of Chile." *Bulletin of U.S. Bureau of Mines*, no. 474 (1948).

Torres, Víctor. *Una casa en Lota Alto*. Havana: Casa de las Américas, 1973.

Trabucco Godoy, Luis. *Tesis sobre la Ley no. 8987 (de Defensa Permanente de la Democracia)*. Licenciatura thesis, Universidad de Chile, 1953. Santiago: Editorial Jurídica de Chile, 1953.

Trask, Roger R. "The Impact of the Cold War on United States–Latin American Relations, 1945–1949." *Diplomatic History* 1 (Summer 1977): 271–84.

Troncoso, Ramiro. *El turismo en la provincia de Concepción: Obra publicada bajo los auspicios del Club de Turismo del Sur de Chile*. Concepción: Tipografía y Litografía Concepción, n.d.

Ulianova, Olga. "Develando un mito: Emisarios de la Internacional Comunista en Chile." *Historia* 41, no. 1 (January–June 2008): 99–164.

————. "La figura de Manuel Hidalgo a través de los archivos de la Internacional Comunista." In *Por un rojo amanecer: Hacia una historia de los comunistas chilenos*, compiled by Manuel Loyola Tapia and Jorge Rojas Flores, 189–210. Santiago: ICAL, 2000.

————. "Levantamiento campesino de Lonquimay y la Internacional Comunista." *Estudios Públicos* 89 (2003): 173–223.

Ulianova, Olga, and Alfredo Riquelme Segovia, eds. *Chile en los Archivos Soviéticos, 1922–1991*. Vol. 1, *Komintern y Chile, 1922–1931*. Santiago: LOM / Centro de Investigaciones Diego Barros Arana, 2005.

Uribe Ulloa, Héctor. *Folklore y tradición del minero del carbón*. Concepción: Editora Anibal Pinto, 1998.

Urzúa Valenzuela, Germán. *La democracia práctica: Los gobiernos radicales*. Santiago: CIEDES / Editorial Melquiades, 1987.

————. *Historia política de Chile y su evolución electoral desde 1810 a 1992*. Santiago: Editorial Jurídica de Chile, 1992.

————. *Historia política electoral de Chile, 1931–1973*. Santiago: Colección Documentos de Chile, 1986.

U.S. Tariff Commission. *Mining and Manufacturing Industries in Chile*. 1945. Reprint, Washington, D.C., 1949.

Valdés López, Marcos. *Todo Penco: 1550–1990*. Concepción: DELTA, 1990.

Valdés Urrutia, Mario. "Chile, ruido de sables en 1948: La conspiración en contra del Presidente Gabriel González Videla." *Revista de Historia* (Universidad de Concepción) 7, no. 7 (1997): 111–36.

————. "Notas para la historia de la inteligencia política chilena: El Departamento Confidencial de la Policia de Investigaciones, 1933–1945." *Historia Nuestra*, no. 2 (1990): 75–87.

Valdivia Ortiz de Zárate, Verónica. *Las Milicias Repúblicanas: Los civiles en armas, 1932-1936.* Santiago: DIBAM / Centro de Investigaciones Diego Barros Arana, 1992.

———. "Las Milicias Socialistas, 1934-1941." *Mapocho* 33 (1993): 157-80.

———. *El nacionalismo chileno en los años del Frente Popular, 1938-1952.* Investigation Series 3. Santiago: Universidad Católica Blas Cañas, Dirección de Investigación, 1995.

———. *Nacionalismo e ibañismo.* Investigation Series 8. Santiago: Universidad Católica Blas Cañas, Dirección de Investigación, 1995.

———. "Las nuevas voces del nacionalismo chileno: 1938-1942." *Boletín de Historia y Geografía,* no. 10 (1993): 119-39.

Vannucci, Albert P. "The Influence of Latin American Governments on the Shaping of United States Foreign Policy: The Case of U.S.–Argentine Relations, 1943-1948." *Journal of Latin American Studies* 18 (November 1986): 355-82.

Varas, Augusto, comp. *El Partido Comunista en Chile: Estudio multidisciplinario.* Santiago: CESOC / FLACSO, 1988.

Vásquez A., David, and Lionel Zúniga. *Producción y recolección marginal de carbón: Diagnóstico de las comunas mineras de Coronel y Lota.* 2 vols. Working paper nos. 3-4. Concepción: INPRODE, 1987.

Vega, María Eliana, and Alonso Carrasco Valenzuela. *Cuando la luz se apaga: El día en que se cerró la mina de Lota.* Santiago: n.p., 1999.

Venegas Valdebenito, Hernán. *El carbón de Lota: Textos y fotografías a fines del siglo XIX. Las visiones de Francisco Marcial Aracena y Guillermo E. Raby.* Santiago: Pehuén, 2008.

———. "Crisis económica y conflictos sociales y políticos en la zona carbonífera, 1918-1931." *Contribuciones Científicas y Tecnológicas* 25 (November 1997): 125-53.

———. "La huelga grande del carbón, 1920." *Revista Chilena de Historia y Geografía,* no. 160 (1992-93): 225-49.

Veneros Ruiz-Tagle, Diana. "El epistolario de la pobreza: Nexos entre mujer y estado, 1946-1952." *Dimensión Histórica de Chile,* nos. 13-14 (1997-98): 111-37.

———. "Sufragismo y roles femeninos: De las paradojas de 'la mujer moderna,' 1946-1952." *Nomadias Monográficas* 1:239-63. Santiago: Editorial Cuarto Propio / Facultad de Filosofía y Humanidades, Universidad de Chile, 1999.

———. "Testimonio histórico: Rosa ('Miti') Markmann de González." *Dimensión Histórica de Chile,* nos. 13-14 (1997-98): 385-94.

Vergara, Angela. *Copper Workers, International Business, and Domestic Politics in Cold War Chile.* University Park: Penn State University Press, 2008.

Vergara, Ignacio. *El protestantismo en Chile.* 2nd ed. Santiago: Editorial del Pacífico, 1962.

Vergara, Marta. *Memorias de una mujer irreverente.* Santiago: Zig-Zag, 1961.

Visita oficial del Excmo. Sr. Henry A. Wallace, Vice-Presidente de los Estados Unidos de Norte América: Programa de festejos: 26 de marzo-4 de abril de 1943. Pamphlet. Santiago: Imprenta la República, 1943.

Vitale, Luis. *Interpretación marxista de la historia de Chile.* Vol. 6, *De Alessandri P. a Frei M., 1932-1964: Industrialización y modernidad.* Santiago: LOM, 1998.

Vivallos Espinoza, Carlos, and Alejandra Brita Peña. "Inmigración y sectores populares en las minas de carbón de Lota y Coronel, Chile, 1850-1900." *Atenea* 501 (2010): 73-94.

Wallace, Henry A. *Después de la guerra debe comenzar el siglo del hombre del pueblo.* Mexico City: Universidad Obrera, 1942.

————. *El siglo del pueblo.* New York: Hispanic-American Section, International Workers Order, 1943.

Wallace, Henry A., et al. *Christian Bases of World Order.* New York: Abingdon Press, 1943.

Walton, Richard J. *Henry Wallace, Harry Truman, and the Cold War.* New York: Viking, 1976.

Watson, Thomas J. *Visita del Excelentísimo señor don Gabriel González Videla, Presidente de la República de Chile, a los Estados Unidos de América, 12 de abril–3 de mayo de 1950.* N.p.: IBM, 1951.

Weisz, Morris. "The Labor Diplomacy Oral History Project." *Labor History* 36, no. 4 (1995): 588–98.

Whitney, Robert. "The Architect of the Cuban State: Fulgencio Batista and Populism in Cuba, 1937–1940." *Journal of Latin American Studies* 32 (May 2000): 435–59.

————. *State and Revolution in Cuba: Mass Mobilization and Political Change, 1920–40.* Chapel Hill: University of North Carolina Press, 2001.

Williams, Raymond. *Marxism and Literature.* New York: Oxford University Press, 1977.

Winn, Peter. *Weavers of Revolution: The Yarur Workers and Chile's Road to Socialism.* New York: Oxford University Press, 1986.

Yopo, Boris. *El Partido Radical y Estados Unidos: 1933–1946.* Working paper no. 230. Santiago: FLACSO, December 1984.

Zapata, Francisco. "De la democracia representativa a la democracia 'protegida': Movimiento obrero y sistema político en Chile." *Labouragain Publications* (online publications of International Institute of Social History; IISG) (March 2007): 1–29. http://www.iisg.nl/labouragain/documents/zapata-chile .pdf/ (accessed September 2007).

Zeitlin, Maurice. *The Civil Wars in Chile (or the Bourgeois Revolutions That Never Were).* Princeton: Princeton University Press, 1984.

Zeitlin, Maurice, W. Lawrence Neuman, and Richard Earl Ratcliff. "Class Segments: Agrarian Property and Political Leadership in the Capitalist Class of Chile." *American Sociological Review* 41 (December 1976): 1006–29.

Zeitlin, Maurice, and Richard Earl Ratcliff. *Landlords and Capitalists: The Dominant Class of Chile.* Princeton: Princeton University Press, 1988.

Zemelman Merino, Hugo. "El movimiento popular chileno y el sistema de alianzas en la década de los treinta." In *América Latina en los años treinta,* edited by Pablo González Casanova, 378–450. Mexico City: Instituto de Investigaciones Sociales, UNAM, 1977.

INDEX

Page numbers in *italics* indicate figures, maps, and tables.

government mediation of industrial conflicts. *See* contract negotiations; industrial relations system; labor department
officials
government spies, 133–35. *See also* company
informants and spies
Goyenechea Gallo, Isidora, 31, 32, 33
Grandin, Greg, 19–20
Great Britain, 5, 31–32, 35, 36, 39, 77, 178, 187,
241
Great Depression, 3, 5, 61, 107–8, 190
Great Strike of 1920. *See* strikes in coal mining zone, 1920–22
Grove Vallejo, Marmaduke, 65, 97, 100,
113n49, 179n18, 204n98, 209, 232n93,
278, 282–83, 307, 308n25. *See also* Authentic Socialist Party (PSA)
Gulf of Arauco, 5, 36, 273

health and safety in the workplace, 43, 44,
55, 124, 130, 138, 195, 253, 262. *See also*
accidents and explosions
Hijo de las piedras, 15–16
Hoffman Hansen, Alfredo, 237n125, 239, 261,
264, 265, 269, 271, 281, 290–92
Holger Torres, Immanuel
accusación constitucional against,
224n60, 279n55, 296–97
emergency zone chief, 224, 237, 238–39,
240
interior minister, 258–59, 278, 303, 330
Hoover, J. Edgar, 223n54, 232, 234
Horowitz, Daniel L., 185–86, 186n39, 188n44
observations by, 188–90, 192, 195–99,
203–6, 210–12, 215n27, 216–17, 222–25,
240, 241
hospitals
Berguño Report discussion of, 130
company hospital in Lota Alto, 40, 48, 69,
70, 159, 182
housing, 70–76
Berguño Report discussion of, 130, 138
coal company provision of, 45, 48–50, 71–
74, 167, 292
earthquake damage to, 110
in Lota, description of, 72–74
row houses (pabellones), 72, 73, 154
Hughes Cerna, Arturo, 94n88, 95–96, 114,
114n51
Huneeus, Carlos, xiv, 2n6, 19
hunger strikes of political prisoners, 64,
327–28
hydroelectric plant Chivilingo, 8, 39

Ibáñez Aguila, Bernardo
CTCh secretary general, 128n21, 137,
230n84, 233
CTCh Socialist faction leader, 235–38
Socialist congressman, 129n26, 211n12
Socialist Party leader, 129n26, 209–10,
240, 247, 249, 286, 293
Ibáñez del Campo, Carlos
coup attempt (1942), 179
dictatorship of (1927–31), 44n40, 57–62,
79, 166, 267n3, 272, 340
presidential elections (1938), 97, 102, 104
presidential elections (1942), 144, 167
presidential elections (1952), 302n1
industrial relations system (modern, tripartite), 6–7, 35, 126, 166, 171, 173
debates over, 54–55, 63
ideal of capital–labor harmony with state
mediation, 22, 29, 56, 124, 145, 146, 151–
53, 187–88, 192, 193–94
leftist and worker acceptance of, 56–57,
63, 151
See also laws on labor relations and social
system; Labor Code of 1931
internal state security laws. *See* laws on internal state security
internment camps, 177–78, 178n9, 273–74,
287–88, 292, 301
denounced as concentration camps, 288,
292, 328, 338
Quiriquina Island, 273, 287, 288, 319, 321,
324, 325, 326, 329, 335
See also deportations from coal zone;
exile, internal; Pisagua

Jiménez, Max, 13, 14
Juventudes Comunistas de Chile (JJCC). *See*
Communist Youth of Chile

Klubock, Thomas, 18, 19, 72n12, 172, 258,
258n48

Labor Code of 1931
alleged violations of, 12, 90, 269
altered by Law for the Permanent Defense
of Democracy, 313–15
on contract negotiations, 155n9, 189, 268
consolidation of 1920s laws, 35, 55n75, 56
foundation of industrial relations system,
6, 56, 61–62, 145
foundation of national development
model, 199–200
on freedom to work, 275
restrictions on labor organization and action, 61–62

work shifts, 131, 131n36, 154, 155, 271n25. *See also* workers' rights, eight-hour workday
Workers' Insurance Fund, 55, 102
workers' rights
  eight-hour workday, 45, 45n42, 55, 131, 131n36
  freedom of assembly, 45, 101, 106, 162, 170, 172, 200, 268–69, 279, 279n55
  freedom to work, 139, 240, 275
Workers' Socialist Party (PST), 63n108, 88n64, 114–15, 180n19, 202n90
World War II
  Battle of Midway, 151

Battle of Stalingrad, 151, 176, 187
as context for Popular Front strategy, 3
effects on coal industry, 5, 121
end of, 207
German invasion of USSR, 129, 177
Nazi-Soviet Nonaggression Pact, 177n3
Pearl Harbor bombing and U.S. entry, 140
San Francisco Conference, 206
Teheran Conference, 187
Yalta Conference, 203
See also anti-Fascism

Zañartu Prieto, Enrique, 10–14
Zapata Díaz, Emilio, 12, 63, 63n108
zona carbonífera. *See* coal mining zone